THE WAYS OF PHILOSOPHY
Searching for a Worthwhile Life

SCHOLARS PRESS
Studies in the Humanities

Editorial Board

Number 17

THE WAYS OF PHILOSOPHY
Searching for a Worthwhile Life

A. L. Herman

THE WAYS OF PHILOSOPHY
Searching for a Worthwhile Life

by

A. L. Herman

Scholars Press
Atlanta, Georgia

THE WAYS OF PHILOSOPHY
Searching for a Worthwhile Life

by

A. L. Herman

©1990
Scholars Press

Library of Congress Cataloging in Publication Data

Herman, A. L.
The ways of philosophy : searching for a worthwhile life / by A. L.
Herman.
    p. cm. -- (Scholars Press studies in the humanities ; no. 17)
    Includes bibliographical references and index.
    ISBN 1-55540-515-0 (alk. paper). -- ISBN 1-55540-516-9 (pbk. :
    alk. paper)
    1. Life. 2. Conduct of life. 3. East and West. I. Title.
II. Series: Scholars Press studies in the humanities series ; no.
17.
BD435.H45 1990
170--dc20   90-48124
                                             CIP

Printed in the United States of America
on acid-free paper

For Barbara and Helen

For no light matter is at stake;
the question concerns the very manner
in which human life is to be lived.
                    -Plato-

Philosophy is an activity which by
discussions and arguments secures
the happy life.
                    -Sextus Empiricus-

What is the use of studying philosophy if all
that it does for you is to enable you to talk
with some plausibility about some abstruse
questions of logic, etc., and if it does not
improve your thinking about the important
questions of everyday life?
                    -Ludwig Wittgenstein-

CONTENTS

ACKNOWLEDGEMENTS

For permission to print copyrighted material in excess of fair use I would like to thank the following publishers:

Excerpts from "Letter From Birmingham Jail" from *Why We Can't Wait* by Martin Luther King, Jr. Copyright 1963, 1964 by Martin Luther King, Jr. Reprinted by permission of Harper & Row, Publishers, Inc.

Excerpts from *Stride Toward Freedom* by Martin Luther King, Jr. Copyright 1958 by Martin Luther King, Jr. Copyright 1986 by Coretta Scott King, Dexter King, Martin Luther King III, Yolanda King and Bernice King. Reprinted by permission of Harper & Row, Publishers, Inc.

Excerpts from Aldo Leopold, *A Sand County Almanac.* Copyright 1966 by Oxford University Press. Reprinted by permission of Oxford University Press.

Excerpts from *The Basic Works of Aristotle.* Edited by Richard McKeon. Copyright 1941 by Random House. Reprinted by permission of Oxford University Press.

Excerpts from Diogenes Laertius, *Lives of Eminent Philosophers,* Two Volumes. Translated by R.D. Hicks. Copyright 1950 Harvard University Press. Reprinted by permission of Harvard University Press.

A number of people have very willingly donated their time and their talents in the preparation of the manuscript. In particular I wish to thank the following: All of my super-colleagues at the University of Wisconsin, Stevens Point, but especially Gary Alexander, John Bailiff, Donald Fadner, Richard Feldman, Alan Lehman, Thomas Overholt, Joseph L. Schuler, and John Vollrath; J. Baird Callicott, my colleague for many years, and Russell T. Blackwood of Hamilton College, both of whom are always there when needed the most; Barbara H. Herman who has an unerring ear for good English; Kathy Halsey of Inter-library Loan for her speed and efficiency; Carolee Cote who, more than any person alive, made everything possible; and Dennis Ford of Scholars Press who is the most perspicacious editor I've ever worked with. The comments and criticisms of these people have saved this work and me from flagrant errors and conspicuous embarrassment. The errors that this book does contain, and there are errors, are entirely the result of my own blunders. Whatever merit this book possesses is due entirely to the collective kindness, wit, and attention of all of the above extremely generous persons.

A.L.H.
June, 1990

PREFACE

One of the central tasks of philosophy has always been the solving of human problems. And one of the most urgent human problems that philosophers have attempted to solve is the problem first posed as a question by Aristotle, What is the best and most worthwhile life that a human being can live? Using some twenty different thinkers from both the Western and Eastern philosophic and religious traditions, this book offers to students of comparative philosophy, religion, and the humanities examples of ways of philosophy that have served as answers to Aristotle's question. Each of the fourteen chapters provides an historical context for the lives and views of the philosopher under consideration. His way of philosophy is presented and examined under four heads: The *problem* that he was trying to solve; the *cause* of the problem; the *solution* that he found; and, finally, the *way* that he proposed to secure that solution. Following this presentation the major accomplishments of the philosopher are discussed together with an examination of the problems and puzzles which he managed to solve. Each chapter concludes with a discussion of the new criticisms and problems that might accompany the way of philosophy under consideration together with the possible defense against such difficulties. Each way of philosophy is judged by its success or failure in meeting three standards which any "adequate" way of philosophy ought to meet; those standards are common sense, a subjective standard resting on ordinary meanings and ordinary comprehensibility; consistency, a logical standard; and completeness, a practical standard that asks, Has the problem under discussion been solved? and Have new unsolved problems been introduced by this way of philosophy?

These three standards should give us a foundation from which to critically examine the ways of philosophy presented in this book; and they should also allow us to critically examine any way of philosophy that attempts to answer Aristotle's question.

ONE
THE WAYS OF PHILOSOPHY
❯❯·❮❮

PHILOSOPHIES FOR TIMES OF CRISIS

In his *Nichomachean Ethics* Aristotle, in a discussion of *eudaimonia* or happiness, asks, What is the best and most worthwhile life that a human being can live? Aristotle's question is the central question of this book on the ways of philosophy.

It is perhaps a truism to say that we live in a time of urgent crisis* for I don't know of any age, any historical period, about which that assertion could not be made. But our age differs from all others in that at no previous time, not even after the introduction of the battle chariot, the long bow, the musket, or the machine gun, has life seemed so precariously balanced between existence and non-existence, as it is in the 1990s: If nuclear radiation doesn't get us, then environmental pollution surely will.

What Erich Fromm, the noted psychoanalyst and critic of Western culture, wrote over thirty years ago about that culture is even more poignantly true today. Our society, the whole of Western society, Fromm claimed, was sick, and that sickness was displayed in the intolerably high incidence of suicides, alcoholism, drug addiction, homicides, insanity, poverty, pollution, and war generated by and within the society. Taking war as an example, Fromm observed:

> Let us, in good psychiatric fashion, look at the facts. In the last one hundred years we, in the Western world, have created a greater material wealth than any other society in the history of the human race. Yet we have managed to

---

* "Crisis" is from the Greek verb *kriein*, to decide, and *krisis* is "a point of decision."

kill off millions of our population in an arrangement which we call "war." Aside from smaller wars, we had larger ones in 1870, 1914 and 1939. During these wars, every participant firmly believed that he was fighting in his self-defense, for his honor, or that he was backed up by God. [Erich Fromm, *The Sane Society* (Fawcett Publications, 1967/1955) p. 13.]

Thus guided by their disparate philosophies of life, the various participants in Western civilization, whether individually or collectively, have brought together the greatest wealth the world has ever known and the greatest anguish and misery that it has ever known. It was and it is a time of collective social madness.

Western views of happiness, the goals at which we all aim, and the philosophies that attempt to reify those goals whatever the cost, may lie, ultimately, at the root of all this suffering. Fromm continued his 1955 study which he titled, *The Sane Society*, by observing:

Happiness becomes identical with consumption of newer and better commodities, the drinking in of music, screen plays, fun, sex, liquor and cigarettes. Not having a sense of self except the one which conformity with the majority can give, he is insecure, anxious, depending on approval. [*Ibid.*, p. 309]

The kind of person that we have managed to produce and that we take as the norm as the best that we can produce is a person "alienated from himself" which means that,

He is incapable to love and to use his reason, to make decisions, in fact incapable to appreciate life and thus ready and even willing to destroy everything. The world is again fragmentalized, has lost its unity; he is again worshipping diversified things, with the only exception that now they are man-made, rather than part of nature. [*Ibid.*]

And Fromm concluded,

This alienation and automatization leads to an ever-increasing insanity. Life has no meaning, there is no joy, no faith, no reality. Everybody is "happy" - except that he does not feel, does not reason, does not love. [*Ibid.*, p. 312]

Ian McHarg, a professor of landscape architecture and another pungent critic of Western civilization, writing some fifteen years after Fromm, felt that the major cause of the world's moral as well as its environmental dislocation was to be found in the values espoused by Western philosophies and religions, in particular those religions in the Judeo-Christian tradition:

The great western religions born of monotheism have been the major source of our moral attitudes. It is from them that we have developed the preoccupation with the uniqueness of man, with justice and compassion. On the subject of man-nature, however, the Biblical creation story of the first chapter of Genesis, the source of the most generally accepted description of man's role and powers, not only fails to correspond to reality as we observe it, but in its insistence upon dominion and subjugation of nature, encourages the most exploitative and destructive instincts in man rather than those that are deferential and creative.

McHarg concludes, speaking about the philosophy of life that may have sanctioned the practices that have proved so environmentally destructive in our time:

The creation story in Judaism was absorbed unchanged into Christianity. It emphasized the exclusive divinity of man, his God-given dominion over all things and licensed him to subdue the earth. [Ian L. McHarg, *Design With Nature* (Doubleday & Company, 1969), p. 26]

If one joins Fromm's observation, that our civilization is sick, with McHarg's insight, that what we do and say and believe is traceable to the philosophy or religion that we are guided by and have faith in, then we must conclude that adopting or believing in philosophies and religions, whether intended or not, can lead to terrible and destructive consequences, indeed.

What makes this entire matter so poignantly true today, as we said above, is that some thirty years after Fromm wrote and some twenty years after McHarg, very little has been done to change the situation that they have described and, in fact, things may even be getting worse. Here, for example, is the anthropologist, Marvin Harris, with a recent catalogue of fears and concerns that confronts both American conservatives and liberals in the crisis of the 90s:

Violent crime is at an all-time high. Children are disrespectful. Vandalism is rampant. Premarital and extramarital sex for both men and women have become the norm; the birthrate is at an all-time low. There are more divorces and broken families than ever before, and there is a sharp rise in the number of homosexuals or at least in the number of people who publicly express and advertise homosexual preferences. There has also been a proliferation of California-style cults, a great burgeoning of interest in shamanism, astrology, witchcraft, exorcism, fundamentalism, and mind-changing sects ranging from est to the "Moonies" and Jim Jones's jungle temple.

Harris extends his list to the bizarre events in recent American economics:

> At the same time people have lost pride in their work. Sales help are unco-
> operative and ill-informed. It's hard to find competent secretaries, waiters
> and waitresses, bank clerks, and telephone operators. Also, America has lost
> its reputation for producing high-quality industrial goods. Automobiles and
> appliances are in constant need of repair and many items break as soon as
> their warranties expire. The whole economy seems to have gone berserk....
> Billions doled to people on welfare get spent on shoes and clothing made in
> Taiwan or Korea while American shoe, clothing, and textile factories go out
> of business. [Marvin Harris, *America Now* (New York: Simon and Schuster,
> 1982), pp. 7-8]

Harris concludes by stating an assumption on which his book, as well as
this book, rests with respect to times of crisis:

> In writing this book, I have proceeded on the premise that people cannot
> rationally offer a solution to a problem unless they understand its cause. It
> seems to me that if we act on the basis of sterile political formulae, irrational
> impulses, or unsound knowledge we are likely to make matters worse
> rather than better. [*Ibid.*, p. 174]

What has brought us to this particular time of crisis, it must be apparent by now, is our own fault, our own doing. It is not God's judgment
on us, divine necessity, Fate or chance, or mysterious unconscious powers beyond our knowledge or control, but our own doing and a doing
that is invariably the result of our own conscious and rational choices.
Chance and unconscious mental drives have a part to play in human actions to be sure, but they are undoubtedly minimal. We are what we
think, and, on occasion, what we don't think, and yet we have the kind of
world that, paradoxically, we want, i.e., we made it by our own choices,
and that we don't want, i.e., life is becoming intolerable.

If history is inclined to repeat itself, or if it is inclined to appear to be
terribly similar to itself through time, and if human nature is inclined to
be somewhat the same through time, then it ought to be possible to do
two things with respect to the past: First, to discover the origins of past
errors in thought that have brought us to our own time of crisis; and second, to discover what solutions previous generations had developed to
meet problems in their own times of crisis. It is an assumption that this
book makes that error in thought can be discovered by examining the
past and that the course of the future can be altered as a consequence of
that discovery.

Past answers to Aristotle's question have proved faulty in some fashion or they would not have led us into our present condition. Examples
of faulty thinking abound in the 20th century and one has only to recall

the many forms of imperialism, nationalism, fascism and colonialism which have led to human suffering and misery to make the point clear. Examples from the past that embody faulty systems of thinking will become apparent as our investigation of past philosophies proceeds. This present study is going to examine representative traditions and systems of thought from the past that have attempted to define the worthwhile life. These traditions and systems will be embodied in the various ways of philosophy from both Western as well as Eastern sources. The questions that are to be raised are simply, What went wrong? and What can be done now to correct it? Both of these questions are a natural consequence of attempting to answer Aristotle's question, What is the best and most worthwhile life that a human being can live?

What is philosophy?

"Philosophy" is a Greek word, a conjoining of a Greek verb, *philein*, "to love," and a Greek noun, *sophos*, "wisdom"; hence "philosophy" means "the love of wisdom" and the philosopher is then one who loves wisdom. In early Greece the best examples of professional philosophers were said to be the group of enterprising and itinerant wise men called "Sophists" who, for a fee, would teach Athenians and others the art of wisdom, which meant for them the art of being successful, of getting along in the world. Getting along in the world meant, ultimately, being happy in the world by pursuing wealth, reputation, and honor. It is not unfair to say, then, that these early philosophers, these professional wise men, taught the art of happiness. They might, for that reason, be said to be among the foremost teachers of a way of philosophy.

Most famous of the ancient wise men, though he would probably reject the title "sophist," just as he rejected their way of philosophy, was the Athenian philosopher Socrates (469-399 B.C.). Socrates' fees were modest; for his labors he received, as often as not, merely a good supper with sufficient wine and the attentions of challenging and attentive companions. Unlike the Sophists, Socrates' traveling was primarily confined to Athens and environs; but, as we shall see below, he did manage, nonetheless, through his vigorous questioning and the simple mode of his life, to focus the attention of the Greek world on himself and on the way of philosophy which to him lay through "the greatest improvement of the soul." Socrates, too, would probably have regarded his endeavors as teaching the art of wisdom, viz., a philosophy by which to guide one's life.

Philosophy, in its more technical and traditional sense, has been defined as that intellectual discipline that seeks to set and solve problems arising in some four traditional areas of human concern. Those four areas are: *metaphysics*, where the problems are concerned with the nature of ultimate reality, e.g., with Matter, Mind and Spirit; *epistemology*, where the problems are concerned with the nature of knowledge, e.g., with belief, truth and justifications; *value theory*, where the problems are concerned with both *ethics*, which deals with problems relating to right and wrong in human conduct, and *aesthetics*, which deals with problems relating to beauty and ugliness in works of art; and *logic*, where the problems that are set and solved are concerned with the nature of inference, e.g., with necessity, consistency and validity. To these four subfields of philosophy can be added a fifth, viz., *agōgē*,* philosophy as a way of life. Philosophy now becomes that intellectual discipline that sets and solves problems about, as the Sophists would say, how to get along in the world in order to find happiness, or, as Socrates might say, how to care for the greatest improvement of the soul in order to find happiness.

The wise person, to the Sophists and to Socrates, is the person who, at the very least, has learned the art of living well and happily. As an art, then, it would seem that wisdom can be taught and, if it can be taught, then it can be learned. We are speaking of philosophy now, in this fifth sense, as that intellectual discipline which sets and solves problems concerned with the philosophies of life, ways of life, *agōgēs*, that attempt to answer Aristotle's question.

The Prescription for Happiness

Philosophy as a guide of life has then an ancient and honored beginning in the West with the Sophists and Socrates. But it has just as ancient and honored a beginning in the East, as well. Nowhere is this more clearly seen than in the philosophy, or religion, of Gautama the Buddha (563-483 B.C.). He has been likened to a physician who practiced the art of diagnosis and cure perhaps in the same way as Socrates, likening himself to a midwife, helped the young men of Athens to bring forth their ideas in an intellectual birth.

Gautama the Buddha provides us with a formula for neatly summarizing any philosophy of life, a formula patterned after the four stages of

---

* *Agōgē*, from the Greek meaning "to carry away" or "to lead to a point," in Hellenistic Greece meant a way of philosophy or a way to happiness. Thus Epicureanism, Stoicism, Cynicism and Skepticism, each of which we shall examine below, are instances of 4th century B.C. *agōgēs*.

a physician's diagnostic art: First, the doctor discovers the symptoms of the disease, the *problem*; next, he or she seeks the origin of the problem, the *cause*; next, the prognosis, the future course of the cure, is calculated, the *solution*; fourth, finally, and most importantly, the physician prescribes the medicine for the cure, the *way*. The origin of this formula or prescription for happiness is found in the following recounting of the life of the Buddha: After achieving *nirvana* or liberation at the age of 35, we are told that the Buddha journeyed to the city of Banaras in India to preach his first sermon. The sermon, known as the turning of the wheel of the law, enunciates for the first time the Four Noble Truths that lie at the heart of ancient and modern Buddhism. It is on these four truths that the Buddha establishes his own *agōgē* or way of philosophy.

1. Now this, O monks, is the noble truth of suffering: birth is suffering, old age is suffering, sickness is suffering, death is suffering, sorrow, lamentation, dejection and despair are suffering....

2. Now this, O monks, is the noble truth of the cause of suffering: desire....

3. Now this, O monks, is the noble truth of the cessation of suffering: release....

4. Now this, O monks, is the noble truth of the way that leads to the cessation of suffering: the Noble Eightfold Path....
    [*Samyutta-nikāya* V. 420 in Edward J. Thomas, *The Life of the Buddha as Legend and History* (London: Routledge & Kegan Paul, Ltd., 1949/1927) p. 878.]

The Four Noble Truths are in a very real sense paradigmatic of any way of philosophy for in them the Buddha has described the four essential elements that any such way must have. First, the Buddha has indicated the *problem* with which he intends to deal, and for the Buddha that problem is suffering; suffering lies at the heart of not only the Buddha's prescription for happiness but at the heart of human existence, itself.

Second, the Buddha has indicated the *cause* of the problem; any way of philosophy, if it is to be useful in solving the problem of suffering, would have to seek the causes of that suffering.

Third, the Buddha has indicated, as any optimistic philosophy of life ought, that a *solution* is at hand; any way of philosophy, it would seem, must state that the problem of suffering can be solved else what's the use of having such a philosophy?

Fourth, the Buddha has indicated that there is a *way* to the solution and that it lies in treating the cause of the problem; any way of philosophy, it would appear, again, must provide the method by which suffering can be overcome.

Suppose we refer to this four stage model for any philosophy of life as "the way of philosophy." The way of philosophy that the Buddha has laid before his followers would in outline, then, look like this:

The Way of the Buddha

1. Problem: Suffering
2. Cause: Desire
3. Solution: Release, *Nirvana*
4. Way: The Noble Eightfold Path

We shall be examining the Buddha's prescription in some detail below. For the present, let us assume that this brief four stage schema allows us to get at the heart of any philosophic way. We shall be using it as the model for summarizing all of the ways of philosophy throughout this book. Before we turn to our first philosophers, however, consider for a moment the question, What constitutes an adequate, satisfactory or good way of philosophy? In other words, What would be a satisfactory answer to Aristotle's question? and What would constitute an unsatisfactory answer?

What is an Adequate Way of Philosophy?

It has often been stated that there is one thing that everyone ought to change at least once in their lives, viz., their philosophy. And perhaps this is so. In making this change, it might be well to keep in mind that it is never a rational justification for a way of philosophy to claim for it:

1. that it was taught to you as a child and you have always believed it;
2. that everyone you know believes it;
3. or that it is the only philosophy of life that you understand.

These three propositions may be *causes* for a belief or for a way of philosophy; but stating the causes or origins of a belief are not *reasons* or justifications for maintaining or accepting the belief, or for persuading someone else to hold that belief or that philosophy.

As a child, you may have been taught that Santa Claus will reward all good children at Christmas; but that is not a reason to continue believing now that Santa Claus will reward all good children at Christmas. Or the fact that everyone that you know believes that women are inferior to men is not a reason for you to accept that prejudice or to defend it to others; recall that many people used to believe that the earth was flat. Or you may believe that blue fairies turn the wheels inside your watch because that is easier to understand than the chronological mechanics of watchmaking; but ease of understanding is not a reason for persuading someone else that your views on watches are better than theirs. Discovering and describing the origins and simplicities of beliefs and ways of philosophy are not rational justifications for accepting any belief or way of philosophy.

Finally, it may well be the case that any one of these three causes of beliefs could be grounds for questioning and then changing one's beliefs or way of philosophy. Thus discovering that my way of philosophy, i.e., my prescription for happiness, was something that I have believed or held since childhood because my family and friends believed it or because it was the easiest philosophy for me to understand may be a reason now for questioning it, criticizing it, and getting rid of it.

But there are other reasons for challenging or even discarding a way of philosophy. We shall concentrate on three such criteria and say that when any of these three standards are not met, we can then be said to have an inadequate way of philosophy; and that when all of them are met, we can then be said to have an adequate way of philosophy. The chief reason for using these three standards to judge the philosophies that we shall be meeting in this book is that they will give us a ground on which to critically examine these philosophies. After presenting the various ways of philosophy, we shall want to know in what fashion they may have proved to be inadequate, i.e., to be incomprehensible, self-contradictory, or incomplete. In other words, in keeping with the aim of philosophy as a problem-hunting and problem-solving discipline,* we shall be concerned with the problems that these ways of philosophy fail to raise or fail to solve such that when they do fail they cannot be regarded as adequate philosophic ways, and when they do not fail, they can be regarded as adequate philosophic ways. Consider now these three standards that any way of philosophy must meet if it is to be called "adequate," "best" or "most worthwhile," viz., common sense, consistency, and completeness.

Common sense (a comprehensibility standard)

Any acceptable way of philosophy must be stateable in ordinary and non-technical language, and what is expressed ought to be compatible

---

* Recall William James' wise words about problem-solving: "The transition from a state of puzzle and perplexity to rational comprehension is full of lively relief and pleasure."

with common sense. For example, Aristotle will attempt to justify both slavery and the inferiority of women. But this attempt, because it seems so bizarre, would probably be grounds for calling his way of philosophy, insofar as it depends on or leads to such weird views, "inadequate." And Gorgias of Leontini's unexplained and curious claims that nothing exists; and that even if something did exist, we couldn't understand it; and that even if we understood it, we couldn't explain it to anyone, would also appear *prima facie*, to violate our standard of comprehensibility. The criterion is admittedly hazardous because "common sense" is not only vague (having no clear meaning) but notoriously ambiguous (having too many meanings), as well. But using the standard with care will prove to be extremely useful in judging adequacy.

Any way of philosophy which cannot be stated in a common sense or comprehensible language is inadequate.

Consistency (a logical standard)

Any acceptable way of philosophy must be or stateable in language and arguments that are neither self-contradictory nor logically unsound. For example, popular hedonism will claim that all pleasures are good. But this claim overlooks the fact that some pleasures can cause pain and even kill; hence, the way of popular hedonism leads to the self-contradictory conclusion that some pleasures are both good and not-good. Or consider Aristotle's proof of the existence of a First Mover (God): If there were no First Mover then there would be no effects now; but there are effects now (look around); therefore, there must be, or must have been, a First Mover. The argument is valid, i.e., it follows the rules of logic, but unsound, for the first premise is probably false.

Any way of philosophy which contains logical inconsistencies is inadequate.

Completeness (a practical standard)

Any acceptable way of philosophy must be capable of solving or resolving the kinds of problems that compel us to invent ways of philosophy to begin with. If the way of philosophy being considered fails to *raise* problems that it should have raised or it fails to *solve* those problems that it does raise, then that way of philosophy must be considered inadequate.

For example, Martin Luther King, Jr. will ask us to recognize injustice wherever it occurs and to take a stand against it whenever it occurs. But he fails to raise the question, How do we know when injustices do occur?, and he fails to solve the problem of what is to be done with every case of recognized injustice. It's easy to recognize the obvious cases of injustice, such as brutal attacks against peaceful marchers. But what about the claims of injustice in less obvious cases. Good men and women conscientiously and honestly disagree over abortion, divorce, capital punishment, gun control, contraception, flag burning, and so on, where public law and private morality clash repeatedly. Without *raising* the problem of the nature of injustice in all cases, and without *solving* the problem of what is always to be done when injustice is recognized, King's way of philosophy may lay itself open to charges of incompleteness in both senses.

Any way of philosophy which is incomplete, either because it fails to raise or it fails to solve obvious problems, is inadequate.

Conclusion

The three criteria for an adequate way of philosophy, viz., common sense, consistency, and completeness, are not always going to be satisfied in the philosophies that we are about to discuss. And it will not always be clear when they are not met or satisfied. Common sense, for example, is the most subjective of the three criteria, resting, as often as not, on the background and training of the reader, besides being relative to the time and place in which the philosophy was developed. Consistency is a formal and objective criterion and its violation should be the easiest to isolate. Completeness is a practical criterion but, like common sense, it is relative to time, place, and the reader's sophistication, for its application. The best way to understand these criteria of adequacy is to see them in action and test each of them under direct battle conditions, as it were.

The search for an adequate way of philosophy will involve applying our three standards to the various philosophies and philosophers to be discussed in this book. Our search will presuppose that all of these philosophies and philosophers were attempting to answer Aristotle's question; and that they were attempting to answer it by applying the four-stage way of philosophy that identifies the problem, the cause of the problem, the solution to the problem, and the way to that solution.

In what follows, the standards of common sense, consistency, and completeness will all be closely examined as we apply them to our various philosophies and philosophers. Our task, in addition to this application, will involve presenting as clearly and sympathetically as possible some twenty ways of philosophy, as we poke, probe, and pry into them in order to see just how good, how adequate, they actually are. In other words, our examination of these ways of philosophy is intended to be both descriptive and critical. Penultimately, it will be up to the reader to judge both the fairness of the description and the aptness of the criticism. Ultimately, it will also be up to the reader to judge whether any of these ways of philosophy, adequate or not, can answer Aristotle's question, What is the best and most worthwhile life that a human being can live?

TWO

THE WAY OF RELATIVISM
❖·❖

PROTAGORAS OF ABDERA: THE FIRST PHILOSOPHER

"Philosophy is an activity which by discussions and arguments secures the happy life." [*Sextus Empiricus*, Four Volumes, translated by R. G. Bury, Vol. III, "Against the Ethicists," (Harvard University Press, 1968), pp. 465-467. Sextus is quoting Epicurus and discussing, and then attacking, Epicurus' "art of life" in order to present his own skeptical "art of life."] Thus the Greek Skeptic philosopher, Sextus Empiricus, (ca. 200 A.D.), defined "philosophy." In so stating, Sextus was following a tradition that saw philosophy as a way of life, a tradition that predates the Western world's two greatest philosophers, Socrates and Plato, by some one hundred years. For the first person to use the word "philosophy" was Pythagoras of Samos (572-497 B.C.) who was also probably the first person in the West to treat philosophy as a way of life. For Plato (427-347 B.C.) says of Pythagoras:

> Such was Pythagoras, who was himself especially loved on account of having transmitted to posterity a certain way of life which even to this day is called "Pythagorean." [Plato, *Republic* 600 b. The Pythagorean Order was a brotherhood of men following a social, ethical and religious life in and near Crotona in southern Italy shortly after 530 B.C. This way of life involved following the precepts of Pythagoras relating to such diverse topics as medicine, food, hygiene and mathematics in what can now be best described as a secretive monastic society.]

The Greek tradition of philosophy that evolved between the times of Pythagoras (530 B.C.) and Sextus (200 A.D.) was one which provided men and women with a way of life and a method for securing happiness.

Foremost among those who eagerly pursued this ancient tradition and who sought a way to the happy life were the Sophists of the fifth century B.C.

The Rise of Athens

When the eastern Persian hoards invaded Greece and the Grecian outposts, first under Darius the Great (King from 521-486 B.C.) and then under his son, Xerxes the Great (King from 486-465 B.C.), they swept all and everything before them. From about 500 B.C. until 480 B.C., they roamed through the north and eastern Greek isles and inland cities, burning, pillaging, murdering the males, and taking the women and children as slaves. Aside from a few modest and temporary Greek victories and several well-executed delaying actions, the Persians moved inexorably south, their hundreds of thousands devouring in their slow but deadly progress the tens of thousands of the Hellenic community.

At last they were poised for a final triumph to take and destroy the city of Athens, herself. The terrified Athenians sent an assembly to Delphi to plead with the God Apollo for a sign, a strategy for survival. The God spoke through His priestess saying that only a wall of wood could save them: "Safe shall the wooden wall continue for you and your children." [Herodotus, *The Persian Wars*, VII. 141.] This cryptic response to a desperate situation turned out to have more wisdom in it than was usual for the mysterious prophetess at Delphi. Themistocles, a highborn Athenian, came forward having divined the meaning of the oracle, and urged his compatriots to build a fleet of ships. His interpretation and urgings won out. The wooden wall was built. Themistocles was put in command and the Athenian navy decisively defeated the Persians at Salamis in 480 B.C. Subsequently, Athenian sea power and Athens went on to dominate the eastern Mediterranean and then the entire civilized Western world for three quarters of a century.

But the sea power that defeated Xerxes the Great also enfranchised the lower class citizens of Athens who had been called upon to pull the oars and man the sails in Themistocles' new and now victorious navy. With Athenian hegemony of the Aegean Sea, there came wealth, culture, and democracy to the Greeks and especially to Athens, the capital of what now became a new Hellenic empire. Under the inspired leadership of Pericles (died 429 B.C.), the city was rebuilt, more beautiful than ever as seen even in its 20th century ruins. Athens prospered and grew, spreading Athenian ways and learning, science and culture, throughout the civilized and uncivilized world, attracting to itself workers, artisans, merchants, and visitors from all over that world. Athens became the Paris-New York-London and Washington of the Mediterranean.

The newly enfranchised citizens of victorious Athens enjoyed a prosperity unprecedented in the ancient world. In casting about for ways to spend and enjoy their new-found wealth and leisure, they discovered, or were discovered by, the Sophists.

If necessity is the mother of invention, then wealth and leisure are surely the father. The needs that the Sophists claimed to meet were the needs that related directly to the question with which we began this study of the ways of philosophy: What is the best and most worthwhile life that a human being can live? The Sophists seem to have answered the question for many Athenians and, in the process of enriching their clients or students, they enriched themselves and posterity as well. For their answers to Aristotle's question are answers that remain practical and vital to this day. Their answers laid the foundation for that modern philosophy of life called "secular humanism."

The Sophists and Their Accomplishments

Before turning to the greatest exponent of Hellenic secular humanism, Protagoras, and his way of philosophy, let's first examine some of the basic principles of Sophist doctrine.

First, the Sophists claimed to be able to teach people how to be successful, how to be good and, ultimately, how to be happy. This seems like an innocuous enough claim. Don't churches, synagogues, parents, and schools teach children how to be good or virtuous?; don't books on success stream constantly from publishers claiming to show the way to wealth and happiness through the stock market, through investments in cities, housing and land, and through learning to be a lawyer, a broker, an auctioneer, an artist, a gourmet, a yogi? And don't they all claim to teach shortcuts to happiness by giving tips on good banks, good food, good investments, good music, good health, good sex, good religion, good you-name-it? Don't television, radio, magazines, and newspapers offer to teach the way to heavenly happiness, earthly bliss, and psychological stability through prayer, recorded music, painting at home, writing or reading in one's spare time, dieting, exercising, drinking only this beverage but not that one, or using only this soap, that aspirin, that laxative, that diet drink, reducing potion, antacid, or skin lotion, and so on? And won't this lead to better investments, better health, better middle age, old age, and in a word, a better life? But what's wrong with all of this? Isn't using these products and isn't success in these matters essential for the good life? for happiness? Isn't this the attitude of the new YUPies (young urban professionals) seeking their proper place in the world of the 90s? And isn't it the job of some persons to fill needs like this, needs that we deem essential for the good life? In other words, if people feel the need to be successful and happy, then why shouldn't someone teach them how to achieve success and happiness?

In ancient Athens those who first attempted to teach people how to be virtuous, to be morally upright, politically and socially successful, financially secure, and, in a word, happy, were probably the Sophists. They were foreigners who appeared to the more conservative among the Athenians to be intellectual hucksters, pandering to the puerile tastes and vulgar needs of the *hoi polloi*, the many. It is no wonder that the Sophists came to be seen by many Athenians, just as many conservative Americans today see the secular humanists, as

> ostentatious imposters, flattering and duping the rich youth [the ancient YUPies] for their own personal gain, undermining the morality of Athens public and private, and encouraging their pupils to unscrupulous prosecution of ambition and cupidity. They are even affirmed to have succeeded in corrupting the general morality, so that Athens had become miserably degenerated and vicious in the latter years of the Peloponnesian War [431-404 B.C.], as compared with what she was in the time of Miltiades and Aristeides [about 470 B.C.]. [G. Grote, *History of Greece* (London: 1883) Vol. VIII, p. 156, quoted in G.B. Kerferd, *The Sophistic Movement* (Cambridge University Press, 1984), p. 5.]

Nowhere is the claim that the Sophists taught virtue and taught people to be virtuous more easily seen than in Plato's dialogue *Protagoras*. In this dialogue, Protagoras has claimed to teach political *aretē*, political virtue, and Socrates has expressed his doubts that this is possible. *Aretē*, the tradition said, was a quality of human excellence which made a man, among other things, a good man and a natural born leader. *Aretē* was, consequently, something that you were born with; it depended on natural or divine gifts and was a mark of good parents as well as good upbringing by those virtuous parents. The conservative tradition that defended the rights and privileges of the aristocratic class held that *aretē*, virtue, was a matter of *physis*, nature, and not *nomos*, nurture. Hence, some people, people from the right class, were born to rule. The question then is, Could *aretē* be taught and learned by someone who didn't have it to begin with?, thereby allowing anyone who learns political virtue to rule. Protagoras was striking at the very foundation of Athenian society.

Second, the Sophists claimed to be able to teach people how to be successful, good, and happy through a series of paid courses of instruction. The various virtues, therefore, the keys to acceptance in society, could be acquired through university-type educational lectures. Those who had the money and the leisure could take the lectures and thereby become virtuous, i.e., good, just, wise, temperate, and courageous, or at least they could get the reputation for being so. Anyone could now become a gentleman, a member of the elite and upper classes, by learning the art, the *technē*, that led to the virtues. It's as if a vocational-technical school were to teach people how to behave as if they had college degrees in the liberal arts even though they don't have them. Nowadays we read books like *How to Make Your Friends Believe That You Know All About Wine*, or *All About Latin*, or *All About History*, or *All About Music*, or *Classical Literature*. It has a snob appeal; but it was and is all so superficial; it was a sham, an illusion; it was, to quote the later conservative critics of the Sophists like Socrates and Plato, all about appearances, opinions, and falsehoods, and not about reality, knowledge, and truth. The Sophists had set out, through their paid courses, to produce what we have come to call "the sophisticated man."

Third, the Sophists claimed to be able to teach people how to win their cases in courts of law. In particular, they are probably responsible for introducing the disputatious or adversarial method into Western legal practices. In the adversarial method one tries to convince a jury of the rightness of one's own case by both disputing one's opponent's claims to rightness and at the same time making one's own case appear to be as right as possible. No matter if one's case is the worst or the least just; persuasion by confrontation is everything; swaying the jury is everything. It was an attempt, as Socrates put it, to make the worst cause appear to be the better cause. Winning was everything; compromise was nothing. In addition, the Sophists were the first to introduce in their courses in public speaking formal, logical techniques for courtroom debating by employing the methods for recognizing fallacious and invalid arguments. Their adversarial arts came clothed in rhetorical armor. It will be interesting to compare this adversarial approach to legal adjudication with the compromise approach, used so successfully by Mohandas Gandhi, later in this book. The adversarial method is neatly illustrated and marvelously satirized in Aristophanes' hilarious 5th century B.C. comedy, *The Clouds*, where two adversaries appear on stage as fighting cocks labeled "the just" and "the unjust" laws. They debate in a clownish, slapstick manner and, of course, the unjust rooster always wins.

Fourth, the Sophists recognized a basic distinction in what was called *nomos*, or convention, and *physis*, or eternal nature, and they exploited that distinction. *Nomos* came to have the sense of that which is artificially contrived, sometimes what is false though commonly believed. *Physis* came to have the sense of that which is real and true. If you were to ask the question, What is the source of our ideas of right and wrong?, the answer, of course, is *the law*, the moral, i.e., the subjective and personal, law or the ethical, i.e., the objective and public, law. But where do *those* laws come from? Are our laws only conventions (*nomoi*), established by human beings?, conventions that can change with time, place and circumstance? Or do our laws ultimately rest on and reflect something in the very nature (*physis*) of the universe, something eternal and in itself unchanging. For example, what is the source or foundation of the law that says, Honor thy father and thy mother? Is that commandment absolute, i.e., unchanging and established for all eternity? Or is it relative, i.e., applicable to human beings at a particular time and place? If God established that law, does that make it absolute? Couldn't God change His mind today and alter the law saying, Honor thy mother only, thereby making the original commandment relative? Does God's approval of the law make it absolute in any sense? Or does God approve the commandment because it is absolute?

In Plato's dialogue *Euthyphro* we find a young man taking his own father to court, charging him with murdering one of the father's slaves. Socrates questions the young man, Euthyphro, and the discussion centers on the very issue that had earlier separated the Sophists from the more conservative Athenians, viz., what is the relation between the Gods' approval of a particular law, such as honoring parents, and the good inherent in the law over and apart from that approval. Socrates puts the question this way:

> Is what is sacred [like the law] sacred because the Gods approve it?, or do they approve it because it is sacred? [Plato, *Euthyphro*, 10a, author's translation.]

If the former is the case, then the holiness of the law depends on the Gods, and the law could change just as soon as the approval of the Gods turned to disapproval: The law is then *nomos*, conventional, social custom, and relative. If the latter is the case, if the Gods approve of the law because it is sacred, then that sacredness does not depend on the Gods, and the law is separate from the Gods, eternal and holy independently of their approval or disapproval: The law is then *physis*, natural, real, and absolute.

The Sophists recognized this basic difference between *nomos* and *physis*, and they, with one or two exceptions, argued that all laws are man-made, dependent on communal approval and disapproval, and that convention, common practice, is the final arbiter of right and wrong. And just as languages, politics, dress, and social customs may differ from community to community, so also may the laws of those communities differ. They are based on *nomos*, not on *physis*.

Fifth and finally, the Sophists recognized and in general seem to have accepted the theory that later 17th and 18th century philosophers, such as Thomas Hobbes, John Locke, and Jean Jacques Rousseau, would call "the social contract." This theory follows from the Sophists' defense of *nomos* as the origin of law and justice, and it is the view that "human societies rest upon implied and so non-historical, or on an actual and historical, agreement to establish an organized community." [G. B. Kerferd, *The Sophistic Movement, Op. Cit.*, p. 147] The social compact or social contract theory assumes that prior to the contract being drawn up, man lived in a state of nature in which there were no social or ethical obligations and each person pursued his or her own interests independently of, and in competition with, others. But if such a contract was agreed upon, and if social and ethical obligations, rights, and duties followed, then the concept of *nomos* applied. However, the question arose as to whether or not there were rights that existed independently of and prior to such a humanly constructed social contract. If there were "self-evident and inalienable rights," for example, grounded in nature, itself, then the concept of *physis* applied.

The commitment to a social contract theory, as opposed to an eternal law theory, was the one thing to which all of the Sophists seem to have been bound. The theory of *nomos* or social contract is nowhere more clearly and fairly expressed than by Plato who puts the theory into the mouth of the greatest Sophist of them all, Protagoras. Protagoras gives us a mythic account of the origin of the human race and the political skills by which humans live. After humans were created, the myth says, they lived in scattered groups for there were no cities. Hunted down and devoured by beasts stronger than themselves, they survived in a desperate condition because they lacked the art of defending themselves. And they lacked this art becaues they were without the art of war which depended on another art which they also lacked, viz., the art of politics:

> They sought therefore to save themselves by coming together and founding
> fortified cities, but when they gathered in communities they injured one
> another for want of political skill, and so they scattered again and continued
> to be devoured.

This natural condition of man described by Protagoras is similar to that
later described by Thomas Hobbes (1588-1679). Men are by nature nasty,
mean, brutish, quarrelsome and selfish, Hobbes contended. Before contracts, cities, and civilization existed, it was a war of all against all in
which each man attempted to pursue his own advantage whatever the
cost, a theme now sounded by the Sophists, like Callicles, Thrasymachus,
and Critias. It was nature red in tooth and claw.

Protogoras continues his mythical story of the origin of law and civilization:

> Zeus therefore, fearing the total destruction of our race, sent Hermes to im-
> part to men the qualities of respect for others and a sense of justice, so as to
> bring order into our cities and create a bond of friendship and union.

Zeus orders Hermes to distribute respect and justice equally, to all, and
not to only a few as talent and skill in the arts are apportioned. Thus it is
that in politics, Protagoras concludes, every man is an expert if only he
be taught correctly, for every man can be taught political wisdom, justice
and moderation. It is on this assumption, of course, that democracy is
built and civilization established wherein the citizens "listen to every
man's opinion, for they think that everyone must share in this kind of
virtue; otherwise the state could not exist." [Plato, *Republic* 322 b, c; 322a,
in *The Collected Dialogues of Plato*, Edited by Edith Hamilton and
Huntington Cairns (Pantheon Books, 1961), pp. 319, 320.]

The laws that men make when they come together, when they contract together, are all *nomoi*, i.e., man-made laws, differing at times from
one contracting group to another. Further, the sense of justice and the respect for others, the capacity for moderation and civic virtue, are, for
Protagoras, not innate but acquired virtues. And they are acquired by
"instruction and taking thought," as he is quick to point out. From the 45
drachma course on virtue one can make a silk purse out of a sow's ear,
after all. It is in this sense that virtue can be taught, social contracts executed, and human beings made safe and happy.

The Sophists' names were well-known to the young men of Athens
just as the names of popular Rock stars are known by today's youth. And
the influence then on young Athenians may have been as mind-blowing

to them, and as disturbing to their elders, as the Garbage Galoots and the Yahoo Screamers are today.

There was, for example, the rhetorician Gorgias of Leontini who lived in the latter half of the fifth century B.C. He introduced a hearty scepticism into the Sophists' bag of philosophic tricks by outrageously claiming and defending:

First, that nothing exists
    a.   Not-Being does not exist.
    b.   Being does not exist....
    c.   A mixture of Being and not-Being does not exist.
Second, even if anything exists, it is incomprehensible.
Third, even if it is comprehensible, it is incommunicable.
[Kathleen Freeman, *Ancilla to the Pre-Socratic Philosophers* (Harvard University Press, 1983/1948), p. 128.]

It is just this sort of sophistry that subsequently led Cato the Elder (234-149 B.C.) to ban philosophers forever from Rome. The story is that Carneades, a famous head of Plato's Academy, came on a mission in 155 B.C. from Athens to Rome with Diogenes the Stoic. Like the young men of Athens who clamored after the Sophists before him, the "most studious youth immediately waited" on Carneades who "gathered large and favourable audiences, and ere long filled, like a wind, all the city with the sound of his oratory." The young men of Rome were so impressed "that quitting all their pleasures and pastimes, they ran mad after philosophy." [Plutarch, *The Lives of the Noble Grecians and Romans*, translated by John Dryden (New York: Modern Library, n.d.), p. 428.] Carneades then went before the Roman Senate and through an interpreter gloriously expounded the virtues of justice as taught by Plato and Aristotle. The next day he returned and just as movingly expounded the evils of justice, arguing that great states had become great by unjust acts against their weaker neighbors. The youth of Rome loved it, but the great conservative moralist and statesman, Cato the Elder, also called "the Censor," the defender of all the ancient and noble Roman virtues, did not. He got the Senate to pass a law banishing the Greek visitors and forbidding all philosophers forever after from entering Rome. Sophists and Skeptics have been popular with the young but unpopular with their elders since the times of ancient Athens and Rome.

Protagoras' Life

But the greatest of all of the Sophists was Protagoras of Abdera. He is the one Sophist on whom Plato spends most of his critical time and he is the Sophist that the modern world most remembers. In what follows I shall say something about his life, his general philosophy, and then conclude with a discussion of the four elements of his way of philosophy that are based on that life and philosophy.

Protagoras was born in Abdera, Thrace, and lived from about 490 B.C. until about 420 B.C. Very little is known about his early personal life and what we do know is taken from the reports of the 3rd century A.D. gossip and essayist, Diogenes Laertius. Diogenes reports, for example, that Protagoras gave public readings for a fee, that he was the first to distinguish the grammatical tenses of verbs, that he invented the shoulder pad on which porters carry their burdens, for he had been a porter himself at one time, and, finally, that he was responsible for the following charming but paradoxical tale:

> The story is told that once, when he asked Euathlus his disciple for his fee, the latter replied, "But I have not won a case yet." "No," said Protagoras, "if *I* win this case against you, I must have the fee, for winning it; if you win, I must have it because *you* win it."
> [Diogenes Laertius, *Lives of Eminent Philosophers*, Two Volumes (Harvard University Press, 1950), Vol. II, p. 469.]

He spent many years in Athens, traveling throughout the neighboring districts, attracting large crowds of admirers and the curious wherever he went, speaking in a voice so deep that other orators were drowned out by it. He was a close friend of Pericles, the Athenian statesman, and he aided Pericles in the latter's attempts to bring and to keep democracy in Athens. His writings, save for brief fragments from works with interesting titles such as "Of the Misdeeds of Mankind," "Of Wrestling," and "On the Dwellers in Hades," have not survived. Most of what we know of him comes, unfortunately, from his enemies or from those who strongly took issue with him. He is said to have died when his ship went down while on a voyage to Sicily.

But Protagoras is a seminal figure in Western intellectual history. He set the standards for empiricism, relativism, subjectivism, scepticism, and probably materialism and atheism, standards which later ages will follow. For all of this he might justifiably be called "the first philosopher in the Western world."

Man as the Measure of All Things

All of the essentials of Protagoras' philosophy can probably be logically deduced from two well-known statements that have been attributed to him:

> Man is the measure of all things; of the things that are as to how they are, and of the things that are not as to how they are not.

> Concerning the Gods, I am not able to know whether they exist or do not exist nor what they are like; because the things preventing knowledge are many, the subject is obscure and human life is too short. [Kathleen Freeman, *Ancilla, Op. Cit.*, pp. 125, 126 with some changes.]

To say that man is the measure or standard for all things can be taken in either of two ways: Either each individual is his or her own standard of value, truth and reality; or men and women taken as a group are the standard.* Further, Protagoras may not only be describing what he has found people doing as he traveled about Hellas, but he may also be telling us what he believes those people ought to be doing; that is to say, not only *is* man the standard but he or she *ought to be* the standard, as well. The position that Protagoras is speaking to here has been called "relativism," the view that two contradictory judgments could both be correct. Thus the acceptance of contradictory judgments in ethics where, for example, I might claim that abortion of human fetuses is never morally right, and you might claim that it is sometimes morally right, means that we could both be correct according to *ethical relativism*; similarly, the acceptance of contradictory judgments in epistemology where, for example, I might claim that it is true that women should have the same rights as men and you claim that it is false, means that we could both be correct according to *epistemological relativism*; similarly the acceptance of contradictory judgments in metaphysics where, for example, I might claim that I know that God is real and you might claim that you know that God is not real, means that we could both be correct according to *metaphysical relativism*. The relativism that Protagoras' first quotation leads to is frequently stated as, Well, it's good to you, or true for you, or real for you, but it's not good, or true, or real for me; but we're both right! In other words, whatever turns you on is okay, and the fact that it turns you on, or turns your group on is, alone and by itself, a sufficient measure or warrant or standard or reason for calling the statement "correct" or "okay."

If man, individually or collectively, is the standard, then, Protagoras' anthropocentric philosophy says, that there can be no absolute rules or Rulers that can bind all human beings forever; i.e., there are no absolute, unchanging, eternal criteria for measuring goodness, knowledge, or real-

---

* Here is the beginning of the controversy between individualism and communalism. See Chapter 13, *The Ways of Individualism and Community*, below.

ity. What each person or group of persons says is what goes. There is no one true morality, no one true religion, no one right political system, no one true standard for correctness in anything, whether in grammar, beauty, humor, cake baking, car driving, etc.: Whatever you do, or your group does, is correct as long as you or your group thinks it's correct.

This Protagorean relativism will be soundly bludgeoned by Socrates, as we shall see shortly.

But if man is the standard, then how does man* measure? Not by the past traditions of measurers, not by God or by Revelation or by Faith or by Intuition for they are all relative and open to the charge that they too were measured, at one time or another, by another individual or measurer or by groups of individual measurers. The measuring must be done by each person using and trusting to his or her own senses. All values, knowledge, and reality are measured, when all is said and done, by the senses and reason of individual measurers. In epistemology the position that says that all knowledge ultimately is based on or comes from the five senses, is called *empiricism*, i.e., the view that there is nothing in the mind that was not first in the senses. Protagoras is an empiricist: Man with his and her senses is the measure of all things, a view which leads us, naturally, to Protagoras' second quotation, above.

As an empiricist, Protagoras cannot claim to know whether the Gods exist or not for the senses cannot give us knowledge about the transempirical Gods. The consequence is that Protagoras must be a *sceptic* on matters relating to the knowledge of the Gods. *Epistemological scepticism* maintains that knowledge is impossible. Protagoras is an epistemological sceptic with respect to the existence of and nature of these things, if there are any, that transcend sensory investigation.

Diogenes Laertius tells us that after Protagoras wrote the above statement about the Gods in the introduction to his book, *On the Gods*, the Athenians immediately expelled him. They sent around a herald to collect all of his existing works and then burned them in the marketplace in Athens. [Diogenes Laertius, *Op. Cit.*, Vol. II, p. 465.] The sceptic's life has never been an easy one.

But Protagoras is a *pragmatist* with respect to the conduct of life. His empiricism and skepticism notwithstanding there are sufficient grounds for maintaining that Protagoras believed that what works, or what is

---

* I have not yet found a neutral and easy way of rendering pronoun gender that does not sound either awkward or grotesque. I apologize to all of those persons whom I shall no doubt offend.

THE WAY OF RELATIVISM

useful, is what should be followed and accepted as right or correct. He says,

> Teaching needs endowment and practice.

and

> Art without practice, and practice without art, are nothing. [Kathleen Freeman, *Ancilla, Op. Cit.*, pp. 126, 127.]

Thus, the book burning incident aside, he attempted to be consistent with his ethical relativism and to follow the customs and commitments of those cities in which he lived; and he seems to have urged others to do the same. If a thing works well for yourself or your community, in other words, then it is good, true or real. Stay with it, keep it, follow it, protect it. This is Protagorean pragmatism, pure and simple. That advice ought to have led Protagoras to accept the Gods of the Athenians or at least it ought to have forced him into keeping silent about his sceptical doubts concerning those Gods. But as we shall see in our discussion of Socrates, the Greek world in general was going through a cultural revolution in the latter half of the 5th century B.C. All the traditional customs and commitments were being called into question, including the current religious practices and beliefs in Athens. Things were changing so rapidly that it was very difficult to know what the mores of a given society were and what customs were to be followed at any given time.

PROTAGORAS' ACCOMPLISHMENTS

From Protagoras' two statements quoted previously, we have been able to deduce several philosophic views that remain popular and viable in the 20th century: Relativism, empiricism, scepticism and pragmatism. It will remain for other later philosophers to sharpen, as well as to attack, these positions; but their presence here, by inference at least, in the philosophy of Protagoras justifies us, once again, in calling him "the first philosopher of the Western world."

We turn finally to Protagoras' way of philosophy. The questions that we are attempting to answer are, Can the Sophists or Protagoras speak to our condition and to our problems in the 20th century? What have they to offer to those looking for a philosophy to guide their lives in these times that they also offered to the troubled youth of Athens?

THE WAY OF RELATIVISM: PROTAGORAS OF ABDERA

The Problem

From what has been said previously about the Sophists and Protagoras, it ought to be possible to reconstruct the problem that Protagoras was attempting to solve for the Athenians and other Greeks of his time.

In Plato's dialogue, *Protagoras,* Socrates' young friend, Hippocrates, has just wakened Socrates shortly before dawn. The lad is all excited about the arrival in Athens of "the wisest man now living" and urges Socrates to come and introduce him to this greatest Sophist of them all, viz., Protagoras. The dialogue then turns to two important questions, What is a Sophist? and, Why would anyone want to go to visit a Sophist?

The young man, and we must assume all young men of the time as well, wants to see Protagoras in order to become wise, because a Sophist is, "one who has knowledge of wise things and teaches that knowledge to others": Socrates' young and eager friend wishes to become a Sophist. At the house where Protagoras and several other Sophists have gathered the youth is introduced to Protagoras who proceeds to recount the aims of Sophism to Hippocrates:

> Young man, if you come to me, your gain will be this. The very day you join me, you will go home a better man, and the same the next day. Each day you will make progress toward a better state. [Plato, *Protagoras* 318a in *The Collected Dialogues of Plato, Op. Cit.,* p. 317.]

On closer questioning by Socrates, Protagoras states that the subjects that he teaches to his pupils are not arithmetic, astronomy, geometry, and music, topics which the other Sophists teach, but something much more general wherein the subject is:

> The proper care of his personal affairs, so that he may best manage his own household, and also of the state's affairs so as to become a real power in the city, both as speaker and man of action. [Plato, *Protagoras,* 318d, *Ibid.*]

So what is the problem that the Sophist attempts to solve? The problem might have been merely the very general fear of failure, a fear as common today as it was 2400 years ago. The fear that all sensitive young men and women have of not being a success, of not measuring up to the demands and the goals set by family and society.

Plato, though an arch opponent of the Sophists, has managed in the *Protagoras* to present fairly and well the problem, the solution to which made the Sophists so popular. They taught the art of success as a way of overcoming the problem of the fear of failure.

The Cause

The cause of the problem of anxiety about one's future success in private and public affairs was ignorance of the art of successful living. They were saying to the youth of Athens and elsewhere that they had only their own ignorance to blame if they ended up a failure. The cause was in them. The virtues, those qualities that lead to success, can be "instilled by education." They had only to pay the fees, take the courses in the art of happiness, and get ready to be successful. The magic words, then as now, for selling a product, are words like "gain," "better person," "better state," "progress," and "success."

The Solution

The solution to the problem was being successful, becoming a better household and estate manager, becoming a real power in the city. The acquisition of all or any of these qualities would lead to happiness. And happiness defined in this fashion is precisely what the Sophists were selling and guaranteeing. To this extent the Sophists of yesteryear are not altogether different from the Sophists of today, as we have seen, who claim that if you only buy their product, use their way or method, follow their philosophy or religion, then you will be happy. "Happiness" is an ambiguous word that, as we shall see, can take on many meanings throughout the world. It is an ultimate goal of human endeavor and it can mean "pleasure," "knowledge," "love," "salvation," and so on. Saying it is "ultimate" means that people seek it for its own sake and not in order to reach something else by using it. Happiness is not a means to something else. It is the final goal of all of our endeavors; it is, as Aristotle says, that at which all things aim.

The Ways

The ways to happiness (the solution) must attack the ignorance (the cause) of the anxiety or fear of failure (the problem). These ways for the Sophists were many and varied. They involved taking courses in astronomy, geometry, arithmetic and music, and lectures in grammar, logic, rhetoric, and whatever else would help the pupil "get ahead." Protagoras tells Hippocrates that he will go home a better man, making progress daily towards a better state. The art of success, if it is an art (technē), can be taught, and one can gain wealth, reputation, fame and honor by following the teaching imparted by Protagoras and the Sophists. The specifics of the way, however, must remain a secret since none of the Sophists' works on success have survived in any great detail.

PROBLEMS WITH SOPHISM

The three criteria that we had previously established for an adequate way of philosophy, viz., common sense, consistency and completeness, have been met in part. The way of philosophy is stated in a language that all can understand and there seems to be no logical contradictions in the philosophy, itself. But the claim to meet the problems for which it was established is admittedly incomplete since we have either only fragments of the Sophists' writings or we hear about them and their philosophies through philosophers such as Plato who were their ideological enemies.

But, this textual incompleteness aside, another issue emerges that is worth pursuing for it directly challenges the basic Sophist claim that the way to success can be taught. Both Socrates and Plato appear to have argued that the virtues that the Sophists claimed to teach in their courses, virtues such as courage, wisdom, piety, self-control, and the like, cannot be taught. That, as a consequence, there is a radical incompleteness about Sophism for the common sense that they preach is simplistic if not false, and that in claiming to teach what is essentially unteachable they are, in fact, being self-contradictory. Therefore, this argument concludes, Sophism and the way of philosophy for Protagoras are woefully inadequate.

Protagoras had claimed "that virtue can be instilled by education." It sounds so modern, natural, and agreeable. With all reasonableness he even raises his own objection to the claim asking, Why is it then, if goodness, morality, courage, wisdom, and all the other virtues are teachable, that the sons of noble and good men turn out so badly? Well, one answer is that they all had a bad teacher. So find a better teacher (and here he is!):

> My claim is that I am one of these, rather better than anyone else at helping a man to acquire a good and noble character, worthy indeed of the fee which I charge and even more, as my pupils themselves agree. [*Protagoras*, 328b, *Ibid.*, p. 324.]

Socrates leads the attack against this very popular belief that goodness can be instilled in people by instruction and what he says can be put into a contemporary context. When teenagers drink too much, or drug too much, we ask the schools to teach temperance or abstinence. When stealing and murder become more than the public can bear, we blame the schools for not offering moral inspiration in courses in ethics or theology. When youngsters show lack of obedience or respect to authority, we blame the teachers, or lack of instruction in the schools, or permissiveness in society, and the cry goes up, Get a Sophist!, or nowadays we cry, Get a teacher!, or Get a new minister!, or Change presidents!, and so on. The question is then, Can anyone teach someone to be good? Protagoras seems to have said, Yes, I can!, and Socrates and Plato said, No, you can't!, and no one can!

When the schools were called upon to handle the problem of teenagers' drinking and their deaths by auto accidents, they didn't teach temperance in the schools; they taught defensive driving. Preaching abstinence wouldn't work to control teenage drug problems; but teaching human physiology and what happens to the human body when drugs are introduced into it was taught. Morality and goodness cannot be taught, the defenders who agreed with Socrates would say. The individual must teach himself or herself. No one but you can carry out the task of becoming virtuous. How would courage be taught? How would self-control be taught? The Sophists' claim to teach virtue is simply false; therefore, his entire program is false for it rests upon this seemingly simple claim. Thus the response from the Sophists' critics.

I leave it to the reader to ponder the following questions, Does one become moral by instruction from another? Does one learn to be virtuous through courses of instruction? Can integrity be taught? Can one be taught to be courageous?, or self-controlled?, or honest? Presumably, the Sophist would answer all of these questions in the affirmative.

THREE

THE WAY OF *PSYCHĒ*
❯•❮

SOCRATES OF ATHENS: THE FATHER OF WESTERN PHILOSOPHY

Socrates' Life

Socrates was born, raised and, in time, died in Athens (469-399 B.C.). What we know about him comes from three Athenian citizens whose writings survive and who knew him directly but who remembered him in quite different ways: Aristophanes, the comic dramatist who hilariously satirized Socrates as an unregenerate pedantic Sophist; Xenophon, soldier of fortune and essayist, who saw Socrates as an eminently practical but eminently wise man of affairs; and Plato, the greatest philosopher of the ancient and maybe any other world, who has given us the picture of Socrates as a martyr whose life became a sacred mission in obedience to the command of God.

We know that Socrates' mother was a midwife, that he, like his father, may have been a sculptor or stonecutter by trade, that he was something of a physical oddity in appearance being snub-nosed, "ugly" by his own admission, propelling himself along with a curious duck-like walk. We know that he was married, that he had three sons, and that he spent much time away from home, first as a soldier and then as a kind of Sophist. As a soldier and military hero, he fought in the Peloponnesian War (431-404 B.C.) where he served with distinction at Potidaea, Amphipolis and Delium, becoming by 424 B.C. a hoplite or fully armed infantryman. Subsequently, he emerged as a sort of "town character," a debater, teacher, "seer" and mystic, living only for his "mission" and for the probing conversations and embarrassing debates which he held with any citizen of Athens who thought himself wise and who would stay around long enough for a verbal scuffle with Socrates. We know that he lived a simple life, often wearing the same garments both winter and summer, going barefoot in the coldest times, indifferent to the elements, priding himself on how little he needed to stay well and alive. Socrates' strength of will and sense of honor and rightness were legendary. Equally well-known were his long periods of intense concentration when, like an ancient yogi, he would remain in the same meditative position for hours on end. He himself admitted to receiving divine signs, an inner voice that spoke to him, a conscience or *daimōn* that guided him in various moral ways. Finally, as we shall see below, Socrates was perhaps the first Western philosopher to argue repeatedly for the immortality and divine nature of the soul or *psychē*.

Socrates' life reached a climax in 431 B.C. when, at the age of 38, he was plunged into a spiritual crisis. His friend Chaerephon had asked the oracle of Apollo at Delphi, the greatest source of divine prophecies in the ancient world, this question: "Is any man wiser than Socrates?" When Socrates heard that the God had answered "None!", he was astonished. He knew that he was not wise at all, for he knew nothing. But then, believing that it was probably in this knowledge of his own ignorance that the God's claim for Socrates' wisdom lay, Socrates saw Lord Apollo's curious response as a divine command to him to test the claim. He was to dedicate the remainder of his life to that testing, and it was to earn him the deadly enmity of his fellow Athenians, the loving admiration of his devoted and youthful companions, and the honor and respect of the remainder of the civilized world ever since.

Plato's Dialogues

Plato's picture of his beloved friend is found in the famous dramatic dialogues in which Socrates is the central figure. It is in the earliest of these dialogues, or conversations, that we get the truest portrayal of the great philosopher at work. We have a total of some 27 dialogues by Plato of which about 15 are "Socratic," i.e., they give us a fair picture of Socrates and his philosophy, while the remainder of the dialogues are "Platonic," i.e., Socrates' own philosophy fades into the background and Plato's philosophy gradually emerges. In the last three or four of Plato's dialogues, finally, Socrates appears in only a minor role or not at all, and Plato's own mystical and metaphysical philosophy is presented, separate and distinct from Socrates' religious and moral philosophy.

The topics of the early Socratic dialogues from which our own view of Socrates will come are very varied. In *Charmides* (from about 390 B.C.) the topic is self-control; in *Euthyphro,* as we saw above, the topic is piety and service to God; in *Meno* the topics are education and virtue as gifts of God; and in *Laches* the topic is courage. These dialogues, probably along with *Apology, Crito* and *Phaedo,* where the subjects are Socrates' trial, defense and execution, are all concerned with the virtues and how they are acquired. They were all, with the exception of *Phaedo,* probably composed within ten years of Socrates' death.

To see Socrates at work and to understand what the nature of his method and pursuit of finding a man wiser than himself was like, consider this brief exchange from *Laches.* The subject is the fighting man's virtue, courage or valor, and whether it can be taught as the Sophists claimed. And what better persons to ask about courage than two military men, two generals, whose business is concerned with courage? These two men, Nicias and Laches, both claim to know what courage is, at least they know until Socrates begins to poke and probe them with his dialectic, i.e., his curious method of asking embarrassing and pointed questions. The conversation with Laches begins by centering on the issue that if virtue, particularly courage, is going to be taught, then we'd better know what it is before we proceed:

> SOCRATES: Then, Laches, suppose that we first set about determining the nature of courage, and in the second place proceed to inquire how the young men may attain this quality by the help of studies and pursuits. Tell me, if you can, what is courage.
> LACHES: Indeed, Socrates, I see no difficulty in answering. He is a man of courage who does not run away, but remains at his post and fights against the enemy. There can be no mistake about that.
> SOCRATES: Very good, Laches, and yet I fear that I did not express myself clearly, and therefore you have answered not the question which I intended to ask, but another.
> LACHES: What do you mean, Socrates?
> SOCRATES: I will endeavor to explain. You would call a man courageous who remains at his post, and fights with the enemy?
> LACHES: Certainly I should.
> SOCRATES: And so should I, but what would you say of another man, who fights flying, instead of remaining?
> LACHES: How flying?
> SOCRATES: Why, as the Scythians are said to fight, flying as well as pursuing, and as Homer says in praise of the horses of Aeneas, that they knew 'how to pursue, and fly quickly hither and thither,' and he passes an

encomium on Aeneas himself, as having a knowledge of fear or flight, and calls him 'a deviser of fear or flight.'

LACHES: Yes, Socrates, and there Homer is right, for he was speaking of chariots, as you were speaking of the Scythian cavalry. Now cavalry have that way of fighting, but the heavy-armed soldier fights, as I say, remaining in his rank....

SOCRATES: [But] I was asking about courage and cowardice in general. And I will begin with courage, and once more ask what is that common quality, which is the same in all these cases, and which is called courage?...

LACHES: I should say that courage is a sort of endurance of the soul, if I am to speak of the universal nature which pervades them all.

SOCRATES: But that is what we must do if we are to answer our own question. And yet I cannot say that every kind of endurance is, in my opinion, to be deemed courage. Hear my reason. I am sure, Laches, that you would consider courage to be a very noble quality.

LACHES: Most noble, certainly.

SOCRATES: And you would say that a wise endurance is also good and noble?

LACHES: Very noble.

SOCRATES: But what would you say of a foolish endurance? Is not that, on the other hand, to be regarded as evil and hurtful?

LACHES: True.

SOCRATES: And is anything noble which is evil and hurtful?

LACHES: I ought not to say that, Socrates.

SOCRATES: Then you would not admit that sort of endurance to be courage—for it is not noble, but courage is noble?

LACHES: You are right.

SOCRATES: Then, according to you, only the wise endurance is courage?

LACHES: It seems so.

SOCRATES: And yet men who thus run risks and endure are foolish, Laches, in comparison with those who do the same things, having the skill to do them.

LACHES: That is true.

SOCRATES: But foolish boldness and endurance appeared before to be base and hurtful to us?

LACHES: Quite true.

SOCRATES: Whereas courage was acknowledged to be a noble quality.

LACHES: True.

SOCRATES: And now on the contrary we are saying that the foolish endurance, which was before held in dishonor, is courage.

LACHES: So we are.

SOCRATES: And are we right in saying so?

LACHES: Indeed, Socrates, I am sure that we are not right....

SOCRATES: Suppose, however, that we admit the principle of which we are speaking to a certain extent?

LACHES: To what extent and what principle do you mean?

SOCRATES: The principle of endurance. If you agree, we too must endure and persevere in the inquiry, and then courage will not laugh at our faintheartedness in searching for courage, which after all may frequently be endurance.

LACHES: I am ready to go on, Socrates, and yet I am unused to investigations of this sort. But the spirit of controversy has been aroused in me by what has been said, and I am really grieved at being thus unable to express my meaning. For I fancy that I do know the nature of courage, but, somehow or other, she has slipped away from me, and I cannot get hold of her and tell her nature.

SOCRATES: But, my dear friend, should not the good sportsman follow the track and not give up?

[*Laches* 190d-194b, *The Collected Dialogues of Plato, Op. Cit.*, pp. 134-137, *passim.*]

But for all of their attempts, in the end they do give up. The generals, whose lives are devoted to the virtue of valor, are unable to define or explain that to which they have been devoted. The question of teaching courage to others is left in the air since no one really knows what in the world courage is. How can you teach something to others when you don't know what it is yourself?

Socrates undoubtedly angered many of the more prominent and conservative citizens of Athens, including famous generals, with his challenging questions. The young men must have loved his exposure of the pomposity and ignorance of those in authority and power, for they gathered about wherever he went knowing that a spectacular exchange of wit, intelligence, and philosophic barbs was in the offing. But the attempt to carry out what he regarded as the will of God led to his final troubles with the democratic authorities in Athens. In 399 B.C. Socrates was brought to trial on a capital charge, *asēbeia*, blasphemy against the Gods, and it is in the defense of himself and his mission during and after this trial that we get the clearest portrayal of his way of philosophy.

Socrates' Trial

In the dialogue, *Apology*, ("defense"), Socrates through Plato gives the clearest description yet of what his life was all about. The dialogue is actually a long monologue wherein Socrates attempts to do three things: First, present the charges for which he is being tried; second, answer those charges; third, describe his life's mission out of which the charges have come and in which they must now be answered. Meanwhile Plato, besides giving Socrates a chance to speak to the above three issues, provides us with a dramatic and continuous description of the courtroom, the jury of Athenians, their reactions to Socrates' speeches as they shout, interrupt, and hector him throughout his passionate defense to them. Socrates' philosophic intention, together with Plato's dramatic background, give us probably the greatest and most famous dialogue ever written by a devoted pupil as he movingly recalls the final days of his beloved teacher.

Socrates' accuser is one Miletus, supported in turn by Anytus and Lycon, who has finished the case for the prosecution as the *Apology* begins. They have warned the jury, 501 male citizens of Athens over the age of 30, against Socrates' eloquence, so, as he rises to defend himself, he is surrounded by a generally hostile audience. He reviews the charges against himself:

> "Socrates is an evil-doer, and a curious person, who searches into things under the earth and in heaven, and he makes the worse appear the better cause; and he teaches the aforesaid doctrines to others." [*Apology* 19b, *The Dialogues of Plato*, Benjamin Jowett, translator, Two Volumes (New York: Random House, 1937/1892), Volume One, p. 402]

Socrates begins by saying that these charges are really based on the nonsense in the comedy of Aristophanes who had a person in it called "Socrates," but that person is not he. He says that he is not a student of natural philosophy, that he receives no money for his instruction, that he is not a Sophist, and that therefore these charges, old charges to be sure for they had probably been around since 423 B.C. when Aristophanes' play was first produced, have all been answered.

But there are some more recent charges, he continues, far more dangerous and far more difficult to answer. These charges come from his carrying out the will of God, viz., his mission. Here he recounts an incident, typical we must assume, that followed hard upon that mission, as he tests Apollo's claim that there is none wiser than Socrates:

> Accordingly I went to one who had the reputation of wisdom, and observed him—his name I need not mention; he was a politician whom I selected for examination—and the result was as follows: When I began to talk with him, I could not help thinking that he was not really wise, although he was thought wise by many, and still wiser by himself; and thereupon I tried to explain to him that he thought himself wise, but was not really wise; and the consequence was that he hated me, and his enmity was shared by several who were present and heard me....[*Apology* 21c, d, *Ibid.*, pp. 404-405.]

The one difference between the man that he examined and himself was that the man "knows nothing, and thinks that he knows; I neither know nor think that I know." This is *Socratic irony* at its best; for, as it turns out, there is a great deal that Socrates does know. And it is this irony together with the carrying out of his mission that earns him the enmity and hatred of those in power with pretensions to wisdom.

This second and more recent accusation is then read by Socrates:

> It says that Socrates is a doer of evil, who corrupts the youth; and who does not believe in the gods of the state, but has other new divinities of his own. [*Apology* 24b, *Ibid.*, p. 407]

Socrates easily, too easily perhaps, and quickly, too quickly perhaps, dismisses these two charges and their parts. To the charge that he corrupts the young Socrates argues:

1. No one intentionally harms those who could then harm oneself.

2. To corrupt the young would be to harm those who could then harm oneself.

3. Therefore, Socrates could not have done this intentionally.

The argument assumes that no one willingly tries to harm himself or herself; man is not a pain-seeking creature. Corrupting the youth would mean that one was intentionally a pain-seeking creature. Since that's impossible, Socrates must be guilty of nothing more than ignorance of what he was doing, i.e., he did it involuntarily or unwillingly. And that's not a serious crime!

Socrates asks how is it that he corrupts the young? By teaching them to believe in new deities, is the reply, in false gods. Miletus, his prosecutor, then charges Socrates with atheism, and it is to this charge that Socrates then argues:

1. Anyone who believes in supernatural beings is not an atheist.

2. But Miletus had said that Socrates believes in supernatural beings because he believes in supernatural activities (his theories about the heavens and below the earth in the first and older charge against him).

3. Therefore, Socrates is not an atheist.

Keeping the charge of the corruption of youth in mind, the question is then raised, If these are things that he does not do, then what is it that he does do? First, Socrates says, since "God appointed me, as I supposed and believed, to the duty of leading the philosophical life, examining myself and others," it would be "wrong, wicked and dishonorable" now to desert that duty. It is in obedience to God, consequently, that he willingly pursued that path and for which he now willingly faces the consequences here in court of that obedience.

Second, in one of the greatest speeches ever penned, Socrates eloquently states that he owes a greater obedience to God than to the Athenians. Then he states what that obedience has compelled him to do and become, and herein lies the description of his divine mission:

> Men of Athens, I honour and love you; but I shall obey God rather than you, and while I have life and strength I shall never cease from the practice and teaching of philosophy, exhorting any one whom I meet and saying to him after my manner: You, my friend, - a citizen of the great and mighty and wise city of Athens [United States of America?], - Are you not ashamed of heaping up the greatest amount of money and honor and reputation...

These three were the very things, of course, that the Sophists claimed to teach men to "heap up."

> ...and caring so little about wisdom and truth and the greatest improvement of the soul, which you never regard or heed at all.

In one swoop Socrates has distinguished himself from the Sophists and stated wherein the difference lies, viz., his concern for *psychē*, the soul.

> And if the person with whom I am arguing says: Yes, but I do care; then I do not leave him or let him go at once; but I proceed to interrogate and examine and cross-examine him, and if I think that he has no virtue in him, but only says that he has, I reproach him with undervaluing the greater, and overvaluing the less.

And for whom does Socrates carry out this cross-examination?

> And I shall repeat the same words to every one whom I meet, young and old, citizen and alien, but especially to the citizens, inasmuch as they are my brethren. For know that this is the command of God; and I believe that no greater good has ever happened in the state than my service to the God.

And what are the specifics of that service, the carrying out of which has gotten him indicted and will shortly get him convicted and executed?

> For I do nothing but go about persuading you all, old and young alike, not to take thought for your persons or your properties, but first and chiefly to care about the greatest improvement of the soul. I tell you that goodness is not given by money, but that from goodness comes money and every other good of man, public as well as private. This is my teaching, and if this is the

doctrine which corrupts the youth, I am a mischievous person. [*Apology* 29d-
30b. *Ibid.*, pp. 412-413.]

Socrates concludes his defense to the jury by stating that his mission for
God has forced him to neglect his family and has left them all in poverty.
He mentions his divine or supernatural voice "which comes to me...and
dissuades me from what I am proposing to do," and has been with him
from early childhood. This divine voice, the voice of God *(daimōn)* within   being
him, told him not to enter politics, not to establish himself as a teacher   within
and not to take fees for the performance of his mission. And the voice of
God has spoken to him in other ways as well: eudaimonia
    ↓.
> Now this duty of cross-examining other men has been imposed upon me by   well being
> God; and has been signified to me by oracles, visions, and in every way in
> which the will of divine power was ever intimated to any one. [*Apology*, 33c.
> *Ibid.*, p. 416.]

After asking whether any of his pupils wish to come forward to accuse
him now, and none do, Socrates rests his case.

By a vote of 280 to 221 Socrates is found guilty. The crime for which
he is finally convicted was probably not *anosion*, unholiness, offending
the Gods and the community, but *asebeia*, blasphemy, which could result
from any number of activities none of which Socrates had ever been
guilty of, e.g., desecrating an altar dedicated to the Gods, studying astronomy, saying impious things or revealing the secrets of the mystery
cults.* *Asebeia* was a capital crime and it may have been what the
Athenians were thinking about when they handed down their conviction
and subsequently their penalty.

According to Athenian law, the convicted person could propose his
own fine, sentence or penalty. Socrates now angers the jury even further
by proposing an utterly outrageous penalty:

> And if I am to estimate the penalty fairly, I should say that maintenance in
> the Prytaneus at state expense is the just return. [*Apology* 36d. *Ibid.*, p. 419.]

But then noting the furor that his proposal has caused, he relents and
proposes an outrageously small fine, one mina, about $100. Then he re-
lents yet again and proposes 30 minas as an appropriate penalty. This
teasing causes the jury to vote for the death penalty; he is sentenced to
death by 80 more votes than had previously voted him guilty.

---

* Consider also the Greek word, *blasphēmia*, which means "impious or profane
speaking of God or of sacred persons or things."

In the context of his bantering with the jury over the nature and size of his penalty, Socrates utters the most well-remembered phrase of his entire career: "The unexamined life is not worth living." If someone were to propose as a penalty that he spend the rest of his life living quietly, minding his own business, then, he says, he could never do that:

> Now I have great difficulty in making you understand my answer to this. For if I tell you that to do as you say would be a disobedience to the God, and therefore that I cannot hold my tongue, you will not believe that I am serious; and if I say again that daily to discourse about virtue, and of those other things about which you hear me examining myself and others, is the greatest good of man, and that the unexamined life is not worth living, you are still less likely to believe me. [*Apology* 37e-38a. *Ibid.*, pp. 419-420.]

And in this he was undoubtedly correct, once again.

The *Apology* closes as Socrates looks forward to death without any sign of fear. He explains that death is either a wonderful dreamless sleep or a grand migration of the soul to a region where he can continue searching peoples' minds to find out who is really wise and who only thinks that he is wise. Nothing, he concludes, can harm a good man in life or after death. Then, realizing that it is God's will that he die, Socrates forgives his persecutors:

> I am not angry with my condemners, or with my accusers....

And the *Apology* comes to its conclusion as Socrates makes a last request for his sons:

> When my sons are grown up, I would ask you, O my friends, to punish them, and I would have you trouble them, as I have troubled you, if they seem to care about riches, or anything, more than about virtue, or if they pretend to be something when they are really nothing—then reprove them as I have reproved you, for not caring about that for which they ought to care, and thinking that they are something when they are really nothing. And if you do this, both I and my sons will have received justice at your hands.

And it ends with Socrates' final words:

> The hour of departure has arrived, and we go our ways—I to die, and you to live. Which is better God only knows. [*Apology* 41e-42. *Ibid.*, p. 423.]

Within a month Socrates will be dead.

Socrates last earthly moments are described in minute detail in Plato's *Phaedo* where the subjects for discussion are, appropriately enough, death and dying, arguments for the immortality of the soul, and, once again, what is the best and most worthwhile life that a human being can live? The *Phaedo* ends as Socrates drinks the deadly hemlock and requests that a friend make a payment for him to the God of healing. Plato then says of his master:

> Such was the end of our friend, concerning whom I may truly say, that of all the men of his time whom I have known, he was the wisest and most just and best. [*Phaedo* 118. *Ibid.*, p. 501.]

It is no wonder that Socrates has been called the Jesus of Nazareth of the ancient Greek world: born of humble parents, an artisan by trade, called by God to undertake a divine mission that would anger the mob and lead to his public trial and execution on a charge of blasphemy after he had forgiven his enemies.

SOCRATES' ACCOMPLISHMENTS

Socrates has left an intellectual legacy to Western civilization that more than justifies calling him "the father of Western philosophy." He was directly or indirectly responsible for the schools of Platonism (385 B.C.) through Plato, of Cynicism (399 B.C.) through Antisthenes, and of Aristotelianism (330 B.C.) through Plato's pupil, Aristotle. Earlier, through other companions and friends, he influenced atomism through Democritus, logic through Euclides, and rhetoric through Aristotle who happily attributes inductive argument and general definition to Socrates. Aristippus, the founder of Hedonism and of later Epicureanism (306 B.C.), was a companion, as was Antisthenes, who influenced Diogenes the Cynic, who had a profound effect on Zeno, the founder of Stoicism (300 B.C.). Finally, Anaxarchus of Abdera (340 B.C.) and his pupil Pyrrho of Elis (360-270 B.C.), the founders of Skepticism, were both profoundly affected by Socrates' life and his claim that he knew nothing, nothing at all, a claim that was to become the foundation of Western Skepticism. All of these schools that Socrates influenced managed to survive and flourish, in one fashion or another, following his death and on into the 20th century.

In addition, Socrates was the first man to insist on or to teach:

That the human soul, "that within us that makes us wise or foolish and by which we are judged good or bad," is immortal, eternal and divine. That tending it, knowing it and making it good are ways of living that can lead to happiness.

That the true self is rational, that it can be discovered and that that true self is the eternal soul.

That the unexamined life is not worth living and that the examined life involves knowing the soul or self.

That reason can be made the guide of life, that the divine and eternal part of man can always lead one on right paths.

That no person knowingly does evil, for no one would knowingly hurt himself, and evil persons always end by injuring themselves. That, further, no one knowingly does evil, for ignorance alone is the cause of evil, that it is ignorance of the soul and of who one really is that leads to harm to others and to oneself, and that to know the good is to do the good.

That civil authority is frequently wrong, as it was in sentencing him to death, and that it can be challenged as Socrates challenged it through his mission.

That education is not a memorizing but a remembering prompted by the dialectic of question and answer whereby one comes to know the soul, its nature and its role in the good life.

That coming to know anything is coming to know the nature of a thing, and that this is arrived at by seeking through the dialectic, i.e., through progressively higher and more complete levels of understanding and clarification, the essence of that thing, i.e., its necessary and sufficient conditions, or as Plato will later call it, the "Form" of the thing.

That the Sophists are dead wrong in what they have to say about the nature of law, morality, knowledge, truth and even beauty. The Sophists had argued that the judgments about these ideas are grounded in convention, *nomos*, and that two contradictory moral, epistemological or, even, aesthetic judgments could both be right. Socrates argues that the law, knowledge and beauty are all ultimately grounded in the nature of things, *physis*, that their essence is fixed, eternal, and unchanging. Consequently, one person's opinion need not be as good as another person's opinion. Socrates' destruction of relativism begins very simply as he points out that when one wants certain tasks performed, we turn to the professionals in the field to perform them, i.e., we turn to the man or woman who has knowledge in the field and who is the expert. If everyone's opinion were equally valuable, then when you have a toothache or an appendicitis, you could turn to your roommate or close friend to tend to your tooth or appendix. You don't. You turn to the person who knows, the expert. And so it is, Socrates claims, that relativism is false. There are experts, there is knowledge, in those areas that relate to the conduct of life, and some views are, consequently, better than others.

But does Socrates have anything to offer to men and women encountering the problems of the 1990s? Even if he did influence a large number of his contemporaries and those philosophers who came after him, does he speak to anyone's condition today? At a time when more and more people are looking to the security of wealth, position, success and reputation that the Sophists talked about, what does Socrates have to offer as an alternative? Let's keep these questions in mind as we turn to the way of philosophy of Socrates.

THE WAY OF *PSYCHĒ*: SOCRATES OF ATHENS

The Problem

From what has already been said, it is probably clear that the central problem that Socrates was attempting to solve both for himself and for those who associated with him was the problem with which this entire book is concerned: What is the best and most worthwhile life that a human being can live? More specifically, the problem involved the suffering that one would face both in this life and in the next for the person who failed to find that best and most worthwhile life. It is with this kind of suffering in mind that Socrates sets out on his mission.

The Cause

The cause of suffering for Socrates lies in human ignorance. It is in ignorance that wrong choices are made, that wrong decisions are arrived at, and that the wrong goals are pursued. In particular it is ignorance of the soul and the soul's real nature that brings suffering to human beings. This ignorance of who you are is a double ignorance of both the soul's divine and eternal nature, and its mundane and human nature. The God within that spoke to Socrates is present in all of us, Socrates seems to be saying. To hear that voice, to let one's own life be guided by it, is to say that all humans have a "mission" in this world. To know what one's own mission is is to erase the ignorance that prevented life from having meaning. Similarly, on the mundane and human level, to know the soul's own capacities and limitations is to ensure that one will go to one's outer limits while at the same time one won't go beyond those limits.

The Solution

The solution to the problem of suffering lay in getting at the ignorance that caused the problem. For Socrates that solution lay in the greatest improvement of the soul, which is another name for happiness, *eudaimonia*, or the state of well being.

The Way

The ways to self-knowledge and happiness must lie in meeting the cause of the problem of suffering. The way for Socrates was through the care, tending and knowledge of the self or soul. This attention and knowledge was, in turn, brought about by the dialectic, the adamantine art of question and answer that Socrates practiced on the citizens of Athens and also on himself. The dialectic forces one to face oneself with honesty and forthrightness. In the spotlight of that honesty and under the microscope of that questioning the self is exposed. From that exposure ignorance of the real nature of the self vanishes. You come to know who you are on two levels, the spiritual and the human. On the spiritual level, the divine nature of the self is revealed, its eternal and God-like essence is uncovered. On the human level, the practical, earthly nature of the self is exposed. You come to the realization, following the discovery of the eternal nature of the self, of who you are, what your capacities are, i.e., what you can become, and what your limitations are, i.e., what you can not become. Suppose that you want to be a lawyer but you discover from looking closely at yourself that you don't like studying history, political science or philosophy. Maybe you should look at your goals again. Suppose you want to be a physician but you realize that you have no interest in biology, chemistry or mathematics. Better look again at your career plans. This is the kind of self-analysis that leads to self-discovery, and this is the dialectic in action.

But it is probably modern psychoanalysis that comes as close as we can get now to the kind of dialectic that Socrates practiced on himself and on others. Through the psychoanalytic experience knowledge, change and transformation of the self occur. Erich Fromm, speaking of the efforts of Sigmund Freud in the field of self-transformation through self-knowledge, comments:

> The principle to be mentioned here first is Freud's concept that *knowledge leads to transformation*, that theory and practice must not be separated, that in the very act of *knowing* oneself, one *transforms* oneself. It is hardly necessary to emphasize how different this idea is from the concepts of scientific psychology in Freud's or in our time, where knowledge in itself remains theoretical knowledge, and has not a transforming function in the knower. [Erich Fromm, "Psychoanalysis and Zen Buddhism" in Erich Fromm, D.T. Suzuki, and Richard DeMartino, *Zen Buddhism and Psychoanalysis* (Harper Colophon books, 1970), pp. 82-83.]

For Socrates "mental health" lay through rigorous self-searching and self-examination wherein one reified, i.e., made real, the ideals of wisdom, justice and courage in one's own life. In other words, spiritual self-knowledge led to the recognition of certain moral virtues in the self and it led, as Socrates said, to the certainties that a just man harms no one, that all the virtues are ultimately one, that that one all-important virtue is knowledge, that without knowledge, i.e., knowledge of the self and who you are, all the other virtues are impossible, that it is better to suffer wrong than to do wrong, that anyone who knows the good will always choose it, and that a person can never really be harmed by being deprived of his property or pleasures.

Socrates' beliefs about the nature of the self and of human nature stand in sharp contrast to the Sophists' belief that the self was "a rather simple amalgam of natural greediness and conventional habit." [Robert S. Brumbaugh, *The Philosophers of Greece* (State University of New York Press, 1981), p. 128.] Such a Sophistic self was ideally suited for amassing property, gaining prestige and pursuing pleasure so much so that it rejected precisely the ideals that Socrates sought.

Socrates summarizes this way to the care of the soul, i.e., to this art of the knowledge of the spiritual self and all that follows from it, in this fashion:

> Can we mention anything more divine about the soul than what is concerned with knowledge and thought? Then this aspect of it resembles God, and it is by looking toward that and understanding all that is divine—God and wisdom—that a man will most fully know himself. [Plato(?), *Alcibiades* 133c in W.K.C. Guthrie, *Socrates* (Cambridge University Press, 1979), p. 153. While the *Alcibiades* may or may not have been written by Plato, it is useful and quotable, nonetheless, "as a sort of introduction to Socratic philosophy for beginners" (p. 150).]

The "looking toward" that is carried out through the dialectic results in "an intellectual and a moral insight "into the *psychē*. [*Ibid.*, p. 152.] It is this double insight into the divine and human nature of the self that leads to the wisdom that for Socrates was the goal of life.

PROBLEMS WITH SOCRATES

Socrates leaves us with a number of problems that Plato himself will attempt to solve as the latter's own philosophy matures and develops. As far as our three criteria for an adequate way of philosophy are concerned, viz., common sense, consistency, and completeness, Socrates seems to satisfy all of them to a degree. On common sense, some modern readers might be taken aback by Socrates' talk about the soul and its apparent divine and human nature. But in the context of his time, as well as of our own, the talk about knowing the dual-natured self, particularly in the light of modern psychoanalytic theory and some very popular 20th century religious beliefs about the self or soul, is understandable and even acceptable.

On consistency, the problem of the existence of an object like the soul which is reputed to be both divine and human (not-divine) may seem objectionable. Can something have *contradictory* properties (like red and not-red) or are these properties merely *contrary* properties (like red and green)? If the latter is the case, then there may be no problem with the logical consistency of Socrates' apparent claim about the dual nature of the soul nor, it would seem, about knowing that divine-human entity.

On completeness, however, we may find the greatest difficulty with Socrates' philosophy of life. Specifically, can this way of philosophy solve the problem that it has set out to solve when several vital questions probably remain unanswered: How can my knowing who I am keep me from suffering? Couldn't it lead to more suffering? Take the case of Oedipus, a myth and a play by Sophocles that Socrates knew all too well. Oedipus lived in complete ignorance of his true identity and his past crimes, viz., that he had killed his father, married his mother, and had four children by her. Is he better off knowing who he is? When his wife/mother finds out she kills herself. When Oedipus finds out who he is, he blinds himself and, blinded, leaves his city to wander the roads, a polluted outcaste for the rest of his wretched life. Can self-knowledge destroy as well as ennoble? Was Oedipus ennobled?

Further, Socrates, by following his way of philosophy, got himself executed by the state. Is that a way of philosophy worth following? Who wants to die? But being killed for your beliefs is going to be a problem to be faced with respect to three other philosophers that we shall be discussing, viz., Anaxarchus the Skeptic, Mohandas Gandhi, and Martin Luther King, Jr. Are their ways of philosophy null and void if their authors end in execution or assassination?

Finally, the charge of incompleteness may extend to Socrates' dialectic itself. How is it to be practiced? What techniques are there to its practice that have been left out in these early dialogues about Socrates? Is it really like self-analysis or psychoanalysis?

These are questions that relate to the incompleteness of Socrates' way of philosophy as presented by Plato; there are things in that way of philosophy that Socrates either failed to consider or, when they were considered, the details about them are simply lacking. It will be left to Plato, in his more mature and later writings, to solve the problems of incompleteness found in his master's earlier way of philosophy.

FOUR
THE WAY OF JUSTICE
≫·≪

PLATO OF ATHENS: THE FOUNDER OF WESTERN PHILOSOPHY

If Socrates was the father of Western philosophy, then Plato, his greatest and most famous pupil, must be considered its founder. What we know of that father is known primarily from what this founder has written about him. The historical Socrates is really a Socrates as Plato created him and conceived of him which makes it as difficult to separate Plato from Socrates as it might be to separate a founder from a father.

Plato set standards in the search for both the meaning of life and the philosophy of life which later generations of philosophers in the West have attempted to follow. In a very real sense Plato invented philosophy and he took his invention very seriously, indeed. He says in his greatest work, *Republic*, "For no light matter is at stake; the question concerns the very manner in which human life is to be lived," [*Republic* I. 352d.] anticipating thereby the sentiment of his own pupil, Aristotle, who asked the question that we are pursuing in this book, What is the best and most worthwhile life that a human being can live?

Plato's Life

Plato was born in Athens in 427 B.C. His real name was "Aristocles" but a nickname, "Platon," which in Greek means "wide" or "broad," was given him perhaps because of his broad, stocky size, and it is the name by which he is known to this day. Plato's family was from the aristocratic ranks, but strongly supported Pericles' administration of democratic Athens. He counted among his father's ancestors one of the last kings of Athens and among his mother's ancestors was Solon, the great lawgiver.

An uncle, Charmides, and his mother's cousin, Critias, were both deeply involved in Athenian politics, and both were pupil-friends of Socrates. Plato grew up during the devastating Peloponnesian War (427-404 B.C.) and was only 23 when it finally ended with totalitarian Sparta triumphant over democratic Athens. As a young man he fought in three battles in that war and won a medal for bravery. He excelled in his studies in music, mathematics, rhetoric and poetry. He wrestled at the Isthmian games and wrote love poetry, tragic verses and epigrams. Plato, though acquainted with Socrates all of his life, may have been only twenty when he first heard Socrates speak in public. One source says that the experience moved him so much that he went home and burned a tragedy that he had just written, and renounced poetry, wrestling and women to follow this odd but compelling personality.

He had cherished the hope for a political career, as he tells us in one of his many letters that have survived, but gave up politics when he saw what horrors the rule of the notorious Thirty Oligarchs (among whom were both Charmides and Critias) brought to defeated Athens when the pro-Spartans seized power in 404 B.C,. and especially when he saw later how the anti-Spartan democracy dealt with his beloved Socrates after they recovered power in 403 B.C. Athenian politics was no place for a political moderate, a well-educated and promisingly brilliant philosopher. Following the tragic death of his dear friend and teacher, Plato spent twelve years traveling. He probably fled Athens to avoid any problems with the democratic executioners of Socrates.

The Academy

Plato, on his return to Athens in 387, proceeded to establish a school, the Academy, one mile outside the walls of Athens in a place sacred to a hero, Academus. The place consisted of a grove of trees, gardens, gymnasium and several other buildings. It was here in this sacred spot that Plato gathered about him the young men who were to form a religious fraternity, the nucleus of one of the first universities of its kind in the ancient world. [The first university was probably that of the Pythagoreans at Crotona in Italy in about 520 B.C. Plato was probably copying them in offering several courses of instruction to a united community of scholars. Further, Isocrates of Athens established a university or college in Athens eight years prior to the Academy's founding.] The school was dedicated to the Muses, the nine daughters of Zeus and Memory, who preside over the arts and sciences. [These nine goddesses who inspired artists and poets were: Clio (history), Euterpe (lyric poetry), Thalia (comic drama and idyllic poetry), Melpomene (tragedy), Terpsichore (choral dance and song), Erato (love verse and mimicry), Polyhymnia (hymns), Urania (astronomy), and Calliope (epic poetry).] The scholars ate their meals in common, and the meals were occasions for long drinking, reading, and talking sessions, "symposia,"* as they were called.

Outsiders were welcome to the public lectures and people came in large numbers, especially for lectures with catchy titles like "On the Good." Having come, they expected, we are told, to hear some wonderful sort of prescription for human happiness; but, as often as not, they went away disappointed when the master's lecture was all about mathematics and astronomy, Plato's prerequisites to virtue and the good life. Over the portals of the Academy, carved in the face of the rock, was the motto by which this school, established on sacred ground and dedicated to the divine Muses of learning, was guided: Let No One Ignorant of Geometry Enter Here, a reference to the order and harmony and reality of the numbers and ideal figures which Plato, like his Pythagorean predecessors, revered. Besides lectures on the good, mathematics, and astronomy, Plato also taught political theory. For Plato it was essential that the exact sciences be a preliminary to any education in political theory. The curriculum of the Academy probably followed the same educational lines developed later in his *Republic*, which we shall discuss below. Natural science was taught even though Plato regarded the things and objects of the sensible world as metaphysically inferior to the higher world of intelligible reality of number and ideal figures, i.e., of the Forms, to which mathematics pointed.

But the principal aim of the education at the Academy, the entire reason for its existence, was to produce those men and women who would become philosophers, statesmen, counselors, rulers, and even kings in the world outside its sacred confines. The pupils of Plato, we are told by Plutarch and others, traveled far and wide as political troubleshooters helping colonies, cities, and states revise their constitutions, govern better their subjects, citizens and colonies, adopt milder forms of government, and more agreeable and enforceable laws. The Academy became a School of Political Science and Diplomacy for the entire Mediterranean world for several hundred years and remained an educational force in the West until its abrupt closing by the Roman Emperor Justinian in 529 A.D. The memory of Plato's Academy stands, even to-

---

* "a drinking together"

day, as a model for educational inspiration and reform, a bright intellectual light that the passage of the years has neither extinguished nor dimmed. [See the bibliography and accounts of Plato's life in A. E. Taylor *Plato, The Man and His Work* (London: Methuen & Co., Ltd., 1978/1926); W.K.C. Guthrie, *A History of Greek Philosophy*, Volume IV, *Plato, The Man and His Dialogues* (Cambridge University Press, 1975).]

Plato died in 347 B.C. and, following a funeral procession at the Academy, was buried within its sacred grounds while the entire city mourned the death of the greatest philosopher and Athenian since Socrates.

The Dialogues

What we know of Plato's own philosophy comes to us from the dialogues that he wrote. The twenty-seven or so works which survive can be divided into three categories. The early dialogues, such as *Apology, Crito, Laches*, and *Euthyphro*, were probably composed before Plato was thirty-six and before 388. The general aim of these early "Socratic" dialogues, as we have seen in our discussion of Socrates previously, is to make clear Socrates' philosophy of life and to defend him as a harmless and affable human being but a penetrating and critical thinker.

The middle dialogues, such as *Symposium, Phaedo, Republic, Parmenides*, and *Theaetetus*, were probably composed in the next twenty years when he was at the Academy and before 367. The general aim of these mature dialogues is to present Plato's own philosophy of the Forms or Ideals as he wrestles with Socrates' hunt for the essences of the meanings of concepts in the ever-changing world in which those ideals are to be reified or realized.

The later dialogues, such as *Philebus, Timaeus*, and the *Laws*, were probably composed shortly before and then following 361. The general aim of these final works is to present Plato's ultimate metaphysical views tinged as they were with Pythagorean influences.

The early dialogues, consequently, are principally concerned to present the philosophy of Socrates. But as Plato's own views developed, he grew beyond Socrates' moral concerns and his hunt for the essential meanings of concepts such as courage, knowledge, temperance and justice, and how to get along in this world. Instead, by the time he gets to his later dialogues, Plato's concerns became more abstract, more "other-worldly" and coldly metaphysical. He leaves off the hunt for meanings and the Socratic pursuit for the man who is wiser than Socrates, he leaves behind the flashy and brilliant verbal joustings that make the early and middle dialogues so enjoyable to read. Instead, in their place, we find a Plato who preaches a message; a Plato who in old age has discovered the true, the good and the beautiful, who has stopped searching for knowledge because he has found it; a Plato who dispenses with Socrates as a central figure and opts instead for more positive, adamant and absolute professors of the truth. Using Socrates to give him a leg up on the best life one can live, he finally kicks him away and soars off on his own to ontological heights where Socrates would have had a grand critical time but where he could never have followed his now other-worldly pupil.

In the process Plato created for the Western world a wholly original vocabulary of technical terms, terms such as "generation," "action," "passion," "essence," and "power" — all muscular, strong, dynamic words matching Plato's kinetic personality and broad, athletic somatotype. In the process he grappled with the two major influences of his youth, Socrates and the Sophists; later, he will struggle with the three major influences of his middle years, the Pythagoreans, Parmenides and Heraclitus. In the throes of these contests and struggles he will create a new and powerful way of philosophy. Let's look at several of these influences before we turn to Plato's answer to the question, What is the best and most worthwhile life that a human being can live?

The Synthesis of Parmenides and Heraclitus

Socrates tried in his lifetime to answer the Sophists and their claims that the virtues were different from one another and that each one could be successfully taught to whomever would pay and listen. Socrates taught instead that the virtues are one, i.e., you can't have one virtue unless you really have them all, and the most important virtue for this unification of them all was knowledge, specifically knowledge of the eternal and divine soul, i.e., your self. Plato has a similar view about unification and it lay in finding a solution to a problem which he may have inherited from Socrates, viz., the dilemma of knowledge. What is at issue is the very possibility of knowledge, itself. The dilemma turns on metaphysical questions about the nature of reality.

Parmenides (ca. 500 B.C.) had held that the Real is characterized as that which is unchanging, eternal and uncreated, and independent from all other entities. This is an explication of the Real that will be accepted by philosophers and theologians into the 1990s. Plato, too, will follow Parmenides and accept this view of the nature of Reality and in doing so, he will have to wrestle with the dual problems regarding the status of the world of change in which we all live (if its not real, then what is it?), and the possibility of knowledge in and of that world.

Parmenides had come to hold that the Real is "the One." There cannot be any entity other than the One, for if there were a second, an other, then it could not be the One for it would be different from the One. But then, if it could not be (the One), it could not be (in existence) at all, i.e., it could not exist. So the One must be all that there is. [Parmenides' invalid argument, as Plato will subsequently point out, rests on his confusion of the *is of predication*, as in "could not *be* the One," with the *is of existence*, as in "could not *be*." Parmenides *Proem* is in Kathleen Freemàn, *Ancilla to the Pre-Socratic Philosophers* (Harvard University Press, 1948) and Plato's reply will be found in his *Sophist* 258 ff.] Parmenides based his conclusion on an analysis of "negation" and on the impossibility of anything being a *not*. Thus it is impossible for anything to be nothing, for nothing is inconceivable. Try to conceive of nothing! And if you can't think it, then it can't exist. What Parmenides is saying is that anytime we introduce *nothing*, *not* or *un* or any other negative concept into our thinking, we are being irrational, for we are dealing with what doesn't exist, i.e., the *unthinkable*, the impossible, the irrational and the unreal. From which it follows that it's the same thing that can be thought and that can be.

Take the concept of change. For anything to change it must become something which it is *not* and *cease* to be what it is. The leaf appears to change from green to red in the autumn, i.e., it goes from being not red and becomes not green. But to become what it is *not* is to become *nothing* and we've already seen that *nothing* is irrational, unthinkable, and therefore unreal. Hence, change is impossible. The leaf doesn't *really* change from green to red. It only *appears* to change. From which it follows that reason is more reliable than the senses.

Heraclitus (ca. 500 B.C.) held, on the contrary, that change was the essence of Reality. The world is locked into constant flux, and while this change is ordered and measured by what he called *Logos*, Word or Principle, which made change occur in a smooth and harmonious fashion, it is still change that characterizes the Real. It was Heraclitus who said, "One cannot step into the same river twice for new waters are ever flowing in," and by saying so attacked the entire Parmenidean notion that there could ever be a One which was unmoving, unchanging, and ever the same from moment to moment. Heraclitus' pupil, Cratylus, went his master one better claiming, "One cannot step into the same river even once." [See Kathleen Freeman, *Ancilla, Op. Cit.*, for Heraclitus pp. 29-31, and for Cratylus p. 90.] Heraclitus likened Reality to an ever-living fire, that flashes, changes, and sparkles, its restless and dynamic nature constituting the model for the universe, just as for Parmenides it was the solid and perfect and static sphere that was the model for the universe.

The Dilemma of Knowledge in *Sophist*

These two philosophies, the philosophy of Being for Parmenides, and the philosophy of Becoming for Heraclitus, were to influence Plato's mature thought as much as the philosophy of Socrates was to influence his early thought. Nowhere is this later influence more clearly presented than in the later dialogue, *Sophist*, where Plato calls attention to the dilemma of knowledge, a dilemma generated by the two views under discussion. For if Parmenides is right and there is no *becoming* or change of anything, then there could never be any *becoming known* of anything and knowledge would be impossible, for I could never *change* from a state of ignorance to a state of knowledge. On the other hand, if Heraclitus is right and there is no *being* or permanency, then there could never be any *being known* and, again, knowledge would be impossible.

Plato concludes *Sophist* by arguing that both being and becoming are essential to knowledge, that neither Parmenides nor Heraclitus is wholly correct. And yet, each philosopher is correct in the metaphysical sphere to which his philosophy applies. For Plato, Parmenides triumphs with his philosophy of Being, because it will provide Plato with the foundation for his intelligible and transcendental world of the Forms; while Heraclitus triumphs with his philosophy of change and motion because it will provide Plato with the ground for his sensory world of space and time. This metaphysical dualism that recognizes the significance of both worlds is to become Plato's greatest legacy to the modern world. To live the best life possible it is essential that one learn to balance both worlds. And in showing how to balance both worlds, the Parmenidean world of Being, and the Heraclitean world of Becoming, Plato answers the question, What is the best and most worthwhile life that a human being can live? That answer comes in his greatest dialogue, and perhaps the greatest Western philosophic work ever written, *Republic*.

REPUBLIC: A BEST PLACE THAT IS NO PLACE

Republic consists of an opening chapter in the style of an early Socratic dialogue and nine remaining chapters in the style of Plato's middle period. The subject throughout is *dikē* (pronounced "dee-kay"), justice, which refers to the best and most worthwhile life that a human being, or society, can live, i.e., the just life is the best and most worthwhile life that a human being can live. [The subject throughout *Republic* is "What kind of life should one live?", and "What is the best life for a real human being?" See *Gorgias* 500c and *Republic* 352d.]

What is Justice?

The *Republic* is undoubtedly Plato's finest and, except for the *Laws*, his longest work. In it Plato, through his hero Socrates, undertakes to describe the ideal state in which every human being will be happy. It is the first and in many ways the most finely described Western utopia that we have, setting a model that later utopia builders, from Aristotle to Aurelius Augustine, to Francois Rabelais, Jonathan Swift, Karl Marx, Edward Bellamy, and Aldous Huxley, will try to match and surpass.

The *Republic* is set sometime around the year 421 B.C., following a religious festival. The action takes place in the house of one Polemarchus in the Piraeus, the port of Athens and six miles from the city. Plato's two brothers are present along with a company of young men and several older men. The subject of discussion quickly turns to *dikē*, justice, the normal rule of behavior, i.e., the best life that one can live. What is it?, is the question. The first book of *Republic* is a dialogue in the grand old Socratic tradition of the early dialogues of hunting for the meanings of concepts through the analysis of suggested definitions. Before the first book concludes, some seven definitions of *dikē* will have been offered and rejected. But what is needed, Socrates discovers at the end, is a lengthier and larger examination of justice in the context of a state or society before it can be determined what justice in the small, i.e., personal justice, is all about. That is to say, before they can determine what is the best life for the individual to live, justice in the small, it will have to be discovered what is the best life for a community to live, justice in the large. It is then that Plato turns to the construction of his utopian society, and the remaining nine books of *Republic* will have that as their concern.

In Book I Cephalus, the aged father of Polemarchus, offers the first definition of *dikē* by stating that justice is simply telling the truth and paying back what you've borrowed. In other words, you'll be happy if you abide by the ordinary moral rules that all good men follow. Our society is grounded in such rules as this. The foundation of all economic contracts and most social relations are built on the trust that telling the truth and honestly giving back what you've borrowed demand. There couldn't be an easier and simpler way of stating the essence of the good life. But it just won't do. Socrates objects to the definition by suggesting that there are problems in trying to live by such a meaning. For suppose you borrow a weapon, and then the owner of it goes mad several days later and shows up at your house demanding its return. It would be foolish to live by this first meaning of *dikē* and admit that you had the weapon and even more foolish to give it back to the mad man.

Polemarchus comes to his father's rescue with a second definition of justice by stating that justice is giving to each man his due, i.e., what is owed that person. Now this too is a fine and defensible definition, much used even today. One is just in giving punishments to whom punishments are due, and rewards to whom rewards are due. But, Socrates objects, "what is due" is precisely what is at issue and it is what we are trying to define, viz., justice. Hence, the definition is circular in saying that justice is what is due, for that means quite trivially that justice is justice. Moreover, that madman who wants his weapon back is still there banging on the door. And what is his due?

A third definition is offered which states that justice is rendering benefit to one's friends and harm to one's enemies. But this won't do either, Socrates points out, for then one could steal if it benefited one's friends or did harm to one's enemies. And that would make stealing right just as long as it fulfilled those ends; and such a view is morally reprehensible.

A fourth definition tries to cover the above difficulty by stating that it is just to benefit the friend if he is good and harm the enemy if he is bad. That makes stealing right if it punishes the bad person or rewards the good. But this is wrong, as well, Socrates states, because those whom you harm may become unjust; therefore this kind of justice, harming enemies, makes them unjust. And this too is morally reprehensible. The rule ought to be to harm no man lest you produce injustice. At this point, knowledge of some sort seems to be clearly called for in the definition of the best life.

A fifth definition is offered by an angry Sophist, Thrasymachus, who bursts into the dialogue stating that justice is whatever is to the advantage of the stronger, that what the ruling party in the state says is just is what is just; in other words, might makes right, according to Thrasymachus. This cynical but perhaps realistic account of what the best life is (It's what I tell you it is!, shouts the angry parent, the infallible theologian and philosopher, or the power-drunk tyrant.) has much to be said for it, too. But Socrates demolishes the new definition by showing that a stupid ruling party (or a close-minded parent, a muddled theologian or philosopher, or an imbecile tyrant) may ignorantly order what is not to their advantage or to the advantage of the stronger.

A sixth definition is then brought out as Socrates attempts to repair the previous definition stating that justice is what *appears* as the advantage to the stronger party. This attempt fails as Thrasymachus refuses to accept the definition possibly seeing that what appears may be false thereby leaving the way open for Socrates to get to the point that he has made throughout his life regarding the virtues like justice: To be virtuous demands knowledge; hence the unjust man is always ignorant and vice versa, and justice is ultimately inseparable from the other virtues like courage, temperance and wisdom: You can't really have one unless you have them all.

A seventh and final definition of justice is attempted that states that justice is the advantage of the superior but the definition and the discussion of it is to be left to another occasion.

A Conclusion About Justice

The dialogue turns briefly to the nature of the soul and how one can live happily in this world. We know a number of things from the previous exchange of views even though no acceptable definition of justice has been discovered. For example, we know that the unjust man is stupid, that he is, in some sense, out of control, that he goes too far, that he is out of balance. In other words, his soul is not governing him well, whereas the good soul, we are led to believe, governs well. This leads Socrates to the following argument:

First, when justice exists in a person, then that person's soul is governing properly.

Second, when that soul is governing properly, then that person is happy.

Third, therefore, when justice exists in a person, then that person is happy. In other words, the just man is the happy man; therefore to be just is more profitable than injustice because it leads to the happy life, i.e., the best and most worthwhile life that a human being can live. And there the first book of *Republic* ends.

The Ring of Gyges

In Book II, Plato's brother, Glaucon, steps in with an eighth definition, challenging Socrates' conclusion about justice, stating that justice is a compromise between the best and the worst. Glaucon, playing the devil's advocate, reaches this odd definition by assuming two things:

First, that all men are selfish and that they would do anything that would benefit themselves personally; and second, that the life of the unjust man is by far the best life that a person can live. The only thing that keeps people from expressing their basically selfish nature is fear of being caught. Those who follow their nature and don't get caught are happiest. As proof of the point he tells the story of Gyges.

Gyges was a shepherd in the service of the ruler of Lydia. Following a terrible storm and earthquake the earth opened up into a great chasm. Gyges entered the chasm and found a corpse inside. On the hand of the corpse was a gold ring which he removed and then climbed back onto the level ground. Later when he went to make a monthly report to the king about the flocks that he tended, he wore the ring. He chanced to turn the stone in the ring and lo, he became invisible. With this new found power of invisibility he went about doing all sorts of unjust things, seducing the queen, killing the king, unlawfully seizing the kingdom, and so on. And he did all these things because he knew he could never be caught. [*Republic*, 359d-360b, *The Collected Dialogues of Plato, Op. Cit.*, p. 607. Herodotus has another version of the popular story at *Persian Wars* I. 8-13.]

Glaucon makes the point that Gyges was happy at last, because he could do whatever he wanted with impunity, i.e., without ever being punished. And, Glaucon says, that even the just man would behave this way. For it's human nature, *physis*, to be selfish and to our own advantage to be selfish, unless we get caught. Only human laws and conventions, *nomoi*, keep us in check. Therefore, he concludes, the unjust life is ultimately the most profitable and the best life.

After some brief verbal skirmishing, all now turn to Socrates. The lines of the just and the unjust life have been drawn and the company appeals to Socrates to set matters clearly and straight. The search for justice begins. Socrates had earlier reminded his listeners of the importance of the search on which they are now all engaged:

> Do you think it a small matter that you are attempting to determine and not the entire conduct of life that for each of us would make living most worth while? [*Republic*, 344e, *Ibid.*, p. 594.]

Justice in the Large: Utopia

Now Socrates suggests that in order to see what justice in the small or the individual soul is like, it might be better, first, to see justice magnified. And therefore he recommends looking at justice in the large in the only place where it can exist, i.e., in the state. Then after finding what justice is like there, written large where all can see it, we can return to justice in the small for a look at justice in the human soul. Now begins Plato's construction of an ideal community, a community which is happy, where all may seek the best and most worthwhile life possible. Here is Plato's utopia, a best place (*eu-topos* in Greek) which is no place (*ou-topos* in Greek).

Plato starts by focusing on the three classes of citizens who compose the state, i.e., the rulers or philosopher-kings, the warriors or defenders, and thirdly, the craftsmen, farmers, and producers. The warriors are the guardians of the state, and, like the rulers, they possess no private property, wealth or money lest they become corrupted by bribery and greed; they eat in a common mess, share and share alike, live together like campaigning soldiers, and handle no gold or silver. These guardians are the helpers of the rulers and, like the rulers, they are chosen for their vocation according to their inborn, or hereditary, natures. Plato's community is based on the natural talents, abilities, and capacities with which everyone is born but which may differ from one person to another.

Censorship and Eugenics

In the beginning everyone over the age of 10 will be driven from the society. Education must begin with the children only, for adults are already corrupted and uneducable and cannot be trained for utopia. The children of the state will develop and be trained under the watchful eyes of Plato's philosophers. Strict censorship exists and even Homer is prohibited lest his immoral tales of the Gods corrupt the young. Plato would have been shocked by today's romantic movies about religion, like *The Ten Commandments, The Robe, Jesus Christ Superstar*, and *The Last Temptation of Christ*, as well as by the cute Sunday school stories of Biblical heroes. Music is censored and only strong military music is allowed, not sentimental, romantic tunes; Plato would have been horrified were he living now by our modern sentimental love songs, as well as by our country-western and rock and roll, rock jazz, and acid rock. John Philip Sousa would have pleased him however. Plato's entire culture is to be rigidly controlled in its intellectual, emotional and religious life in the controversial belief that what you are exposed to today will determine the kind of person that you will become tomorrow. Everything that is done is to ensure that the young and growing citizens will be surrounded only by the best, at least "the best" as determined by the wisest minds available, at least "the wisest minds" as determined by Plato. The society is a totalitarian state from top to bottom, with the aim of making all of the citizens happy, and producing the best and most worthwhile life for all.

The citizens are trained to accept the class that their soul natures determine they belong in. Through an elaborate "golden lie," a falsehood or great myth, the citizens are induced to believe that it is God's will that they remain in the class that they test out in and that that class is the best. [*Republic* 414c-415c, *Ibid.*, pp. 658-659.] Socrates states:

> It seems likely that our rulers will have to make considerable use of falsehood and deception for the benefit of their subjects. [*Republic* 459c, *Ibid.*, p. 698.]

But the lies are *golden* lies because they are harmless and ultimately for the best, just as our lies to our children are profitable and for the best regarding Santa Claus, Easter Bunny, Tooth Fairy, and so on. Individual security and social stability are the end results.

Eugenics is practiced among the rulers and the guardians as the best mate only with the best "like race horses," Plato states. Abnormal infants are allowed to die by the chief method of birth control known throughout the ancient world, exposure. But women are treated on an equal level with men, sharing the direction and defense of the society where their natural vocations lead them. Plato is thousands of years before his time on the issue of women's rights. While men's and women's natures differ, Plato says, it is not a difference that will make a difference to this society.

The Organic Theory of the State

The utopia that Plato envisions is an organic state in which the citizens are like the cells in a body with the three classes forming the body's major parts. [*Republic* 462d, *Ibid.*, p. 701.] The ruling class is the head, the defenders are the arms, and the farmers-workers-artisans are like the loins, stomach, and legs. All the parts are necessary to the happy functioning of the whole. No one part is more important than another, and all are equally important. Cicero, the Stoic Roman statesman of the 1st century B.C., tells a story that best illustrates this organic theory of the state. It seems that a violent dispute broke out in the body between the head and the arms as to who was the most important. The head maintained that without it the body would never find food and would wither and die. The arms maintained that the head was wrong for without arms the food would never be gathered and the body would surely perish. And on they shouted and raged at one another until all their wrangling woke up the stomach who sleepily asked what all the racket was about. On being told the stomach lazily stated that as far as truth was concerned, it, the stomach, was the most important member of the body. Whereupon the arms and head began to roar with laughter at the impertinence of this lazy, good for nothing interloper in their fight. So the stomach promptly stopped accepting the food which the head found and the arms fed it. The body, after several weeks, began to wither and was only saved from death when the head and arms acknowledged the importance of the stomach to the total health of the body.

That is the very point that Plato is making in his description of his state: All the parts are important to the total well-being of the whole; if each part is happy and doing its assigned task, then the whole state will be happy. Thus the need for strict central control of the classes by censorship and the lies: Justice (well-being) in the parts yields justice in the whole. That is to say, there will be justice in the state when the ruler is ruling, the defender is defending, and the farmer-artisan-businessman is doing what the state needs, viz., producing and exchanging goods.

Similarly, following a kind of microcosm-macrocosm parallel, there will be justice in the soul, which also has three parts, when its parts are doing their appropriate tasks. Socrates states:

> Then a just man too will not differ at all from a just city in respect of the very form of justice, but will be like it.
> Yes, like. [Glaucon answers]
> But now the city was thought to be just because three natural kinds existing in it performed each its own function, and again it was self-controlled [the *aretē* or chief virtue of the farmer-artisan-businessman], brave [the *aretē* of the soldier-defender], and wise [the chief virtue of the philosopher-king] because of certain other affections and habits of these three kinds.
> True, he said.
> Then, my friend, we shall thus expect the individual also to have these same forms in his soul, and by reason of identical affections of these with those of the city.... [*Republic* 435b, *Ibid.*, p. 677.]

But how does one know to which class one belongs? And what does it mean to be happy in following one's vocation, one's calling? and Who calls one to one's task or vocation, anyway? The answers to these questions, as we shall see, are that through education one discovers one's appropriate class; to be happy means to have the parts of one's own soul working in harmony and balance just as happiness in the state means that the classes of the state are working in harmony and balance; and each person calls himself or herself to the class and the vocation that one enjoys in the state, i.e., your soul calls you and you'd better listen. These questions and answers will be explored as we turn finally to Plato's philosophy of self-realization in his *Republic*.

Justice in the Small: Self-realization

There are four assumptions that underlie Plato's description of his ideal state which, if accepted, would probably make that state work, i.e., produce the best and most worthwhile life for all of its citizens. Taken together these assumptions constitute Plato's description of justice in the small and his theory of self-realization as the way to that best and most worthwhile life of the soul:

1. Each person has one of three distinct soul natures.

Plato assumed that every human being has a soul, that it has three parts, and that these parts determine the kind of person one will be. The theory of the tri-partite soul is essential to both justice in the state, "justice in the large," and justice in the soul, "justice in the small," that Plato is advancing in *Republic*. The three parts of the soul are: First, the rational or reasoning part which predominates in the naturally contemplative and thoughtful person; second, the spirited or active part which predominates in the naturally pugnacious or aggressive person; third, and finally, the appetitive or acquisitive part of the soul which predominates in the naturally wealth-directed, material-object-loving person. The kind of person that you are essentially, whether a thinking, aggressive or acquisitive person, depends on which of the three parts of your soul is dominant.

Plato's assumption about the soul may not be as strange as it first looks. For example, in *The Wizard of Oz* by L. Frank Baum we meet a scarecrow, a lion, and a tin man who splendidly represent the three soul natures that Plato is discussing. Each of the three seeks the virtue appropriate to his calling in life, viz., wisdom, courage, and feeling, respectively. Baum understood his Plato all too well. Moreover, many physiologists now suggest that the basic goals of modern Western society, viz., knowledge, honor or fame, and money, may be associated with different parts of the brain, the site of modern man's soul, viz., the cerebral cortex, the motor centers, and the hind brain, respectively. Further, W. H. Sheldon has proposed that the three somatotypes, or body postures and physique, viz., ectomorphy (thin), mesomorphy (muscular), and endomorphy (fat), have corresponding mental or personality types to which they can be correlated, viz., cerebrotonia (brain-oriented), somatotonia (muscle-oriented), and viscerotonia (stomach-heart oriented), respectively. Again, the ancient *Upanishads* of the Hindus have stated that the three qualities or *gunas* of the soul determine to which caste or class one will belong arguing that one of the three *gunas* predominates in one class and not in others. Thus the *guna* of wisdom (*sattva*) predominates in priestly souls and the brahmin class, the guna of action (*rajas*) predominates in warrior souls and the *kshatriya* class, and the guna of acquisitiveness (*tamas*) predominates in producing souls and the *vaishya* class in a system that directly parallels Plato's. What is shared by all of these parallels and symmetries from the humors of the time of Shakespeare to the current classifications of personalities in contemporary psychology is Plato's first assumption, that people have soul natures and that there are three such natures. The first assumption may not be as wild and unfamiliar as it first seemed. [See also A.L. Herman, *An Introduction to Indian Thought* (Prentice-Hall, Inc., 1976), pp. 152-158, for a discussion of personality types, East and West.]

   2.   A person can live the best and most worthwhile life, i.e., be happiest,
        when he or she is living according to his or her own soul nature.

Plato assumed that the soul nature that one had was the key to happiness. There are vocations, in other words, to match soul natures. Part of the task of Plato's educational system, as we shall see, is to match soul natures to jobs. Plato joins three specific vocations to the three predominant soul natures in the following manner: Corresponding to the soul that is predominantly rational and contemplative is the vocational class of the philosopher-kings whose task it is, like the head of the human body, to lead and direct the state; corresponding to the soul that is predominantly aggressive and assertive is the vocational class of the guardians and warriors whose task it is, like the arms of the body, to protect and defend the state; corresponding to the soul that is predominantly appetitive and acquisitive is the vocational class of the artisans, merchants and farmers, whose task it is, like the stomach and intestines, to nourish the state.

Socrates points out to Glaucon that justice in the state, as well as harmony and happiness in the soul, depend, in the end, on the same thing, viz., each person and thereby each class, doing what they are best fitted by their own nature to do. The state is the soul writ large:

   Through these waters, then, said I, we have with difficulty made our way
   and we are fairly agreed that the same kinds equal in number are to be
   found in the state and in the soul of each one of us.

That is so. [Glaucon answers.]

Then does not the necessity of our former postulate immediately follow, that as and whereby the state was wise, so and thereby is the individual wise? Surely. [*Republic* 441c, *Ibid.*, p. 683.]

And in the same way as the state and the individual are wise, so also will it be with respect to bravery and self-control in the state for the two remaining classes and in the individual for the two remaining parts of the soul. Further, the state will be just in exactly the same way as the individual is just:

...that the state was just by reason of each of the three classes found in it fulfilling its own function. [*Republic* 441d, *Ibid.*, pp. 683-684.]

From the parallel with the state, then, the soul will be just and happy when all of its parts are performing their proper functions and working in harmony with one another.

3. A person's soul nature can be empirically discovered.

Plato assumed that education in the state could be employed to determine which citizens were by nature best suited to handle the three main tasks of the society: Governing it, defending it, and nourishing it. There is to be every opportunity for the demotion of the unworthy and the promotion of the worthy. The educational plan that he developed in *Republic* and later in his *Laws* worked somewhat as follows:

Ages	Educational Activity
1-5	The children of the workers are kept at home and the children of the rulers and soldiers are raised together in the state nurseries.
5-15	Reading, writing, music, the arts and gymnastics are taught with the teachers keeping a watchful eye in order to see what natures or abilities predominate in their charges. *The working class, the common people, begin to drop out.*
15-17	Mathematics is taught and examinations, verbal, written, and physical, are given as future *farmers, craftsmen, and merchants continue* to *drop out.*
18-20	Military and physical training is taught and more tests are given as future *warriors drop out.*
20-30	Higher mathematics instruction and tests are given as the *lower ranks of philosopher-kings drop out.*

| 30-35 | Pure reasoning is taught and higher training in moral reasoning is given. |
| 35-50 | More advanced instruction in running the state is given and the *higher ranks of philosopher-kings emerge.* |

Socrates describes Plato's aristocratic (literally "the rule of the best") vision of a state directed by men and women with the highest practical expertise backed by the purest theoretical knowledge:

> Unless, said I, either philosophers become kings in our states or those whom we now call kings and rulers take to the pursuit of philosophy seriously and adequately, and there is a conjunction of these two things, political power and philosophical intelligence, while the motley horde of the natures who at present pursue either apart from the other are compulsorily excluded, there can be no cessation of troubles, dear Glaucon, for our states, nor, I fancy, for the human race either. [*Republic* 473c-d, *Ibid.*, pp. 712-713.]

Unhappy states are the result of unhappy people who are the result of unhappy souls which are caused by people doing what is unnatural, i.e., what they are not fitted by their soul natures to do. The wrong people in the wrong jobs makes them unhappy, "unjust" in Plato's words, and they cause nothing but trouble for everyone else in the state. In a way, our modern educational system from our high schools to our vocational schools, to our colleges and universities, serve the same function today as Plato's state schools were designed to serve his citizens: Education properly carried out helps each student to find out who he or she is, to know themselves, and to discover what in life they will be happiest doing, whether it be political service, the professions, police and military work, business, agriculture or the arts. Plato's educational theories and his underlying educational assumption is still very much with us today. (Plato's fourth and final assumption is on p. 69, below.)

The Allegory of the Cave

Plato offers one of the most memorable similes ever written to graphically illustrate what the educational process is like. We are, he says, like prisoners in a darkened cave, chained to a wall, unable to move about or to see beyond what is directly in front of us. And what is in front of us are dark shadows cast on the wall of our prison which in our ignorance we take for real things as these images move and appear to speak. But then one of us is freed from his bondage, stands up, turns around, and sees the cause of the shadows, viz., a fire at the back of the cave with objects being passed in front of it. Now he understands dimly the causes of the shadows, and in so doing, part of his former ignorance is over-come. But he is still in the cave. Suppose next, Plato says, that someone should forcibly drag him out of the cave, up the steep ascent to the mouth of the cave, away from the shadows and darkness and the fire and objects. Now he is out in the sunlight, seeing at first only the shad-ows and reflections caused by the Sun. His education continues as he is gradually able to raise his eyes upwards to the cause of it all, the Sun.

This is Plato's theory of education cast into the form of the myth of the cave. The visible world of the cave is the Heraclitean world of change, of shadows, of appearances and ignorance; the intelligible world of the sun is the Parmenidean world of non-change, of Ideals and Forms, of Reality and Knowledge. Plato's dualism of the unreal and the real, of ignorance and knowledge, of the visible or sensational and the invisible or intellectual is now complete. The dualism, furthermore, is enshrined in his educational system as the escaped and educated prisoner (the soul) now returns to his former home to teach and to lead others out of the darkness (*educare*, in Latin, means "to lead out") even as he was led:

> If such a one should go down again and take his old place would he not get
> his eyes full of darkness, this suddenly coming out of sunlight?
> He would indeed. [Glaucon agrees.]

The men and women of vision, the true seers, prophets and reformers, return to the cave in which we all unhappily exist, their eyes still dazzled by what they have seen, as they try to tell us of their vision:

> Now if he should be required to contend with these perpetual prisoners in
> 'evaluating' these shadows while his vision was still dim and before his eyes
> were accustomed to the dark...would he not provoke laughter...

One immediately thinks of reformers and visionaries and idealists like Jesus of Nazareth, Mohandas Gandhi, and Martin Luther King, all of whom drew laughter and ridicule in their lifetimes. Socrates continues:

> ...and would it not be said of him that he had returned from his journey aloft
> with his eyes ruined and that it was not worthwhile even to attempt the
> ascent? And if it were possible to lay hands on and to kill the man who tried
> to release them and lead them up, would they not kill him? [*Republic* 517a,
> *Ibid.*, p. 749.]

This is the martyr of Athens speaking, of course, and Plato was all too conscious of the irony that Socrates' words must have produced.

The Forms

The education of the philosopher-king, that gives him or her the vision that Plato speaks of in the allegory of the cave, is an education in apprehending the so-called Forms or Ideas or, better, *Ideals*. These Forms are abstract entities, neither mental nor material, that the soul grasps through the process of the dialectic, the technique of intellectually mounting to higher and higher levels of abstraction or generalization, leaving the visible world behind as one climbs higher and higher into the rarefied atmosphere of pure rationality. So what's going on here, anyway?

Let's begin with a question: Do you believe in love? Now love is an abstraction, a concept that has many instances, i.e., it is instantiated or exemplified, here and there, between people who love one another. But love, itself, perfect love, is never found here, in the cave. It's an ideal, and as such, it is imperfectly produced in our space-time, cave-world. Love, then, like Justice, Brotherhood, Equality, Truth, Goodness, Beauty and a host of other concepts which end in -ity, -ness, -hood, and -icity, are all Ideals, or Ideas, as Plato called them: They are the Forms. They are perfect, unchanging, independent, uncreated and eternal. They are the only Reality. The particulars which instantiate them, e.g., this couple in love, this act of Brotherhood, this just action, this red instance of Redness are imperfect, changing, dependent on the Form for their properties, and all are created and are now decaying: They are appearances and illusions and they are, therefore, compared to the Forms, unreal.

To know the Form of anything is to command the knowledge of everything that the Form instantiates. Suppose I want to know what a book is? I can have that knowledge in two ways. The first way, the way of sensation, is tedious, incomplete, open to doubts and further questions, and involves looking at this book and then looking at that book, and examining and coming to sense an infinitely large number of particular books; they all differ from one another, they all give me a bit more information about what a book is. This is *cave learning*, this is the way of opinion and probability. The second way, the way of dialectic, is instantaneous, intuitive, sudden, complete and final, and comes from apprehending or grasping the Form Bookness. Now I know what all particular books actual and potential have in common. I possess by one simple act the essence or nature of book. This is *Sun learning*, this is the way of knowledge and certainty. It is the way, in a sense, that both Socrates and Parmenides recommended to the best and most worthwhile life, and it is the way that Plato, himself, ends by recommending for his philosopher-kings.

4.   Therefore, in order to find the best and most worthwhile life that a human being can live, i.e., in order to be happy, a person must discover his or her soul nature and then live according to that nature.

Plato assumed that justice in the soul paralleled justice in the state such that to be happy, to live well, one must let reason rule the soul just as the philosopher-king rules the state. All persons can be happy—the key lies, as it did for Socrates, in self-knowledge.

With these assumptions out of the way, let us turn next to a list of Plato's accomplishments. I shall forego repeating the accomplishments mentioned above with Socrates, all of which apply to Plato, as well, but add a brief comment to Plato's own attack on philosophical relativism.

PLATO'S ACCOMPLISHMENTS

Plato's influence on subsequent political, social and intellectual history is enormous, as one might expect. Let me select those influences that directly relate to the subject of this book, the best life that a person can live:

Plato catalogued for the first time the four possible types of government that states could adopt, and he demonstrated how these governments must inevitably regress in time, thereby passing through all four types from the best to the worst: The best government, of course, is aristocracy, the rule of the best, the government which Plato favors and which he has just described; timocracy, the rule of the warriors, which he condemns because seeking honor is at the root of this state and the government is by those least fitted by nature to rule, viz., the soldiers and police; oligarchy, the rule of the few, wherein only the rich rule as in a plutocracy, the rule of the wealthy, where the ruler's sole aim is to make money; fourth and finally, democracy, the rule of the many, which Plato condemns as the worst government of all, arises when the poor scorn the rich and band together to produce the violence and terrorism that easily follows from an excess of equality, freedom, and license.

And just as states can evolve, as Plato predicts, from aristocracy to the tragedy of democracy, so also with individuals. This happens when lust and license seize control of the soul and it pursues, not wisdom, courage, and self-control, but fame, reputation, wealth, and finally to its utter destruction, pleasure and the satisfaction of its baser appetites. [*Republic* 555c-559e, *Ibid.*, pp. 784-788.] Plato has warned all who support democracy as the best form of government to be continually on guard lest his predictions of the inevitable and regressive de-evolution of government occur.

Plato introduced what later came to be called "faculty psychology" wherein the soul is divided into three parts, viz., a rational, a spirited or kinetic, and an appetitive part; each part has a certain capacity or faculty, viz., thinking, willing, and feeling, which, if the part is out of balance, can lead to an imbalance and sickness of the whole soul, the entire self. Just as each part has a particular virtue or *aretē*, at which it aims, viz., wisdom, courage, and self-control, respectively, so also each part has a particular vice, viz., ignorance, dishonor, and intemperance which is manifested in the condition of imbalance or disharmony, i.e., injustice or unhappiness. Faculty psychology was to have important influences on the development of both philosophy and psychology in subsequent centuries.

Plato probably had more to do with introducing religious mysticism into Western theology than any other ancient philosopher. The education of the philosopher-king was to include the study of the Forms. The Forms were divided into the lower Forms, such as Circularity, Bedness, Brotherhood, and progressively higher and more real Forms, like Truth, Beauty, and Justice. Finally, by the dialectic, the process of purely rational inquiry, one leaves all these Forms behind and suddenly beholds the highest Form of all: The Idea of the Good. Here, at the ultimate mystical moment, the interconnectedness of all Forms, their interdependence and place in the scheme of Reality, is intuitively apprehended.

The Idea of the Good is likened to the symbol of the Sun in the allegory of the cave. Like the physical sun that makes all things visible, the mystical Sun makes all the other Forms real and intelligible, thereby making possible all those created physical objects that depend for their existence and intelligibility on the Forms. For just as the images in the cave (our physical and sensible world) depend on the Forms outside (the intelligible and transcendental world) so also those Forms depend in turn on the highest and most real Form of all, the Idea of the Good. Such a Form cannot be discussed except in hyperbolic metaphors and symbols, i.e., It is a mystery. [*Republic* 505e-511e, *Ibid.*, pp. 741-747.] The mystical vision of the Good is the greatest experience that a human being can have. This marks the beginning of religious mysticism in Western theology for Plato's description of the contemplation of the Idea of the Good went on to influence both Jewish and Christian mystics.

Plato established absolutisms in various branches of Western thought that served to drive relativism from the scene for centuries to come. Philosophic absolutism states that if two judgments, whether in aesthetics, epistemology, metaphysics or ethics, contradict one another, only one of the judgments can be true or right. Consequently, and it is aristocratic Platonism that seizes the initiative here, there is only one standard, one rule, one truth, one reality, and one right in all of the preceding disciplines. When I say that aristocracy is the best form of government and you say that aristocracy is not the best form of government, the political absolutist says that since these judgments contradict one another, only one of them can be right; the political relativist, on the other hand, will say that both judgments could be right and it all depends on, its all relative to, time and place, 4th century B.C. Athens or 20th century A.D. Washington, D.C.

Following Socrates' attack on Sophistic relativism, Plato attacked the democratic notion that all opinions are equally valid or worthwhile. There are experts in shipbuilding and medicine, so why not in ethics and politics? When your tooth hurts, do you consult your grocer? Why not?, he'd be cheaper! But if all women and men are equal, then your grocer and your dentist are equal. And if they're not equal in dentistry and grocering, then why are they equal in ethics and politics? Plato's absolutist, aristocratic, anti-relativist point is that when you want to know what is beautiful, true, good or real, then you should ask the expert, the person who has apprehended the Forms of Truth, Beauty and Goodness, an apprehension that turns amateurs into experts. That person is an expert because knowledge is the result of training, discipline, and a certain natural capacity not shared equally by everyone. Thus Plato's attack on relativism and his defense of absolutism.

Does Plato have anything to offer specifically to men and women in the 1990s? Can his warnings about democracy (for example, if, as has been claimed, the United States Senate is a rich man's club, is this reason for concern?), his insights into the nature of the soul, his religious mysticism, and his attack on philosophical relativism speak meaningfully to our condition today? More specifically, Can Plato teach us what is the best and most worthwhile life that a human being can live? To pursue the latter we turn to Plato's way of philosophy.

THE WAY OF JUSTICE: PLATO OF ATHENS

The Problem

The central problem for Plato is really two-fold, viz., a personal problem involving the soul and a political problem involving the state. There are evils aplenty waiting to seize either the soul or the state and suffering abounds at both levels.

The Causes

Injustice is the concept that Plato uses to describe the imbalance that produces the suffering spoken of previously. Injustice is the imbalance and disharmony of soul and state that leads to the vices or excesses of ignorance, dishonor, and intemperance in the soul or to military oligarchy, tyranny, timocracy, and democracy in the state. The cause, in turn, of this injustice is primarily ignorance, and in particular ignorance of one's own nature through lack of proper education. If the citizens knew who they were, what their soul natures or natural abilities were, then presumably they would follow the vocation that they were naturally fitted for and the state would be harmoniously balanced as those fitted by nature to rule, to defend, and to produce became rulers, defenders, and producers, respectively. And in following that vocation, they, in turn, would be happy, and the state, in turn, would be happy.

The Solution

The solution to the problem of suffering lay, as it did for Socrates previously, in stopping the ignorance, establishing justice in both the soul and the state, and thereby producing happiness for everyone. The solution is happiness at both levels.

The Ways

The ways to happiness in the soul and happiness in the state lay through self-realization, i.e., through establishing justice through erasing ignorance, finding out who you are and working at that vocation that you are suited by your nature to follow. This view that Plato is expressing makes sense and sounds familiar because his self-realization philosophy has become part of the common *patois* of the 20th century. When we speak of going to school in order to develop our potentials or to find out who we are, we are speaking Platonese. This belief that we have capacities that are hidden or concealed and which education in the proper political setting will bring out owes its origin to Plato. The view that we are happiest when we are realizing the potentials of the soul, when reason is directing us in what we do and what we feel, is Platonic in origin and a view still common and popular today.

PROBLEMS WITH PLATO

Probably the chief problem with Plato's way of philosophy lies in his absolutism, both political and moral. Let's examine the ramifications of his absolutism with respect to the three criteria of adequacy for a way of philosophy.

As regards common sense, most readers of Plato would probably agree that the best and most qualified should make all the decisions in the state, but most readers would disagree with Plato's claim that he knows who those best are. Plato has reminded us of a number of important facts about the political life of the state, e.g., that just because you're rich doesn't mean that you're fit to govern, that the political state can become sick and degenerate, that there are bad, rotten, and corrupt forms of government, and so on. But when he says that only the most intellectually gifted ought to rule, only those who can think in icy abstractions and commune with the Forms (and what and where are those Forms, anyway!?), then we might tend to think that he has gone too far, that aristocracy in our century is a thing of the past because no one now really knows who or what *the best* are.

But if Plato's views about aristocracy can be successfully challenged because they defy common sense, then all that depended on those views must be challenged as well, viz., his views on education, on justice in the large and justice in the small, and the philosophy of self-realization itself, together with his faculty psychology and his way of philosophy. Plato's philosophy of life is so carefully constructed and interconnected that if you pull out one piece, such as challenging the view that the best, the most intelligent, can ever be found or ever identified, the rest topples, as well.

On consistency we may be affronted by Plato's totalitarian state that promises peace, prosperity, and happiness, but at a price that threatens to take as payment the very thing that it promises to offer, viz., individual and free choice about how one can spend one's life. As with most utopias, something is lost in the parts, viz., freedom and individual liberty, for the sake of the whole, viz., conformity and communalism. Thus the heavy censorship, the planned eugenics, the crushing communalism and military uniformity of this Spartan utopia must give us all second thoughts about becoming Platonic utopians; especially so, when we realize that Socrates would probably have been executed much sooner in Plato's state than he was in the Athenian state, for Plato was to come to argue, in the *Laws*, that any serious questioning or threatening of the political power or the religion of the state was to be a capital offense. [See Plato, *Laws* X. 910d, "Any person who is guilty of a sin against piety...shall suffer death for doing sacrifice in a state of defilement." *Op., Cit.*, p. 1465.] There may be a fundamental inconsistency in claiming that all can be happy in such a state when it's obvious that a silenced Socrates would be miserable.

On completeness Plato may fail as well, and he may fail on the very grounds that Socrates failed earlier. Has Plato solved the problem of human suffering that he set out to solve when self-knowledge may make one more miserable than self-ignorance (remember Oedipus who found out to his utter destruction who he was)? That is to say, self-realization philosophies, such as those of Socrates, Plato, Aristotle, and the Stoics, may all suffer from the same charge unless they can demonstrate more fully how knowledge of the eternal Soul can lead to the happiness that such knowledge has promised. [See the sharp and more detailed criticism of Plato and Platonism in Karl R. Popper, *The Open Society and Its Enemies*, Two Volumes, (New York: Harper Torchbooks, 1963), especially Volume Two, "The Spell of Plato."]

The Platonist has an answer, of course, to all three of the charges against the adequacy of Plato's way of philosophy, not the least of which is a defense of man's rational faculty for solving problems, personal and political, and the numerous benefits to civilization that such solutions have brought. Aristotle, as we shall see, has also chosen to take a similar tack in his way of philosophy, but only after criticizing Plato and launching a new approach to the problem of human suffering. We turn to Aristotle next.

THE WAY OF SELF–REALIZATION
❖

ARISTOTLE OF STAGIRA (384-322 B.C.): THE LAST MAN WHO KNEW EVERYTHING

"Every person is born either a Platonist or an Aristotelian."

If Socrates was the father of Western philosophy, and if his greatest pupil, Plato, was its founder, then Plato's greatest pupil, Aristotle, might easily be called their most influential descendent. But oddly enough that descendent is considered the chief opponent of things Socratic and Platonic, for Aristotle set the stage for an opposition between the mystical and the medical, between religion and science, that has continued to exist into the 1990s.

Samuel Taylor Coleridge (1772-1834), the poet and literary critic of the English Romantic Movement, once observed that every person is born either a Platonist or an Aristotelian. The wisdom of that remark will become evident as we proceed, but a word at the beginning on the way of Platonism and its most distinguished alternative way might be very much in order.

Rationalism (Platonism) and Empiricism (Aristotelianism)

Coleridge's remark if true would seem to divide the ways of philosophy into two major categories and to suggest that the divisions are each a matter of inherited temperament. But whatever the source of one's Platonism or Aristotelianism, whether nature or nurture, heredity or environment, this much is certain: The two ways stand opposed in all areas of philosophy, from metaphysics and epistemology to ethics and aesthetics. The consequence is that each must, of necessity, offer quite different views on the nature of the best and most worthwhile life.

The fundamental opposition between Platonism and Aristotelianism can be stated in terms of the two central ways of philosophy that grew out of them. Those two ways have come to be called "rationalism" and "empiricism," and they offer two entirely opposed views on the origin of our ideas, on the nature of reality, on what is most valuable, i.e., on what is the nature of the good, the right and the beautiful, and, finally, on how to achieve the best life possible.

Rationalism has its roots in Parmenides of Elea's philosophy of the One and in Plato's incorporation of that philosophy into his own Socratic views. Empiricism, on the other hand, has its roots in the school of atomism, particularly in the views of its founder, Democritus (460-352 B.C.), and in the school of the Sophists, particularly in the views of its chief luminary, Protagoras, and, of course, in the influence that these schools and views had on Aristotle's own thinking.

Rationalism argued that some of our ideas do not originate with, or are not dependent upon, the senses or sense perception. Instead, it held that our ideas have an extra-sensory, transcendental or spiritual source. Empiricism, on the other hand, had denied this, arguing instead that all of our ideas are rooted in sensory experience. While Aristotle is not a consistent empiricist, as we shall see, the tradition of the natural sciences and of Western anti-rationalist philosophy, particularly that of the modern British empiricists, John Locke, George Berkeley, and David Hume, will trace its origins back to Aristotle and to Aristotelianism and its empirical leanings. The tradition of the mathematical sciences and of metaphysical system-building, particularly that of the modern Continental rationalists, Rene Descartes, Baruch Spinoza, and Gottfried Leibniz, will trace its origins back to Plato and to Platonism and its rationalist leanings.

The Tender-minded and the Tough-minded

William James (1842-1910), the American philosopher of pragmatism long-interested in the intellectual battles waged in the name of the rationalist-empiricist controversy, has nicely described the two positions, perhaps with Coleridge in mind. James claims that what you are philosophically is all a matter of what you are born with:

> Temperaments with their cravings and refusals do determine men in their philosophies and always will. [William James, *Pragmatism* (Harvard University Press, 1978), p. 24.]

And what you are born with philosophically is either a rationalist temperament which James describes as "tender-minded" and "intellectual" or an empiricist temperament which James describes as "tough-minded" and "sensational":

> ...'empiricist' [means] your lover of facts in all their crude variety ["*physis*"?], 'rationalist' [means] your devotee to abstract and eternal principles ["*nomoi*"?] ....*nature* seems to combine most frequently with intellectualism an idealistic and optimistic tendency. Empiricists, on the other hand, are not uncommonly materialistic, and their optimism is apt to be decidedly conditional and tremulous. Rationalism is always monistic. It starts from wholes and universals [abstractions?, Forms?], and makes much of the unity [order?, balance?, Justice?] of things. Empiricism starts from the parts [particulars?, substances?], and makes of the whole a collection—is not averse therefore to calling itself pluralistic.

James then concludes with several more familiar items apparently to challenge the reader to classify himself or herself as a tender-minded rationalist or a tough-minded empiricist:

> Rationalism usually considers itself more religious than empiricism.... It is a true claim when the individual rationalist is what is called a man of feeling, and when the individual empiricist prides himself on being hard-headed. In that case the rationalist will usually also be in favor of what is called free-will, and the empiricist will be a [determinist].... The rationalist finally will be of dogmatic *temper* in his affirmations, while the empiricist may be more sceptical and open to discussion. [*Ibid.*, p. 13, brackets and emphases added.]

Maybe Coleridge is right. Perchance one is, indeed, born tender-or tough-minded. And what you are born with you supposedly can never change, or you change at a certain risk. In a way, this is precisely what Plato's theory of the tri-partite soul and the hunt for one's proper and natural vocation really came down to. Aristotle will argue in a similar fashion that discovering who you are, realizing your self and actualizing the potential within your soul, is the only way to reach *eudaimonia*, i.e., happiness, i.e., the best and most worthwhile life. Both Plato and Aristotle are in agreement on this point: Philosophy is a matter of natural, i.e., soul, temperament and knowing that soul is essential for happiness.

Aristotle's Life: Teacher, Scientist, Philosopher

Aristotle was born in Stagira, a small town in northern Greece, in 384 B.C. His father, Nicomachus, was a physician at the court of Amyntas, King of Macedon. Nichomachus' occupation in the medical and biological sciences of his time and its influence on Aristotle's temperament as well as his father's connection to Macedonia will have far reaching implications for Aristotle's later life as a biologist and as a teacher. When he was 17, Aristotle entered Plato's Academy in Athens as a student. He was to remain there for almost 20 years, "overwhelmed by the best education in the world," according to W. D. Ross.

Following Plato's death in 347 B.C., Aristotle became one of three candidates to succeed him but lost out when the position passed to Plato's nephew, Speusippus. Several reasons for his being passed over are known, chief among them being that although he was clearly the best man, after all who remembers Speusippus?, he had probably been critical of Plato and Plato's attempt to turn philosophy into mathematics. [Aristotle was later to write at *Metaphysics* 992.a.32: "But mathematics has come to be identical with philosophy for modern thinkers, though they say that it should be studied for the sake of other things." *The Basic Works of Aristotle*, Edited by Richard McKeon (New York: Random House, 1941), p. 710.]

Leaving Athens he traveled to Assus in Asia Minor where one of his former fellow-students, Hermeias, had recently risen from the status of a slave to become the ruler. Aristotle remained with his friend for three years marrying Hermeias' niece. Upon her death he moved to Lesbos, and then in 342 B.C. he went on invitation to Pella in northern Greece and to the court of Philip of Macedon. Philip had needed a cultured teacher for his son, Prince Alexander, a young hellion of about 13 years of age. Aristotle was to remain Alexander's tutor for four years. He returned later to Athens in 335 B.C., the year when Philip died and Alexander became King of Macedonia.

The Lyceum

Aristotle set about renting some buildings in a grove sacred to Apollo Lykeius. Here he established his school, the Lyceum, in direct competition with the Platonic Academy. Because of his reputation not only as the teacher of the future dictator of the world but in his own right as a wise man, as well, he quickly attracted pupils from among the best and the brightest. He was to remain the director of the Lyceum and its chief teacher for the next 13 years.

The library of the Lyceum held thousands of manuscripts and maps; it contained a museum of specimens garnered from the ends of the world, many of which, legend has it, were sent back to his old tutor by the world-conquering Alexander of Macedon. The Lyceum library and museum were to become paradigms of educational superiority for universities and centers of learning to emulate for centuries to come.

The students at the Lyceum ate their meals in common much as students at universities do today, and the food was probably just as bad. Once a month, we know, Aristotle held a symposium (a seminar accompanied by the drinking of wine) with his pupils which was extremely popular. The curriculum for the students at the Lyceum is easily discovered from the volumes of Aristotle's notes and lectures which have happily survived times' decay. We know that in the mornings he would walk about lecturing, talking on specialized topics for advanced students in logic, physics and metaphysics. It is this habit of Aristotle's walking around, *"peripatetikos,"* that gave the name "Peripatetics" to Aristotle's followers and his way of philosophy became known as the "peripatetic philosophy." In the afternoons Aristotle gave more general and public lectures on popular topics for both students and visitors. The subjects that were covered ranged from ethics and rhetoric to politics and aesthetics, attracting a following of devoted and attentive followers and disciples.

The Writings

Aristotle's enduring reputation as a teacher and administrator is overshadowed, of course, by his legacy to future generations as a scientist and philosopher. For those future generations he did four things for which the modern world is still much in his debt: First, he fixed the classification of the sciences; second, he founded the study and subject of logic still taught in universities to this day; third, he made the study of this world of first importance as opposed to abstract speculations on Platonic other worlds; and, finally, he focused attention on concrete events and particular objects as opposed to a focus on abstract Platonic Forms. In other words, he saved science and philosophy from Platonism. There was, as a matter of fact, no area of human endeavor that Aristotle did not attempt to investigate, to master, and to speak or write the final word upon. Of his surviving books, scientific investigations, and general knowledge, Julia Annas has written:

> The *Physics, On Generation and Corruption* and *On the Heavens* explain natural events in terms of highly theoretical principles, and give an account of the structure and physical constitution of the universe. But Aristotle's energetic appetite for explanation does not stop there; it comes down to more mundane levels. In the *Meteorology,* for example, he produces an

(understandably primitive) geology, meteorology, and chemistry: in *On the
Senses* we find a theory about colors.

From the inorganic world Aristotle turned his greatest efforts and attentions to the organic where he became the first biologist:

> *On the Soul* and *The Short Physical Treatises* (*On Memory, On Dreams* and *On
> Prophesying Dreams*), essays which create the science of the psychology of
> living things, are followed by massive studies of various aspects of the
> animals (including humans): *On the Generation of Animals* discusses their
> reproduction, *On Motion* and *On the Movement of Animals* their modes of
> movement, *On the Parts of Animals* their parts and structures. The *History of
> Animals* is a record of animals' behavior and habits, a record that must have
> been compiled in collaboration with others and that, although often wrong
> and sometimes credulous, is a famous historical monument of empirical
> science. [Julia Anna, "Classical Greek Philosophy," in *The Oxford History of
> the Classical World*, Edited by John Boardman, *et al* (Oxford University Press,
> 1988), p. 246.]

Realizing, as he says, that "there is something of the marvellous in all
natural things," Aristotle painstakingly identified over 500 different
species of animals, dissecting over 50 species, himself. He identified and
classified their parts and systems all the while proclaiming, as a good
empiricist ought, "We must trust the evidence of the senses rather than
theories, and theories as well, so long as their results agree with what is
observed." [See G.E.R. Lloyd, *Aristotle*, (Cambridge at The University
Press, 1968), pp. 68-79.] It is no wonder that later generations would
come to call Aristotle "the last man who knew everything."

The End

In 323 Alexander died. Athens had some years earlier been
conquered and occupied by Alexander's troops and great resentment
had been built up by patriotic Athenians against the dictator and against
all Macedonians and their collaborators. Aristotle, long identified with
all things Macedonian, thereupon fled the city, "So that," as he said,
"Athens would not sin twice against philosophy." He died in Chalcis the
following year at the age of 62.

The Aristotelian Task: Finding and Bringing Value
into a World of Facts

Aristotle's greatest works, and the ones that have had the most
telling impact on later generations of theologians and philosophers, are
his *Metaphysics* (supplemented with *On the Soul*) and his *Nicomachean*

Ethics (supplemented with *Politics*). To fully understand Aristotle's way of philosophy and his own answer to his own question regarding the best and most worthwhile life, we shall concentrate on these seminal texts while at the same time recognizing the importance of his other writings in the history of Western science, logic and the arts.

One of Aristotle's intentions in engaging in a long life of philosophic work was to solve a problem left by his predecessors, the Atomists or materialists, and Plato. The problem was that of finding value in an everchanging impersonal, value-neutral, material world. Specifically, the problem was that of finding the best and most worthwhile life in a world that, as the Atomists had discovered, consisted merely of atoms in motion in an uncaring emptiness, a place indifferent to, and care-less of, right and wrong, good and bad, beauty and ugliness; or, as Plato had argued, a material world that was everchanging, temporal, dependent, and, in a word, valueless (recall that dark and gloomy Platonic cave). It will be Aristotle's task to show that Plato's Forms, with all their reality, value and beauty, can exist in the Atomists' material world of changing particulars. In other words, Aristotle is going to attempt a synthesis of the two opposing views, of the Atomists and of Plato, in the same way that Plato had previously attempted a synthesis of the views of Heraclitus, who held that everything was in motion, and of Parmenides, who held that nothing real could be in motion. But where Plato's efforts had led to an uncompromising dualism, Aristotle's efforts will end with a new and challenging pluralism by finding and bringing values into a world of facts, thereby making the search for, and the discovery of, the best and most worthwhile life in this world both possible and meaningful.

In order to describe Aristotle's way of philosophy it will be best to start with his metaphysics, his views on ultimate reality, as it relates to God, the world and man, and then conclude by focusing on his ethics as it relates to man and the world. It is important to remember that through all of the theoretical joustings in metaphysics and ethics that follow, Aristotle will be leading up to that all-important problem regarding the nature of, and the attainability of, human happiness.

The Nature of the Real: Aristotle's Metaphysics

Plato's Dualism

Plato had argued that only the Forms are real and that the Forms are utterly transcendent to the world of atoms, space, motion, and physical objects. Platonic Forms are neither mental nor material but spiritual entities that are unchanging, eternal and completely independent of all other things. The world that we live in, on the other hand, the world of space and time, is devoid of the Forms and is, like the world inside Plato's darkened cave, the place of ignorance, of opinion, of change, time, and unreality.

Plato's dualism consisted of these two worlds, then, two distinct metaphysical "reals," two disparate epistemological "truths," and two divided ethical and aesthetic "values," totally separated one from the other.

Plato's legacy to the modern world would subsequently come to be regarded as an icy metaphysical otherworldliness that tended to neglect and even despise this world in preference for that perfect heavenly world beyond. It must follow then that human happiness must depend on apprehending that other world of perfect order and beauty and value. What order and beauty and value this world has is there imperfectly and only by a rank and defective imitation of that transcendent world of Forms.

Take, for example, this book. It consists of a congeries of restless atoms held precariously together in this current space-time region. Its pages are oxidizing, sulphurizing, fading, and falling apart ever-so-slowly but ever-so-certainly. It is a poor, unreal imitation of its paradigm, the Ideal Book, i.e., Bookness, in the realm of Forms, which is unchanging, eternal and independent, i.e., real. The existence of this book depends on the reality of the Bookness, such that without the latter the former would never have existed or been known. Thus classic Platonic dualism.

Aristotle and Substance

Aristotle will have none of this. There are Forms alright, but they are not transcendent to the changing world of things. They are, instead, immanent within that world. Aristotle brings Plato's Forms out of the heavenly world down into the material world: Aristotle brightens Plato's darkened cave with the splendor of the Forms. Physical objects are no longer unreal entities striving to imitate their transcendental betters. Instead, physical objects are one kind of substance, viz., formed matters, and each physical object is a combination of a form (we can drop the honorific 'F,' now) with some particular matter in which it is embedded. Thus this book for Aristotle is a substance composed of the form of the book together with material water, air, fire, and earth, i.e., matter, in varying combinations.

Aristotle, having rejected Plato's dualism, now sets about erecting a metaphysical system of his own using as a key his conception of substance.

God, the World and Man

For Aristotle there is, however, one pure Form (bring back that 'F' temporarily) that originates motion and subsequently causes all other motions in the world. This is God, the Prime or First Mover, whom Aristotle conceives of as God. In addition to this one pure Form there is the universe of substances, formed matters, that includes man, animals, plants, as well as the inorganic world of clouds, mountains, dirt and waters. Third and finally, in this ontological hierarchy, we have at the bottom "prime matter," i.e., pure matter with no admixture of any form at all. Prime matter, however, is a purely ideal entity and can have no existence, Aristotle admits, since it lacks any form at all. In summary, then, Aristotle's metaphysical system consists of pure Form, God, at the top, with pure matter, i.e., prime matter, at the bottom, and an array of substances, formed matters, in between. In what follows, we shall briefly examine Aristotle's concept of Prime Mover as well as those all-important substances which include man. We shall, like Aristotle, have nothing more to say about prime matter since nothing can be said about that which lacks a form.

The Prime Mover as God

Aristotle's system requires a Being that gets motion going in the world of substances. This Being, for Aristotle, does not create nor is It created. It is unchanging, hence It is unmoved, Itself, and It is totally indifferent to the world. Aristotle's Prime or First Unmoved Mover (and there are some 47 or 55 other lesser unmoved movers though none are Prime) cannot serve as a foundation for any religion, consequently, for It neither hears prayers nor answers them nor receives offerings nor performs miracles. Aristotle's Prime Mover, or God, is transcendent but moves the world and causes its motion by virtue of the world's being attracted to It, much as a beautiful person will cause motion in others, getting heads to turn and eyes to stare, while doing nothing other than just being itself.

The Prime Mover has no body since It is "pure actuality," i.e., It lacks nothing and is always in action. The only action that It need perform is that action that fully expresses Its own perfect and essential nature. For Aristotle that nature is reason, and the exercise of that nature is thinking.

Consequently, the Prime Mover does nothing but think. But It's thinking is always immediate, complete and perfect, i.e., It doesn't have to go through stages of reasoning as man does from premises to conclusions; instead, It sees things suddenly, clearly and without error. God is a pure, intuitive reasoner, a thinker, a super-yogi, a contemplator. And what does God contemplate? It contemplates that which is perfect and best, viz., Itself.

Aristotle referred to his Prime Mover as "God" and thereby founded the discipline of theology, the "discourse on god." His proof for the existence of God is as ingenious as it is unsound. He begins with the fact that there is motion in the world and then asks, Where did the motion come from? Through a series of cause and effect connections he traces motion back through time to a first cause. The argument, quite valid but quite unsound (since the first premise is clearly false), looks like this:

1   If there were no Prime Mover or first cause then there would never be effects now.
2.   But there are effects now (look around you).
3.   Therefore, there must be (or must have been) a Prime Mover or first cause.

There cannot be an infinite regress here, of Movers or causers, for an infinite regress has no beginning; and without a beginning, there is no middle; and without a middle there is no end, and, therefore, no present moment. But there is a present moment—here you are! Therefore, an infinite regress is impossible.

Aristotle has his God but a God who is wholly indifferent to everything and everyone; and why not?, since It lacks for nothing. So Aristotle has a God, a Prime Mover, a perfect being, but no religion. And since his God is perfect, It is a being to be admired and emulated. Man's emulation of Aristotle's super-rational God, as we shall see below in our discussion of Aristotle's ethics, is the key to the best and most worthwhile life for man.

The World of Substances

Aristotle argued that in order to understand any particular thing in the world, i.e., to understand any created substance, it was necessary to understand what caused that substance, what was responsible for that individual thing, whether this book or this man, being what it was. The Atomists and Plato had already disagreed on what was necessary in order to understand a thing, the former claiming that if one knew the matter of any thing then the thing was known, and the latter claiming that if one knew the Form of any thing then the thing was known. Aristotle agrees up to a point with both views, claiming that matter and form, as necessary causes of any thing, are both necessary to understanding that thing. However, matter and form are only half of the story of a being or a substance, and therefore only half of the story for the understanding of that being. To matter and form Aristotle now adds two more causes. Let's look at those four causes of being and knowledge.

The Four Causes

In the *Metaphysics* Aristotle develops his theory that reality is four-dimensional and explores the factors responsible for a thing being the kind of thing that it is. He states that each thing in the world, whether artificial or natural, is caused, i.e., owes its existence as well as its essential nature, to four "causes":

> 'Cause' means (1) that from which, as immanent material, a thing comes into being, e.g., the bronze is the cause of the statue and the silver of the saucer.... (2) The form or pattern, i.e., the definition of the essence and the classes which include this... and the parts included in the definition. (3) That from which the change or the resting from change first begins; e.g., the adviser is a cause of the action, and the father a cause of the child, and in general the maker a cause of the thing made and the change-producing of the changing. (4) The end, i.e., that for the sake of which a thing is; e.g., health is the cause of walking. For 'Why does one walk?' we say; 'that one may be healthy'; and in speaking thus we think we have given the cause. [Aristotle, *Metaphysics* 1013a, *The Basic Works of Aristotle*, Edited by Richard McKeon (New York: Random House, 1941), p. 752.]

Consider first an artificial substance such as this book. The paper and ink are its *material* cause; it has a shape, a pattern, which, if copied, could produce another book, and this blueprint is, so to speak, its *formal* cause; in order for the book's matter to have this shape it had to be made by someone, a book maker or book binder, who is its *efficient* cause; finally, to understand the nature of the book completely it is essential that its purpose be known, i.e., the reason for its being made in the way that it has and this means knowing its *final* cause. For artificial or constructed things the final cause is the purpose or use to which they are designed to be put; for natural things, however, like trees and human beings, the final cause is the goal of self-realization which guides the stages of development and maturity, drawing actions towards itself.

Consider, then, a natural substance such as the tree outside my window. Its *material* cause is the water, air and earth that compose it, nourish it and make it grow; the genetic code that directs that nourishing into the shape and the ends for which it grows constitutes its *formal* cause; the source of the tree, the seed or seedling from which it sprang, constitutes its *efficient* cause; finally, the end that it grows towards in fulfilling its plant-like purpose in becoming a fully matured tree and reproducing its own kind constitutes its *final* cause directed to that end by its formal cause, its "genetic program," we would say. For Aristotle, the formal and final causes of all natural substances, i.e., all living things, i.e., all things with souls, are treated as a single cause.

Consider, finally, another natural substance, a human being. Your *material* cause is the stuff out of which you are made, your organs, tissues and cells; your *formal* cause is, in a sense, the species that defines you and to which you belong, *homo sapiens*. For Aristotle, there are a limited number of such natural kinds created in the beginning, once and for all, not evolving but fixed in nature. That species defines the pattern that your growth will take as you develop and mature into a human being. Your *efficient* cause is your parents for, unlike the book but like the tree, you were generated and not manufactured. Fourth, and finally, your *final* cause, your goal, is found in that within you which, with your free choices, directs you to your final end, self-realization. In order to see what the formal and final causes of human beings are like and why they can be said to work as a single cause, we must say a word about Aristotle's concept of the soul. It is in the soul, whether vegetable, animal or human, that formal and final causes lie buried.

Three Souls and Their Natures

The soul, Aristotle contended, is the principle of life, the form of the body as well as that which drives living substances to their proper ends. In *On the Soul* Aristotle defined a soul as the determining principle of the living body, as "the essential and enduring character of a body possessing the capacity of life." In other words, soul is the power of life, it is life, and as such it is present in all living things:

> What is soul?... Among substances are by general consent reckoned bodies and especially natural bodies.... Of natural bodies some have life in them, others not; by life we mean self-nutrition and growth (with its correlative decay)....

Having defined "soul" in good empirical fashion as the form of a natural body with life potentially in it, i.e., whatever has soul *exhibits* life, i.e., certain kinds of publicly sensed powers or properties, Aristotle goes on to talk of the three kinds of souls and their powers.

Aristotle established three grades of living things from a lowest to a highest, viz., the vegetative, the animal and the human. Growth and change in plant, animal and human substances do not take place haphazardly and chaotically but in an orderly and progressive fashion guided by their forms, i.e., their souls.

Those [powers of the soul that] we have mentioned are the nutritive, the appetitive, the sensory, the locomotive and the power of thinking. All *plant souls* have none but the first, the nutritive, while another order of living things [animals] has this plus the sensory. If any order of living things has the sensory, it must also have the appetitive; for appetite is the genus of which desire, passion, and wish are the species. All *animal souls* have one sense at least, viz., touch, and whatever has a sense has the capacity for pleasure and pain and therefore has pleasant and painful objects present to it, and wherever these are present, there is desire, for desire is just the appetite for what is pleasant.... Certain animal souls possess in addition the power of locomotion, and still another animal soul, the *human souls* ...possess the power of thinking, i.e., mind. [Aristotle, *On the Soul* 412b, 412a, 414b, *The Basic Works of Aristotle, Op. Cit.*, pp. 555, 557, 559.]

Living things actualize, i.e., make known, their powers through their matters as soul provides the life and power and energy for that actualization. *Plants* have the plant soul that makes nutrition and reproduction possible; *animals* have the plant soul within an animal soul that makes locomotion and sensation possible; and humans (with the odd exceptions of females and natural slaves whom Aristotle argued were without a rational soul) have a human soul which has both the animal soul and the plant soul within itself that makes thinking, as well as sensation, locomotion, reproduction and nutrition, possible.

The human or rational soul which includes the functions of the other two souls is, of course, superior, Aristotle felt, to those other two souls; hence man is superior to all other living organisms. Aristotle believed that the superiority of the rational to the plant and animal souls lay in the rational soul's ability to freely choose the means as well as the ends it wished to pursue. Carrots and camels are predestined, as it were, in the choices they make for their futures. The rational soul, on the other hand, has its destiny within its own hands. The rational soul can override the dictates of instinct, desire and appetite at any time that it chooses. It is, consequently, of the utmost importance, then, to discover what man's destiny is, what the good for the rational soul is, and how best to achieve that end. So how does man go about actualizing the form of his rational soul in order to lead the best and most worthwhile life?

Self-realization: Aristotle's Ethics

Actualizing, or making publicly observable, one's potentialities, is carried out as the rational soul is pursuing its proper end or goal, its *aretē* or virtue, capacity or excellence. All substances aim at some goal or end, whether consciously or not. And that end is their happiness. Earth, air, fire and water, plants, animals and man all have their appropriate ends, their final causes, their appropriate happinesses. It may sound odd, indeed, to speak of happy rocks and carrots but why should it? We speak about happy camels and happy cats and even, on poetic occasions, of happy daffodils and daisies. So why not happy carrots and happy rocks?

Take this book, for example. Place it on the ground and dig away the dirt beneath. What happens? It goes down. Why? Because it's trying, however metaphorically, to actualize its chief good as a material substance which is to get to its appropriate place, its final goal, in the universe. Where is that? Aristotle thought that it was the center of the earth. As far as the four prime substances are concerned, each one has a good, a goal, toward which it aspires. Thus fire goes up, air lies between it and water in the Aristotelian scheme of things, and earth, the heaviest of all, together with books, go down. Those places are their rightful or just places, and those places are the ultimate ends for all four of the elemental substances.

Further, and here Aristotle agrees with Plato, when a thing is doing what its final cause or form dictates as its proper end, then it is happy. When it is not allowed to reach that end, think of stunted trees, diseased carrots, deformed camels, then its good becomes unattainable and it is said to be unhappy.

Happiness As Final Cause

For man, his happiness lies in reaching his ultimate end or final good through soul actualization or, as we might call it, "self realization." When man strives for and achieves that final goal, then he, too, like the rock, the carrot and the camel, will be happy. So what is the good for man, what is this self-realization, at which his rational soul aims, and how is it to be achieved?

Aristotle raises this question in what may be his greatest philosophic work, the *Nicomachean Ethics*. He says that opinions differ as to what constitutes human happiness. We only know that human happiness is "something final and self-sufficient, and is the end of action," i.e., it is that at which all human endeavors aim. For consider this: Suppose that I ask you why you are reading this book, i.e., what purpose have you in trying to understand Aristotle? If you are a student, you are probably trying to pass a course of study. Why? In order to get certain academic credits. Why do you want the credits? In order to graduate. Why do you want to graduate? In order to get a better job, perhaps. Why do you want a better job? In order, you might say, to make more money. Why do you want more money? In order, you might say, to buy not only the necessities of life, e.g., good food, clothing, a house, better health, and so on, but to make life more enjoyable, to meet more interesting people, and to be challenged physically, emotionally and intellectually, things that those with money can choose and that those without it cannot. Even Aristotle will argue that the poor, the involuntary poor, can never be happy, and for good reason: Their choices are woefully limited.

Now, why do you want all of these things that money can bring? In order, you might reasonably say, to be happy. And why do you want to be happy? But this is an odd question, surely. Happiness is not like the other intermediate goals already mentioned, "instrumental ends," Aristotle will call them. Happiness is not at all like passing a course, getting an academic degree, finding a better job, making more money, and so on. Happiness is an "ultimate end," that for the sake of which everything else is done. We have, as a matter of fact, reached the end of our "in-order-to's" and have arrived finally at that which all things aim— happiness, *eudaimonia*.

Happiness As Living Well By Doing Well

But what is this happiness, anyway? In the *Nichomachean Ethics* Aristotle opens the investigation, seeming to pick up the thread of his discourse where we left it, above, following the discussion of rational souls and final causes:

> Let us resume our inquiry and state, in view of the fact that all knowledge and every pursuit aims at some good, what it is that political science [i.e., philosophy] aims at and what is the highest of all goods achievable by action. Verbally there is very general agreement; for both the general run of man and people of superior refinement say that it is happiness, and identify living well and doing well with being happy; but with regard to what happiness is they differ, and the many do not give the same account as the wise.

So what is happiness then, the ultimate object, the final goal, of all the purposive pursuits that you and I are engaged in continuously and energetically?

At this stage of the search the least we can say is that happiness is a direct consequence of "living well and doing well," and that "it is achievable by action." In other words, happiness, *eudaimonia*, is identified by Aristotle with the best and most worthwhile life that a human being can live. But what is the nature of that life of living and doing? What is the essence of the happy life peculiar to man? Aristotle begins his answer:

> For the general run of common men think it is some plain and obvious thing, like pleasure, wealth, or honor; they differ, however, from one another—and often even the same man identifies it with different things, with health when he is ill, with wealth when he is poor.... Now some [the Platonists of the Academy are meant] thought that apart from these many goods there is another [the Platonic Forms] which is self-subsistent and causes the goodness of all these as well. [Aristotle, *Nichomachean Ethics* 1095a, *Op. Cit.*, p. 937.]

Aristotle's own aristocratic view, however, is that the good of man lies in that virtue, or capacity, which is peculiar to man, alone. The result is that happiness for man, i.e., the best and most worthwhile life, must involve those abilities or powers peculiar to his human soul. In other words, the best and most worthwhile life for man must be directly related to man's ability to reason. The conclusion for Aristotle is that the best and most worthwhile life will be a life of rational contemplation, a life which ultimately imitates God, the Arch-contemplator, in the highest and most perfect degree:

> If the function of man is an activity of soul which follows a rational principle...and we state that it is the function of man to live a certain kind of life, and this to be an activity or action of the soul implying a rational principle...then human good turns out to be an activity of soul in accordance with virtue [i.e., its own proper ability] and if there is more than one virtue then in accordance with the best and most perfect. [*Ibid.*, 1098a, p. 943.]

So the goal of man conforms to what his soul is and does uniquely and best. And that is that it reasons: Man is, Aristotle insists, the only rational animal. But out of all the various kinds of human lives and human types possible, which is the best? Aristotle distinguishes three types of human lives.

Three Types of Human Lives

Some say that there are other virtues peculiar to man, abilities other than the capacity for reasoning and contemplation. Aristotle locates these other ways to happiness in a discussion about human types in the

Nichomachean Ethics. First, there is the *vulgar type* who identifies the best
and most worthwhile life with the life of enjoyment. This is the goal, of
course, of the hedonists whose school in Athens with Epicurus at their
head was shortly to rival Aristotle's Lyceum. Of the vulgar type Aristotle
states:

> Now the mass of mankind are evidently quite slavish in their tastes, prefer-
> ring a life suitable to beasts, but they get some ground for their view from
> the fact that many of those in high places share the tastes of Sardanapallus
> [a prominent voluptuary and sensualist of the time]. [*Ibid.*, 1095b, p. 938.]

Aristotle had earlier in his writings rejected the life of pleasure by pointing out that while the life of a child, or the states of drunkenness and
sleep, are all pleasant, none of us would care to return to or remain in
any of those states for very long. Furthermore, none of these conditions
would be enjoyable at all if reason, *phronēsis*, itself, were absented from
them: "For if a man had everything, but the thinking part of him was
corrupted and diseased, life would not be desirable for him." [The quotation is from Aristotle's earliest work on ethics, *Protrepticus*, and is in
Werner Jaeger, *Aristotle*, Second Edition (Oxford University Press, 1962),
p. 252.] The life of reason is superior to the vulgar life of pleasure.

Second, there is the *political type* who identifies the best and most
worthwhile life with achieving public honors. This is the goal, of course,
of the political life. But this is rejected as too superficial for a best possible life for, as Aristotle says, "... it depends too much on those who
bestow honor rather than on him who receives it." [Aristotle,
Nichomachean Ethics, 1095b, *Op. Cit.*, p. 938.] The good for man must be
something that will not destroy him (as pleasure can) and that will also
"be something proper to a man and not easily taken from him" (as
honors can). [*Ibid.*]

The two types of lives that we have mentioned thus far, it should be
mentioned, relate directly to the two classes of citizens of Plato's state as
found in his *Republic*. The similarity between the three classes of citizens
in *Republic* and Aristotle's three types of human beings continues as
Aristotle presents his own version of Plato's superior human being, the
philosopher-king.

Third, there is the *contemplative type* who identifies the best and most
worthwhile life with the active exercise of the soul's highest virtue,
reason:

> If happiness is activity in accordance with virtue, it is reasonable that it should be in accordance with the highest virtue; and this will be that of the best thing in us.

Aristotle concludes by associating this best of all possible lives with a spiritual calling, a view which Socrates and Plato had both held:

> If reason is divine, then in comparison with man, the life according to it is divine in comparison with human life. But we must not follow those who advise us, being men, to think of human things, and, being mortal, of mortal things, but must, so far as we can, make ourselves immortal, and strain every nerve to live in accordance with the best thing in us; for even if it be small in bulk, much more does it in power and worth surpass everything....

The consequence is that the best life a man can live will be the life of reason:

> And what we said before will apply now; that which is proper to each thing is by nature best and most pleasant for each thing; for man, therefore, the life according to reason is best and pleasantest, since reason, more than anything else is man. This life therefore is also the happiest [i.e., the best and most worthwhile]. [*Ibid.*, 1177b-1178a, p. 1105.]

But what is the life of reason? And how does one arrive at or reach such a blessed, spiritual existence? And if happiness lies in action in accordance with, or guided or energized by, moral virtue or excellence then how is all of this to come about? In other words, what must I do in order to be happy?

The Happy Life of Reason and How to Get It

Aristotle has argued that well-being, the best and most worthwhile life, lies in well-doing. Happiness is not possible without activity and, unlike Plato, Aristotle argues that merely knowing the good is not enough for well-being. Hence, happiness is an activity guided by reason. But reason is of two sorts: First, it is a faculty that understands the world; and, second, it is a practical activity that acts in accordance with what is understood. When I know, in the first sense, what my society recognizes as good or right, then I can develop a skill for knowing, in the second sense, how to achieve those goods by doing the right thing.

Aristotle knew the moral virtues from observing the ordinary Greek citizens of his day. These virtues were the capacities for excellence in each soul waiting to be actualized, and included such obvious goods as courage, self-control and justice, as well as pride, friendship, gentleness and prudence.

The Golden Mean

These potential capacities discovered by the cognitive reason had now to be brought into existence by the exercise of the practical reason through, among other things, the avoidance of the harsh excesses of which each is capable. Aristotle's famous doctrine of the golden mean illustrates the use of practical reason in avoiding those excesses. For example, take the moral virtue of courage. Suppose that you are facing a situation where you could lose your life. The fear of death which you experience could lead to two extremes where too much fear would produce the vice of cowardice and too little fear could produce the vice of foolhardiness and carelessness. The moral virtue of courage is a mean between those two extremes. All of the moral virtues, Aristotle felt, were means between extremes. The moral life guided by reason is a life of moral moderation (*sōphrosynē*) that avoids such excesses.

The Practical Syllogism

Morality is taken by Aristotle to be simply intelligent conduct that flows deductively after the fashion of a logical syllogism. To this end, practical reason devises the practical syllogism as an aid in making moral decisions for moral action. The syllogism with a major premise, a minor premise and a conclusion is a tentative and highly probable business at best for making decisions to act because, as Aristotle wisely noted, ethics is an inexact science, it does not, unlike Plato's moral views, rest on absolute knowledge of some transcendental good.

Instead, Aristotle's ethics is a naturalistic science and, ultimately, a learnable and copyable skill wherein judgments of right and wrong, and the actions to which they lead, follow from perceived facts. It is from such facts that the major premise of the practical syllogism is derived; it is, as such, a principle of right conduct that reason will use to guide action.

The major premise states the character of a virtue or a vice and takes the form "X acts are bad for us," or "X acts are always good for us," or "One ought always to do X acts." Second, the minor premise asserts that the character described belongs to the mode of conduct under consideration at the moment. The minor premise of the practical syllogism is arrived at by observation of a particular moral situation. The minor premise will be of the form "This is an X act." Finally, the conclusion of the practical syllogism is always a directive to do X or not to do X depending on what results reason has drawn from the major and minor premises. In other words the conclusion to the practical syllogism is really an action. Here is one such example of the practical syllogism:

Major premise: Excessive drinking is bad for everyone.
Minor premise: What you are doing is excessive drinking.
Conclusion: So stop drinking right now!

For children and other humans who lack the rational ability to know the moral principles which ought to guide life, moral training and the instilling of moral habits can still make them good citizens. They know both the facts and the differences between right and wrong but do not know the reasons, i.e., they lack both the knowledge of those major premises of the practical syllogisms and the ability to draw conclusions from them. But habits of virtuous conduct can be built up in such persons by conditioning, by training them to take pleasure in noble acts and by demonstrating to them the pain that is involved in the ignoble. Finally, when in doubt as to what one ought to do, and this advice goes for everyone, then follow the moral example of the virtuous and wise men around you: Copy their behavior. The moral life is ultimately a life of developing good moral habits.

But the good life and especially the life of contemplation which is the best life depend upon public and private peace, order and prosperity, at the very least. Further, the life of reason would seem to demand wealth and leisure, at the very least. So where are we to get our peace, order and prosperity?, our wealth and leisure?, in order to live the good life.

The Necessary and Sufficient Conditions for the Good and Happy Life

Aristotle answers these questions in part by carefully defining the conditions that must be present in order for the best and most worthwhile life to exist. In the *Nichomachean Ethics*, having already laid down the internal conditions for happiness, viz., "the goods of the soul" that we have discussed above, Aristotle goes on to list the external goods or conditions for happiness. He states what appears to be the *necessary* conditions, without any one of which you can never be happy, and the *sufficient* conditions, with all of which you are guaranteed to be happy, for the life of complete well-being. In other words, if happiness is an activity directed by reason then doing noble acts is the key to happiness. But for such acts it is obvious that certain external goods are needed:

...for it is impossible, or not easy, to do noble acts without the proper equipment. In many actions we use friends and riches and political power as instruments; and there are some things the lack of which takes the lustre from happiness, as good birth, plenty of children, beauty; for the man who is very ugly in appearance or badly-born or solitary and childless is not very likely to be happy, and perhaps a man would be still less likely if he had thoroughly bad children or friends or had lost good children or friends by death. As we said, then, happiness seems to need this sort of prosperity in addition [to the internal goods like courage, temperance and justice] for which reason some identify happiness with good luck.... [*Ibid.*, 1099b, p. 945.]

But how are all of these external and necessary goods for happiness to be realized? What is the proper arena wherein happiness can be attained?, wherein virtuous action can be carried out?, and wherein the contemplative life can be lived to its fullest? The answers to these questions will draw us into Aristotle's political theory and into his version of the ideal state in which human self-realization is made possible.

Aristotle's Ideal State

The best life for man, Aristotle has already argued, is the life of contemplation. But that life, in turn, depends upon the life of virtuous action. And the life of virtuous action depends, in turn, upon a community. So we might well ask, What kind of community does Aristotle have in mind in which the best and most worthwhile life of action and contemplation can be lived? These questions are dealt with at great length in his *Politics* which is Aristotle's response to Plato's *Republic*.

Politics begins with a statement about the purpose of the state or city-state, i.e., about its final cause:

Every state is a community of some kind and every community is established with a view to some good. But... the state or political community... aims at good in greater degree than any other, and at the highest good. [Aristotle, *Politics* 1252a, *The Basic Works of Aristotle, Op. Cit.*, p. 1127.]

So what could be the degrees and nature of "good" at which the state aims?

The Middle Class

Like Plato before him, Aristotle recognized that in order to make the good life or good lives possible certain basic necessities had to be satisfied. Thus every viable state had to include farmers and producers, merchants and tradesmen, soldiers and defenders, as well as leaders and governors. He lists three kinds of possible states from which a choice for his own best state will be made. There is, first, a *monarchy* where one man rules; second, an *aristocracy* where the few best men rule; and third, a *polity* where the many rule in the interests of the entire state. While monarchy is the best form of government and aristocracy the next best, Aristotle unpredictably but rationally opts for a polity as the most practical form of government. In a polity it is the *middle* class, the mean between the classes of the very rich and the very poor, that actually rules:

> Thus it is manifest that the best political community is formed by citizens of the middle class, and that those states are likely to be well-administered in which the middle class is large, and stronger if possible than both the other two classes..., for the addition of the middle class turns the scale, and prevents either of the extremes from being dominant. [*Ibid.*, 1295b, p. 1221.]

Unlike the poor, the middle class does not covet its neighbors' goods; nor are its goods coveted by the poor. It neither plots against others, nor is it plotted against. Being the most secure, therefore, it forms the soundest fabric and foundation for the good state. Hence, it is in this class, a mean between the other two, that political power ought to lie.

The Rule of Law

Finally, this middle class will in turn be guided by a constitution and laws. Aristotle was one of the first political scientists to realize the importance of the rule of law as opposed to the rule of men as the chief source for justice and legal adjudication in the state. The rule of law, like the middle class, is a mean between extremes, in this case a mean between the excesses of anarchy, on the one hand, and tyranny, on the other. Anarchy is having no law at all and tyranny is merely injustice of a different order:

> Tyranny is just that arbitrary power of an individual which is responsible to no one, and governs all alike, whether equals or betters, with a view to its own advantage, not that of its subjects, and therefore against their will. No freeman, if he can escape from it, will endure such a government. [*Ibid.*, 1295a, p. 1219.]

The law, on the other hand, functions as passionless reason. When we have the rule of law then the application of justice by reason is unaffected by human emotions, feelings and desire. And even though the law may be tainted by the imperfections of those men who established it, it still remains superior to the rule of men. The reasons are clear and compelling:

> He who bids the law rule may be deemed to bid God and reason alone to rule, but he who bids man rule adds an element of the beast; for desire is a

wild beast, and passion perverts the minds of rulers, even when they are the best of men. The law is reason unaffected by desire. [*Ibid.*, 1287a, p. 1202.]

Unfortunately for Aristotle's argument the origins of the laws as well as their application remain in the hands of men. This entire defense of the rule of law runs hard against Plato's views on the question of who or what should rule. Recall that Plato's philosopher king was nothing more than embodied reason unaffected by desire. [See Plato's *Statesman* 294a-295c.]

Like Plato, Aristotle discussed the size and population of his utopia (keep the state small, no more than 10,000, so that all citizens may participate directly; Aristotle was deeply suspicious of representative government), together with a detailed plan for educating those citizens. Further, unlike Plato, Aristotle focused his attention on the family which he seems to have regarded as the social foundation of the community.

Finally, classes, law, form of government, family and education all seem to come together in one of the most important concepts ever considered by a community or by any political scientist or philosopher. It is a concept that Plato had ignored, but about which both Aristotle and the world of the 1990s will have much to say: Leisure. It is, for Aristotle, the most important condition of the most worthwhile life.

Leisure

Action and leisure are both necessary to the good life. But leisure is better than action for there could never be action without leisure:

> Nature herself requires that we not only be able to work well but to use leisure well; for, as I must repeat once again, the first principle of all action is leisure. Both are required, but leisure is better than occupation and is its end; and therefore the question must be asked, what ought we to do when at leisure? [*Ibid.*, 1337b, pp. 1306-1307.]

Without leisure there can never be real happiness, according to Aristotle; hence, those who work for a living and have no leisure can never be happy:

> For he who is occupied [and not at leisure] has in view some end which he has not attained;.... [*Ibid.*, 1338a, p. 1307.]

This belief lies at the heart of Aristotle's *aristocratic* state, his democratic, middle class tendencies to the contrary notwithstanding.

Education in this state, the Greek word *scholē* means "leisure," is undertaken primarily to train these aristocrats, these gentlemen, to enjoy their leisure, since mere amusement, which has pleasure as its goal, is not the aim of life nor should it be the aim of leisure:

> What ought we to do when at leisure? Clearly we ought not to be amusing ourselves, for then amusement would be the end of life. [*Ibid.*, 1337b, p. 1307.]

The education of the citizens is aimed at perpetuating the state which will then make possible the good life, the life of reason and leisure for the best men, the *aristos*, but not for all.

As far as Aristotle is concerned, a citizen is a person who is a free male and who has political power. But many of those who live in the state do not have either the right sex, the leisure, the education or the intelligence to participate in the political power of the state. Thus not only are children and women excluded from citizenship but slaves and those who work for a living, are excluded, as well. Those who work include laborers, traders, and peasants. This means that citizenship and the exercise of political power are effectively left to the three classes of citizens, viz., the warriors, citizens who in their youth protect the state from within and without; the rulers, citizens who in their middle age perform the state's deliberative and judicial functions; and, finally, the priests, citizens who in their old age attend to the religious ceremonies of the state. All three classes, in turn, are drawn from the propertied, land-holding, well-educated, leisured middle class. Thus citizens who do manual labor will be unable to enjoy the good life and the leisure that is both its cause and its effect. This may be too high a price to pay, the critic must feel, merely to ensure the happiness of the free and well-born gentlemen of this utopia.

ARISTOTLE'S ACCOMPLISHMENTS

Again, as with Plato, above, let me select for discussion only those items that have a direct bearing on the subject of this book, the best life that a human being can live.

First, Aristotle gave to future generations a viable philosophic alternative to Plato's way of philosophy and to Platonic rationalism. Aristotle's empiricism, i.e., his focus on the investigation of particulars, of individual substances, together with his reliance on the senses as the surest grounding for knowledge claims about those particulars, set metaphysics, epistemology and value theory on a path that they remain committed to to this day. Most important of all, Aristotle made plain common sense a viable standard against which to test all metaphysical, epistemological and value theories. To the person seeking reality, knowledge and value one need look no farther than the end of one's nose.

The interior of Plato's cave now redesigned and redecorated by Aristotle contains reality, knowledge and value. That cave is where we all live and Aristotle made living in it more meaningful more exciting and more enjoyable for future generations. He brought value back into the world of facts.

Second, and more specifically, Aristotle vigorously attacked both Platonic transcendentalism as well as Socratic ethicism. That ethicism included the so-called Socratic paradoxes and the following indefensible claims: That virtue is merely knowledge; that no one does wrong willingly; that if a man knows the good, he will always do the good; that wrong action is always a case of ignorance (overlooking the fact that some men are by nature vicious); and that all the virtues are one.

Third, on the matter of pleasure Aristotle attacked the hedonists and successfully argued that while pleasure always accompanies right action pleasure is never *the* good, i.e., the one and only good, of life. Pleasure is merely a sign of proper human functioning.

Fourth and finally, Aristotle, in the tradition of the Sophists and the Atomists before him, made naturalism in metaphysics, empiricism in epistemology, and humanism in ethics, respectable alternatives to supernatural transcendentalism, Platonic rationalism and other-worldly theism. His way of philosophy was to provide a workable alternative to the other ways of philosophy that were to be set going in the world in the Hellenistic period that followed his death. The Aristotelian way was to become an alternative not only to Platonism but also to the philosophic ways of Stoicism, Epicureanism and Skepticism, all three of which we shall be examining below.

THE WAY OF SELF-REALIZATION: ARISTOTLE OF STAGIRA

The Problem

As with Plato, the central problem for Aristotle was two-fold: First, there was a personal problem involving the individual soul, viz., how can a human being achieve happiness; and, second, a political problem involving the state, viz., how can the state be made amenable to human needs. As with Plato, also, the possibility of suffering at either the psychological or the political levels was real, for then as now instances of the corrupt soul and the corrupt state were evident everywhere. Both problems can be encompassed by a single question, however, the question with which this entire book is concerned, viz., What is the best and most worthwhile life that a human being can live?

The Cause

Ignorance, as Plato well knew, is probably the chief cause of the psychological and social suffering just mentioned. It is an ignorance of what constitutes the best life for the individual and especially for individuals living in a community or city-state. It is an ignorance of the role of reason, man's chief virtue, in one's own life and of the ability to secure the internal and external conditions that make happiness and the most worthwhile life possible in a community.

The Solution

The solution to the problem of suffering is happiness, *eudaimonia*, that well-being or well-living that is identified with the best and most worthwhile life.

The Way

The way to happiness lies in treating the problem of ignorance. That way is best summed up by the concept of self-realization. This way of philosophy entails discovering one's own nature, the form of the self, which is the rational part of the soul. This way of philosophy includes not only knowledge but also action, action guided by reason, following the golden mean between excesses, securing all of the *internal conditions* necessary to happiness, such as courage, temperance, wisdom and justice. This way of philosophy seeks to establish a state that will enable all of those qualified citizens to secure the *external conditions* necessary to happiness, as well, such as wealth, friendship and leisure. The only condition that this way of philosophy cannot secure but that remains necessary to happiness is good fortune, i.e., luck; for that condition reason is powerless to help. Finally, this way of philosophy entails making the conditions right for the select few in the state such that the highest good of man, the contemplative life, can be lived with mental ease and physical comfort. Pursuing these ways, Aristotle felt, was the best way of guaranteeing the happiness which he so artfully sought.

PROBLEMS WITH ARISTOTLE

There are three problems with Aristotle's way of philosophy, two troublesome but minor difficulties, and one major problem.

The Problem of Women

Aristotle's attitude towards women is quite different from Plato's. Where Plato was able to give women equal status among men in the running of the state and in the chance for happiness, Aristotle balks. For Aristotle, woman is an incomplete man, "an infertile male," "a deformed male." Her soul, among other things, lacks mature reason, a lack that makes Aristotle say of her, "The male is by nature fitter for command than the female" and "the inequality is permanent." [Aristotle, *Politics* 1259a, *Op. Cit.*, p. 1143.] And why is this? It is because the souls of women being incapable of reasoning are also incapable of ruling and commanding. Unlike the slave who has no reasoning faculty whatsoever in his or her soul, the free woman has it but it remains stunted, without authority, without force or power. Thus while she may on occasion seem to demonstrate the virtues, they are not the same as man's virtues. Take courage, for example; it cannot be the same in both sexes for "the courage of a man is shown in commanding, of a woman in obeying." [*Ibid.*, 1260a, p. 1144.]

The overall consequence is that "Silence is a woman's glory," [*Ibid.*, 1260a, p. 1145.] a view subsequently shared by St. Paul when he commanded, "Let women keep silence in the churches" [I *Corinthians*14.33.] and "Wives be subject to your husbands as to God." [*Ephesians* 5.21.] This future double barreled attack from the Greek and from the Christian sides against women has led to other equally atrocious and specious crimes against women. Aristotle's legacy to the modern world is unfortunate as far as women are concerned. The Aristotelian view of women served to reinforce the medieval Christians' equally prejudiced attitudes about woman, an attitude from which women and men remain burdened to this day.

The Problem of Slavery

The question Aristotle raised regarding slavery and to which he then attempted an answer was this: Is slavery natural? Aristotle responds:

> There is no difficulty in answering this question, on grounds both of reason and of fact. For that some should rule and others be ruled is a thing not only necessary, but expedient; from the hour of their birth, some are marked out for subjection, others for rule. [Aristotle, *Politics* 1254a, *Op. Cit.*, p. 1132.]

That slaves are "living possessions" Aristotle does not doubt. The difficulty arises in determining who is in fact a natural slave and who is not, since slave-nature while congenital is not inherited, i.e., children of slaves are not necessarily slaves.

Despite all of this, however, Aristotle argued that since the interests of the master and the slave are the same, viz., the enhancement of the master's interests, the master should be a friend to his slave and all slaves should be given the hope of emancipation. But slavery as an institution must remain for, just as with the sexes in general, "the male is by nature superior, and the female inferior, the one rules, the other is ruled," so also with masters and slaves. It thereby follows with those who are slaves by nature, i.e., persons who lack a rational soul [*Ibid.*, 1260a, p. 1144.], that "slavery for them is both expedient and right." [*Ibid.*, 1255a, p. 1133.]

The slaves not only make possible the leisure of Aristotle's cultured contemplatives, but slaves left to their own devisings are simply incapable of living well or being happy. For even if they had the leisure for happiness, they would still lack the one all important ingredient that makes happiness possible, viz., reason. They wouldn't be happy, couldn't be happy, even if they were free.

Twice now Aristotle's reliance on his senses and logical abilities for an impartial and objective evaluation of the world have failed him. His empirical observations of slaves and women and the implications which he drew from those observations seem to have fallen wide of the mark of even Greek common sense. We blush and pass on to the third and most important problem with Aristotle's way of philosophy.

The Problem of Self-realization

The center of Aristotle's way of philosophy is the way of self-realization. The essence of this way to the goal of happiness consists of actualizing certain potentials in the soul and through that discovering what you are. In other words, what you are is what you actualize. And what you actualize is going to be your potential to reason, to think, to go deductively from general principles to specific actions. Man becomes happy by the unfolding of his own soul through reasoned activity. Man is a rational animal as well as a political animal, who is happiest when he is exercising, actualizing, and reifying his unique natural potentials. Thus the way of self-realization.

But the problem lies with the contention that what you are is what you actualize. Many other potentialities are also actualized in the course of a lifetime of reasoned actions such as stupidity, laziness, ignorance and wickedness. Aristotle rejects these as signs of defective character and they are, as such, not part of the truly rational animal that he is investigating. But hasn't Aristotle really assumed then what he is attempting to prove? As with Plato, who started the whole self-realization business, Aristotle has presupposed that the human soul, except for slaves and women, will be rational. But doesn't this then jeopardize not only his much-touted empiricism but doesn't it also, once again, fly in the face of plain common sense? Aristotle's view of the self seems woe-fully one-sided, as if he had overlooked or rejected a part of the self, viz., what we now recognize as the affective or non-cognitive side of being human, our propensity for benevolence and philanthropy.

This refusal to see the emotional, loving, and feeling side as a significant partner, a necessary feminine adjunct to the masculine, rational side of human nature, has led to some important omissions in Aristotle's psychology, ethics and political theory. It is bound to have a significant impact on his much-touted way of self-realization. [In line with this it is interesting to note that the Greek word *aretē*, "excellence," is usually translated as "virtue" from the Latin *virtus*. Both *aret ē* (from "Ares," the Greek God of war) and *virtus* (from *"vir,"* a male) imply masculine excellences; the feminine excellences or capacities or abilities were obviously misogynously neglected by both classical and modern linguagenators.]

For those who will have something to say directly about human suffering and pain, compassion and pity, we shall have to await the coming of the ways of philosophy of the Buddha, the Epicureans, and the Stoics. They will speak to the anxieties, terrors and tortures of the average man and woman possessed by more than the ordinary fears and foibles of Aristotle's self-realized cultured gentleman.

SIX

THE WAY OF *NIRVANA*
≫·≪

The Life of the Future Buddha

The man known as "the Buddha" was born in Lumbini in northeastern India (modern Nepal) sometime around 563 B.C. His father, Shuddhodana, most Buddhists believe, was a great king who had his palace-capital in Kapilavastu, and the son, the future Buddha, was therefore a high-born Hindu prince. After his birth a soothsayer had predicted that the young Gautama, as he was called, would grow up to be either a great king, a world monarch, or he would become a great religious saint. King Shuddhodana was intent on keeping his son a prince and on straight political paths, and being fearful that Gautama would turn to the religious life, devised a scheme to make sure that the child would remain innocent of any experiences that might turn his head away from monarchy. Hence the king kept Prince Gautama a virtual prisoner in the royal residence and surrounded him with all possible distracting and pleasant experiences. All sources of unhappiness, pain and anxiety were forbidden in what finally became a palace of pleasures. At the age of 16 the young prince was married and it seemed as if his future, however boring and pleasure filled, was safe and secure. And so matters continued for the next 14 years of Gautama's life.

But then something happened to change his life and the future of the world.

The Four Signs

Shuddhodana, fearful that his son would ever experience pain and grief, had left strict orders forbidding him to be taken from the sanitized precincts of the palace grounds. But one day during Gautama's twenty-ninth year, his charioteer, a man named Channa, disobeys the king's orders and takes the prince outside the royal walls and into the real world. As the horses carry them down this altogether new and strange road, Gautama sees a man by the side of the road, his body covered with pus-running sores, his face flushed and his limbs trembling with fever. Shocked, Gautama asks his charioteer what is happening. "Sire," the charioteer replies, "this is sickness. It is the condition to which all human beings must sooner or later come." Disturbed by his first sight of human suffering and perplexed even more by his driver's explanation of it, Gautama asks to be driven back to the palace. He spends a sleepless night, consumed with his first sight of human suffering, the suffering of sickness.

The next day he's out once again with the charioteer. As the vehicle leaves the palace grounds, Gautama sees an old man tottering along by the side of the road, his face wrinkled with age, his hair white, his emaciated and withered body tremblingly supported by a staff. Again, perplexed, Gautama asks Channa about this man. "Sire," the charioteer replies, "this is old age. It is the condition to which all human beings must sooner or later come." Deeply moved, once more, by what he hears and sees, Gautama asks to be driven back to the palace. Again, he spends a wearisome night considering this second sight, the suffering of old age.

The third day, undaunted by the sights of the previous two days, Gautama is outside the palace walls, once again. This time he encounters a funeral procession and a corpse being carried to the cremation grounds. Moved by the sight of the dead man, Gautama asks Channa what is happening. "Sire," the charioteer replies, "this is death. It is the condition to which all human beings will at last come." Disturbed, yet again, by the experience, Gautama is driven back to the palace and spends the night considering this third sight, the suffering of death.

The fourth day events proceed as before but this time Gautama encounters a man in the yellow robes of a religious ascetic, his face tranquil and peaceful, walking by the road. Channa informs Gautama that the man is a sannyasi, a wandering beggar, one who has renounced the world of temptations and pleasures in order to conquer the anguish and suffering of sickness, old age and death. Brooding on this fourth experience, Prince Gautama is driven back to the palace where his wife has just given birth to a son. Gautama promptly names the son Rahula, "bondage," and resolves that he too will give up the life of a prince and follow the way of the religious saint. Late that night he leaves the palace and the easy life of pleasure, taking with him only the clothes on his back. He has renounced the world in order to find the solution to human suffering.

Gautama's Teachers and Companions

Gautama was 29 years old at the time of his renunciation of the world. As he travels into his new life as a renunciate, he encounters two master yogis, each of whom will teach him the art of yoga meditation. Strenuously practicing the techniques of yoga he soon reaches the deep trance of total nothingness surpassing thereby his first master. Realizing the yoga powers of his young pupil, this first teacher invites Gautama to become partners with him in directing his other disciples in the art of yoga. But Gautama refuses and travels on to another teacher.

Studying with this second yoga master Gautama soon surpasses him as well in the depth and quality of his meditation. This second teacher, recognizing the superiority of Gautama's attainments, then offers to become Gautama's pupil. But Gautama is seeking neither disciples nor trance states of nothingness in meditation. He is searching for a positive and permanent state of mind, one of peace and tranquility that does not vanish when one ceases meditation. He is searching for liberation from suffering and liberation into permanent happiness. He is searching for what will come to be called *nirvana*.

Leaving his second teacher behind, Gautama falls in with a group of five fanatical ascetics. These men believe that the condition for which Gautama searches can be found through the harsh physical disciplining of body and mind. Trustingly, he follows their example and for several years practices their way of the mortification of the body. He drinks only water, sleeps on the hard ground, eats sparingly of fruits and herbs, existing finally on one grain of hemp a day. His body wastes away until after two years he can push his hand through his emaciated abdomen and grasp his spinal cord. Weak and undernourished he nearly dies, realizing only at the last moment that this way of pain, like the way of pleasure previously, is not the way to be liberated from suffering, for this ascetic way will lead only to death. There must be another way, a middle way, a path between the two harsh extremes of pleasure and pain. He now sets out to find that middle way, a way that will forever after memorialize Buddhism as "the religion of the middle way."

Enlightenment

Recovering his strength and wits, and now rejected by his five ascetic friends for his faint-heartedness, Gautama resolves to find the way to *nirvana* by his own means. Journeying to Gaya in modern Bihar, Gautama seats himself under a Bo or Bodhi tree ("the tree of wisdom"), a tree sacred to Hindus and, from this time forward, sacred to Buddhists, as well. He resolves not to rise until he has achieved the goal for which all of his efforts over the past six years have been directed. During the night which follows he experiences four states of meditational trance. Finally, with the coming of dawn, Gautama sees intuitively into the fundamental nature of all things. He became the Buddha, "the awakened one."

Following his *nirvana* the Buddha journeys to Banaras, the most sacred city of the Hindus, seeks out his former five companions who now become his first disciples, and at the Deer Park in Banaras he preaches the first sermon of his ministry called "Setting in motion the wheel of the law." The substance of that first sermon constitutes the Buddha's original and essential teaching.

The Four Noble Truths

The Buddha is said to have summarized his teachings in one sentence, viz., I teach but one thing: Suffering and the release from suffering. Ultimately the matter is far more complicated than that, but penultimately that is precisely what Buddha's doctrine comes to. And the Four Noble Truths which he preached at Banaras are merely an extension of that one compact summary. The first three noble truths are about the essential nature of suffering; and the last noble truth is about how to be released from it. And yet upon the foundation of these four truths an enormous corpus of theological and philosophical literature has been erected; dozens of separate sects, schisms and individual interpretations have sprung from them, underscoring both their singular complexity and their extraordinary influence.

Here is the first of the four noble truths that the tradition says were enunciated by the Buddha in the Deer Park at Banaras around 528 B.C.:

> Now this, O monks, is the noble truth of suffering: birth is suffering, old age is suffering, sickness is suffering, death is suffering, sorrow, lamentation, dejection, and despair are suffering. Contact with unpleasant things is

suffering. [A.L. Herman, *An Introduction to Buddhist Thought* (University Press of America, 1984), p. 56. The sermon is from the Pali text of the *Samyutta-Nikāya* v. 20.]

Buddha is mindful here of the three signs of suffering or anguish, viz., sickness, old age and death, which some six years previously had set him off on his long search for peace and tranquility.

It seems fair to ask, following such an apparently pessimistic cata- logue, Is that the way life really is? And isn't the middle way on which Buddha has established his philosophy a rather one-sided way at that? But it would be unfair to characterize what Buddha says as a pessimistic doctrine, for he does not say that life is always suffering or painful. The catalogue of sorrows or pains that he lays before us does, indeed, consist of painful elements. But all of life is not characterized by these elements, nor does the passage quoted above suggest that it is. To believe that life is always painful would be pessimistic in the extreme.

Finally, to argue that life is always painful would be simply false, if not pure non-sense, and for several reasons: First, without some plea- sure, or the absence of pain, in some form or other, the identification of pain would be psychologically impossible. Moments of pain are recog- nized only because there are moments when there is no pain. To argue otherwise would be to fly in the face of common sense.

Second, right at this moment are you feeling any pain? I suspect that you are not, but pause and check. Doesn't this prove then that life is not always painful? And even if you are experiencing toothache or headache, depression or tension, you know they won't last.

Third, it would seem to be logically impossible for the word "pain" to have any meaning as a comparative noun unless there was a concept with which to compare it, viz., non-pain. That is to say, it would be logi- cally impossible to have a meaningful concept, pain, unless there was another meaningful concept, non-pain.

Fourth, and finally, the very fact of *nirvana* as a condition beyond all pain means that, to the Buddhist, life is not ultimately painful; hence, life cannot be characterized as *always* "painful." To argue otherwise would make non-sense of this ultimate optimism of Buddhism.

Faced with exceptional, extraordinary suffering, people turn to any number of means for escaping from it; Buddha sought release in "religious conversion" or metaphysical transformation; today, many people confronted with exceptional suffering in themselves turn to psy- choanalysis, drugs, religious and aesthetic distractions, and the like. And many people confronted with exceptional suffering in others turn to

THE WAYS OF PHILOSOPHY

political and social conversion, to politics, social reform, philanthropy, and the like.

Recall that it had been prophesied at Gautama's birth that he was to become either a Buddha or a great universal monarch. One might speculate that had Gautama's initial discovery of suffering not been existentially grounded in his own being, if he had been able to transcend the egocentric thrust of the three signs, he might have become that great world monarch that his father had hoped he would become. Or instead of renouncing the world in order to find peace and tranquility for himself, he might instead have become a physician (at the sign of sickness), a geriatric social worker (at the sign of old age) or a laconic wit noted for his ironical quips and homilies (at the sign of death). But Gautama chose the option of the way of the religious seeker because the pain he saw was, we must suppose, *his* pain and not the pain of the sick man, the old man and the dead man.

We turn next to the second noble truth:

> Now this, O monks, is the noble truth of the cause of suffering: that craving which leads to rebirth, combined with pleasure and lust, finding pleasure here and there, namely, the craving for passion, the craving for existence, the craving for non-existence. [*Ibid.*, p. 59.]

Buddha, whether aware of it or not, here follows the Hindu teaching that craving or desire is the cause of suffering. And this is no commonplace utterance but a tremendously important discovery. The cause of suffering is existentially grounded in the individual; suffering is not the result of metaphysical evil, like original sin, resulting from some ancestral Fall, as suggested by many Christians; nor is it simply due to actions performed by the individual in society and against God, as detailed in the Hebrew *Decalogue* and *Pentateuch* by Moses; nor is it one economic class in society exploiting another, as pointed out by the Marxists. In fact, original sin, individual sin, and societal sin can all be neatly subsumed under that cause that all three sins have in common, viz., they are all expressions of craving and desire.

Paradoxically, suffering lies in wanting what you can't get, and suffering also lies in wanting what you can get. The former is easy to see, the latter is not, but both seem to be important truths. When I get what I want then I worry and feel pain wondering if I can keep it. I want the 'A' on the test, the love of a friend, the summer job, the prize for being best, the inheritance from my rich aunt, and so on. If I don't get them, I'm pained and disconsolate. If I get them, then I worry about the 'A' on the next test, keeping the friend's love, the next job, the next prize, another aunt.

The nature of the mind seems to be characterized by wants; it moves restlessly from one obtainable or unobtainable object to another. You no sooner pass from one desire than another appears to take its place. Man is the anxious animal because he's the only desiring animal, living fretfully and forever in a future of anticipated wants. Satisfaction of the wants doesn't stop them; it only fuels them and feeds them. Frustration doesn't stop them; hope springs eternal, but with hope the fearful round of desiring continues. Buddha has wisely pointed to the cause of pain and suffering by calling attention to this one essential element of the suffering human mind: Desire exists.

We turn next to the third noble truth:

> Now this, O monks, is the noble truth of the cessation of suffering: the cessation without a remainder of that craving, abandonment, forsaking, release, non-attachment. [*Ibid.*, p. 60.]

Buddha would have been a negligent religious guide, indeed, if he had identified both the existence of suffering and its cause, desire, but had said nothing about the fact that anguish can be stopped.

In a way this is a curious "truth." It seems only half finished, for the listener wants to ask immediately, Okay, how? What's the way? But the answer to that question is found in the fourth noble truth, below. The third noble truth doesn't seem as noble as the other three, particularly because it leaves one hanging, waiting for some second eschatological shoe to fall.

Furthermore, the third noble truth is out of chronological and, even, logical, order with the fourth noble truth that describes the way to stop suffering. For how could Buddha know that the third is true unless he knew that the fourth was true? After one sees the way and follows it (the fourth noble truth) only then would one know that the possibility of stoppage (the third noble truth) was an actuality and worthy of being included as a noble truth. Why is it included at all? Why not have three noble truths, viz., there is suffering, its cause is desire, and there is a way to stopping desire and with it all suffering. That's neat, elegant and tidy. So what's the point of introducing this third noble truth that simply says cessation or ending of desire is possible?

I would suggest that it's mentioned as it is in order to underscore, to stress, the fact of stoppage. The fourth noble truth, as we shall see, repeats the stoppage motif in order to reinforce this most significant truth of Buddha's meditations: You're suffering but there can be a complete and total ending of that suffering. This deliverance, or salvation, motif is essential to any religion: "Come to me ye that labor and are heavy laden and I will give you peace." [See *The Gospel of St. Matthew* 11:28 and *Jeremiah* 31:25 for the expressions of this Christian and Jewish stoppage of suffering.] Without such a promise, without such a possibility of the stoppage of suffering, religions would be empty and useless, indeed. Buddha, in citing this third truth and in placing it where he does, emphasizes the promise and the optimism of the Buddhist way: Suffering can be permanently stopped.

We turn, finally, to the fourth noble truth:

> Now this, O monks, is the noble truth of the way that leads to the cessation of suffering: this is the Noble Eightfold Path, namely, right views, right intentions, right speech, right action, right livelihood, right effort, right mindfulness, right concentration. [*Ibid.*, p. 61.]

Buddha ends his first sermon at Banaras with this description of the way to the cessation of pain and suffering. It must appear as both simple and disappointing at first glance. We might have expected something more complicated, something more esoteric and mystical, than this list appears to offer. But the simplicity and the disappointment are assuaged when one realizes that there is a great deal that is practical and common sensical packed into each one of these "rights." For the listener is told that there is something that he or she can do, must do, and is able to do, *here and now*, in order to overcome desire and thereby destroy pain and suffering.

The Noble Eightfold Path

The eight "rights" are easily divisible into three quite distinct categories. The first category we might label "the internal path"; it comprises the first two rights, viz., right views about the nature of suffering, and right intentions not to increase the suffering in the world. The internal path is concerned with mental activities in relation to the world of suffering where those mental activities can be seen as necessary preliminaries to action or inaction in that world: For as your mind is, so are your actions.

The second category we might label "the external path"; it comprises the next three rights, viz., right speech in relation to others in the world, right acts towards others in the world, and right livelihood or vocation while living in the world. The external path is concerned with the actions that one performs and that directly concern other human beings and not merely oneself. Consequently, Buddhists respect truth, life and property, they refrain from occupations in the military and other businesses that involve killing in any form, e.g., the occupations of herdsman, tanner, leather worker, butcher and the like.

The third and final category of the paths we might label "the meditation path"; it comprises the last three rights, viz., right endeavor to control the qualities of the mind through yoga, right mindfulness achieved again through meditational yoga in which one rises above the wants, lusts, and desires of the body and mind, and finally, right concentration, the deepest stage of yogic meditation or penetration where one advances by further levels to the highest stage of realization, viz., *nirvana*. Yoga meditation is then the *sine qua non* of the Noble Eightfold Path and it is the cornerstone not only of Buddhism but of all the major philosophies and religions of India, China and Japan.

The Death of the Buddha

Following the first sermon in Banaras, where the Four Noble Truths were preached, Buddha set about gathering converts to the new doctrine. The tradition tells us that at first a few, and then hundreds, and finally thousands, flocked to his religion's standard as he preached and traveled (up to 20 miles a day!) throughout northeastern India, to the cities of Rajagriha, Sravasti, the capital of Kosala, Pataliputra or Patna, Vaishali and Kushinara and elsewhere for the remaining forty-five years of his life.

Beginning with his five ascetic associates, other disciples soon joined him, including one Yasa, the son of a wealthy guildmaster of Banaras. The tradition says that Yasa left his riches behind in disgust, sought out the Buddha in the Deer Park at Banaras and after hearing the Four Truths from him became the sixth disciple of the new movement. Buddha accepted a meal at Yasa's house and soon Yasa's mother and former wife became members of the lay or secular Order. Then four of Yasa's companions entered the Order as monks, and soon fifty other men of Banaras became *Arhats* or enlightened monks of the Order. As monks they engaged in a ceremony still practiced today of shaving their heads, wearing yellow robes, and reciting the vows three times, promising to take refuge or have faith in the Buddha, in the Doctrine, or *Dharma*, that he preached, and in the Order, or Sangha, of monks. The number of adherents eventually grew to such a number, we are told, that Buddha ceased to direct the ceremony personally and left its performance to the monks, themselves.

After three months of seclusion because of the rainy season, Buddha went to the town of Uruvela making converts along the way. One event that the later tradition relates is worth mentioning. Buddha came across a group of thirty young men having a picnic with their wives. One of them, who was without a wife, had brought a prostitute with him and she had stolen everyone's valuables and fled. All were looking for her when they came upon Buddha and asked him if he had seen the woman:

> "What do you think, young men," Buddha replied, "which is better for you to go in search of a woman, or to go in search of yourselves?" "It is better, Lord, for us to go in search of ourselves." [*Ibid.*, p. 75.]

With that Buddha preached to, converted and ordained them.

Grumblings were heard from the people of Magadha, the kingdom in which he was making these early conversions, and it is not surprising. The people complained that Buddha was bringing about childlessness and widowhood by dissolving the families of the young men he converted. The new converts were expected, after all, to leave their homes, parents, wives and children, much as the young Gautama, himself, had done originally, and to join the celibate, womanless Order. This abandonment could produce economic hardship on the abandoned families, one can well imagine, for Buddha's disciples were not all wealthy as Buddha, himself, had been.

Why did young men abandon the world and their families? What was the attraction? What drove them to it? Undoubtedly the charismatic personality of Buddha had very much to do with the conversions to monkhood. These conversions were not merely "decisions for Buddha" after the manner of evangelical tent meetings so familiar in the West, today. The young men didn't merely resolve to devote their lives to the new ideal, sign a pledge, sing a hymn and then return to their former lives (although the lay conversions of householders may have been something like this, to be sure). The monkish conversions required total abandonment of their previous lives, positions, duties and responsibilities. The personality of Buddha must have been overwhelming, indeed, to effect such a change, for the conversions were, if we can believe the tradition, true "turnings around" in the most radical sense. And so complete were they that backsliding is hardly mentioned.

There is another legend, a powerful story, from the period of Buddha's forty-five years of preaching that is worthy of mention as well. Kisa Gotami's beloved son had died when he was just a toddler. In her anguish she carried the body of the dead child to Buddha hoping for a miracle, for the tradition attributed many miraculous powers to Buddha, e.g., walking on water, flying through the air, knowing events before they happen, reading the hearts and minds of men, as well as raising the dead. Perhaps it was this reputation that brought her, sorrowing and in despair, to him. Buddha tells her that she was wise in coming to him for medicine, and promises to help her. He tells her to return to the city and to seek for a mustard seed from a house in which no one has died. Full of hope for her innocent, dead babe she goes to the city enquiring from door to door for the mustard seed from a house that cannot be found. Realizing her own folly and the wisdom that Buddha has shown her, that death touches everyone, she returns to Buddha. The sorrowing mother takes up the body of her child and carries him to a cemetery. Gently laying her son down for the last time and holding his tiny hand she says, "My little son, I thought that death had come to you alone; but it is not so; it happens to all people." She leaves him there, returns to Buddha and asks him for help in her despair. And Buddha says to her,

> Him whose mind is set upon the love of children and cattle, upon him as on
> a sleeping village comes a flood, Even so comes death and seizes him. [*Ibid.*,
> p. 80.]

In the twentieth year of his preaching he chooses Ananda as his bowl-bearer and heir-apparent leader of the Order. Converting kings, princes, and commoners, the wealthy and the poor, he travels about the northeastern parts of the subcontinent firmly establishing his reputation and the Order.

One day, towards the end of his long ministry, Buddha falls dangerously ill. Ananda became concerned because Buddha had made no official provision for the continuation of the Order. He enquires of Buddha what he has determined for the Order. Buddha, now in his eightieth and final year, replies rather sharply, we may suppose, saying, in effect, what more would you have from me?, I have told you everything that there is to be told.

> Therefore, Ananda, dwell as having refuges in yourselves, resorts in your-
> selves and not elsewhere, as having refuges in the Doctrine, resorts in the
> Doctrine and not elsewhere. [*Ibid.*, p. 81.]

That Buddha wished not to be revered as a God and that he desired not to fix attention on the Order as an institution seems clear from these remarks. The only source for enlightenment for future Buddhists is to be in the Doctrine or *Dharma* that he has preached, i.e., in essentially, but not exclusively, the Four Noble Truths, and what each man and woman will make of this Doctrine within himself or herself; that, he seems to be saying, is where the real strength and power of Buddhism must rest.

Moving on to Pava he stops at the mango grove of a blacksmith named Chunda. The latter provides a meal that brings on the Buddha's final sickness. He is taken ill with gushing blood and violent pains, but he controls his mortal illness and sets off with Ananda for Kusinara. On the way he rests and speaks further about the Doctrine. He indicates that there are four places worthy to be visited by monks: The place where the Buddha was born; where he attained enlightenment; where he first turned the wheel of the law; and where he attained *parinirvana*, or complete *nirvana*, i.e., where he died. Thus the way is prepared for the raising of future stupas (relic-chambers for Buddha's bones) and temples at these holy places. Now dying, Buddha speaks to the sorrowing Ananda,

> The Doctrine and Discipline, Ananda, which I have taught and enjoined upon you, is to be your teacher when I am gone.

And then addressing all the monks gathered at the sacred spot at Kusinara he speaks to them for the last time:

> And now, O monks, I take my leave of you; all the constituents of being are anitya, transitory; work out your salvation with diligence. [*Ibid.*, p. 83.]

And then, surrounded by his sorrowing disciples, Gautama Siddhartha Shakyamuni, he who was called 'the Buddha,' dies.

THE BUDDHA'S ACCOMPLISHMENTS

There is one basic truth about human existence to which the Buddha first drew attention, a truth that has only recently been given the attention that it deserves by Western philosophers, theologians and psychologists. This is the truth which lies at the very foundation of the four noble truths at Banaras, a truth which the Buddha reiterates with his dying breath at Kusinara. It is the truth of *anitya*, universal change, which in time will become one of the central dogmas of Buddhism. Let's look at this dogma very briefly and see what implications it carries. [I see nothing sinister in the use of the word "dogma" ("established point of view") to describe a fundamental precept, a definitive or authoritative tenet. Many Buddhists like to believe that they are dogma-free. I would suggest that no one is entirely dogma-free, and that to believe otherwise is to believe in at least one dogma.]

The Dogma of *Anitya* and Five Curious Implications

The dogma of *anitya* makes its appearance early in the history of Buddhist thought where we find it stated by Buddha in an early 3rd century B.C. text:

> Whether Buddhas arise, O monks, or whether Buddhas do not arise, it remains a fact and the fixed and necessary constitution of being, that all its constituents are transitory [*anitya*]. [*Ibid.*, p. 108.]

Anitya means "impermanence, transient, or perishable." Its primary sense for the Buddhists is that of ceaselessly flowing and changing. Buddha concludes:

> Impermanent, alas! are all compound things. Their nature is to rise and fall. When they have risen they cease. [*Ibid.*]

The dogma of *anitya* is simply this: All existence is characterized by ceaseless change.

One doesn't have to search Buddhist texts to see the truth and force of this dogma. Look around you. See the trees and grass grow and die, the day turn into night, the seasons wax and wane, the years, decades and centuries roll inexorably past. Look at your hands that are holding this book. Dermatologists tell us that all the lovely colored flesh that you see is really dead epithelial tissue, cells pushed up from the growing dermal layer of the skin that lies beneath them. These dead cells are scraped, washed and sloughed off as the growing tissues live and die. Your body is a colony of such cells, a microcosm of the changing, flowing universe, never the same from moment to moment, in its orderly processes of creation, maintenance and destruction, producing life, growth and death.

Furthermore, things that seem permanent really only seem that way. Look at this book. If we were to place it on a table and take a motion picture of it at the rate of one frame per year for the next thousand years, and then show a movie of those one thousand frames, what we'd see would be a gradual disintegration of the seemingly permanent book as it oxidized and sulfurized its way into decay and eventual dust. All this should surprise no one. The Buddhists have simply taken a rather ordinary, common-sense property of objects in the space-time world and by calling philosophical attention to that property's universality they have made it an essential dogma of their doctrines.

The Buddhists, however, have gone further with the implications of the dogma than many of us would care to go. First, from the dogma of *anitya* it follows logically that there can be no Gods, i.e., no ultimately real, permanent and unchanging, divine beings. Thus one of the implications of *anitya* is atheism.

Second, if the dogma of *anitya* is accepted, then from it one can generate the doctrine of universal suffering or anguish, *duhkha*, which, as we have seen, lies at the heart of all Buddhist doctrine. Recall the three signs of suffering witnessed by Gautama in his early life, viz., sickness, old age and death. It was the impermanence of the body that led to these three states of pain and it was the search for a way to permanent peace and tranquility that finally drove Buddha to leave his household life and set out on the path to that permanence.

Alvin Toffler, in an enormously popular book on change and suffering, says in his opening sentence, "This is a book about what happens to people when they are overwhelmed by change." Toffler defines change as "the process by which the future invades our lives." [Alvin Toffler, *Future Shock* (New York: Bantam Books, 1971), p. 1], and he uses the term "future shock" to describe "the shattering stress and disorientation that we induce in individuals by subjecting them to too much change in too short a time." [*Ibid.*, p. 2.]: Future shock, in other words, is anguish. Summarizing the research on what happens to people subjected to repeated change, Toffler states:

> ...those with high life change scores were more likely than their fellows to be ill in the following year. For the first time, it was possible to show in dramatic form that the rate of change in a person's life—his pace of life—is closely tied to the state of his health. [*Ibid.*, p. 330.]

One of the researchers whom Toffler quotes had said that the results of their work were so spectacular that "at first we hesitated to publish them." Toffler concludes:

> In every case, the correlation between change and illness has held. It has been established that "alterations in life style" that require a great deal of adjustment and coping, correlate with illness—whether or not these changes are under the individual's own direct control, whether or not he sees them as desirable. Furthermore, the higher the degrees of life change, the higher the risk that subsequent illness will be severe. [*Ibid.*]

The physiological relationship between change (*anitya*) and illness (*duhkha*) has been known for some time in both the East and West. The experiments that Toffler cites give dramatic reconfirmation to that previous knowledge.

Third, the existence of *anitya* manifested as *duhkha* drives one to seek an escape from it into the bliss of *nirvana*. Buddha summarizes the reasons for this setting out on the path to escape the effects of *anitya:*

> Impermanent, alas! are all compound things. Their nature is to rise and fall. When they have risen they cease. The bringing of them to an end is bliss. [*Ibid.*, p. 111.]

Hence, the knowledge of the fact of *anitya* drives one into seeking its dissolution in the peace and serenity of *nirvana*. Thus a third implication of *anitya* is the search for *nirvana*.

A fourth implication of the concept of *anitya* involves the notion of *trishna*. *Trishna* means "thirsting or lusting or desire." *Trishna* results from being caught in *anitya*, for when one is faced with continuous change and mounting *duhkha* and anxiety, one desires to cling to whatever one already possesses. In other words, *anitya* is a cause of *trishna*, for desire has its origin in the attempt to clutch at things, as well as states or conditions, that are, once and for all, safe and secure from change. Thus a fourth implication of *anitya* is *trishna*.

Fifth and finally, the concept of *anitya* leads to the doctrine of *anatman*, the doctrine that the self is unreal or impermanent. For if everything is in perpetual flux, then it follows that there can be no abiding or permanent self. The doctrine of non-self is not as far out and silly as it must first sound. In fact the doctrine has received a lot of support from both Western philosophers and psychologists who probably began by trying to experience the so-called "self" directly. Can we experience or know the self?, is a legitimate question. When you look for it, you can't find it. What do you find? Look into your mind right now; can you discover anything there other than sets of particular momentary thoughts, perceptions or desires? Is there anything else besides these, such as a person, or an ego, or an I, or a self?, over and beyond those particular changing and ephemeral phenomena? Consider the following statement:

> For my part, when I enter most intimately into what I call *myself*, I always stumble on some particular perception or other, of heat or cold, light or shade, love or hatred, pain or pleasure. I never catch *myself* at any time without a perception, and never can observe anything but the perception. When my perceptions are remov'd for any time, as by sound sleep; so long am I insensible of myself, and may truly be said not to exist. [David Hume, *A Treatise of Human Nature* (Oxford: Clarendon Press, 1888), p. 252.]

The author of that very Buddhist sentiment is David Hume (1711-1776), an empiricist and phenomenalist philosopher of the British

Enlightenment. For Hume, as for the early Buddhists, the self is a fiction, an artifice, Hume says, of memories held together by the force of imagination. And, though the terminology is different, Hume's meaning and intent are the same: There is no self.

B. F. Skinner, a contemporary Western behaviorist and psychologist, says some things about the self that, again, might help us to grasp the Buddha's insight a bit more securely. Recalling Western notions of a permanent and substantial self, Skinner observes:

> It is often said that a science of behavior studies the human organism but neglects the person or self. What it neglects is a vestige of animism, a doctrine which in its crudest form held that the body was moved by one or more indwelling spirits. When the resulting behavior was disruptive, the spirit was probably a devil; when it was creative, it was a guiding genius or muse. Traces of the doctrine survive when we speak of a *personality*, of an ego in ego psychology, of an *I* who says he knows what he is going to do and uses his body to do it, or of the role a person plays as a person in a drama, wearing his body as a costume. [B. F. Skinner, *About Behaviorism* (New York: Alfred A. Knopf, 1974), p. 171.]

The behavioral analysis of "person" or "personality" leads to the abolition of this modern devil or genius, the homunculus in mufti, an illusion created out of our ignorance. The behaviorist, like the Buddhist, seeks the exposure of this illusion, its exorcism and abolition:

> What is being abolished [say the defenders of this person or self] is autonomous man, the homunculus, the possessing demon, the man defended by the literature of freedom and dignity. His abolition has long been overdue... He has been constructed from our ignorance.

> The purpose of the dispossession is made clear by Skinner when he says, again, sounding, in part, very much like a Buddhist:

> Only by dispossessing him can we turn to the real causes of human behavior. Only then can we turn from the inferred to the observed, from the miraculous to the natural, from the inaccessible to the manipulable [controllable]. [B. F. Skinner, *Beyond Freedom and Dignity* (New York: Alfred A. Knopf, 1971), p. 200, 201.]

In the West, the concept of the self has evolved, first, from the staunch belief in an indwelling demon or spirit, then to a ghost in a machine, a notion attacked by Hume and ridiculed by Skinner, and finally, to a fiction for Hume and a behaving organism for Skinner. Thus a fifth implication of *anitya* is *anatman*.

In conclusion we might say, then, that *anitya* is, indeed, one of the central and, apparently, common-sensical concepts in early Buddhism. Later Buddhism will accept it also, but it will not accept all of the implications to which that concept seems inexorably to lead. Those implications, as we have seen, are bound up with five concepts, viz., atheism (there are no real Gods), *duhkha* (anguish is the chief characteristic of this bodily life), *nirvana* (liberation is what one is driven to search for by the realization of the fact of *anitya*), *trishna* (desire is manifested by the presence of *anitya*), and *anatman* (there is no real self).

THE WAY OF *NIRVANA*: GAUTAMA THE BUDDHA

The way of *nirvana* or "the way of tranquility and liberation," as it might now be called, is rather simple to describe since the Buddha, himself, created the model, the Four Noble Truths, that we have been using throughout this text for summarizing the various ways of philosophy. (See above Chapter 1, *The Ways of Philosophy*, pp. 6-8.)

The Problem

From what we have learned from the first sermon of the Buddha at Banaras, the problem that must be solved is *duhkha*, best translated as "anguish" or "anxiety." It is the heart-rending fear that my present condition will change and that I will become sick, old or dead. Becoming sick, becoming old, becoming dead are the verbs that describe the changes that describe my suffering.

The Cause

The cause of suffering is desire or craving. Once desire is controlled and eliminated, the suffering will end. But as long as the possibility of craving exists, just so long will the possibility of anxiety exist.

The Solution

The solution to the problem of anxiety and pain lies in stopping or preventing the cause of the pain. In other words, the solution lies in stoppage, cessation, bringing desire to an end. For the Buddha that stoppage is *nirvana*, the blowing out, the extinguishing, of the flame of desire.

The Way

The way to end the craving that leads to suffering, anxiety and pain is to follow the Noble Eightfold Path. By properly controlling change in the body and the mind, desire can be brought to an end. That proper control is carried out by recognizing that some forms of *anitya*, viz., the various changes recommended by the way of the Noble Eightfold Path, can be used to end *anitya*, to end craving, to end suffering.

But a problem, at least one, develops with this way of philosophy and it lies in the Buddha's attempt to find the best and most worthwhile life.

PROBLEMS WITH THE BUDDHA: THE PROBLEM OF *ANITYA*

The problem of *anitya* is simply this: If *anitya* is true then how is *nirvana* possible? The problem can be generated by turning the epistemological tables on Buddha and asking Plato's question (see The Dilemma of Knowledge, above, p. 55) of him: Plato's question was, How can there be knowledge, which for Plato was the final objective of the metaphysical struggle and the Socratic dialectic, if there is no being (known) as well as becoming (known)? Since the final objective for Buddha is *nirvana*, a condition of being or non-change, we might ask: How can one reach *nirvana* unless there is both *being* (the final blissful unchanging condition) as well as *becoming* (the changing condition of transformation by and through which the condition of *being* is attained)? In other words, *anitya* cannot be as pervasive as the Buddhists claim or else *nirvana* would be impossible. The problem of *anitya* points to an apparent logical inconsistency in the way of philosophy of the Buddha. Finally, the problem of *anitya* points to an essential incompleteness in that way of philosophy since the dogma of *anitya* would seem now to be in some jeopardy once unchanging *nirvana* is accepted as the solution to the problem of suffering.

We turn next to a way of philosophy that the Buddha, himself, had rejected. His early life in his father's palace had been a life surrounded by luxury and sensual satisfactions. But that way of pleasure proved incapable of solving the problem of suffering for the future Buddha. Let's examine that rejected way of philosophy and see if the Buddha might have missed something in his encounter with it.

SEVEN

THE WAY OF PLEASURE
⇒•⇐

HEDONISM: POPULAR AND ENLIGHTENED HEDONISM

If the Sophists sought happiness through worldly success, and if Socrates sought happiness through self-discovery, the philosophers we are now investigating sought the ultimate good through pleasure. They have been called "hedonists," from the Greek *hedonē*, "pleasure," but because they differ so much with respect to just what pleasure is, we shall have to make some distinctions in dealing with them. Those distinctions are best made by speaking first of "popular hedonism" and second of "enlightened hedonism." We begin with two representatives of popular hedonism, Aristippus of Cyrene and Omar Khayyam, and conclude with two enlightened hedonists, Epicurus and John Stuart Mill.

The hedonist again raises the question with which we began our study, What is the best and most worthwhile life that a human being can live?, and he or she answers the question by saying that the best life is one that produces the most pleasure and avoids the most pain. Who would want it any differently? Problems arise, however, in explaining *what kinds* of pleasure are being produced and *for whom* they are being produced. If I seek only the pleasures of the senses and the body in food, sex, and drink, and avoid the higher pleasures of the mind and the spirit, such as knowledge, friendship, creativity and the like, then aren't I behaving like some sort of animal? And if I'm just going to go after and increase my own pleasures, then aren't I being selfish? So doesn't hedonism really end in a philosophy of crude and selfish beastiality? These are questions that hedonism, in fashioning a way of philosophy out of pleasure, will have to answer.

Popular Pleasure: Aristippus and Omar Khayyam

Aristippus of Cyrene (435-350 B.C.)
The Founder of Popular Hedonism

Aristippus was born in the city-state of Cyrene, "a land of wealth and beauty" near the Mediterranean Coast in modern Libya. Founded by Greek colonists in 631 B.C., Cyrene was a city not only of trade, business and commerce, but a home for scientific and intellectual pursuits, as well. Within one hundred years of her founding, Cyrene's school of scientific medicine was famous throughout the ancient world. The Cyrenians lived in prosperity and showered their wealth on temples, palaces, houses, the arts and sports, devoting much of their time and concerns to the breeding and racing of horses to compete at the Greek games at Olympia, Delphi, and elsewhere. [See Kathleen Freeman, *Greek City States* (New York: W. W. Norton & Company, 1950), pp. 191-220, for a grand description of Cyrene.]

We are told that Aristippus left Cyrene and came to Athens attracted by the fame of Socrates, "the wisest man in the world." In Athens he sought out and remained with Socrates until the latter's execution in 399 B.C. It is said that he was the first of Socrates' companions to charge fees for his teaching and that once on sending his master the sum of 20 minae, Socrates returned it saying that his supernatural voice would not let him accept it. Leaving Athens after Socrates' death, he traveled widely and then returned to Cyrene where he taught until his own death in 350 B.C. The titles of two of his many lost books are illustrative of his life-long commitment to pleasure: "To those who blame him for his love of old wine and of women" and "To those who blame him for extravagant living." [*Ibid.*, p. 213.]

Xenophon (420-354 B.C.), another of Socrates' companions, tells us that Aristippus was intemperate or lacked self-control with respect to drink, sex, and sleep. Holding slaves and keeping servants, Aristippus lived luxuriously and expensively. He had no occupation, slept late, and freely indulged his passions. Defending his sensual life style Aristippus stated: "As for me, I classify myself among the men who want to live as easily and pleasantly as possible." [Xenophon, *Recollections of Socrates and Socrates' Defense Before the Jury*, translated by Anna S. Benjamin (The Library of Liberal Arts, 1965), p. 35.] Aristippus' fondness for rich food, drink, fine clothes, perfumes, women, and a life of luxury and unrestrained pleasure became proverbial in the ancient world. He claimed that one's possessions unlike one's shoes could never be too large for comfort.

And yet he displayed a certain wisdom about possessions and pleasures that may have gone largely unnoticed. Thus he advised his friends to limit their possessions to what they could save from a shipwreck; and he counselled "...it is not abstinence from pleasures that is best, but mastery over them." [Diogenes Laertius, *Op. Cit.*, Vol. I, p. 205.] This latter remark was well illustrated when he was reproached for his relationship to the infamous courtesan Lais. He retorted, "I possess Lais, she does not possess me." [*Ibid.*] He enjoyed his pleasures fully, never going out of his way or exerting himself in pursuit of them but taking only those near at hand and easily obtainable.

Aristippus believed that since the future was never present, it was unreal and therefore "nothing to us." Hence one had to derive pleasure from what was immediately present and not work to get pleasure from things not present. It followed, then, that one must pursue only those pleasures that are immediate and certain, i.e., the physical and sensuous pleasures: You only go around once in this life so grab all the gusto you can, is a motto to which Aristippus would have readily assented. Let's call this philosophy of pleasure "popular hedonism," and let's say that anyone who seeks the physical, as opposed to the intellectual, pleasures of the present moment is a popular hedonist. Aristippus was a popular hedonist.

Popular Ethical Hedonism

Aristippus' followers were called "Cyrenaics." They accepted the popular hedonism that stated that all pleasures are good but that immediate sensual pleasures are best. That is to say, pleasure, and in particular sensual pleasure, is the only thing that is desirable for its own sake, i.e., pleasure is the only intrinsically good thing. Other ends or goals of life, such as wisdom, love, prudence or friendship, or other pursuits such as success, wealth or honor, are good only instrumentally, i.e., only if they lead to pleasure. This view, that all pleasure is good and that pleasure is the only thing that is intrinsically good, is called "ethical hedonism"; it says that any action that is right leads to pleasure, and any action that leads to pleasure is right. In other words, *popular ethical hedonism* holds that an action is right if and only if it leads to pleasure. Suppose that I have a choice between reading further about the Cyrenaics or going to a movie. Suppose that I'm pretty certain that I'll get immediate pleasure from the movie and I won't get anything but pain from reading on. And suppose that I'm a popular ethical hedonist. According to the definition of a right action above, it would be right for me to go to the movie. Moreover, for the sake of completeness, my ethical code also tells me that it would be *wrong* for me to continue to read on, and that it is my *duty* to go to the movie and to avoid reading further, and that I have a *moral responsibility* to go to the movie. All this follows from my popular ethical hedonism.

Underlying and supporting this ethical hedonism is another view with which it ought not to be confused, viz., psychological hedonism. The latter holds that it is human nature to pursue pleasure and to avoid pain. The Cyrenaics put it this way:

> That pleasure is the end [to be pursued] is proved by the fact that from our youth up we are instinctively attracted to it, and, when we obtain it, seek for nothing more, and shun nothing so much as its opposite, pain. [*Ibid.*, p. 217.]

Ethical hedonism, the view that pleasure *ought* to be pursued by man, is constructed on the foundation of psychological hedonism, the view that pleasure *is* instinctively pursued by man. So to the question, Why ought I seek as many pleasures as possible?, the popular hedonist can answer, Why, it's human nature. The *ought* rests on the *is*, and ethics finds its roots in psychology.

The *Rubaiyat* of Omar Khayyam

Popular ethical hedonism can be stated in a form that is quite congenial to human tastes. Consider the poem, the *Rubaiyat*, of the 12th century Persian poet and astronomer, Omar Khayyam.

The poem that we attribute to Omar is perhaps better attributed to the Victorian translator of the *Rubaiyat*, Edward Fitzgerald. That the latter used an extremely free hand in his translation is accepted now by most critics. With this in mind, let's look at this greatest of all celebrations of popular hedonism. Omar, or Fitzgerald, begins his encomium to life and pleasure, reminding us to eat, drink, and be merry, with the momentous cry:

> Wake! For the Sun, who scatter'd into flight
> The Stars before him from the Field of Night,
> Drives Night along with them from Heav'n,
>   and strikes
> The Sultan's Turret with a Shaft of Light.
>
> Before the phantom of False morning died,
> Methought a Voice within the Tavern cried,

"When all the Temple is prepared within,
Why nods the drowsy Worshipper outside?"

Come, fill the Cup, and in the fire of Spring
Your Winter-garment of Repentance fling:
 The Bird of Time has but a little way
To flutter—and the Bird is on the Wing.

Whether at Naishapur or Babylon,
Whether the Cup with sweet or bitter run,
 The Wine of Life keeps oozing drop by drop,
The Leaves of Life keep falling one by one.

A Book of Verses underneath the Bough,
A Jug of Wine, a Loaf of Bread—and Thou
 Beside me singing in the Wilderness—
Oh, Wilderness were Paradise enow!

Some for the Glories of This World; and some
Sigh for the Prophet's Paradise to come;
 Ah, take the Cash, and let the Credit go,
Nor heed the rumble of a distant Drum!

[*Rubaiyat of Omar Khayyam*, translated into English by Edward Fitzgerald
(New York: Random House, 1947), pp. 53, 56, 58-59.]

We turn next to the way of philosophy as envisaged by popular hedonists like Aristippus and Fitzgerald's Omar Khayyam.

THE WAY OF POPULAR HEDONISM:
ARISTIPPUS AND OMAR

The Problem

From what we have said above, it ought to be simple to quickly reconstruct the popular hedonism of Aristippus and Omar. The problem
that the hedonists in general were trying to solve was the problem of
suffering. Since, according to psychological hedonism, human beings
will innately avoid pain and by nature pursue pleasure, it follows that
the problem to be solved is how to best carry out these two natural aims,
i.e., how to avoid suffering and how to achieve pleasure: That is the
double edged problem of suffering. The pain that humans seek to avoid
is both physical and intellectual. The pleasures that they pursue are primarily physical, though both Aristippus and Omar give recognition to
intellectual pleasures since both have constructed philosophies of happi-

ness, intellectual guides in themselves, by which to pursue those physical pleasures and to avoid the anxiety of not having them.

The Causes

The cause of the problem of suffering is equally double edged. It is ignorance of how to avoid pain and ignorance of how to acquire pleasure. As we shall see, it is the inability to adequately handle this ignorance that will prove to be the major problem for popular hedonism.

The Solution

The solution to the problem of suffering lies in getting as much pleasure, bodily pleasures, as possible, and avoiding as much pain as possible.

The Ways

The ways to the solution of the problem involve knowing where the bread, the wine, and the thou are, and knowing how to get to the table, the tavern, and the bough.

PROBLEMS WITH POPULAR HEDONISM

But problems arise when we consider that some pleasures may not be good, or good for you. Contrary to what the Cyrenaics said some pleasures can be painful. Further, suppose that I want to do two things and they are both pleasant. How do I decide between them? Call these problems "the problem of bad pleasures" and "the problem of choices between pleasures." Consider the following Cyrenaic view:

> Pleasure is good even if it proceed from the most unseemly conduct.... For even if the action be irregular, still, at any rate, the resultant pleasure is desirable for its own sake and is good. [Diogenes Laertius, *Lives*, *Op. Cit.*, Vol. I, pp. 217, 219.]

The problems that such a view creates should be obvious. "Irregular" actions, moreover, especially if they are "immoral" according to common sense, may also lead into a blatant contradiction as we see that one and the same action can be both right, because it produces pleasure, and wrong, because it produces pain. For example, according to popular ethical hedonism, it would be right for me to get drunk if doing so leads to pleasure; but the hangover and sickness that accompanies or that follows is painful. Hence the same act leads to both pleasure and pain. Hence the same act is both right and wrong. In both instances popular ethical hedonism manages to violate our standards of common sense and consistency for a way of philosophy. Thus the problem of bad pleasures.

Suppose that I want to go to a movie but I also want to continue reading about the hedonists. In other words, suppose I get pleasure from both. How do I choose between two pleasures? Popular ethical hedonism tells me that both actions are right but it doesn't tell me how I can go about deciding whether to go to the movie or continue reading in this book. To that extent popular ethical hedonism violates the standard of completeness for a way of philosophy for it won't help me to solve a very simple ethical problem. Thus the problem of choices.

Following our three criteria of common sense, consistency, and completeness for an adequate way of philosophy, popular hedonism appears to lose on all three counts. Popular hedonism violates common sense and contradicts itself to the very degree that it unrestrainedly pursues physical pleasures: Too much pleasure can lead to pain, suffering and death. It would be a violation of common sense to gather as much pleasure as one could under such circumstances. To begin with, if the pleasures that one is unrestrainedly pursuing become pains, because one has left caution, moderation and restraint behind, then pleasure has become pain and we have a flaring inconsistency in the way of philosophy of popular hedonism. The person who eats or drinks to excess, or the drug addict painfully hooked on coffee, tobacco, alcohol, or cocaine, are outstanding examples of instances in popular hedonism where the logical inconsistency of the position is apparent, i.e., where pleasure becomes not pleasure and one ends by pursuing pain as one's pleasure.

Finally, the incompleteness of popular hedonism is glaringly apparent not only from the problem of choices but also from the realization that physical pleasures are only temporary ameliorations of suffering. When the pleasures die down, if one hasn't burned oneself out already with too much booze, too many drugs, too much food, sex, titillation, and stimulation, or when the tavern closes, the beloved dies, the bread is gone, and the bottle is empty, the problem of suffering returns. The problem has been there all along, really, hidden, covered over, waiting, biding its time, ready to pounce. Popular hedonism is incomplete in failing to find a permanent solution to the problem of suffering, viz., how to escape suffering and achieve lasting pleasure.

The consequence is that the way of philosophy according to popular hedonism fails on all three counts of adequacy. It is because of this failure that most hedonists turn from this naive and simple-minded hedonism of Aristippus and Omar to what we shall now refer to as *enlightened hedonism.* Repairs to hedonism as a way of philosophy can be made and it will be left to enlightened hedonists like Epicurus and, subsequently, John Stuart Mill to make them.

Enlightened Pleasure: Epicurus

Epicurus of Samos (341-271 B.C.): The Founder of Enlightened Hedonism

Epicurus was born of Athenian parents on the Aegean island of Samos in 341 B.C. It is said that he turned to philosophy in disgust when his schoolmasters could not tell him the meaning of *"chaos"* in Hesiod. At first he followed the philosophies of Democritus the atomist and Aristippus the hedonist before combining their views into a highly original philosophy of his own.

He came to Athens when he was eighteen. After studying what was available, he became disenchanted with the welter of philosophies then being taught in the city, the Platonic philosophy at the Academy ("the toadies of Dionysius"), the philosophy of Aristotle ("a profligate") at the Lyceum, as well as the up and coming Pyrrhonist, Sophist, Stoic, Cynic and Skeptic doctrines elsewhere. So, after much study and at the age of 37, he purchased a secluded garden for 80 minae (about $8,000) and set up his own school of philosophy, a place where his friends could gather about him and seek answers to questions about pleasure and its relation to a man's life. It was on pleasure that he came to focus his principle attentions saying:

> I know not how to conceive the good, apart from the pleasures of taste, sexual pleasures, the pleasures of sound and the pleasures of beautiful form.
> [Diogenes Laertius, *Op. Cit.*, Vol. II, p. 535.]

But Epicurus' hedonism, which here sounds like unregenerate Cyrenaicism, is far more complex, as we shall see, than this passage would seem to indicate.

In opposition to the other reigning schools, he set about finding his own answer to the question on which all were focusing attention, What is the best and most worthwhile life that a human being can live? Epicurus and his friends answered the question directly and practically by adopting lives of the utmost simplicity and frugality. Epicurus, the founder of the view that intellectual pleasure is the highest and only good of life, was content to live on plain bread and water, surrounded by quiet conversation and loving companions. Writing to a friend who had asked him what he could send to the most famous philosopher of pleasure in Athens, Epicurus answered, "Send me a little pot of cheese, that, when I like, I may fare sumptuously." [*Ibid.*, p. 541.] Epicurus was no epicure.

He suffered greatly during his life from kidney stones and died in 271 B.C.:

> ...he entered a bronze bath of lukewarm water and asked for unmixed wine, which he swallowed, and then, having bidden his friends remember his doctrines, breathed his last. [*Ibid.*, pp. 543, 545.]

His unsurpassed good will earned him the praise and friendship of whole cities of men and women who honored him and his doctrines with statues in bronze. Such was his life and his death. But what were his doctrines?

Empirical Atomistic Hedonism

Epicurus' Hedonism

Epicurus defined philosophy as "the daily business of speech and thought to secure a happy life." That happy life for Epicurus centered around pleasure which is,

> ...our first and kindred good. It is the starting point of every choice and every aversion and to it we come back and make feeling the rule by which to judge of every good thing....

But, as we've seen above, Epicurus was no unabashed follower of Aristippus. The Epicurean guides his pleasures by reason and not by passion and it is this intelligent pursuit of pleasure that makes all the difference between the popular hedonist and the enlightened hedonist. In a letter to his young friend and disciple, Menoeceus, from which the previous and the following passages come, Epicurus speaks to this very point:

> And since pleasure is our first and native good, for that reason we do not choose every pleasure whatsoever, but oftentimes pass over many pleasures when a greater annoyance ensues from them. And oftentimes we consider pains superior to pleasures when submission to the pains for a long time brings us as a consequence a greater pleasure.

Where the rule of the popular hedonist was to grab all the pleasures that you can, whatever they are like, for tomorrow you die, the rule of the enlightened hedonist is one of intelligently weighing pleasures to see which are better and then choosing those: Quality is more important than quantity of pleasures in that choosing. All pleasures are good, Epicurus never denies that basic hedonistic doctrine, but, and here he differs again from the muddled popular hedonist, not all pleasures should be chosen:

> While therefore all pleasure because it is naturally akin to us [Epicurus' version of psychological hedonism] is good [Epicurus' version of ethical hedonism], not all pleasure is choiceworthy, just as all pain is an evil and yet not all pain is to be shunned. It is, however, by measuring one against another, and by looking at the conveniences and inconveniences, that all these matters must be judged.

It is that "looking at" and measuring that turns popular, naive hedonism into enlightened, intelligent hedonism. Epicurus concludes, modifying his hedonism even further:

> When we say, then, that pleasure is the end and aim, we do not mean the pleasures of the prodigal or the pleasures of sensuality, as we are understood to do by some through ignorance, prejudice, or willful misrepresentation. By pleasure we mean the absence of pain in the body and of trouble in the soul. [Both physical and intellectual pleasures are important and necessary to the good life for Epicurus.] It is not an unbroken succession of drinking-bouts and of revelry, not sexual love, not the enjoyment of the fish and other delicacies of a luxurious table, which produce a pleasant life; it is sober reasoning, searching out the grounds of every choice and avoidance, and banishing those beliefs through which the greatest tumults take possession of the soul.

Epicurus then turns from this praise of intelligently guided pleasures to one of the virtues, *phronēsis*. *Phronēsis* is usually translated "prudence" or "good sense" and in Plato's dialogues *phronēsis* is generally identified with "knowledge" or "wisdom." [See W.K.C. Guthrie, *A History of Greek Philosophy*, *Op. Cit.*, Vol. IV, p. 265: "Both in Plato and elsewhere one must translate *phronēsis* and *sophia* as either 'knowledge' or 'wisdom' according to the context. Plato uses this feature of Greek language and thought to further the thesis that virtue is knowledge, and of course the knowledge which unites the virtues is not knowledge as understood by the ordinary man; but he did not invent it." Epicurus follows the same convention.] It is the latter meaning that our enlightened hedonist intends in his final words to Menoeceus:

> Of all this the beginning and the greatest good is phronesis, wisdom. Wherefore wisdom is a more precious thing even than philosophy; from it spring all the other virtues, for it teaches that we cannot lead a life of pleasure which is not also a life of wisdom, honor, and justice; nor lead a life of wisdom, honor, and justice, which is not also a life of pleasure. For the virtues have grown into one with a pleasant life, and a pleasant life is

inseparable from them. [Diogenes Laertius, *Op. Cit.*, Vol. II, pp. 655, 657. R. D. Hicks translates *"phronēsis"* as "prudence" rather than "wisdom" throughout.]

Through his stress on *phronēsis* Epicurus has managed to solve both of the problems that confronted the popular hedonist, viz., the problem of bad pleasures and the problem of choices. Enlightened hedonism recognizes that some pleasures are bad because they lead to future states of pain. Epicurus would advise us to avoid the addictive pleasures because pursuing them leads either to pain or to death thereby making the pursuit of pleasure in the future either difficult or impossible. Thus the problem of bad pleasures.

Finally, enlightened hedonism recognizes that not only are some pleasures, even though they are all good, to be avoided but some pleasures are better than others. Wisdom, prudence or *phronēsis* alone can determine which of the really good pleasures are to be chosen. If going to a movie or reading about the hedonists are the two choices of pleasure open to me, then wisdom chooses the pleasure with the greater chance for knowledge, honor and justice. And a movie about the life of Mohandas Gandhi or Martin Luther King or Epicurus or even Aristippus might take hedonic precedence over reading this book, everything else being equal. Thus the problem of choices between two pleasures.

Epicurus' hedonism is accompanied by two other views, views which seem, invariably, to coexist with hedonism, viz., empiricism and materialism. We turn next to Epicurus' empiricism and materialism.

Epicurus' Empiriciam and Atomism

Epicurus was an unabashed empiricist. He believed that all of our ideas are derived from sensation and that nothing can refute or challenge the senses for they are the standards by which truth and falsity, knowledge and ignorance, and everything else, are to be judged:

> For the existence of bodies is everywhere attested by sense itself, and it is upon sensation that reason must rely when it attempts to infer the unknown from the known.

> Next, we must by all means stick to our sensations, that is simply to the present impressions whether of the mind or of any criterion whatever, and similarly to our actual feelings, in order that we may have the means of determining that which needs confirmation and that which is obscure. [*Ibid.*, p. 569.]

Epicurus' final view was that,

...all of our ideas are derived from sensations, either by actual contact or by analogy, or resemblance, or composition with some slight aid from reasoning. [*Ibid.*, pp. 561-563. Italics added.]

The world that the senses range over, furthermore, consists of material bodies in space and whatever can ever be known about the world is about those bodies. Epicurus was strongly influenced by the atomism espoused by the Greek philosopher Democritus, a contemporary of Socrates from around 400 B.C., who had said that the world consists of only two entities, viz., *atoms* (Greek "indivisibles") of all shapes, weights and sizes, and the void or space in which these atoms move. Moreover, these atoms combine together to form material objects which continuously give off films or layers of their atoms into the surrounding space:

> For particles are continually streaming off from the surface of bodies, though no diminution of the bodies is observed, because other particles take their place. [*Ibid.*, p. 577.]

And as they stream off, these particles strike sense organs thereby producing sensations. But the sensory qualities that are observed in sensation, oddly enough, are neither in the atoms nor in the physical objects from which they come; they are rather in the observer whose senses are being stimulated by the atoms:

> Moreover, we must hold that the atoms in fact possess none of the properties belonging to things which come under our observation, except shape, weight and size.... [*Ibid.*, p. 583.]

In other words, the atoms that stream off this book that you are holding cause you to sense colors, smooth and rough feels, inky and papery smells, and so on; but the colors, feels, odors, sounds and tastes that you have are neither in the atoms nor in the book that the atoms compose. These sensory qualities are in your mind. What the book possesses are only the objective *quantities* (shape, weight, size), not the subjective *qualities* (color, odor, sound, feel, taste) according to both Democritus and Epicurus. The objective quantities are those mathematically measurable properties, such as rectangular shape, two pounds weight, and 8-1/2 by 5-1/2 inches by 1 inch in size, and these objective properties of the book are the properties of the gross atoms that compose the book.

The whole of being, then, consists of atoms and space. We know there is space because atoms and bodies or objects move, and motion would be impossible without space:

> And if there were no space (which we call void and place and intangible nature), bodies would have nothing in which to be and through which to move, as they are plainly seen to move. Beyond bodies and space there is nothing which by mental apprehension or on its analogy we can conceive to exist. [*Ibid.*, pp. 569-571.]

Moreover, while the atoms are infinite in number, dense, solid and finite in size, they are incapable of being split or divided.

Mind and Intelligence

In addition to the gross atoms composing physical bodies and giving them size, shape, and weight but not color, taste, smell, feel and sound, there are, Epicurus holds, many extremely refined atoms that compose the material soul. Notice that this material-atomic conception of the soul is quite contrary to the Socratic-Platonic idea of *psychē* as a non-material, spiritual entity. Epicurus states:

> ...we must recognize generally that the soul is a corporeal thing, composed of fine particles, dispersed all over the frame [body], most nearly resembling wind with an admixture of heat. [*Ibid.*, p. 593.]

In addition to this *psychē* with its fine atoms spread throughout the body, there is a third class of atoms, even more ethereal than the second group, that are capable of communicating between the finer soul atoms and the grosser body atoms. This is Epicurus' way of introducing the material mind and what we would call "nerves" into his metaphysical catalogue:

> But, again, there is the third part which exceeds the other two in the fineness of its particles and thereby keeps in closer touch with the rest of the frame. And this is shown by the mental faculties and feelings, by the ease with which the mind moves and by thoughts, and by all those things the loss of which causes death. [*Ibid.*, pp. 593-595.]

Armed with his hedonism, empiricism and materialism Epicurus now moves to dispel the three greatest fears known to Hellenistic men and women, fears relating to God, death and the world. Let's examine these anxieties and Epicurus' way of curing them within the historical context of the 4th century B.C. and within what we shall call "the problem of self-WORLD."

The Tragic Fall of the City-State

One of the noble and ancient goals of philosophy as we have seen was to provide a wise guide of life for men and women caught in the world's puzzles and perplexities. These wise guides or philosophies of

life are nowhere more clearly presented than during the Hellenistic period from the birth of Alexander the Great in 356 B.C. to the death of
Caesar the Great in 44 B.C., about 300 years. It was a time of rapid tech-
nological and social change dominated by the disintegration of the comforting security and warm, nurturing order provided by the ancient city-
states. Insuperable forces beyond the grasp and control of ordinary
citizens suddenly held those citizens in thrall. The small and defenseless
towns and cities of the Hellenic world were suddenly gobbled up by the
big and well-armed leagues and confederacies. Military might and political power, big armies, big business, and big governments left the individual citizen of the small city lost and afraid. What the Persian hoardes
had begun, what Athens, Sparta and Thebes had continued, Macedonia,
under King Philip and Alexander the Great, now copied, soon to be followed by the might and terror of the Roman Empire. It was the beginning of the modern world.

The history of this period is captured best in considering the rise and
fall of that unique political institution known as the city-state (*polis* in
Greek from which "politics" is derived). These free, resourceful, and independent units of pre-Hellenistic government were distinguished by
their different and separate constitutions, unique coinages, laws, linguis-
tic dialects, ways of life, social customs and religions. The city-state
provided a social system in which nearly everybody knew everybody
else, where food, shelter, clothing, and work were plentiful, where the
immortal gods were known, worshipped, and present throughout the
year, where life was on the whole beautiful, bountiful, and blessed. The
person who was a citizen, a person who belonged to a city, had it made.
Listen to the chorus from *Antigone* (played in Athens in 441 B.C., ten
years before the Peloponnesian War began) singing the praises of the
man or woman who is a citizen in those best of Hellenic times:

> Many the marvelous things; but none that can be
>> More of a marvel than man!
>
> He has taught himself speech, and wind-like thought, and the lore
>> Of ruling a town. He has fled the arrows of rain,
> The searching arrows of frost he need fear no more,
>> That under a starry sky are endured with pain.
> Provision for all he has made—unprovided for naught,
>> Save death itself, that in days to come will take shape.
> From obscure and deep-seated disease he has subtly wrought
>> A way of escape.

THE WAY OF PLEASURE

Resourceful and skilled, with an inconceivable art,
   He follows his course to a good or an evil end.
When he holds the canons of justice high in his heart
   And has sworn to the gods the laws of the land to defend,
Proud stands his city; without a city is he
   Who with ugliness, rashness, or evil dishonors the day.
Let me shun his thoughts. Let him share no hearthstone with me,
   Who acts in this way!

[Sophocles, *Three Theban Plays*, Translated by Theodore Howard Banks
(Oxford University Press, 1956), pp. 11-12.]

The last lines are the most revealing: Man without a city, without laws, is
a barbarian; but to belong to a community, to be citified, is to be civilized. The first act of the tragedy of the fall of the city-state began with a
barrage of bitter quarrels among the older mainland Greeks as well as
the newer overseas colonized Greeks. These antagonisms, disputes, and
fights reached a climax in 431 B.C. as the two chief rivals of the ancient
Greek world, viz., Athens with its empire and Sparta with its confederacy, engaged in a violent and exhausting war, the Peloponnesian War,
from 431 to 404 B.C. The uncivilized consequences of the war are reflected in yet another of Sophocles' great plays, perhaps his greatest, the
Oedipus of 430 B.C., composed one year after the war had begun. It is a
pessimistic and gloomy play in which the hero, Oedipus, at the end of
the play is driven from his city, doomed to wander, blind and citiless, for
the rest of his life. The chorus ends the play, prophetically chanting:

In vain
We say a man is happy, till he goes
Beyond life's final border, free from pain.
[*Ibid.*, p. 83.]

The final act of the tragedy of ancient Greece included the gradual
break-up of the city-state and its ultimate dissolution. Philip of Macedon
came to the throne of Macedon in the middle of the 4th century B.C. and
began a series of military incursions that spelled final disaster for the independence and sovereignty of the Greek city-state system. Demosthenes of Athens (384-322 B.C.) saw the catastrophe approaching for all
of Hellas and cried out in vain in speech after speech against the holocaust that would end Greek civilization, once and for all. Athens was
crushed by Philip at Chaeronea in 338 B.C., and when Philip died in 336
B.C., his son Alexander, called "the Great," took his place and continued
his program of military repression. Alexander conquered and temporarily united practically all of the Western world before dying in a drunken

brawl in 323 B.C. Demosthenes, the bitter foe of Alexander and his collaborators, fled from Athens and in an act that epitomizes the entire history of this late Hellenic period of the city-state matched its civicide with his own suicide to avoid capture.

With Demosthenes' death the history of the tragedy of the Hellenic world and the city-state ends. From its ashes a new period, the Hellenistic, will rise, a period noted for its fears and terrors and for the rise of new ways of philosophy to cope with that insecurity and anxiety. It is a time in which men and women begin in earnest a search for the meaning of life, a search carried on now amid the ruins of a once secure and flourishing civilization that would never rise again. It is against this background that Epicurus, Zeno the Stoic, the Cynics and the Skeptics can all be seen, viz., as philosophers reacting against the rising dehumanization and indifference of the Hellenistic age.

The Problem of self-WORLD

With the destruction of the city-state and with the comfort and security that it afforded its citizens now gone, the inhabitants of the new empire created by Alexander the Great and his generals, faced a monumental psychological problem. That problem was the feeling that one was no longer in control of one's own destiny, that a mighty force, alien and threatening, held all in its power and that the individual, once safe and sacrosanct in the city-state, no longer counted, no longer had any value.

This problem is not unfamiliar even today: A frightened man or woman in a terrifyingly alien world. Call this problem "the problem of self-WORLD" and consider this example: A senior graduates from high school and leaves home. He or she is ceremoniously but precipitously thrust from the maternal, secure environment of the home town, a modern city-state, into the indifferent and even hostile world beyond. The graduate's own Hellenistic period dawns; the comforting customs, the religious and social habits of a lifetime, familiar faces, loving embraces, and the warmth and security of the old and traditional patterns are swept away. The big city, the big university—the big WORLD—is suddenly there to take its place. The challenge of the unfamiliar and the hostility of the wholly-other produces a threat to the self. The familiar and controllable world is gone, the old Gods and the traditional ways have been overthrown. There is a new and terrible freedom that has taken their place. But with that freedom comes separation and isolation together with the thoughts that such terrible solitude can engender, thoughts about God, death, the alien world, and the very meaning of life, itself. Confronted with an impersonal and callously indifferent world over which he had no power, threatened by an environment that rendered impotent all attempts to ameliorate his condition, Hellenistic man, like modern man, will create new ways of philosophy in order to solve the problem of self-WORLD and thereby recover what the new age of indifference had taken away.

Epicurus and the Problem of self-WORLD

Epicurus found that the solution to the problem of self-WORLD involved the shrinking or contraction of the world with the subsequent avoidance of dependence on, and a consequent lessening of, threats from that world. The self is freed, ultimately, from the fear and anxiety that such a world previously held. The Epicureans believed that *death* was not to be feared; for death was merely the scattering and dispersal of the atoms that composed the body and the soul. There was, consequently, no threat of a life after death that could disconcert or upset a person. In his famous letter to his disciple Menoeceus, Epicurus offers two arguments that conclude that death is not to be feared:

> Accustom thyself to believe that death is nothing to us, for good and evil imply consciousness, and death is the privation of all consciousness; therefore a right understanding that death is nothing to us makes the mortality of life enjoyable not by adding to life an illimitable time, but by taking away the yearning after immortality. For life has no terrors for him who has thoroughly apprehended that there are no terrors for him in ceasing to live.

And he continues with a second argument:

> Foolish, therefore, is the man who says that he fears death not because it will pain when it comes, but because it pains in the prospect. Whatsoever causes no annoyance when it is present, causes only a groundless pain in the expectation.

Concluding with these memorable lines:

> Death, therefore, the most awful of evils, is nothing to us, seeing that, when we are, death is not come, and, when death is come, we are not. It is nothing, then, either to the living or to the dead, for with the living it is not and the dead exist no longer. [Diogenes Laertius, *Op. Cit.*, Vol. II, p. 651.]

Moreover, the *Gods* were not to be feared; for the Gods were simply unconcerned and independent congeries of atoms that could neither hurt you nor torment you. It had been believed that the Gods were celestial beings who took an active interest in human affairs from their high perches in the heavens. These Olympian deities terrified human beings with their anger and partiality, and they made their moods known through diseases, wars, earthquakes, and other natural catastrophes. And they supposedly commanded eclipses along with the risings and settings of sun, moon, stars, and planets. But, Epicurus argued, such troubling concerns with human beings would be totally out of keeping with the true and proper blissful and immortal nature of the Gods. [*Ibid.*, pp. 607-609.]

> A blessed and eternal being has no trouble himself and brings no trouble upon any other being; hence he is exempt from movements of anger and partiality, for every such movement implies weakness. [*Ibid.*, p. 603.]

Hence, the Gods are not to be feared.

Neither could *the world* hurt you; for, if you simply avoided it and its entanglements, stayed in your own private world, and cultivated those simple intellectual pleasures, such as friendship, that make life significant, enjoyable and worthwhile, what possible harm could come to you?

> Of all the means which are procured by wisdom to ensure happiness throughout the whole of life, by far the most important is the acquisition of friends. [*Ibid.*, p. 673.]

That is why the world is not to be feared. For one can shrink it to manageable size, to the size of a small garden, and live there with one's world under control and with "the absence of pain in the body, and of trouble in the soul." We turn next to the way of philosophy as seen by the enlightened hedonists such as Epicurus.

THE WAY OF ENLIGHTENED HEDONISM: EPICURUS

The Problem

The problem for all of the hedonists has always been "pain in the body and trouble in the soul." Both the popular hedonist and the enlightened hedonist seem to be agreed on the nature of the problem, although they differ radically on the ways of handling the problem and the goal to be aimed at in that handling.

The Cause

The cause of the suffering in body and soul is best described by the problem of self-WORLD. It is the confrontation of the soul with an alien, intractable world that causes physical pain and mental anxiety. In particular the problem of self-WORLD entails other causes of trouble, such as fear of the Gods, fear of death and the afterlife, and fear of the alien world around us now.

The Solution

The solution that Epicurus sought is *ataraxia*, peace of mind. It is this imperturbability of the soul that becomes the final goal of the enlightened hedonist.

The Way

The way to the ultimate goal of ataraxia lay in solving the problem of self-WORLD. This way was two-fold, really: Shrink the world to manageable size by not seeking notoriety or fame or success or wealth from the world and, in a sense, imitating the very Gods in their tranquility and aloofness; and, second, pursue the katastematic pleasures, i.e., the controllable and stable pleasures of simple food and drink, friendship and knowledge.

PROBLEMS WITH ENLIGHTENED HEDONISM

Following our three criteria of common sense, consistency and completeness, I think it is fair to say that enlightened hedonism proves adequate on all three counts. One reason for being able to say this is simply that enlightened hedonism in one form, utilitarianism, is enormously common, popular and necessary to practically all of the people in the world today as we shall demonstrate when we discuss utilitarianism, below. We have solved both of the serious problems of popular hedonism, viz., the problem of bad pleasures and the problem of choices, wherein enlightened hedonism said of the former "avoid them," and of the latter "choose the stable, intellectual pleasures." In doing so the Epicurean has satisfied not only the standard of common sense but of consistency and completeness, as well. But two new problems of completeness have now cropped up, viz., the problem of whose pleasure?, and the problem of how much pleasure? Let's look briefly at these two puzzles.

Popular ethical hedonism had defined a right action as any action that led to pleasure. That definition in turn led to further problems, as we have noted, not the least of which was the problem of bad pleasures and the problem of choices. But now, with those problems solved, new puzzles haunt us with the new definition of ethical hedonism. Thus enlightened ethical hedonism now defines a right action as any action that leads to *katastematic* pleasures, i.e., to stable, preferably intellectual, but also

simple, bodily pleasures. The key word here is "stable" for the new pleasures that are to decide rightness in an action are stable in the double
sense that we control them and they don't control us, and they don't lead
to future pains farther on.

But how much pleasure can make one action right and another
wrong? And whose pleasure is to be calculated in this new ethical position? Suppose that I am an enlightened hedonist and suppose that I have
a choice between spending an evening with my friend Epicurus eating
and talking about philosophy, or spending a quiet evening at home
reading his letter to Menoeceus. Suppose I can't do both. What is the
right thing to do? Both actions bring *katastematic* pleasures so presumably both actions are right. But enlightened ethical hedonism doesn't
help me decide which right action I should choose. Intuitively one wants
to say that my supping with Epicurus will bring pleasure to both of us,
so it is superior in some sense than reading alone which will bring
pleasure to me alone and may be selfish as a consequence. Thus
enlightened ethical hedonism appears to be incomplete for it fails to
solve the problem of whose pleasure? should be taken into account in
calculating pleasure; and it fails to solve the problem of how much
pleasure? is necessary to make one action right while at the same time
making another appropriate action, but with less pleasure, wrong.

It will remain for the way of philosophy of utilitarianism to solve
both of these problems. Utilitarianism will argue that it is the pleasure of
everyone concerned that must be calculated in determining the rightness
or wrongness of actions, thus the problem of whose pleasure? is answered; and utilitarianism will argue that it is the greatest amount of
pleasure generated by actions that will determine which one of two or
more pleasure producing actions is the right one, thus the problem of
how much pleasure? is answered. The utilitarian, in other words, will
argue that that action is right that leads to the greatest amount of pleasure for the greatest number of people. [See below Chapter 9, *The Way of
Utilitarianism*, especially "Utilitarianism for John Mill," pp. 180-182.] And
according to this principle, the utilitarian would probably argue that
supping with Epicurus would be the right action for me in the situation
described above.

Before turning to utilitarianism and the modern world, however, let's
look at three more of the most popular ways of philosophy of the ancient
world. All three were either antagonistic to, or suspicious of, the way of
pleasure as a proper answer to Aristotle's question regarding the best
and most worthwhile life.

EIGHT

THE WAYS OF LETTING–GO

⇶•⇷

THE LEGACY OF SOCRATES: CYNICS, STOICS AND SKEPTICS

The greatest Stoic of the ancient world was probably Epictetus, a Roman slave who, by his intelligence and unusual character, was to become one of the most famous and honored citizens of imperial Rome. But Stoicism began in Greece where its origins can be found, as happened with so many philosophers of the ancient world, in the life and philosophy of Socrates of Athens. We shall begin by looking at the Socratic roots of Stoicism in the way of philosophy called "Cynicism," then examine Stoicism, itself, as it developed in Greece, and conclude the chapter with the reaction against both in the movement called "Skepticism," also inspired by Socrates.

The problems that all three philosophies are attempting to overcome are the problems of *God*, Does God exist?, and What is His or Its nature?, of *immortality*, What will happen to me after I die?, and of the *world*, What horrors and sufferings await me in this world? Nowhere are all three of these ancient fears spoken of more eloquently and anxiously than in the following lines of Euripides' tragic drama *Medea* of 431 B.C. The lines spoken by a chorus of grief-stricken women from Corinth on the subject of children, suffering and fear:

> And I conclude that those among mortals
> Who are childless have the best fortune.
> For being childless and unaware
> Whether their loss is woe or joy,
> They live free from many a pain.
> But those who have within their homes
> The fragrant flower of tender youth

Are burdened all their days with care.

First to rear them properly,
And then to leave them means to live.
Never sure if all their toil
Is for good or worthless sons.
And then there comes a final fear—
They have found wealth to rear the young,
The bodies have grown to manhood, the mind
Noble—but if a god decrees,

Death comes. Down to the dark of Hades
He takes the bodies of your sons.
How then profits a man, having suffered
All else, to have this pain the more,
The sharpest pang given by the gods,
The bitterest grief imposed on men?

[Euripides, *Medea*, translated by Gilbert Murray (Oxford, 1901).]

It is these problems that those who share in the legacy of Socrates are attempting to solve and, in solving, to answer the question, What is the best and most worthwhile life that a human being can live?

Antisthenes of Athens (446-366 B.C.): The Father of Cynicism

Antisthenes was the son of an Athenian and a Thracian slave. Having studied with some Sophists, he established his own school in Athens sometime around 420 B.C. at the Kynosarges ("dog fish"), a gymnasium frequented by the poor and the working men of Athens, and it was from this place that the Cynic name was originally taken rather than from the charge that their critics made that the Cynics all behaved like dogs (*kynos*). But, it is said, he gave it all up, moving his pupils with him, when he heard Socrates speak.

Socrates' spiritual discipline, self-sufficiency and physical hardiness appealed strongly to the young Antisthenes and nowhere is that appeal more strongly depicted than in Plato's later recounting of Socrates' death in his dialogue *Phaedo* composed sometime shortly after 385 B.C. In *Phaedo* we have a perfect picture of the final moments not only of a great Stoic but a great Cynic, as well. It is difficult to believe that this is the same Socrates that the founder of Hedonism, Aristippus, had also listened to and attempted to emulate, or that this is the same Socrates that the founder of Skepticism, Pyrrho, had heard of and tried to imitate. And yet through the lives and philosophies of these men, whether

Hedonist, Cynic, Stoic, Skeptic, or Platonist, there runs a common inter-woven thread of nobility and dignity that binds them forever to Socrates: Socrates was, most assuredly, all things to all philosophers. Here is Plato's Stoic Socrates, having been tried and sentenced to death, waiting for the executioner in his death cell, surrounded by his friends, joyously discoursing about the nature of the true philosopher to the youthful Pythagorean, Simmias:

Socrates: Do you think that it is right for a philosopher to concern him-self with the so-called pleasures connected with food and drink?

Simmias: Certainly not, Socrates.

Socrates: What about sexual pleasures?

Simmias: No, not at all.

Socrates: And what about the other attentions that we pay to our bod-ies? Do you think that a philosopher attaches any importance to them? I mean things like providing himself with smart clothes and shoes and other bodily ornaments; do you think that he values them or despises them—insofar as there is no real necessity for him to go in for that sort of thing?

Simmias: I think the true philosopher despises them.

Socrates: Then it is your opinion in general that a man of this kind is not much concerned with the body, but keeps his attention directed as much as he can away from it and toward the soul. [Plato, *Phaedo* 64d-e, *The Collected Dialogues of Plato, Op. Cit.*, p. 47.]

And Simmias agrees. So also would Antisthenes have agreed, for he, unlike Plato, was there to hear it all.

Antisthenes once observed that Socrates taught him "to live with myself," and he used to say repeatedly, "I'd rather be mad than feel plea-sure." [Diogenes Laertius, *Lives, Op. Cit.*, Vol II, p. 5.] This motto together with the simple and Spartan style of life that he adopted pretty well encapsulates the way of philosophy of Cynicism as he lived it. He disposed of all of his possessions, keeping a ragged coat to cover his body in winter and summer. Socrates used to chide him for his ragged dress, saying once about his coat, "I can see your vanity, Antisthenes, peeping through the holes of your cloak." [*Ibid.*, p. 21.] He slept on the ground, neglected his body, clothing and appearance, and like many "hippies" of the 1970s, he despised the "squares" or bourgeois good men of society, respecting as the only virtue the self-control and ascetic inde-pendence of the life that he had found in Socrates and that he now taught to others. Where the hedonists like Aristippus had said, "I possess but am not possessed," Antisthenes said, "I do not possess in order not to be possessed."

Like the Stoics whom he was to influence so profoundly, Antisthenes held that self-sufficiency and control of desires were necessary to the best life. His way of philosophy can be easily expressed by a formula that might very well be Hindu or Buddhist in origin:

$$Happiness = \frac{Attainment\ of\ desire}{Desire}$$

The Cynics' solution to the problem of human suffering was to cultivate a general indifference to the world by keeping both desires and attain-ments low. If your desires are higher than your attainments, your happi-ness will be a fraction. But if your desires are lower than your attain-ments, your happiness will be a whole number and the indifference that you seek will have been accomplished. The Cynics may even have thought, like many Hindus and Buddhists of the same period, that the control of desire, while laudable in itself, is not enough to secure true lib-eration and happiness. Only when desire has been completely stamped out, reduced to zero, as it were, is the goal of infinite happiness achieved. Antisthenes' aim in life was to have no desires at all.

Antisthenes died of consumption in 366, his body wracked with ex-cruciating pains up to the very end. Hearing of his suffering, his most famous pupil, Diogenes of Sinope, once brought him a knife. When Antisthenes cried out, "Who will release me from these pains?," Diogenes showed him the dagger and said, "This!" Whereupon, Antisthenes responded cynically, "I said from my pains, not from my life." [*Ibid.*, p. 21.]

The Problem of self-WORLD: The Cynics

The problem of self-WORLD that we touched on previously in our discussion of the Epicureans would be solved quite uniquely by the Cynics. The Epicureans had handled the problem of the misery and suf-fering produced when the self is overwhelmed by a world over which it had little or no control by shrinking the WORLD, living in the Garden, indifferent to, and apart from, all external threats. The Cynics, on the other hand, sought to become indifferent to both the WORLD and the self, by explicitly following the above Formula for Happiness and reducing all desires to zero. This indifference to both self and WORLD is nicely illustrated in the life of Antisthenes' greatest pupil, Diogenes of Sinope (404-323 B.C.).

The Cynic Way of Letting-Go: Diogenes of Sinope on Naturalness, Brotherhood and Love

Diogenes came from a wealthy upper class family of Sinope and his philosophic life story can be easily summarized: He came to Athens and discovered Antisthenes. The latter did not welcome pupils, but by sheer, undaunted persistence and good humor Diogenes wore down his future master until he was accepted. Once, when Antisthenes raised his staff to drive off the would-be disciple, Diogenes offered his head saying:

> Strike, for you will find no wood hard enough to keep me away from you, so long as I think you've something to say. [*Ibid.*, p. 25.]

After that Diogenes was accepted as his pupil. His tutelage under Antisthenes led him to adopt the simple, natural life for which he was to become famous, a life that ultimately was to influence the Stoic philosophy of Zeno, from whom that philosophy spread from Greece to Rome, and from Rome into Christianity and the world.

Diogenes gave up wealth, family, position and his upper class traditions to set out to preach the way of the simple life and the brotherhood of man. He walked barefoot in the snow, lived on plain food and water, carried out his natural functions and love-making in public (hence *kynikos*, the Greek word for "doglike"):

> When Plato styled him a dog, "Quite true," he said, "for I come back again and again to those who have sold me." [*Ibid.*, Vol. II, p. 41.]

Once, when at a banquet some people kept throwing bones to him as they would to a dog, he promptly stood up and urinated on them. So much for Diogenes' cynicism.

On a journey to Aegina he was captured by pirates and later auctioned off as a slave in Crete. When asked what he was good for he replied, "For ruling men." He pointed to a potential buyer and said, "Sell me to this man; he needs a master." And so he was sold, taken to Corinth, and set to tutor the man's children and manage his household.

One time seeing a child drinking water out of his hands, he threw away his cup observing, "A child has beaten me in the plainness of living." Always his aim was to simplify life, reduce his wants, needs and desires and become indifferent to both the self and the world. He lived in a huge cask or jar which he could roll about the city, was loved by the Greeks and all who knew him, and had an international reputation that one time brought the admiring Alexander the Great to Corinth to visit him. "I am Alexander the great king," he said. "And I am Diogenes the Cynic," Diogenes responded. "Why are you called a hound (cynic)?" the universal monarch asked. "Because," was the reply, "I fawn on those who give me anything, I yelp at those who refuse, and I set my teeth in rascals." [*Ibid.*, p. 63.] Upon being asked if there was anything he needed, the old sage replied from the mouth of his jar, "Yes, stand out of my sun light." This prompted Alexander to say, "If I could not be Alexander, I would choose to be Diogenes." The latter did not reply to Alexander with the same courtesy.

He died at Corinth at the age of ninety, some say by "holding his breath," (strangulation). It was at Corinth that he had attracted a close circle of friends and it was there where the world came to visit him.

Diogenes envisioned a world-wide commonwealth, a true community of men, [For more on the concept of community see below Chapter 13, *The Ways of Individualism and Community*, pp. 292-295.] holding everything in common, including property, wives and children. He thought of himself as a true cosmopolite, a citizen of the world [*Ibid.*, p. 65], and under his cosmopolitan ideal was born the ideal of universal brotherhood together with a unique argument: Everything, he maintained, belongs to the Gods [*Ibid.*, p. 73]; hence all men, as the property of the Gods, must share a common nature that makes them brothers. It was this ideal which he preached as he traveled the dusty roads of Attica that made Diogenes the true precursor of Stoicism.

Problems with Diogenes' Cynicism

But the Cynics have not been without their critics:

> To live like a beast, to be indifferent to art, beauty, letters, science, philosophy, to the amenities of civic life, to all that raised Hellenic Man above the beast or savage? How could this be the true end of man? [Gilbert Murray, *Five States of Greek Religion* (Doubleday Anchor Books, 1955/1925), p. 92.]

It will remain for the Stoic philosophers, Zeno in particular, to re-establish the moral life and faith in the "purpose of things" in a form far more acceptable to common sense and the common man. For it was Stoicism that came to dominate the Hellenistic period with an emotional and intellectual power that prompts admiration even to this day.

Zeno of Citium (336-264 B.C.): The Father of Stoicism

Zeno was a Phoenician, a native of Citium in Cyprus who, following a shipwreck off the Piraeus in which he lost all of his goods, came up to Athens at the age of 22. In a bookshop he picked up Xenophon's *Memorabilia*, an account of Socrates' life. He was so impressed that he asked the shop owner, "Where are such men to be found?" As Crates the Cynic happened then to be passing, the shop man replied, "Follow that man." Zeno did and became Crates' pupil. Crates (ca. 325 B.C.), himself, had been a pupil of Diogenes and hence passed on to Zeno the essentials of Cynic philosophy which Zeno, in turn, incorporated into the school of philosophy which came to be called "Stoicism." [The order of succession runs like this: Antisthenes (ca. 400) Æ Diogenes (ca. 350) Æ Crates (ca. 325) Æ Zeno (ca. 300).]

In about 300 B.C. Zeno founded his own school, lecturing while pacing back and forth at the Stoa or Columned Porch in the agora or market place in Athens. Those who came to hear him teach were called "stoics"; and, as with the Cynics, above, the Stoics were named for the place in which they met and in which their master lectured. True to his Cynic inheritance, Zeno ate his food raw, drank plain water with his simple meals, wore a thin cloak throughout the year wholly indifferent to heat, rain, cold and illness. Zeno was loved and honored by the Athenians for his commitment to virtue as the only good, for his attentions to the youth of Athens, and for the consistency between his beliefs and his way of life.

Nature and Natural Law

Zeno taught self-sufficiency and argued that the end of life was to live naturally, i.e., in accordance with nature, two doctrines inherited from his Cynic teacher. He believed that there was a law in nature, a law common to all things, i.e., a natural law, which, if it were followed, would lead to virtue and happiness. The end of life, in other words, lies in living in harmony with the natural, a doctrine that was to influence early Christianity and which survives even today in the condemnation of artificial means of birth control as unnatural and therefore contrary to God's law.*

---

* In the Middle Ages Divine Law, i.e., God's Law, was seen as reflected in Natural Law. The latter, in turn, was subsequently reflected in Human Law and such documents as the Declaration of Independence of the United States with its talk about "self evident truths." All of this, in turn, was a reflection of the ancient controversy between *physis* and *nomos* which, in turn, set the stage for the metaphysical and legal

The Stoics aimed to refrain from every act that was forbidden by natural law. Zeno was the first philosopher to use the word "duty" and to mean by it that which is incumbent on all to perform, a fittingness of behavior in accordance with the nature of things, i.e., with natural law. Actions done on impulse were condemned in favor of actions which were seen to be one's duty and which one ought to perform, therefore. Such dutiful actions were recognized as right by the *Logos*, the indwelling spirit of reason, akin to Socrates' *daimōn*. Actions such as honoring one's parents, country, and friends were fitting and virtuous because they were natural and in accord with reason. Impulsive actions were *alogos*, or irrational, and inevitably involved desire, i.e., irrational appetite, or pleasure, i.e., irrational elation. Both grief and pain were irrational mental reactions and, as such, condemned by Zeno in true Stoic fashion.

Corporeal-Pyro-Pantheism

Zeno believed that corporeal nature is alive with the spirit of God. Moreover, influenced by the philosopher Heraclitus, he believed that the world is like a consuming and changing fire (*pyros*) which he identified with God. This fiery God that fills nature (pantheism) is variously called "Reason" (*logos*), "Fate" (*heimarmenen*) and "Zeus," by Zeno. The consequence of this corporeal-pyro-pantheism is that the world (*kosmos*) is pervaded by Reason just as the human body is pervaded by the Soul. Hence the world like the body is a living organism guided by God or Providence, fated to go the way that it is going, and fated to go the best way possible since God is wholly good. God is the Maker of the universe, the Father of all, Who takes care of the world and Who is living, immortal, rational and happy. God has many names and attributes but He is one God alone. Finally, since the world has a beginning, Zeno argued, it will have an end. A mighty conflagration will consume it all. But following the fiery end of the world, the creation will start again in an endless round of creations, preservations, and destructions that will continue for all time.

Fate and Happiness

All things happen according to the will of Providence or Fate, an endless chain of causes by which things happen as they must. It is the *Logos* or reason unfolding itself, like a motion picture film, according to its

---

battles of the 20th century regarding what constitutes the "natural" and the "unnatural."

own inevitable inner nature. The wise man recognizes this inevitability and lives his life by accepting all that happens because it must happen the way that it does; he is indifferent to good and evil, free from excesses, and totally without passion (*apathē*) or desire. As a result, these wise ones are in actuality the only happy ones, for they have discovered that true happiness lies in the tranquil resignation to the will of Providence.

These sages or wise ones (*sophon*) serve God, recognizing that which is divine in themselves and following that divinity. These wise ones hurt no one, and they are fit to be judges of others, fixing appropriate penalties to crimes, wholly without favoritism, emotion, or pity. These wise ones take part in politics where their aim is to restrain vice and promote virtue. This commitment to the political life will have important repercussions when Stoicism reaches Rome and serves as a guide for emperors, aristocrats, and slaves for several hundred glorious years. They live in society making friends among their equals and not in solitude as their rivals, the Epicureans, unfortunately chose to do. They are Plato's philosophers who have at last become kings, the true aristocrats of society, who have a right to all things because they do all things well and thereby deserve all things, a view not lost on Frederich Nietzsche in the 19th century, as we shall see below.

These wise ones, these superior sages who have chosen a life of reason as opposed to passion, may also voluntarily exit this life either when life becomes intolerable or when moral duty enjoins suicide rather than dishonor. Thus the Stoic who suffers unbearable pain, mutilation, or incurable disease, or to protect his country or his friends, is permitted to commit suicide. Zeno, himself, apparently died in this fashion. As he was leaving his school, he fell, perhaps from a stroke, striking the ground. Crying out to the earth, "I come, I come, why do you call me," [Diogenes Laertius, *Lives, Op. Cit.*, Vol. II, p. 141] and holding his breath, he died.

Problems with Zeno's Stoicism: Fate and Evil

There are two problems which Zeno's Stoic doctrines raise that must be mentioned before we turn to the great Roman Stoic, Epictetus. The first is *the problem of fatalism* which is simply this: If everything is fated to happen as it must then there is no free will and no real choices are open to moral agents; but then there is no responsibility for actions, and, as a consequence, guilt and innocence, blame and praise, make no sense at all. But then how can punishment take place if no one is responsible for what they do since they don't really *do* anything, for events happen *to* them and not *because* of them. What sense does it make, then, to be a judge?, to get involved in politics?, or to try to restrain vice and promote virtue? Fatalism makes a mockery of the moral life and thereby violates our criteria of common sense as well as consistency since it urges us to be moral when we logically have no choice one way or the other; and Stoic fatalism violates our criterion of completeness, since it cannot solve the problem of fatalism. Thus Stoicism fails, it must seem, all three of our criteria for an adequate way of philosophy.

But Zeno has an answer of sorts to the problem of fatalism:

> We are told that he was once chastising a slave for stealing, and when the latter pleaded that it was his fate to steal, "Yes, and to be beaten too." [*Ibid.*, Vol. II, p. 135.]

Thus there is fatalism all around, for judges as well as criminals; so accept your fate and do your duty.

However, the criticism remains that the moral life as ordinarily understood is based on the freedom of the human will to be able to do differently than one did or than one is going to do. Without such freedom the moral life is meaningless.

The second problem is *the problem of evil* which is simply this: If God is all good, all knowing, and all powerful, then why is there evil or suffering in the world. If God because He's all-knowing knew about the six million human beings who were dying in Nazi death camps in Europe from 1942-1945, then He would have wanted to stop the horror because He's all good, and He could have stopped the horror because He's all powerful. But then why did all those people die, and die so hideously, if Providence makes everything happen for the best in this best of all rational, Divine Fire-pervaded, *Logos*-organized worlds? The problem of evil makes a mockery of Zeno's beliefs about the goodness and power of Providence, just as the problem of fatalism makes a mockery of Zeno's beliefs about the possibility of a moral life under Stoicism.

Could fatalism mitigate the problem of evil in some sense and provide us with a solution to the latter puzzle? Perhaps God can't change the way the world suffers because everything is fated. But then God is not all powerful, i.e., God is limited by what has been fated and He can't change it; hence, God is limited by either what he has fated, if He is the cause of events, or He is a tool of impersonal Fate and as much a victim as the rest of us. Once again, Stoicism appears to have failed in meeting the criteria of adequacy of common sense, consistency and completeness.

These problems of fate and free will are problems with which later Stoics will have to deal. One of the foremost Stoics who met these puzzles head-on was the Roman slave turned emancipated Stoic, Epictetus, and we turn to him next.

Epictetus (50-138 A.D.): The Triumph of Roman Stoicism

Epictetus was born a slave in Phrygia in about 50 A.D. Passed from master to master, he had little opportunity for education until he became the property of Epaphroditus, a powerful member of the Emperor Nero's court in Rome. Sickly and crippled because of previous ill-treatment, Epictetus quickly acquired an education when his new and liberal master sent him to study under the most renowned Stoic teacher in Rome, C. Musonius Rufus. After the death of Nero in 68 A.D. Epictetus was freed by his master. He thereupon set himself up as a teacher in Rome. Forced to flee when the Emperor Domitian banished all philosophers in 89 A.D., Epictetus went to Nicopolis in Epirus, not far from Rome, where he proceeded to live as the Cynics before him with but few possessions, a rush mat on which to sleep, the clothes on his back, and an earthenware lamp for light. He became noted for his sincerity, sweetness, gentleness, humility, and charity, a loving attitude toward children, and a personality filled with moral and religious fervor. Ahead of his time and beyond anything Rome ever aspired to, Epictetus denounced slavery, condemned capital punishment, and advocated the treatment rather than the punishment of criminals. He advanced a Stoic golden rule as a guide for behavior, "What you wouldn't want to suffer, don't make others suffer." He urged his followers to return good for evil, to give in and submit to the world's evils, to fast on occasion, and to give up desire for worldly things; it is not without reason that later Christians, like St. John Chrysostum and St. Augustine, loved him well.

He taught patience under suffering and his motto became *"anechou kai apechou"* ("bear and forbear"). The world of Roman intellectuals beat a pathway to his door in Nicopolis where young and old gathered about him. One young Roman Stoic, Flavius Arrian of Nicomedia, recorded Epictetus' lectures and published them in four volumes as the *Diatribai*, or *Discourses*. Epictetus died sometime around 138 A.D.

The Problem of self-WORLD: The Stoics

In the *Discourses* Epictetus urges everyone to the study of philosophy and praises reason as the cure for the problems of the human race. The aim of philosophy is the practice of the good and the inculcation of the virtues. The rational powers of reason within man are parts of World Reason, the *Logos*, a view traceable to Zeno, as we have seen above. The first man was created by God Who is the Father of all, and in virtue of this Fatherhood all men are brothers. In addition, to this theme of the Fatherhood of God and the Brotherhood of man, Epictetus holds that we carry about within us a part, a spark of God:

> But you are a principal work, a fragment of God Himself, you have in your-
> self a part of him.... You bear God about with you, poor wretch, and know it
> not. [Epictetus, *Discourses* II. VIII in *The Stoic and Epicurean Philosophers*,
> Edited by Whitney J. Oates (New York: The Modern Library, 1957), p. 295.]

It is this good news that enables Epictetus to solve the problem of self-WORLD. Now in place of shrinking the WORLD, as the Epicureans had done, or of shrinking both the self and the WORLD through indifference, as the Cynics had done, Epictetus has found something greater, grander, and more than a match for the threatening, anxiety-producing WORLD, viz., a divine Self, a God living within each of us; in other words, a SELF. It is now this good news that Epictetus bids his disciples carry to the world. Here he is, again, sounding very much like a modern evangelist in his enthusiasm for his discovery and its proclamation, "Onward Stoic Soldier":

> God says, "Come and bear witness for me..." Think what it is to be able to
> say, "God has sent me into the world to be his soldier and witness, to tell
> men that their sorrows and fears are vain, that to a good man no evil can
> befall, whether he live or die. God sends me at one time here, at another
> time there; he disciplines me by poverty and imprisonment, that I may be
> better witness to him among men. With such a ministry committed to me,
> can I any longer care in what place I am, or who my companions are, or
> what they say about me? Nay, rather, does not my whole nature strain after
> God, his laws and commandments?" [Epictetus, *Discourses* in *Works*, Two
> Volumes (London: Loeb Library, 1926), I. 29; III, 24; II, 6. See also *The Stoics*,
> Edited by John M. Rist (University of California Press, 1978), especially G. B.
> Kerferd, "What Does the Wise Man Know?" and John M. Rist, "The Stoic
> Concept of Detachment."]

The Problem of Evil

With this passage from the *Discourses*, Epictetus also manages to provide his and Stoicism's future solution to the problem of evil. He claims that evil or suffering is sent by an all-powerful, all-good, and all-knowing God in order to strengthen our characters through the discipline that suffering affords. He states that it is evil, i.e., privations and sufferings, that show what men are truly like and that helps us to develop the "right stuff." Whenever suffering confronts us, we should remember that God, like a trainer of wrestlers, has matched us with a "rough young man," to test us, to temper us and to perfect us; He never sends us more evil than we can properly bear. It is a solution that later Christians, particularly St. Aurelius Augustine, will take up and promote, as well. [See Arthur L. Herman, *The Problem of Evil and Indian Thought* (Delhi: Motilal Banarsidass, 1990/1976), pp. 11-36.]

The Problem of Fatalism

Epictetus' most enduringly successful work, however, was not the four volumes of the *Discourses*, but a brief handbook of some 20 pages called *Enchiridion* or *Manual*. It is a summary of Stoic philosophy as well as an extremely simple introduction to the practical techniques involved in turning Stoic philosophy into a philosophy by which to live. This work was also compiled by Flavius Arrian sometime after 138 A.D. The *Enchiridion* is probably one of the most popular philosophic work ever written, read, and admired by Romans and Stoics, such as the Emperor Marcus Aurelius, the statesman Cicero, and the essayist and biographer Plutarch. It was later adopted as a guide for the monastic life by the Christians. The *Enchiridion* has continued to appeal to such diverse modern intellectuals as Michael de Montaigne, Blaise Pascal, and Frederick the Great who carried the book into battle, as well as to English philosophers like Francis Hutcheson and Adam Smith. The work is simply a compendium of wise insights on how to live the best and most worthwhile life possible.

The *Enchiridion* opens by making an important distinction:

> There are things which are within our power, and there are things which are beyond our power. Within our power are opinion, aim, desire, aversion, and, in one word, whatever affairs are our own. Beyond our power are body, property, reputation, office, and, in one word, whatever are not properly our own affairs. [Epictetus, *The Enchiridion* (Indianapolis, Indiana: The Bobbs-Merrill Company, Inc., 1955), p. 17.]

The advice that follows is good, sound, practical advice, viz., focus your powers only on those matters over which you have control; for the rest, i.e., for those things over which you have no control, those things in the power of Fate or of others, don't waste your time worrying about them, pursuing them or desiring them. In this one paragraph, Epictetus in a sense solves the problem of fatalism by indicating the area of freedom over which Fate has no control, viz., the human will, and the area where it does hold sway, viz., the world outside the will. The "solution" is purchased at a high price, however, for the power of Fate has been considerably tempered. In one famous statement Epicurus makes this tempering quite clear: "Fate leads the willing and drags the unwilling." Hence, one can choose to do differently than one did or will do for while there is freedom in the choosing there is no freedom in the doing.

Which brings Epictetus to the central theme of his Stoic philosophy: the power of the will to control desire. Since "men are disturbed not by things, but by the views they take of things" [*Ibid.*, p. 19], and since we can control the views we take of things, it follows by reason that we can be free of all disturbances by learning to control our views of the world. In particular, it means that we can be liberated from the disappointments of unfulfilled desires that inevitably follow most of our desires. One must learn, therefore, discretion, moderation, and control, and in return nothing need ever bother you again. So whatever comes take it in an unattached way, Epictetus counsels, and the world will become more bearable:

> Demand not that events should happen as you wish; but wish them to happen as they do happen, and you will go on well. [*Ibid.*, p. 20.]

Again, the point is that the way the world goes is not under your control and never can be, so don't desire the impossible. And don't be disappointed at what life passes on to you:

> Remember that you must behave as at a banquet. Is anything brought round to you? Put out your hand and take a moderate share. Does it pass by you? Do not stop it. Is it not yet come? Do not yearn in desire toward it, but wait till it reaches you. [*Ibid.*, p. 22.]

Your life must be played as if it were a role in a stage play: *How* you play it is up to you but *that* you play it, i.e., the part that you have to play, is out of your hands. That you were born when you were in the city that you were, into the family that you were, with parents of the kind that you have, that you are as tall and with the kind of hair, the foot size and nose length that you have, are all out of your control; they are all "fated" and you can't change them. So what's the point of desiring them to be different, to wish that you had been born rich, or beautiful, or an orphan, or in Spain, or whatever. It's not the role you have been given: "It's not God's will," is another way of saying the same thing. In one of the most famous similes in all philosophic literature, Epictetus likens us to actors on a stage:

> Remember that you are an actor in a drama of such sort as the Author chooses—if short, then in a short one; if long, then in a long one. If it be his pleasure that you should enact a poor man, or a cripple, or a ruler, or a

private citizen, see that you act it well. For this is your business [i.e., this alone is in your power] to act well the given part, but to choose it belongs to another. [*Ibid.*, pp. 22-23.]

For the rest, the *Enchiridion* contains homiletic advice on how to behave in the world if you would be contented. We conclude our discussion with some of that practical but often ascetic advice:

Be mostly silent, or speak merely what is needful, and in few words.

Let not your laughter be loud, frequent, or abundant.

Avoid taking oaths, if possible, altogether.

Avoid public and vulgar entertainments.

Provide things relating to the body no further than absolute need requires...but cut off everything that looks toward show and luxury.

Before your marriage guard yourself with all your ability from unlawful intercourse with women.

If anyone tells you that a certain person speaks ill of you, do not make excuses about what is said of you, but answer: "He was ignorant of my other faults, else he would not have mentioned these alone." [*Ibid.*, pp. 31-32.]

Through it all, of course, the ultimate aim is the production of an ideal human being, viz., the Stoic sage:

...he blames none, praises none, complains of none, accuses none, never speaks of himself as if he were somebody, or as if he knew anything. And if any one compliments him he laughs in himself at his compliment; and if anyone blames him, he makes no defense.

He is humility and modesty personified, a person in complete control of himself:

He has got rid of the will to get, and his will to avoid is directed no longer to what is beyond our power but only to what is in our power.... In all things he exercises his will without strain. If men regard him as foolish or ignorant he pays no heed. In one word, he keeps watch and guard on himself as his own enemy, lying in wait for him. [*Ibid.*, p. 37.]

Only the sage is capable of morally right actions, for the praise and blame for actions can only attach to what is freely willed or intended. The consequences of the action depend on others, i.e., the results of what the sage does is out of his control and can, therefore, never be the criterion for judging the rightness or wrongness of moral actions. Stoic ethics, therefore, is an ethics of subjective *intentions* and not an ethics of objective *consequences*. [For an ethics of consequences see below Chapter 9, *The Way of Utilitarianism*, especially pp. 180-182.]

Solutions to the Problems of God, Death and the World

Epictetus also managed through his *Discourses* and the *Enchiridion* to speak to those three most nagging fears of men and women living in the ancient world: First, God is not to be feared for He is a divine force, a true Providence, that guides all of us if we would only let His will be done; moreover, God is in each of us as the *Logos*, the divine Reason, just as Zeno had argued in early Stoicism. Second, death is not to be feared for death, as Zeno had stated, is a co-mingling of Fires, your *Logos* with the world *Logos*, your Spirit with God's; moreover, when pain becomes intolerable, Epictetus counsels in agreement with Zeno, that one may step out of life by one's own hand. Third and finally, the WORLD is not to be feared, as we have seen, for the divine Self within you is more than a match for that WORLD; moreover, a wise and good Providence governs that WORLD and He would not let anything really terrible happen to you. What appears terrible or evil is ultimately good for you, so don't be afraid!

Stoicism's Accomplishments

The Stoics have left a long list of accomplishments in both the law and logic. Under Cicero (106-43 B.C.) Stoicism had a great influence on Roman law, and earlier under Zeno, building on foundations laid by Aristotle, the study of logic made equally great strides. But it is to their accomplishments in *agōgē*, ways of philosophy, that we shall be turning. The Stoics have reminded us of several very basic human truths that continue to have application in the 1990s.

In stating that "men are not disturbed by things but only by the views which they take of things," the Stoics underscored something which we tend to forget: The world is what we make it; the environment that we live in has to a very large extent been created by our individual thoughts, attitudes, and beliefs. If we want to change the world, then we ought to change ourselves first.

In arguing that the things that we get attached to can complicate our lives, the Stoics pointed to and reminded us of a second simple truth about life: Our desires can control us, dominate us and eventually destroy us. The happiest life might well be a life filled with many things, many possessions, for, after all, the Stoics were not Cynics. But where the Cynics believed that by reducing one's possessions one's happiness could be increased, the Stoics wisely saw that even reducing one's possessions can be an obsession. What really matters as far as our happiness is concerned is the control of the mind in relation to those possessions. It's not how much you possess that counts but how much you are possessed.

In their doctrine of limited fatalism the Stoics taught and left as a legacy for all to ponder that what Fate, God, or Providence sends to us is usually bearable. Ask, they said, that events happen as they do happen and not as we wish them to happen. Yielding to Fate, accepting our destiny, bending to the will of God, all these come in the end to the same thing: Saying "Thy will be done" can shape and build the character of the virtuous and happy human being.

We turn next to the way of philosophy as seen by Zeno and Epictetus.

The Stoic Way of Letting Go: Zeno and Epictetus

The Problem

The problems for the Hellenistic Stoics like Zeno and the Roman Stoics like Epictetus were practical problems relating to the fears, really anxieties, that people have about God, death, and the world, and the suffering that those fears engendered.

The Causes

The causes of the mental anguish regarding God, death, and the world were twofold, viz., ignorance of both the divine nature of the Self and the providential nature of God; and second, uncontrolled desires, or what amounts to a lack of self-control.

The Solution

The solution that Epictetus sought was *apatheia*, peace of mind, a condition that results when one has let go of the problems that cause mental anguish and has become the Stoic sage, the ideal human being.

The Ways

The ways to the solution of *apatheia* entail abolishing the causes of suffering, viz., ignorance and desire, by discovering that God is a Divine Force, or *Logos*, within us that wisely governs the world; that death is a mingling of divine Soul fires, ours with God's; and that no fearful punishments follow this life; further, that one must learn to accept one's destiny with a philosophic *amor fati*, love of fate, a total acceptance of all that happens to us. In a letter from about 55 A.D. St. Paul expressed this most Stoic sentiment relating to the best and most worthwhile life that a human being can live:[*]

> Only, let every one lead the life which the Lord has assigned to him, and in which God has called him. This is my rule in all the churches.... Everyone should remain in the state in which he was called. Were you a slave when called? Never mind.... So, brethren, in whatever state each was called, there let him remain with God. [I *Corinthians* 7. 17, 20, 24. Revised Standard Version.]

Problems With Stoicism

Following our three criteria for an adequate way of philosophy, viz., common sense, consistency, and completeness, Stoicism seems to have trouble with all three.

First, there is the problem of fatalism. The critic of Stoicism is eager to point out that a consistently followed belief in *complete fatalism* would lead to total passivity on the part of the believer and would surely violate common sense: No one could seriously believe in complete fatalism, and by our actions and efforts we prove every moment that such a belief is wrong or foolish. After all, if everything that happens to me is going to happen anyway, then why should I try to do anything? And, the critic concludes, no one is totally passive, not even the Stoics themselves who were in the front lines of Roman imperial politics for generations.

But the Stoic might eagerly point out that the total passivity of the believer is also part of what has been fated. So where's the critic's objection then? Furthermore, the Stoic might reply, the critic is missing entirely the salutary effects of the belief in complete fatalism. For consider: Suppose that your dog is killed by a car. Now, won't you be better off by not rushing around blaming people for letting Rusty loose and without supervision, or trying to attack the driver who hit Rusty, or feeling guilty for not paying more attention to where Rusty was at the time he was run down? Isn't it better to simply say, "It was to be, nobody could have done anything," or "There's a car out there with Rusty's name on it and when your number is up, it's up," or "It's God's will," and let it go at that? Everyone does this from time to time and it helps enormously to assuage guilt and grief in such moments.

---

[*] St. Paul was undoubtedly influenced by the Roman Stoic, Lucius Annaeus Seneca (4 B.C.-65 A.D.). See Seneca's *On a Happy Life, On Tranquility, On the Shortness of Life,* and *On Providence,* essays that present him at his Stoic best. Moses Hadas has written of Seneca's 124 extant letters, "Few Roman writings transport readers to the Roman scene so effectively." *The Stoic Philosophy of Seneca* (Doubleday, 1958), p. 13.

But, the critic might respond, it is really *limited fatalism* that is being defended here, and not *complete* fatalism. That this is the case is proved by the fact that the next time I have a dog I check his leash, his whereabouts at crucial times of the day, the fence and gate in my yard, and so on. I don't turn him loose saying, "What will be will be, let him wander as he wills." Our behavior always contradicts a belief in *complete fatalism*. The critics argument looks like this:

1. If Stoic complete fatalism were true then all Stoics would be passive and inactive.

2. But Stoics were not passive and inactive.

3. Therefore, Stoic complete fatalism is false.

The Stoic is quick to respond that while the Greek Stoicism of Zeno may have been a complete fatalism, this is not the case with the Roman Stoicism of Epictetus. As the latter pointed out, the will is free to make choices. "Fate leads the willing and drags the unwilling," Epictetus says, and therein lies the difference: You can choose to accept or reject what will inevitably happen, but you can choose. And in that choosing lies the active life of the Stoic, not the passive quietism that the critic points to. [See William Chase Greene, *Moira, Fate, Good, and Evil in Greek Thought* (Harvard University Press, 1944), pp. 337-365.]

Second, there is the problem of intentional ethics, a problem that follows from both the Stoic view of ethics and the limited fatalism of Epictetus. To begin, let's assume that by an "action" we mean an activity consisting of three parts: An *intention* or motive or desire of an agent for some future state of affairs; an *act* or happening following from that intention; and, finally, the *consequences* or results of the act. An action can be called "right" or "wrong" by looking at any one of these three parts of the action and judging any one of the three as "good," "right," or "best." The Stoic wants to argue that the rightness of an action depends solely on the *intention* of the agent. If my intention is virtuous or right or good, then my action is going to be right.

But, the critic is quick to point out, not only is the road to Hell paved with good intentions but an intentional ethics of the sort that the Stoics propose is the quickest way of driving down that road. For one may intend with one's freely willed acts to do all kinds of good things under Stoic limited fatalism but through ignorance or laziness or some other vice one may be totally unaware that one's well-intentioned act could lead to suffering for many. The worst tyrant in the history of the world may have had the best intentions in the world. Alexander the Great, Napoleon, even Hitler, may have intended to bring about the best of all possible worlds through their violent military acts. But we judge them not on their intentions but on the consequences of their acts. And the world has consistently condemned the actions of all three solely on the basis of the consequences that their acts produced. Stoic *intentional ethics* comes up hard against a more common sense *consequence ethics*, and in doing so appears to violate the common sense of that latter ethics: We judge people by what they do, not by what they say they want to do: The proof is in the pudding, and The road to Hell is paved with good intentions, are both wise clichés.

The Stoic defender of intentional ethics responds that the ethics that is being attacked here is not really Stoic ethics at all. After all, the only person who is really capable of morally right intentions and therefore of morally right actions is the person who has gotten his desires under control, who is free of the ignorance of who he is, and who has achieved *apatheia*, i.e., who is detached and free of mental disturbances and the disease of basic human impulses. The Stoic sage, the ideal man or woman of Stoicism, has removed all such diseased impulses, and is guided entirely by Reason, by the *Logos*, or by God. The Stoic sage has emotions but they do not control or dominate his life.

But, the critic is quick to respond, if this implies that only the sage can perform right actions, then two unacceptable conclusions would seem to follow: First, the ordinary person who is not a sage can never do what is right; and, second, the sage who is not an ordinary person can never do what is wrong. Both conclusions must seem, once again, to violate common sense.

The Stoic would probably then say, "So much the worse for common sense." Only those who are really under control, who know what they are doing and why, can be really virtuous and do what is right. Right actions, contrary to common sense, can never be the result of accident, chance, ignorance or desire. And maybe there is some sense to what the Stoic is saying. Stoic ethics stands in strong opposition to the more conventional ethics of both Epicurus and utilitarians, such as Jeremy Bentham and John Stuart Mill. As a result, Stoic ethics is able to avoid the myriad problems that the teleological or consequence ethics of hedonism will introduce, but not without at the same time encountering some problems of its own. [See Charlotte Stough, "Stoic Determinism and Moral Responsibility" in *The Stoics*, Edited by John M. Rist, *Op. Cit.*, pp. 203-231.]

Finally, the critic, undaunted, points out next that Stoicism violates both criteria of completeness and consistency in its failure to solve the problem of evil. There is a fundamental contradiction in saying that all happens for the best in this world when it obviously does not. All is supposed to happen for the best where God, Who is all-powerful, all-knowing, and all-good, can and wants to prevent useless suffering. But more evil is oftentimes sent than many of us can properly bear, and far from strengthening us such evil can just as easily destroy us. When my dog dies hideously screaming in pain, or your child with cancer suffers for months in agony before finally expiring, what character is being built, what dignity is being strengthened, by such obviously useless suffering? If the problem of evil is not solved, then the Stoics' views about the nature of God remain problematic, and their way of philosophy remains incomplete.

The Appearance of Skepticism

By the year 300 B.C. Athens was playing host to four schools that taught four major *agōgē* or ways of philosophy. They included the Platonists at the Academy, the Aristotelians at the Lyceum, the Epicureans at the Garden of Epicurus and the Stoics in the agora at the Stoa Poikele. All four *agōgē* owed their existence either directly or indirectly to the person of Socrates, to his life as an example and to his way of philosophy as an inspiration for all men and women to follow.

A fifth major *agōgē* now appeared on the Hellenistic scene, a way of life that was to challenge and at the same time depend on the four preceding ways of philosophy. That *agōgē* was Skepticism and its founder was Pyrrho of Elis (ca. 360-270 B.C.). Though Pyrrho, himself, was not directly influenced by Socrates, a later follower in the so-called "Pyrrhonic" tradition, Sextus Empiricus (ca. 200 A.D.), will claim Socrates as the first Skeptic. Skepticism aimed to solve not only the problem of fatalism and the problem of evil but all philosophic problems at one fell swoop. In addition it provided the ancient world with a way of philosophy that is worth considering for the 1990s. We turn to that *agōgē* next.

Pyrrho of Elis (360-270 B.C.): The Father of Skepticism

The reputed founder of the Skeptic school was Pyrrho who was born and died in Elis on the Greek Peloponnesus. It is said that he joined Alexander the Great as a court philosopher in 334 B.C. and traveled with the conqueror all the way to India where he was influenced by certain

Indian "*gymnosophists*," or "naked wise men." [They were probably Jains. Jainism was founded by Mahavira (599-527 B.C.) who held that all knowledge is only probable or partial. Jainism, together with Hinduism and Buddhism, constitutes the third great philosophy of ancient India which survives to this day. Jains believe that reality expresses itself in multiply various views, no one of which possesses the entire truth. That is to say, Jains are Indian sceptics.] Pyrrho returned to Elis in 323 B.C. following Alexander's death. He remained there living in serene poverty until his own death, teaching the doctrines that have become famous since his day.

He left no writings but probably held three views described by his own pupil, Timon of Phlius, who in a series of *Silloi*, or satires, broadcast his master's teachings to the world. These views were: Certainty is unobtainable; second, the wise man will suspend all judgments and seek tranquility rather than truth; and, third, since all views are very likely false, one should accept the myths and mores of one's own society and live one's life according to them. The aim or goal of life is, as we shall see, *ataraxia*, tranquility and quietude, the essence of the best and most worthwhile life that a human being can live.

Pyrrho's own teacher was one Anaxarchus of Abdera, a man with whom he traveled to India. Anaxarchus had maintained in true sceptical fashion that he knew nothing, not even the fact that he knew nothing. Anaxarchus died cruelly by being pounded to death by iron pestles in a large mortar, maintaining a cheerful attitude up to the very last pound apparently. He was one of the first so-called *eudaimonists*, "happy men," and sets the tone for all of those later philosophers among the Epicureans, Stoics and Skeptics whose intention was the pursuit of *eudaimonia*, happiness. [See Diogenes Laertius, *Lives*, *Op. Cit.*, Vol. II, pp. 471-473.]

Three Questions That Lead to Happiness

Pyrrho seems to have inherited this intention, as well as the temperament to go with it, from his teacher. But while Pyrrho was chiefly concerned with finding a happy, independent and peaceful life, he also followed the advice of an Indian philosopher who told him that he would never find the good nor be able to teach it to others unless he sought solitude and independence away from the world. His own quiet nature and his philosophy of happiness through Pyrrhonism attracted the world to Elis. Here came the men who became his pupils, Pyrrhonians classified by such diverse labels as "Seekers," because they were seeking truth;

"Inquirers," because they sought truth but never found it; "Doubters," because of the state of mind that accompanied their search; and "Perplexers," because they were puzzled and confused in their search for truth. To all of them Pyrrho taught his famous three easy steps to happiness all the while trying to maintain that, since he was a Skeptic, he laid down no dogma of his own. If you would be happy, then you need but ask yourself these three questions:

First, what is the real nature of things? The question leads to the discovery that we can never know the true, the hidden nature (adēla), of anything for we are always confined to observing only externals, the phenomena; and these phenomena can only lead us into confusions and contradictions in judgments when we come to describe them. The evidence on one side balances out the evidence on the other side when we deal with the unseen. Does God exist? We never see God, He is one of the unseen. The theist can marshal as much evidence for his or her judgment that God exists, e.g., saying that there is order in the universe (planetary motion, seasons of the year), hence an Orderer must exist, as the atheist can marshal for his or her judgment that God does not exist, e.g., saying that there is disorder in the universe (floods, earthquakes, and terrible suffering, as the problem of evil points out), hence no Orderer exists. The balancing of these judgments, isothenia, one against the other, cancels out each judgment. Hence, the first question leads to the balancing and canceling of judgments.

Second, what is our relation to the things around us thus determined by the answer to the first question? Where judgments cancel out each other we have no choice but to practice epochē, suspension of judgment. For where the judgments that God exists and that God does not exist now stand in equilibrium, neither one deserves our attention, our assent. Hence epochē results. And with epochē we acknowledge our akatalepsia, our lack of understanding, which in turn leads to aphasia, silence.

Third and finally, if you want to be happy, ask yourself what will result from the relation between ourselves and our discoveries about epochē, akatalepsia, and aphasia? The answer Pyrrho gave was that ataraxia, peace and contentment, will result provided that we remain without opinions (adoxastoi), without preferences (aklineis) and without agitations (akradantoi). [See Philip P. Hallie, "Pyrrho" in The Encyclopedia of Philosophy, Paul Edwards, Editor in Chief, 8 Volumes (New York: Macmillan Publishing Co., Inc. & The Free Press, 1967), Vol. 7, pp. 36-37 for a fine discussion of Pyrrho's beliefs.]

It will remain for Pyrrho's later successor, Sextus Empiricus, to expand and systematize Pyrrho's views.

Sextus Empiricus (ca. 175-225 A.D.): The Philosophy of Letting Go

The great codifier of Greek Skepticism has left us precious little information about his life. We know that he was a Greek, that he was born about 175 A.D., that he was a medical doctor, that he headed a school of Skepticism, and that he died about 225 A.D. He wrote two works, *Outlines of Pyrrhonism* from which our central account of his philosophy is derived, and *Against the Dogmatists* in which he attacked the "dogmatic metaphysicians," philosophers like Plato, Aristotle, Zeno the Stoic, and Epicurus. Sextus also opposed the views of the so-called "dogmatic Skeptics" who maintained that knowledge is impossible.

His own view was that the Pyrrhonist Skeptic must learn to suspend judgments on all questions relating to either the certainty of knowledge, which was the view of the dogmatic metaphysicians, or its impossibility, which was the view of the dogmatic, hard-core, Academic sceptics who had taken over Plato's Academy. In this he followed Pyrrho holding that on matters relating to any form of judgment pro and con are both equally probable or improbable, and no one argument, judgment or philosophic view is more worthy of our assent than another. Curiously enough, just as Epicurus before him was no epicure, so also Sextus the Skeptic was no "sceptic," as that word is used today and as it was used by those who revived Pyrrhonism in the 17th century. [See *The Skeptical Tradition*, Edited by Myles Burnyeat (University of California Press, 1983), especially the grand essays by C. B. Schmitt, "The Rediscovery of Ancient Skepticism in Modern Times," and David Sedley, "The Motivation of Greek Skepticism." See also *Sextus Empiricus, Selections From the Major Writings on Scepticism*, Edited by Philip P. Hallie (Hackett Publishing Company, 1985).] He was, instead, an open-minded inquirer, realizing that in the Academic claim that knowledge was impossible there is contained a paradox if not an outright contradiction, and that in the metaphysical claim that knowledge was certain there is contained a conceit completely unwarranted by the evidence. Perhaps a better and more descriptive term for Sextus would be "agnostic" ("I don't know *now*.") rather than "sceptic" ("No one can *ever* know."). We shall refer to his way of philosophy as "Skepticism."

The aim of Sextus' Skepticism is, once again, *eudaimonia*, happiness and peace of mind. Like his predecessor, Pyrrho, Sextus offers a three stage methodology for its realization: *Equipollence, epochē,* and *ataraxia.* Let's examine his methodology as it developed around these three concepts. Again, the claims that Sextus is seeking to be skeptical about are statements or judgments about any object whatsoever including those that go beyond sensory experience, entities such as Plato's Forms, Aristotle's souls, Zeno's Fiery World *Logos,* and Epicurus' atoms, but not judgments about common, everyday entities, such as tables, chairs, water, and grass.

Sextus discusses his philosophy, beginning:

> Skepticism is an ability, or mental attitude, which opposes appearances to judgments in any way whatsoever, with the result that, owing to the *equipollence* [balanced juxtaposition of a judgment and its contradiction] of the objects and reasons thus opposed, we are brought firstly to a state of mental suspense [*epochē*], and next to a state of "unperturbedness" [*ataraxia*] or quietude. [*Sextus Empiricus,* Four Volumes, "Outlines of Pyrrhonism," translated by the Rev. R. G. Bury (Harvard University: Loeb Classical Library, 1939), Vol. I, 8., p. 7.]

The aim of the entire skeptical enterprise is, of course, *ataraxia,* quietude; to seek any other end by any other means than suspending all judgments leads to suffering:

> For the man who opines that anything is by nature good [such as the claim that the virtues are all inherently good, a claim made interminably by all the metaphysicians from Plato to Zeno] or bad is for ever being disquieted: when he is without the things which he deems good he believes himself to be tormented by things naturally bad and he pursues after the things which are, as he thinks, good; which when he has obtained he keeps falling into still more perturbations because of his irrational and immoderate elation, and in his dread of a change of fortune he uses every endeavor to avoid losing the things which he deems good. On the other hand, the man who determines nothing as to what is naturally good or bad neither shuns nor pursues anything eagerly; and in consequence he is unperturbed. [*Ibid.,* I, 27-30, p. 19.]

Sextus is making a case for "letting go," as we shall call it, and his letting go is accomplished through his skepticism regarding the three infamous questions about God, death and the world, viz., Does God exist? and What's His or Its nature?, Is there life after death?, and Can the world hurt me?

In order to get his skeptical program going Sextus begins by introducing ten common tropes or puzzles that prove that all judgments made by men and women are always open to question. Here are several stock-in-trade skeptical tropes:

1. Deceptions of sense impressions, e.g., when an oar that looks bent in water is not really bent.

2. Relativity of sense impressions, e.g., when a hill looks small from a distance but large close up.

3. Judgments of mad men, e.g., when I think everyone hates me and wants to kill me.

4. Wide variation in tastes, likes, and dislikes, e.g., when pickles taste good to me but bad to you.

Such tropes inevitably led to skepticism and to suspension of judgment by compelling us to question and be critical of any inferences that flowed from them.

Previously, Zeno the Stoic had argued that not only was knowledge possible but, further, that certainty in knowledge, even in perception could be obtained. He likened the process of gaining certainty to the four degrees or stages of gradually closing one's right hand to form a fist. The first degree is when we initially sense an object, this book, for example, and form a "mind picture," a *phantasia*, which suggests the statement, "This is a book"; this is like the open right hand. The second degree is when the mind considers what it sees and gives "casual assent"; this is like partially closing the fingers of the right hand. The third degree occurs when the *phantasia* is clear and full assent is given following careful attention in which we get a "fully grasped mind-picture"; this is now like the clenched fist of the right hand. The fourth degree occurs when all of our firmly certain statements interrelate to form a closed consistent system of truths, a system of certainty, which only the Stoic sage possesses; this is like the left hand firmly closed around the clenched right fist. The imagery is singularly apt for consider how often we close our fists and shout, "I know I'm right!"

It was these truths and this system of them that the Skeptic's tropes were designed to question and demolish by simply pointing out, as the first trope does, that sense impressions can deceive us. This may not be a book after all but a bird with papery wings. Think about it.

Consider now this example that the Skeptic used to demonstrate how his philosophy could lead to quietude and contentment. We begin with a *dogma*: God exists. We turn to a *trope*, the problem of evil, that attempts to question the dogma:

> ...when in answer to him who argues the existence of God from the order of the heavenly bodies we oppose the fact that often the good fare ill and the bad fare well, and draw from this the inference that Providence does not exist. [*Ibid.*, I. 32, p. 23.]

Now holding before the mind both the *dogma*, that God exists, and its *contradictory*, that God does not exist, an *equipollence* results, i.e., a balance of judgments which after serious reflection leads to total suspension of all judgments, i.e., *epoché*. With that suspension, i.e., with that letting go or giving up, *ataraxia* results, i.e., tranquility.

The story is told of the great Greek artist Apelles (350-300 B.C.), court painter to Alexander, who was attempting to paint a foaming mouth on one of his horses. It never seemed to come out right. He would paint, step back, see it was wrong, sponge it away. Finally, in disgust he gave up and threw his wiping sponge at the painted mouth. And lo! there it was. The painted foam was perfect. That is the lesson that suspension of judgment and letting go teach. [*Ibid.*, I. 29, p. 21.]

The Problem of self-WORLD: The Skeptics

The problem of self-WORLD is neatly solved by the Skeptics in the sense that the problem need never arise. The practice of letting go has led to a general dismissal of all solutions to the problem of self-WORLD. As a consequence, there are no beings, no theories, and no *agōgēs* to which one can cling; no Epicurean pleasure or secluded Garden, no Cynic Brotherhood or God to which to attach one's hopes and fears, no Stoic natural law or *Logos* to fasten upon. All entities and philosophies have been epoched-away. And since there are no solutions possible, the problem that gave rise to them, the problem of self-WORLD, has been epoched-away, as well.

Recall this story of two women crossing a college campus on a dark and gloomy afternoon. One complains repeatedly to her companion about her personal and academic problems as the two wend their way from the library to the classroom center. In a hectoring and whining voice the complaints reach a crescendo as the two arrive at their destination. There the silent but concerned companion turns to her vociferously troubled friend and in true skeptical fashion speaks: "Margaret," she says, "Be philosophical. Don't think about things."

The problem of self-WORLD, at the hands of the Skeptics, is one more problem that we don't have to think about, if we but adopt the methodology of Margaret's philosophic companion (who has a touch of the Stoic in her, as well) and the Skeptics. Sextus, like Margaret's companion, is asking us to at least put our problems in perspective; and both letting go and not thinking about certain things are salutary ways of responding to that request to stand away from our problems.

But the critic will not be at all happy with this irrational "solution" to a gnawing and grave puzzle about life and its meaning in relation to the world. Margaret's companion has dismissed Margaret's problem, just as the Skeptic has dismissed the problem of self-WORLD without solving it. The real question is, Can the problem of self-WORLD be solved but without dismissing it?, without ceasing to think about it?

Skepticism's Accomplishments

In addition to teaching us all to be more "philosophical," Hellenistic and post-Hellenistic Skepticism has left a legacy to the modern world in teaching us all to be "philosophical." That legacy can be summarized briefly in terms of three major accomplishments:

It taught us all to be cautious in rendering dogmatic and final judgments, and in that caution lay a healthy humility. Violence invariably follows absolutism, totalitarianism and authoritarianism, i.e., fanaticisms under various guises, as the world's religious and patriotic wars of the modern world unhappily attest. Skepticism is the enemy of fanaticism and therefore the enemy of the wars and violence caused by fanaticism. David Hume (1711-1776), the British empiricist and archenemy of both dogmatism and fanaticism in whatever forms they take, whether scientific, political, moral or religious, defends skepticism holding that it makes us humble, tolerant and modest, and reminds us not to overstep the bounds of what our limited human powers can properly know:

> But could such dogmatical reasoners become sensible of the strange infirmities of human understanding, even in its most perfect state, and when most accurate and cautious in its determinations; such a reflection would naturally inspire them with more modesty and reserve, and diminish their fond opinions of themselves, and their prejudices against antagonists. [David Hume, *An Enquiry Concerning Human Understanding* in *The English Philosophers From Bacon to Mill*, Edited by Edwin A. Burtt (New York: The Modern Library, 1939), p. 687.]

Hume adds that "a small tincture of Pyrrhonism" removes pride and replaces it with a "degree of doubt, caution and modesty" which ought always to accompany the judicious reasoner.

It set the stage for modern science where empirical skepticism became the guide for rejecting dogmatic science based on hope, faith, tradition, and bad observations in order to make room for empirical science based on probabilities, sensory testing and public confirmation. Pyrrhonism bids us keep our attentions on matters for which our minds and senses are fitted by nature by, as Hume says, limiting "...our inquiries to such subjects as are best adapted to the narrow capacity of human understanding." [*Ibid.*] It is in this skeptical, or sceptical, atmosphere that contemporary empirical science was born.

It showed that pride goeth before fall, that unhappiness is the inevitable consequence of any desperate clinging to truth and knowledge, and that happiness can result from the cautious abandonment of such clinging. It left a legacy of letting go that more and more people with high blood pressure and anxieties about other people's views of the world are finding more and more salutary. Remembering that the world rests on probabilities and not on certainties is simply good psychological advice for getting through a day dominated by poverty, unemployment, ICBMs, environmental pollution, animal suffering, terrorism, and traffic on the freeway.*

We turn next to the way of philosophy of the Skeptics.

The Skeptic Way of Letting-Go: Sextus Empiricus

The Problem

The problem for the Hellenistic Skeptics like Pyrrho and later Skeptics like Sextus is our old familiar problem of self-WORLD, the same anxiety-producing puzzle that haunted the Cynics, the Epicureans, the Stoics, the Platonists and the Aristotelians. The specific form that the problem of self-WORLD took for the Skeptics was that the overwhelming WORLD included any and every judgment that anyone made about that world. Anxiety and suffering are the result of living in the world, having a rational mind that makes judgments, and then being capable of a peculiar sensitivity when the mind makes those judgments.

---

* Voltaire (1694-1778), the pungent sage of the French Enlightenment, would cry: "The fewer dogmas, the fewer disputes; and the fewer disputes, the fewer misfortunes." To which Frederich Nietzsche (1844-1900) would later add: "Convictions are prisons."

The Cause

The cause of the suffering lies in making decisions or making judgments. Suffering will surely follow whenever anyone unequivocally believes or decides or states that they will (or will not) die; that there is (or is not) life in heaven or hell or neither after death; or that a vengeful or malevolent or benevolent God does (or does not) exist, and so on.

The Solution

The solution to the problem of suffering as a result of the self's confrontation with a WORLD which it cannot control is *ataraxia*, tranquility or quietude.

The Ways

The way to *ataraxia* lies in ceasing to make any and all decisions and judgments beyond the few that are necessary to stay alive ("I will eat and drink when necessary.") and to be a good citizen ("I will outwardly abide by the mores of my community.").* That way lies in taking a *dogma* ("God exists."), taking a *trope* or problem that substantiates the contradictory of the dogma (the problem of evil leads to stating "God does not exist."), realizing that there is a balance of evidence both for and against the dogma allowing a balance between the dogma and its contradictory (an *equipollence* exists between "God exists" and "God does not exist"), leading to a suspension of both judgments (an *epochē* with respect to both judgments), leading to an eventual universal *epochē* with respect to all judgments, and from there to a general *ataraxia*. The letting go of all judgments leads to a letting go of all of the anxiety produced by making judgments.

Problems With Skepticism

One central problem emerges that threatens the adequacy of Skepticism as a viable way of philosophy. The problem involves all three of our criteria for adequacy for it violates common sense, consistency and completeness all together. The problem is that Skepticism is not practicable in the manner in which Sextus and Pyrrho seem to have wanted it to be practiced. It tends to violate common sense for no one can really remain as skeptical about the major problems of life as our two Skeptics

---

* "Adhering, then, to appearances we live in accordance with the normal rules of life, undogmatically, seeing that we cannot remain wholly inactive." Sextus Empiricus, *Outlines of Pyrrhonism, Op. Cit.*, I. 23., p. 17.

desire; it is inconsistent for it recommends a practice the carrying out of which violates the very intent and program of the system, itself, for the simple reason that the Skeptic can't doubt everything without jeopardizing his own extremely rational position; and, finally, following from this inconsistency, it is incomplete in the sense that it leaves one crucial problem unsolved, viz., the problem of not advancing any truths itself in the very act of demolishing other peoples' truths and in advancing its own position. Sextus has a reply to the charges of inconsistency and incompleteness, of course, a reply in which he states that Skepticism had to be a purge that eliminates everything including itself:

> Just as, for example, fire after consuming the fuel destroys also itself, and like as purgatives after driving the fluids out of the bodies expel themselves as well, so too the argument against proof, after abolishing every proof, can cancel itself also. And again, just as it is not impossible for the man who has ascended to a high place by a ladder to overthrow the ladder with his foot after his ascent, so also it is not unlikely that the Skeptic after he has arrived at the demonstration of his thesis by means of the argument proving the non-existence of proof, as it were by a step ladder, should then abolish this very argument. [*Sextus Empiricus, Op. Cit.*, "Against the Logicians" II, 480-481, pp. 487-489.]

This concludes our presentation of Skepticism. We turn next to the ever-popular, much-misunderstood and certainly much-maligned way of utilitarianism.

NINE
THE WAY OF UTILITARIANISM
❧•❦

JOHN STUART MILL (1806-1873): THE GREATEST UTILITARIAN OF THEM ALL

John Stuart Mill, the eldest son of the Scottish reformer and essayist, James Mill, was born in England in 1806. James Mill met Jeremy Bentham, the founder of utilitarianism, two years later, and a friendship that was to have far-reaching consequences for John Mill, Britain, and the world, quickly developed. Just as his son was to do later, James Mill organized a society of Benthamites devoted to the work of, and to the association with, Jeremey Bentham. It included the most powerful and influential reformers of the 19th century, such as Joseph Hume, Francis Place, George Grote, and David Ricardo. It was in this intellectual atmosphere that the precocious and brilliant John Mill was raised.

A Young Man's Education

Under his father's tutelage, young Mill was educated to carry on the Benthamite traditions. He began the study of Greek at three, Latin at eight, with geometry, algebra and differential calculus, all of which he detested, in between. In order to master Greek, a number of common words were written on cards along with their English synonyms, a method of learning a language that was then quite unknown. The child memorized these, turned to Aesop's fables in Greek and, without the grammar which came later, proceeded to translate. By seven he had read most of Plato's dialogues and devoured Herodotus, Xenophon, and Diogenes Laertius. From eight to twelve he read Virgil, Horace, Ovid, Livy, Aristotle, Sophocles and Aristophanes. The father wasted no time with fairy tales, remember that children's books had not yet been invented, but turned to true stories of great and resourceful men like Philip of Macedon, Sir Francis Drake, Captain James Cook, and Frederick the Great. At twelve John mastered logic and the philosophy of the materialist, Epicurean and royalist, Thomas Hobbes, along with all that was then known about the new field of political economy.

John Mill dutifully imbibed all that his father taught him, repeating his lessons to his father on demand in the mornings and then instructing his younger brothers and sisters when his own daily instruction was over. His education continued until his sixteenth year but it was a one-sided education that stressed the science of quantity and facts; there was little room for passion and feeling: reason was his guide and it was his reason that was being educated. John Mill's education was woefully unbalanced, a reflection of his father's needs and interests, and not those of a growing, sensitive, young man. James Mill, whose predilection for the historical, scientific, and factual was too well-known to go unnoticed, was subsequently satirized and immortalized by Charles Dickens in his novel of 1854, *Hard Times*. One of the more depressing characters in the novel is that of Mr. Gradgrind, a man totally without emotion and feeling whom Dickens compels to say repeatedly throughout the book, "Facts, all we want are facts."

In 1823 at the age of seventeen, his home education completed, John Mill entered the Examiner's Office of the East India Company, a London company for which his father also worked. The son was to remain with the company for the next thirty-five years. At the same time he joined and came to dominate the Philosophical Radicals, a group of young men who sought to combine the popular philosophy of Jeremy Bentham with the equally popular associationist psychology of David Hartley, and both of these with the economic theory of David Ricardo. In 1822 he had founded the Utilitarian Society "for the redemption of all mankind," and gradually, over the years that followed, began to pull back from the older utilitarianism of both his father and Bentham.

A Mental Catastrophe

In 1826 at the age of twenty he suffered a deep psychological depression which remained with him for many months. He continued working throughout this period of black gloom and slowly recovered by discovering a part of himself that had been all but drowned through the quantitative, factual, scientific, rational education of his father: John Mill discovered the magic and healing effect of emotion and feeling, particularly in the poetry of William Wordsworth, poetry that may have saved his life:

> I long continued to value Wordsworth less according to his intrinsic merits, than by the measure of what he had done for me. Compared with the greatest poets, he may be said to be the poet of unpoetical natures, possessed of quiet and contemplative tastes. But unpoetical natures are precisely those which require poetic cultivation. [John Stuart Mill, *Autobiography in the Essential Works of John Stuart Mill*, Edited by Max Lerner (Bantam Books, 1965), p. 92.]

In particular, these lines of Wordsworth moved him greatly:

> Thanks to the human heart by which we live,
> Thanks to the tenderness, its joys, and fears,
> To me the meanest flower that blows can give,
> Thoughts that do often lie too deep for tears.
> [Quoted in Michael St. John Packe, *The Life of John Stuart Mill* (New York: Capricorn Books, 1970), p. 82.]

Mill's unbalanced mind became balanced again by the infusion of such thoughts into the emotional side of his nature which his father's influence and education seemed to have all but obliterated. He gradually broke away from that influence to form ideas and thoughts entirely his own.

Romance and Harriet Taylor

In the summer of 1830 John Mill met Harriet Taylor, a woman to whom he was to become utterly devoted. The only problem about their relationship was that Mrs. Taylor was married. But she returned Mill's ardent affection in a purely intellectual but deeply felt association that was to continue for the remainder of their lives. Mrs. Taylor's husband finally died in 1849 and after three of years of proper waiting, Harriet and John were married. He thought her a great genius and she was to have an enormous influence on all of his subsequent writings as well as on his life. Their Platonic love affair ended with her death in 1858 in Avignon, France while the Mills were on tour. The sorrowing John Mill bought a house nearby in order to be close to her grave. He lived there in grief until his own death in 1873. He was later to say of her, ". . .all my published writings were as much my wife's work as mine; her share in them constantly increasing as years advance." [John Stuart Mill, *Autobiography, Op. Cit.*, p. 144.] Finally, Mill was to say of both her and his father's influence on his life and writings, "Who, either now or hereafter, may think of me and of the work I have done, must never forget

that it is the product not of one intellect and conscience, but of three."
[Quoted in Robert L. Heilbroner, *The Worldly Philosophers* (New York:
Simon and Schuster, 1953), p. 121.]

Utilitarianism for Jeremy Bentham

In addition to the emotional and intellectual influence of his father
and Harriet Taylor on his life, Jeremy Bentham's influence was just as
profound. The precocious Bentham was born in London in 1748 and entered Queen's College, Oxford, at the age of 12. He graduated three years
later and began the study of law at Lincoln's Inn. Called to the bar in
1767, he never practiced law but set to work on the system of British
jurisprudence in order to reform and codify both penal and civil law. It is
out of this interest in the law and through a personal commitment to social reform that Bentham's and the modern world's philosophy of utilitarianism was born.

As the leader of the Philosophical Radicals in the fight for social reform in 18th century Britain, Bentham sought a philosophy to guide the
actions of his devoted and dedicated young reformers. Though he believed that the principle of utility, or usefulness, was basically a guide for
legislators, it was also claimed to have, as we shall see, easy application
in one's own personal life.

Bentham met James Mill in 1808 and their friendship became the
foundation of the Benthamite society, each contributing eagerly to the
other's views and principles to the point where it is difficult to distinguish one man's contribution from the others'. Around the two gathered
the leading British intellectuals of the early 19th century and from that
association came eventually the Great Reform Bill of 1832. Unfortunately,
Bentham died on the eve of the Bill's passage. His remains can be seen on
display to this day in a glass case in the public lobby of University
College in London.

Reluctant all of his life to publish any of his writings, Bentham's
greatest work did finally find its way into print in 1789, *The Principles of
Morals and Legislation*. In the opening paragraph of this extremely influential book, the foundations of utility (or "the greatest happiness principle") are clearly laid out as Bentham begins in true Epicurean fashion
with a view about human nature (psychological hedonism) as the foundation for a view about the kinds of actions human beings ought to
perform (ethical hedonism):

> Nature has placed mankind under the governance of two sovereign masters,
> *pain* and *pleasure*. It is for them alone to point out what we ought to do, as

well as to determine what we shall do. On the one hand the standard of right and wrong, on the other the chain of causes and effects, are fastened to their throne. They govern us in all we do, in all we say, in all we think: every effort we can make to throw off our subjection, will serve but to demonstrate and confirm it.... The *principle of utility* recognizes this subjection, and assumes it for the foundation of that system, the object of which is to rear the fabric of felicity by the hands of reason and of law. [Jeremy Bentham, *An Introduction to the Principles of Morals and Legislation* in *The English Philosophers From Bacon to Mill*, Edited by Edwin A. Burtt, (The Modern Library, 1939), p. 791.]

Bentham continues by defining "utility":

By utility is meant that property in any object, whereby it tends to produce benefit, advantage, pleasure, good, or happiness (all this in the present case comes to the same thing), or (what comes again to the same thing) to prevent the happening of mischief, pain, evil, or unhappiness to the party whose interest is considered....

But, it might well be asked, whose interest or pleasure is to be considered when we come to measure the rightness of an action? Bentham answers,

. . .if that party be the community in general, then the happiness of the community; if a particular individual, then the happiness of that individual. [*Ibid.*, p. 792.]

Bentham next argues that an action that is conformable to the principle of utility is right "when the tendency it has to augment the happiness of the community is greater than any it has to diminish it." [*Ibid.*] One final step is needed to make the principle of utility into an ethical principle. Bentham takes that step associating all talk about "utility," "happiness," and "increasing the happiness of the community or the individual," to moral rightness:

Of an action that is conformable to the principle of utility, one may always say either that it is one that ought to be done, or at least that it is not one that ought to be done.... When thus interpreted, the words *ought*, and *right* and *wrong*, and others of that stamp, have a meaning.... [*Ibid.*]

Putting together all that Bentham has given us here, we can say that a "right action" for Jeremy Bentham is an action that tends to promote the greatest amount of happiness or pleasure of everyone.

It will be left to John Mill to sharpen and extend Bentham's work of 1789 into a way of philosophy and into utilitarianism as we know it today. Bentham's principle of utility regarded the *quality* of all pleasures as fundamentally alike wherein, as he claimed, pushpin (a children's game)

is as good as poetry. In other words, physical pleasures were as good as and no different from intellectual pleasures. Epicurus would have been appalled, as John Mill came to be, at this suggestion that the quality of pleasure is relatively unimportant and that quantity alone is what really matters. Mill will attempt to return to Epicurus' view and to escape the piggish Cyrenaicism that Bentham's view threatened.

Utilitarianism for John Mill

In 1863 John Mill published *Utilitarianism* in which he stated clearly the basic doctrine of his recently re-created moral philosophy:

> The creed which accepts as the foundation of morals *utility*, or the *greatest happiness*, holds that actions are right in proportion as they tend to promote happiness, wrong as they tend to produce the reverse of happiness. By 'happiness' is intended pleasure, and the absence of pain; by 'unhappiness,' pain, and the privation of pleasure. [John Stuart Mill, *Utilitarianism* in *The English Philosophers From Bacon to Mill*, *Op. Cit.*, p. 900.]

Like Bentham before him, Mill believed that the "theory of morality" that he is discussing rests upon a "theory of life" that we have previously called "psychological hedonism":

> —namely, that pleasure, and freedom from pain, are the only things desirable [i.e., the only things which can be desired and which it is natural to desire] as ends; and that all desirable things (which are as numerous in the utilitarian as in any other scheme) are desirable either for the pleasure inherent in themselves, or as means to the promotion of pleasure and the prevention of pain. [*Ibid.*]

Mill defends his theory of life against those who probably confused Mill with Bentham, and who now attacked it "as a doctrine worthy of swine," by reminding his readers that this theory assigns "to the pleasures of the intellect, of the feelings and imagination, and of the moral sentiments, a much higher value as pleasures than to those of mere sensation"; [*Ibid.*, p. 901.] and, Mill concludes, "better to be a Socrates dissatisfied than a fool satisfied." [*Ibid.*, p. 902.] Thus Mill separates himself from Bentham on the matter of the quality of pleasures, arguing, as Epicurus before him had, that though all pleasures are good, not all pleasures are worthy of pursuit. Only those pleasures that appeal to the higher faculties of a human being ought to be pursued and, in fact, are pursued by the vast majority of human beings.

In utilitarianism, Mill concludes, the happiness or pleasure that one seeks is never to be the agent's own "but the greatest amount of happiness altogether," i.e., for everyone concerned. Unlike the Cyrenaics who seem to have adopted an *egoistic ethical hedonism* that held that an action is right if and only if the agent's own pleasure is increased, John Mill has adopted a *universalistic ethical hedonism* that holds that an action is right if and only if the happiness "of all concerned," including one's own happiness, is increased. Universalistic ethical hedonism takes two forms, and despite the difficulties which each generates, they help to turn utilitarianism into a powerful and defensible way of philosophy. Let's look briefly at these two versions of Mill's utilitarianism.

Act Utilitarianism

Act utilitarianism simply states that an action is right provided only that 1) it is voluntary or free and not compelled, 2) that it produces more pleasure or happiness for everyone concerned, 3) than any other action, 4) appropriate to the circumstances. Let's look briefly at these four necessary conditions for a right action:

1) The action must be voluntary. We cannot call an action right (or wrong) if the agent was compelled to do it. Suppose that a cancer patient needs a bone marrow transplant, and suppose that you have exactly the kind of blood-bone type that the patient needs. But suppose that you are reluctant to undergo the surgery and the discomfort needed to give up your bone marrow. But suddenly the relatives of the patient overpower you late one night, whip you off heavily sedated to a hospital where your marrow is painlessly but forcefully taken from you. Was your action right? The question is odd. Even if the action led to the greatest happiness for the greatest number and thereby satisfied Mill's principle of utility, we cannot say that *your* action was right. It wasn't, plainly, *your* action at all because it was carried out under compulsion. The first condition for a right action under utilitarianism, that the action must be voluntary, was not satisfied.

2) The action must produce more pleasure for everyone concerned. It is not essential that everyone in the world or every sentient creature in the universe have their happiness increased but only those who are somehow related to the action. With the case of the bone marrow transplant mentioned above, it is essential that the quality of life, or happiness, for the doner, patient, relatives and probably those in close contact with these people be included in any hedonistic calculating.

3) The action must be compared with any other action that one could perform at the time. Here the hedonistic calculus would come into play, once again, measuring, adding, subtracting and comparing units of plea-

sure of the actions available. Suppose that transplanting bone marrow led to 100p (p is a unit of pleasure, let's assume) and not transplanting led to 50p. Then, clearly, transplanting would seem so far to be the right thing to do.

4) The action that is done must be appropriate to the circumstances. Thus if your choices are either to undergo a transplant operation or not to undergo it and your wondering what to do, it would be inappropriate for you to start making and eating a peanut butter sandwich even though such an alternative might give 1000p units of pleasure (you're very fond of peanut butter). Most of us have such hedonic distractions waiting around all the time to help us avoid making moral or social or interpersonal choices.

If all four of these conditions are present, in other words, if our voluntary and appropriate action does lead to the greatest happiness for the greatest number, then act utilitarianism and John Stuart Mill would tell us that the action is right.

But two of the problems with act utilitarianism are that quite frequently there is neither the time necessary to carry out the hedonist calculations nor are we wise enough and unselfish enough to calculate fairly for all concerned in those calculations. In other words, the problems of time, selfishness, and ignorance make fair and just judgments difficult if not impossible under act utilitarianism. We turn, therefore, to rule utilitarianism in order to solve these problems.

Rule Utilitarianism

Rule utilitarianism simply states that an action is right if it is an instance of, or falls under, a moral rule or law which is, itself, already justified by the principle of utility. Should I lie, cheat, steal, or murder? No. Why not? Must I start calculating each time I get myself into a situation where lying, cheating, stealing or murdering is one possible alternative? No, because each of these actions are instances of, or fall under, moral, legal or societal rules that state that instances of these four things are generally wrong. And that rule, it is assumed, has already been sanctified by the majority of voters, citizens or traditions, as one that guarantees the greatest happiness for the greatest number. Why else would a society have laws against lying on contracts, against cheating in business arrangements, if not to protect itself and thereby guarantee a better, happier, more worthwhile life for all concerned. The problems of time, selfishness, and ignorance would all seem to be solved. Mill, himself, seems to be pointing in the direction of what will later be called "rule utilitarianism" when he states:

> ...the beliefs which have thus come down are the rules of morality for the multitude, and for the philosopher until he has succeeded in finding better....To pass over the intermediate generalizations [the laws and rules of society] entirely, and endeavor to test each individual action directly by the first principle [of utility] is...[idiocy]. [*Ibid.*, p. 914.]

In other words, in good conservative fashion, Mill answers the problems of time, selfishness, and ignorance by proposing that we turn to the rules and laws already existing in society, rules and laws sanctified by tradition and justified by their continuing usefulness or utility:

> The answer to the objection is that there has been ample time, namely, the whole past duration of the human species. During all that time, mankind have been learning by experience the tendencies of actions; on *which* experience all the prudence, as well as all the morality of life, are dependent....mankind must by this time have acquired positive beliefs as to the effects of some actions on their happiness. [*Ibid.*, pp. 913, 914, italics added.]

But what's to be done where there are no rules specifically related to our present moral problem?, a problem like the bone marrow transplant. The modern rule utilitarian at this point tells us to theoretically construct a rule or law by generalizing on our current moral dilemma and then ask in good utilitarian fashion, Is the new law right? [Jeremy Bentham has anticipated the modern rule utilitarian when he states, "When an action...is supposed by a man to be conformable to the principle of utility it may be convenient...*to imagine a kind of law* or dictate...and to speak of the action in question, as being conformable to such law or dictate." *Op. Cit.*, p. 792, italics added.] So let's construct a new law relating to the case of the bone marrow transplant:

Bone Marrow Donation Law: Whenever a patient needs a bone marrow transplant and a qualified donor can be found, then that donor must donate his or her bone marrow to the patient provided only that no serious injury shall occur to the donor as a result of the donation.

The law is sufficiently vague to keep an army of lawyers busy for decades. But it does satisfy the first move that the rule utilitarian asks us to make. Finally, we test the newly constructed law against the principle of utility by asking, If the bone marrow donation law became the law of the land, would this lead to the greatest happiness for the greatest number? Here, obviously, calculation is necessary once again and the problems of time, selfishness and ignorance might return to haunt the calculator. But the method of rule-construction in rule utilitarianism goes on all the time in ordinary life when we ask ourselves regarding a particular moral issue, What if everyone did this? What would be the result? What would be the effect on society as a whole if my choice of action became the law of the land? The rule utilitarian is merely stating in a clearer and more precise fashion a common practice carried out daily by the entire moral community. A third kind of utilitarianism, attitude utilitarianism, will follow from this commitment to community. [See below Chapter 13, *The Ways of Individualism and Community*, pp. 298-301.]

Issues and Problems

The case of the bone-marrow transplant raises several issues and problems with John Mill's utilitarianism not the least of which is the matter of privacy and the question of sovereignty over one's life and body. If the majority, i.e., the greatest number, should suddenly decide that all blue-eyes blondes should be forced to give bone marrow whenever it is needed or that all persons under five feet in height should, for the good of society, be stretched five inches, and if greater happiness would be produced for the greatest number of people by showing these spectacles on public television, then it would be right, at least it would be right according to the principle of utility. Any action that brings the greatest happiness to the greatest number is right, after all. What we are suddenly faced with is the possibility of the tyranny of the majority. After all, what the majority wants, in some very loose sense, is always right. But that's patently and common sensically absurd, if you think about it. Suppose the majority wants something that's obviously wrong, like executing Socrates, or crucifying Jesus of Nazareth, or shooting Martin Luther King?, or elongating the bodies of all short people? Or suppose someone wants to read something of which you disapprove, such as *Catcher in the Rye* by J. D. Salinger (because it's vulgar)?, or *The Lord of the Flies* by William Golding (because it's violent)?, or *Brave New World* by Aldous Huxley (because its sexually explicit)?, the three most often censored and prohibited books in high school libraries in the United States. Is that right? But suppose the majority approves!? One of the reasons for having constitutions is to protect the minority from the tyranny of the majority. The Constitution of the United States and, in particular, the Bill of Rights remind the minority and warn the majority that there are certain inalienable and natural rights which all citizens have which can never be taken away. Censorship of books, for example, is a free speech, free press issue, as the federal courts in this country have attested over the years.

Mill is mindful of the tyranny of the majority and nowhere is the issue of freedom of action, freedom of thought and freedom of the press more clearly presented than in his famous little essay called *On Liberty*. The matters raised in this work are part of the general fabric of utilitarianism since Mill firmly believed that happiness could never be achieved in a society where the above freedoms were not present. So before turning to Mill's views of social reform and his way of philosophy, let's look at Mill on censorship in the particular context of his own period.

On Liberty

In 1848 John Stuart Mill published his classic work, *Principles of Political Economy*. The book was a tremendous success, running to seven editions in his own lifetime. He wrote the two volumes effortlessly in just six weeks and in it offered an economic theory of enormous importance which we shall discuss below. In addition, the book laid the foundation for modern socialism together with a vision of man as *homo economicus*, a view strictly consistent with the psychological hedonism and psychological egoism of his philosophy of utilitarianism. The book was condemned by the Roman Catholic Church and placed on the Church's *Index of Prohibited Books* in 1856. As if in response, Mill's remarkable essay *On Liberty*, a defense of freedom of speech and opinion, appeared three years later in 1859. [*On Liberty* was conceived in 1856 while Mill was in Rome and it grew out of a short essay he had written the year before. See Michael St. John Packe, *The Life of John Stuart Mill*, op. cit., p. 376.]

The practice of burning and condemning books as a way of abolishing unpopular opinions lies far back in the Western tradition. The author of the *Acts of the Apostles* in the *New Testament* informs us that, "Many also...came confessing... And a number...brought their books together and burned them in the sight of all." [*Acts.* 19. 18-19. Revised Standard Version.] The first *Index*, or list of banned books, was drawn up by a decree of Pope Gelasius in 496 A.D. In 1467 Pope Innocent III decreed that all books to be published must first be submitted to Church Authority for permission to publish. Pope Leo X at the Lateran Council of 1515 issued a general decree of supervisory censorship over all written books. The Council of Trent in 1564 drew up the first *General Catalogue of Forbidden Books* from which the modern *Index* received its name. The *Index of Forbidden Books* was revised by Pope Leo XIII in 1897 with a final edition published in 1948. The *Index* was quietly dropped in 1966 as a result of the liberalizing trends established by Vatican II in the early '60's.

The Church had held that it was a mortal sin, meaning that one could go to Hell for eternity for disobedience, to read, have written, keep, or publish without permission any book on the *Index*. The Church felt, not without reason, that it had the duty to protect the congregation of the faithful in all matters of faith and morals; after all, Jesus himself had prayed, "lead us not into temptation." And the Church knew, especially after Martin Luther (1483-1546), that ideas are temptations. Permission to read works on the *Index* could be sought, however; but anyone, and this included students, householders and clergy, who knowingly read without permission or disobeyed an order not to read, was subject to condemnation and to excommunication from the Church.

The *Index* contained works by some of the leading intellectuals of the modern world: Frances Bacon, John Locke, John Milton, Edward Gibbon, Jeremy Bentham, J. J. Rouseau, Immanual Kant, Henri Bergson, and, of course, John Stuart Mill. In addition, it was forbidden to read without episcopal permission anything at all written by the following whose complete works had been indexed: Rene Descartes, Thomas Hobbes, David Hume, Voltaire, Emile Zola, and Jean Paul Sartre.

Almost everyone, it now seems, Catholic and non-Catholic alike, thought that the *Index* was silly, defeating the very purpose, i.e., the protection of the unprepared against dangerous ideas, for which it was established. The *Index* was a classic example of the tyranny of the *minority* over the minds of the majority.

Mill's essay *On Liberty* was planned in 1856, the same year that Pope Pius IX declared the dogma of the Immaculate Conception of Mary. This was the same Pope who in 1870 declared Papal Infallibility on matters of faith and morals within the Roman Catholic Church, a declaration which is, even today, a hotly debated issue among liberal Catholics. *On Liberty* has much to say about infallibility in addition to advancing three principal ideas: First, an individual's liberty of *action* can be rightfully constrained only in order to prevent harm to others. Mill writes, "...that the sole end for which mankind are warranted, individually or collectively, in interfering with the liberty of action of any of their number, is self protection." [John Stuart Mill, *On Liberty* in *The English Philosophers From Bacon to Mill, Op. Cit.*, p. 956.] The individual's own good, either physical or moral, is not a sufficient warrant. Thus society has no business to prevent drunkenness, idleness, prostitution, gambling, drug addiction and suicide by saying that it is for the individual's own good:

He cannot rightfully be compelled to do or forbear because it will be better for him to do so because it will make him happier, because, in the opinion of others, to do so would be wise, or even right. These are good reasons for remonstrating with him, or reasoning with him, or persuading him, or entreating him, but not for compelling him. To justify that, the conduct from which it is desired to deter him must be calculated to produce evil to someone else. The only part of the conduct of anyone, for which he is amenable to society, is that which concerns others. Over himself, over his own body and mind, the individual is sovereign. [*Ibid.*]

Second, specific areas of human freedom cannot rightfully be denied to anyone: The freedom to believe, the freedom of taste and preference, and the freedom to unite (for any purpose not involving harm to others). But it is with the third idea that Mill's reputation as the father of modern liberalism emerges and the pertinancy to the *Index* becomes obvious.

Third, open expressions of opinions should *never* be prohibited or repressed, because if the repressed opinion is *true*, one loses the opportunity of discovering the truth; while if the repressed opinion is *false*, discussion of its falsity strengthens the opposing truth making the grounds of truth all the more obvious.

Underlying the entire discussion in *On Liberty* is the doctrine of utilitarianism. For Mill firmly believed that individuals as well as society would be made happier and healthier if the principles of liberty were to be extended throughout society. With the maximum freedom of expression, action and thought, with the maximization of knowledge and unlimited access to it through education, individual growth and happiness would be guaranteed and with that the greatest happiness for the greatest number would at last be truly achievable. Therein lies the utilitarian answer to the question, What is the best and most worthwhile life that a human being can live?

UTILITARIANISM'S ACCOMPLISHMENTS: SOCIAL REFORM

John Mill was elected a member of Parliament in 1865 giving him an even greater opportunity than through his writings alone to help alleviate the plight of the working class of citizens then living in ignorance, filth, and wretched poverty in Victorian, mid-19th century England. The terrible picture of what the times were like can be easily obtained from looking at the various reports of the Royal Commission's investigating the mills, factories, and mines in which men, women, and children worked in the 19th century. And nowhere are these reports more readily accessible than in Karl Marx's classic work, *Capital*, published in 1867.

Marx describes the murderous working conditions in England, acknowledging that matters were far worse on the Continent. The following are taken from newspaper and Royal Commission reports, and Marx titles the section in *Capital*, "Branches of English Industry Without Legal Limits to Exploitation":

> Mr. Broughton Charlton, county magistrate, declared as chairman of a meeting held at the Assembly Rooms, Nottingham, on the 14th of January, 1860, "that there was an amount of privation and suffering among that portion of the population connected with the lace trade, unknown in other parts of the kingdom, indeed, in the civilized world... Children of nine or ten years are dragged from their squalid beds at two, three, or four o'clock in the morning and compelled to work for a bare subsistence until ten, eleven, or twelve at night, their limbs wearing away, their frames dwindling, their faces whitening, and their humanity absolutely sinking into a stone-like torpor, utterly horrible to contemplate..... We are not surprised that Mr. Mallet, or any other manufacturer, should stand forward and protest against discussion..... The system, as the Rev. Montagu Valpy describes it, is one of unmitigated slavery, socially, physically, morally, and spiritually..... We declaim against the Virginian and Carolina cotton-planters. Is their black-market, their lash, and their barter of human flesh more detestable than this slow sacrifice of humanity which takes place in order that veils and collars may be fabricated for the benefit of capitalists?"

Marx continues with another incident:

> "It is impossible," [another] report continues, "for any mind to realise the amount of work described in the following passages as being performed by boys of from 9 to 12 years of age....without coming irresistibly to the conclusion that such abuses of the power of parents and of employers can no longer be allowed to exist."
>
> "At a rolling-mill where the proper hours were from 6 a.m. to 5-1/2 p.m., a boy worked about four nights every week till 8-1/2 p.m. at least...and this for six months. Another, at 9 years old, sometimes made three 12-hour shifts running, and, when 10, has made two days and two nights running." A third, "now 10...worked from 6 a.m. till 12 p.m. three nights, and till 9 p.m. the other nights." "Another, now 13, ...worked from 6 p.m. till 12 noon next day, for a week together, and sometimes for three shifts together, e.g., from Monday morning till Tuesday night." "Another, now 12, has worked in an iron foundry at Stavely from 6 a.m. till 12 p.m. for a fortnight on end; could not do it any more." "George Allinsworth, age 9, came here as cellar-boy last Friday; next morning we had to begin at 3, so I stopped here all night. Live five miles off. Slept on the floor of the furnace, over head, with an apron under me, and a bit of a jacket over me. The two other days I have been here at 6 a.m. Aye! it is hot in here. Before I came here I was nearly a year at the same work at some works in the country.

Began there, too, at 3 on Saturday morning—always did, but was very gain [near] home, and could sleep at home. Other days I began at 6 in the morning, and gi'en over at 6 or 7 in the evening," &c. [Karl Marx, *Capital: A Critique of Political Economy* (The Modern Library, 1906), pp. 268-269, 284-285.]

And so on for another 75 pages.

So what is to be done? For Marx the only solution was violent revolution with the subsequent extermination of the economic conditions that made life a living hell for millions of human beings. For Mill the only possible solution was through reform of the economic, social, and political conditions of 19th century England. The guiding principle for reform remained for Mill utilitarianism, which he found even in the Christian ethics of his day. The philosophy of utilitarianism, his election to Parliament in 1865, and his own way of philosophy all helped to pass the Reform Bill of 1867, the second greatest achievement of social reform in British history. A modern historian comments on that second great reform bill:

The final Reform Bill of 1867 was a major step in the democritization of the country. It provided for a wide extension of the franchise for elections to Parliament and almost doubled the number of voters, which went from about one million to two million.... [Felix Gilbert, *et al*, *The Norton History of Modern Europe* (New York: W.W. Norton & Company, 1971), pp. 1136-1137.]

Why was the addition of so many new qualified voters to the franchise so important? Earlier in his *Principles of Political Economy* of 1848, Mill had made a monumental discovery about the nature of the course of the economic suffering and material poverty in Victorian England. The discovery was very simple: Mill pointed out that the laws of economic production, and here he differed profoundly from Marx, were essentially unalterable; but while such laws could never change, the man-made laws relative to the distribution of goods and wealth were alterable. Robert L. Heilbroner states:

What he meant was very clear: the economic laws of production concern nature. There is nothing arbitrary about whether labor is more productive in this use or that, nor is there anything capricious or optional about such economic phenomena as the diminishing powers of productivity of the soil. Scarcity and the obduracy of nature are real things and the economic rules of behavior which tell us how to maximize the fruits of our own labor are as impersonal and as absolute as the laws of the expansion of gases or the interaction of chemical substances.

But the laws of the economics of production, and this is the real point, have nothing to do with distribution. Once wealth is produced according to laws just as inexorable and unalterable as the other laws of nature, then one can do with that wealth as one pleases, guided only by selfishness, greed, love, hate, or a way of philosophy, or, as Mill proposed, by a personal and social ethic which would reflect the principle of the greatest happiness for the greatest number.

Goods are produced according to rigid and discoverable economic laws which can be used to explain and predict past and future economic behavior. But goods are distributed according to entirely different principles. Mill, himself, states:

> The distribution of wealth, therefore, depends on the laws and customs of society. The rules by which it is determined are what the opinions and feelings of the ruling portion of the community make them, and are very different in different ages and countries, and might be still more different, if mankind so chose.... [Robert L. Heilbroner, *The Worldly Philosophers* (Time Inc., Book Division, 1962), pp. 129, 130.]

Thus the importance of the Reform Bill of 1867 and the enlargement of the suffrage for those who had never voted nor been politically represented before was that voting was the only way into "the ruling portion of the community" and the only way to insure a just distribution of society's wealth.

But while the Reform Bill of 1867 succeeded in enfranchising a million new voters, the bill failed in another respect. The vote was still denied to the urban poor, domestic servants, most agricultural workers and, of course, women. Under Harriet Taylor's influence and from his own profound sense of social justice, John Mill had been one of the earliest champions of women's rights. He proposed an amendment to give the vote to all women who satisfied the same qualifications required of their male counterparts. Mill's amendment failed but his spirited defense of it was to have far-reaching repercussions. For the interest that his amendment generated helped to launch the movement that spawned the National Society for Women's Suffrage which remained in the forefront of the later women's rights movement. But it would take another fifty years, unmitigated brutality, martyrdom, and a world war to make Mill's dream of the suffrage for women a reality.

We turn next to the way of philosophy as seen by universalistic ethical hedonists, i.e., utilitarians, such as John Stuart Mill.

THE WAY OF UTILITARIANISM: JOHN STUART MILL

The Problem

The problem that Mill sought to solve and the question he sought to answer remains the one with which we have been concerned all along, viz., What is the best and most worthwhile life that a human being can live? For Mill that problem expressed itself both personally and publicly through the human suffering that he found in the lives of the working men and women whom he represented in Parliament and in the industrial society of 19th century England.

The Cause

The cause of the suffering at both the individual and societal levels for Mill lay in the inadequate distribution of material goods in the society, i.e., in the hideous poverty of Victorian England. The cause of that economic cause, in turn, was political, viz., the inadequate representation of those who suffered most in society and who lacked the right to vote.

The Solution

The solution to the problems of inadequate political representation and inadequate economic distribution lay in devising laws that would guarantee the greatest happiness for the greatest number. The solution to the problem of the best and most worthwhile life that a person can live lay in living one's life so as to increase the sum total of personal and public happiness in that life.

The Way

The way to the solution of happiness lay in getting at the economic and political causes of the problem of human suffering. For John Mill this way involved adopting utilitarianism as a philosophy of life and so living one's life as to insure the greatest happiness for the greatest number of people.

PROBLEMS WITH MILL

John Mill leaves us with two problems that affect the adequacy of his way of philosophy. The first of these problems relates to the criterion of common sense, call it "the problem of misrepresentation." Mill has assumed repeatedly throughout his *Utilitarianism* that in Christian ethics "we read the complete spirit of the ethics of utility." He goes on to say,

"To do as you would be done by, and to love your neighbor as yourself, constitute the ideal perfection of utilitarian morality." [John Stuart Mill, *Utilitarianism* in *The English Philosophers From Bacon to Mill, Op. Cit.*, p. 908.] Granted that, on the whole, following the ethics of Jesus of Nazareth will lead to the greatest happiness of the greatest number, suppose that it does not. What must the moral Christian do then that the moral utilitarian must not? For suppose that by *not* loving my neighbor as myself I could increase the general happiness. What then? Or suppose I believe that killing is wrong, that to take a human life is contrary to the commandment that we love one another. But suppose that by my killing Jones, a terrorist about to kill ten people, I can save their lives and thereby increase the general happiness. The Christian moralist would have to maintain that the action is eternally and absolutely wrong in an ethic that commands us to love our enemies and to do good to them that persecute us: Killing another human being is wrong and ought not to be done though the heavens fall and earth's foundations depart. The utilitarian, however, would have to maintain that the action in this instance is right. Mill has forgotten that the ethics of Jesus of Nazareth is an *absolutist* ethics; this means that given two contradictory moral choices, to kill or not to kill, only one can be right; and for this kind of Christian, since killing is wrong, not to kill is the only right choice. But Mill's ethics is a *relativist* ethics; this means that given two contradictory moral choices both can be right; killing is right in this context because the general happiness will be increased; but killing could be wrong given another context. For the Christian absolutist it is the moral nature of the acts themselves that are eternal and unchanging; for the utilitarian relativist only the principle of utility seems to be eternal and unchanging, founded as it is on human nature, itself. Mill in discussing Christianity has forgotten this simple common sense point about the difference between these two moral points of view.

The second problem violates the criteria of consistency for an adequate way of philosophy. The problem is called "the paradox of hedonism." While Mill recognized the problem, he did not regard it as serious enough to endanger utilitarianism; but he did regard it as serious enough to bring out his own solution to the paradox. Ethical hedonism had maintained that the only thing good in itself is pleasure and that, consequently, it is our duty to pursue, or try to maximize, pleasure. If anything else is called "good" or "valuable" or "worthwhile," it is only because it leads to pleasure, i.e., these other things are only "instrumentally good," they are not, like pleasure, "ultimately good." So why are love, knowledge, self-sacrifice, honor, wealth, and so on good? Because, the ethical hedonist answers, they lead to pleasure. So we ought to, we have a duty to, pursue, or go after, or attempt to get, as much pleasure or happiness as possible. But, and here's the paradox,* those who go after pleasure will never achieve it. Pleasure is not an object or goal that you can pursue directly. Pleasure is a by-product of doing something else, and doing it well. When you leave your house in the evening and someone asks you where you're going, you don't say, I'm going out to look for happiness. Happiness can never be an object of a search as Mill, himself, recognized and therein lies the paradox: Those who search for happiness will never find it. Mill states the problem and offers a solution:

> I never, indeed, wavered in the conviction that happiness is the test of all rules of conduct, and the end of life. But I now thought that this end was only to be attained by not making it the direct end. *Those only are happy (I thought) who have their minds fixed on some object other than their own happiness; on the happiness of others, on the improvement of mankind,* even on some art or pursuit, followed not as a means, but as itself an ideal end. *Aiming thus at something else, they find happiness by the way....* Ask yourself whether you are happy, and you cease to be so. The only chance is to treat, not happiness, but some end external to it, as the purpose of life. [John Stuart Mill, *Autobiography of John Stuart Mill* (New York: Columbia University Press, 1873/1924), pp. 99-100.]

In other words, happiness or pleasure to be got must be forgot. And here the paradox is seen in all its glory: The aim of hedonism is the attainment of pleasure, but to make pleasure the aim makes it impossible to attain.

The criterion of consistency seems affronted by the paradox for we are told in effect that a goal is not a goal and that there will be a practical frustration in attempting to realize that goal directly. But in saying that pleasure or happiness cannot be pursued directly, aren't we also saying that utilitarianism, which regards pleasure as the only goal worth pursuing, is impossible of attainment as well? For if the only way I can reach happiness is to forget about it and do something else, then what sense is there in regarding pleasure as the only ultimate good?

The real problem may lie in the utilitarian's curious insistence that happiness and pleasure are identical. This surely violates common sense. Many would feel that happiness transcends pleasure or that happiness may include other goods besides pleasure, goods like love, knowledge, beauty, honor, and truth. In fact, 20th century utilitarians like G.E. Moore

---

* "Paradox" is defined as "any statement seemingly contradictory or absurd yet in fact true."

have adopted a position called "ideal utilitarianism" which argues that pleasure is, indeed, not the only ultimate good of mankind but that other goods are equally intrinsically valuable and just as worthy of pursuit.

One of the harshest critics of the way of utilitarianism, as well as of the modern industrial age in which that way played such an important role, was the German philosopher, Frederich Nietzsche. That way and that age will now become targets of Nietzsche's sarcastic jibes and insightful criticisms. Nietzsche's influence will be felt, in turn, by the greatest existentialist of the 20th century, Jean Paul Sartre. We turn next to these two philosophers and to their attempts to answer Aristotle's question about the best and most worthwhile life.

TEN

THE WAYS OF EXISTENTIAL NOTHINGNESS

Frederich Nietzsche and Jean Paul Sartre: The Death of God and Its Aftermath

The Age of Nihilism

Frederich Nietzsche proclaimed to the 19th century and to the modern world that God was dead. In a never-to-be-forgotten passage published in 1882, Nietzsche put God's obituary in the form of a parable about a madman:

> Have you not heard of that madman who lit a lantern in the bright morning hours, ran to the marketplace, and cried incessantly, "I seek God! I seek God!" As many of those who do not believe in God were standing around just then, he provoked much laughter. Why, did he get lost? said one. Did he lose his way like a child? said another. Or is he hiding? Is he afraid of us? Has he gone on a voyage? or emigrated? Thus they yelled and laughed. The madman jumped into their midst and pierced them with his glances.
>
> "Whither is God?," he cried. "I shall tell you. *We have killed him*—you and I. All of us are his murderers.... God is dead. God remains dead. And we have killed him. How shall we, the murderers of all murderers, comfort ourselves?... Whither are we moving now? Away from all suns? Are we not plunging continually? Backward, sideward, forward, in all directions? Is there any up or down left? Are we not straying as through an infinite nothing? [*The Gay Science*, in *The Portable Nietzsche*, Edited and translated by Walter Kaufmann (Penguin Books, 1984), p. 95.]

Nietzsche's prophetic madman proclaims the dawning of the age of nihilism, of nothingism.

The death of God is the death of everything for which the concept of God had stood in previous ages. God had been absolute truth, absolute goodness and absolute beauty; for ages past epistemology, ethics and aesthetics had been securely founded on the Source of all three assumptive absolutes: God had been the one and only absolute reality.

But now the modern age, the industrial age, as Karl Marx and Søren Kierkegaard had both so clearly recognized, had replaced all absolutes with relatives, transcendent truth and value with private truths and temporal values, a traditional moral code with personal greed and collective selfishness, a goal of spiritual change with the bourgeois goals of wealth, security and success. The new truth entailed getting your neighbor before he got you; the new goodness lay in getting as much for yourself as possible; the new beauty was found in the bewitching color of money. And it was the industrial revolution that made all this possible, reinforced, as Kierkegaard, Marx and Nietzsche would all agree, by Christendom, the Christian-bourgeois values of the new industrial age. All three critics knew of the death of God and all three saw with horror the approach of the age of nihilism.

Three Choices for the Age of Nihilism

The question that must be posed in this age of new truth, new goodness and new beauty is this: What is the best and most worthwhile life that a human being can live in the age of nihilism? For what will the men and women of the age of nihilism do when they discover that God is dead?, that the traditional and absolute Source for all values is gone? What are the possibilities for us, for the men and women trapped in the age of nihilism?

Three alternatives have been proposed to fill the value vacuum made by the discovery of the death of God: First, there is the way of initial despair and of final suicide at finding that there is no objective and absolute source for one's beliefs. If God is dead, the pessimistic, despairing suicide says, then I don't want to, and I cannot, go on living. As with the experience of the death of a beloved parent, the realization that God is dead can lead to despair and suicide. The suicidal way out lies through drugs, alcohol, and self-destruction, through giving up on life just as life seems to have given up on the innocent victim. Albert Camus, a modern French existentialist philosopher, arguing that the search for the meaning of life is the most urgent of all quests, comments on the discovery of the meaninglessness of life following the revelation that God is dead:

...in a universe suddenly divested of illusions and lights, man feels an alien, a stranger. His exile is without remedy since he is deprived of the memory of a lost home [the Garden of Eden] or the hope of a promised land [Heaven]. This divorce between man and his life, the actor and his setting, is properly the feeling of absurdity. All healthy men having thought of their own suicide, it can be seen... that there is a direct connection between this feeling and the longing for death. [Albert Camus, *The Myth of Sisyphus*, Translated by Justin O'Brien (London: Hamish Hamilton, 1955), p. 13.]

Suicide is one way out of the despairing realization of the absurdity of life, its essential emptiness and ridiculousness.

Second, there is the way of the new absolutes. In Fyodor Dostoevsky's great novel of 1880, *The Brothers Karamazov*, the discovery is made that if God is dead then all things are lawful:

But what will become of men then?, without God and immortal life? all things are lawful then, and they can do what they like. Didn't you know, a clever man can do what he likes? [Fyodor Dostoevsky, *The Brothers Karamazov*, Translation Revised by Ralph E. Matlaw (New York: W.W. Norton & Company, 1976), p. 558.]

This is the way of the clever man, the selfish man, who seeks the meaning of his or her own existence by pursuing the new absolutes that have taken the place of God; these new absolutes have their origin in the state, in the new religions, in the worship of the physical body, and in the pursuit of wealth and material success. For example, the 20th century has been witness to the spectacle of the rise of nationalism and the new political gods of Nazism, Fascism and Collectivism; to the T.V. evangelisms, and the hopes of the new religions, to the self-help philosophies of est, of primal scream, of Krishna consciousness and the yogas of East and West; to the new fanatical interest in bodily health, through jogging, dieting, health foods and clubs giving us a whole new vocabulary with words like "life-style," "wellness," "bulimia" and "anorexia"; to quite new economic classes of success-through-wealth oriented young professionals and another new vocabulary with words like "Yuppies" and "Dinks" ("Double income, no kids"). The clever man and woman can find God-replacements everywhere, and the new rule is that anything goes as long as it turns you on.

Third, there is the way of the existentialist who, realizing that the old value system is dead, resolves to recreate his or her own value system, and to accept the intellectual and moral consequences of that re-creation. The existentialist is, in this sense, both a true humanist who affirms an identical and common nature uniting all mankind, and a true individualist who recognizes that one's human nature can emerge only when one has confronted the new nihilism and decided neither to run from it nor to adopt any of the prevailing fads of the clever man. Instead, the existentialist, following Kierkegaard or Nietzsche, makes a momentous decision to recreate his or her own life out of, but apart from, the surrounding and prevailing nihilism. The existentialist, alone and solitary in the act of making this choice, affirms that those values that are created out of the confrontation with personal and intimate human existence are the only genuine and truly authentic values.

The existentialist rejects the way of suicide that aborts all values, as well as the way of the new absolutes that leads to slavery to someone else's values. Instead, the way of existentialism adopts a path between these other extremes. The way calls for a daily creation of and re-evaluation of one's own values. It is a way that has its beginnings, as we shall see, in Nietzsche's madman and that has its fulfillment in the philosophic way of Jean Paul Sartre.

Frederich Nietzsche (1844-1900): The Evolution of His Thought

Friederich Wilhelm Nietzsche (hereafter sometimes abbreviated "F.N.") was born in Rocken, Prussia on October 15, 1844. His birthday coincided with that of the reigning monarch, Frederick William IV, and he was joyfully and patriotically named after the king. Years later F.N. was to remark, "There was at least one advantage to the choice of this day: my birthday was a holiday throughout my childhood." [*Ecce Homo* ("Behold the Man") in *Basic Writings of Nietzsche*, Translated by Walter Kaufmann (Modern Library, 1968), p. 682.] F.N.'s father was a Lutheran pastor who died when his son was four. Left in the care of a grandmother, a mother, two aunts and a sister, the young Fritz was raised, adored and spoiled by all five females.

Confirmed in the Lutheran Church at the age of 16, F.N., like Søren Kierkegaard before him, planned on an eventual career in the ministry. But something happened in the next two years that made him change his mind. He lost interest in his high school classes and began to doubt the existence of God as well as his own purpose in life.

Entering the University of Bonn he gave vent to all of his religious and vocational doubts and to his feelings of being oppressed by the five females who had reared him. Turning to alcohol, women and dissipation, F.N. tried to lose himself in the manly student sports of the day that included dueling. But he was really disgusted by the noisy, smoky, hedonistic, boisterous student scene. Bonn and all that he encountered there oppressed him and brought on one of the many emotional crises that he was to experience throughout his long and lonely life. In October 1865 F.N. left Bonn for the University of Leipzig.

At Leipzig Nietzsche turned his attentions to the study of classical languages, an area in which he had always excelled. He became an outstanding pupil winning prizes in essays and scholarship, and he became a favored student and friend of the famous philologist, Professor Friedrich Ritschl. But he also discovered another great man who was to influence his thinking even more profoundly, the German philosopher Arthur Schopenhauer (1788-1860).

Arthur Schopenhauer, Romanticism and Will

Nietzsche at this time, like the Buddha before him, reluctantly renounced the security and comfort of the God and the religion of his childhood; he had already tried the life of unrestrained pleasure and had met disappointment, once again. Life for the bright young scholar seemed vain and futile. But one day in late October 1865 he found his savior. In a bookstore in Leipzig he came across a copy of Schopenhauer's *The World as Will and Representation*. The book began with the arresting assertion that the world "is my representation," i.e., the world is what *I* will make it, and F.N. was hooked. He took the book home and read it through:

> It seemed as if Schopenhauer were addressing me personally. I felt his enthusiasm, and seemed to see him before me. Every line cried aloud for renunciation, denial, resignation. Here I saw a mirror in which the world, life, my own mind were reflected in fearful grandeur. Here the wholly disinterested and heavenly eye of art looked at me; here I saw illness and salvation, banishment and refuge, hell and heaven. [Quoted in the Introduction of W. A. Haussmann's translation of *The Birth of Tragedy* by Friedrich Nietzsche (New York: Russell & Russell, 1964), p. xvii.]

Agreeing with Schopenhauer that *will*, the blind natural force of the universe, and not reason, is the essence of life, F.N. began to see that such a force is cruel, mindless and all-powerful, and that life is strife and hardship, a war for survival.

The German Romantic movement, as exemplified in Schopenhauer, exalted feeling, instinct, and nature, and denigrated reason, logic and civilization. It affected Nietzsche profoundly, and he came to find comfort in the wild savagery of the forces of nature. One day as a storm threatened he climbed a hill. At the top he found a man slaughtering two lambs. Just then the storm broke and standing there surrounded by hail, thunder, lightning, wind and slaughter he reflected on how trivial his personal problems were:

> How different lightning, storms and hail are—free forces, amoral. How happy and how powerful they are; pure will with no intellect to oppress them. [Ronald Hayman, *Nietzsche, A Critical Life* (Penguin Books, 1982), p. 77.]

He had, like Schopenhauer, come to identify 'will' with 'force,' a concept that he will elaborate upon in his first book, *The Birth of Tragedy*. He began to agree further with Schopenhauer that all that a man can do when faced with the realization that existence is nothing but blind and unreasoning will is to resign himself dumbly to it. At twenty-one F.N. was becoming both a pessimist and a renunciate.

As a student, he helped to form a new philology club at the University of Leipzig. As a project for his club, he read an essay on the poems of Theognis to the group. Later he showed his work to Ritschl who was impressed by the rigor and thought of the youthful effort. He became a doctoral candidate under Ritschl and so overwhelmed was the older man with his pupil's abilities that when in 1868 a chair in classical philology became vacant at the University of Basel in Switzerland, he managed to secure the appointment for F.N. The brilliant and youthful 24 year old Schopenhauerian became an associate professor of Greek in January 1869, and the University of Leipzig quickly granted him a doctorate three months later.

Richard Wagner, Dionysus, and Apollo

The year 1869 marked the beginning of a friendship for F.N. with one of the world's greatest composers, Richard Wagner. It was to have permanent and tragic consequences for both of them. Richard Wagner was not yet the internationally famous musical genius that he was soon to become but his intelligence and dynamism appealed to F.N. when they had first met in Leipzig the previous year. In May he went to visit the composer and his wife, Cosima, at the Swiss village of Tribschen. F.N. became a constant and welcome visitor, listening to the composer's work, expostulating to them (and they to him) on the death of Western culture and the philosophies of the will, feeling and force, falling hopelessly in love with Cosima, and making himself useful all around. The Wagners found an exciting, brilliant and devoted friend at a time when one was desperately needed (Cosima had run away from her first husband), and F.N. found a loving home and a caring family at an equally critical period in his own development. But this friendship between these two monumentally egoistic geniuses was doomed from the start.

Nietzsche's first book, *The Birth of Tragedy Out of the Spirit of Music*, was written during this period and published in 1871. In it he attempted to interpret Greek art and life as a conflict between two opposing forces symbolized by the Greek Gods Dionysus, the God of wine, passion, and joyfulness, and Apollo, the God of reason, restraint and order.

The Dionysian force, he argued, is the life force; it is the feeling, desire, and instinct that lies behind all creative change, that drives men to love, to conquest and to mystical ecstasy.

The Apollonian force, on the other hand, is the force that shapes and gives form to changing and chaotic existence; it is philosophy and science imposing sense, meaning and order onto life experiences and the booming, buzzing confusion of daily existence.

The Dionysian force is the intuitive *yin* of Taoism, the dynamic *rajas guna* of Hinduism, and the ceaseless change and flow of life in the philosophy of Heraclitus.

The Apollonian force is the rational *yang* of Taoism, the wisely illuminating *sattva guna* of Hinduism, and the ordering principle of the One in the philosophy of Parmenides.

It is the conflict between, and the eventual joining and balancing of, these two forces, the Dionysian and the Apollonian, that will ultimately give birth to Greek tragedy:

> These two different tendencies [the Apollonian which is best exemplified in the art of sculpture and the Dionysian which is best exemplified in the art of music] run parallel to each other, for the most part openly at variance; and they continually incite each other to new and more powerful births, which perpetuate an antagonism, only superficially reconciled by the common term "art"; till eventually, by a metaphysical miracle of the Hellenic "will," they appear coupled with each other, and through this coupling ultimately generate an equally Dionysian and Apollonian form of art - attic [Hellenic] tragedy. [*The Birth of Tragedy* in *Basic Writings of Nietzsche, Op. Cit.*, p. 33. The idea of Dionysus in F. N.'s later thought will come to stand for the affirmation of life and the positive employment of the passions in creativity in contrast to the Christian negation of life and the suppressing of the passions as vile and sinful.]

In the beginning, the Dionysian spirit dominated Greek art and life from the 8th to the 5th centuries B.C. The epics of Homer, the philosophies of pre-Socratic Greece, the dramas of Aeschylus, and the very soul of ancient Athens were shot through with the exuberance and joy of the dancing and intoxicating spirit of Dionysus. But, gradually, the

Apollonian spirit came to dominate. Greek culture became ordered, restrained, balanced and harmonized. Reason and logic entered and Greek enthusiasm and culture died.

It was Socrates and Plato who instigated this civicide and it was they who best exemplified this death of Greek civilization through their intellectual influence. Socrates, in equating knowledge with virtue, and Plato, in arguing that the man with knowledge can do no wrong, placed intellect above will, placed reason above the passions, put the creative, the affirmative and the instinctive into the judgmental hands of the critical, the negative and the restrictive conscious mind. It made instinct evaluative and consciousness creative, reversing the natural order of matters and subordinating the most valuable. It only remained for Plato to argue that that which was not rational was not real, and that only the real was worthy of pursuit, understanding, and emulation. Logic had triumphed, but Greek musical drama, i.e., Hellenic tragedy, had died. [For a discussion of the distinction between the Western mind and the Eastern mind paralleling these same properties, see below Chapter 13, *The Ways of Individualism and Community*, pp. 277-280.]

It was this discovery and the fear that history was now repeating itself that turned F.N. into the enemy of the science, the religion and the philosophy of the industrial age. "My philosophy-," he cried, "[is] inverted Platonism: the further away from True Being, the purer, more beautiful and better it is." [Quoted in Ronald Hayman, *Nietzsche: A Critical Life, Op. Cit.*, p. 137.] Modern existentialism was born.

The soul-withering Apollonian tradition that insinuated itself into the Platonic world of 5th century Athens has continued into the modern world. It will be F.N.'s task to reverse this tradition, and to call attention to the new artists and thinkers who show signs of this reversing tendency. In this sense he believed that both Richard Wagner in music and himself, as the prophet Zarathustra in philosophy, will bring the Dionysian passion back into the 19th century and rise above the heritage of Apollonian logic, order and reason that had seduced it. Thus we can be comforted, F.N. writes at the conclusion of *The Birth of Tragedy*,

> by indications that nevertheless in some inaccessible abyss the German [i.e., "Dionysian"] spirit still rests and dreams, undestroyed, in glorious health, profundity, and Dionysian strength, like a knight sunk in slumber.... [*The Birth of Tragedy* in *Basic Writings of Nietzsche, Op. Cit.*, p. 142.]

It is Wagner, of course, who must and who will continue to awaken this slumbering Dionysian giant through his operas. They not only combined music with tragic drama, thereby bringing the greatness of the Hellenic past into the modern world, but in recalling the Teutonic mythology of exquisitely suffering heroes and heroines they invited all of those who were able to experience and to emulate.

F.N.'s future aims were now becoming clear. His task was "not the betterment of the majority, who taken as individuals are the most worthless type," but instead "the creation of genius, the development and elevation of superior personalities" of whom the Dionysian man is the ideal. ["Schopenhauer as Educator" #6, in *Thoughts Out of Season* II, Translated by Adrian Collins (New York: Russell & Russell, 1964.]

But Richard Wagner was not to remain F.N.'s ideal Dionysian creator for long. Wagner, according to Nietzsche, soon sold out to the crude and boorish tastes of the decadent age. The break with Wagner was a gradual affair, extending over many months. It may have begun in January 1878 when Wagner sent to his young friend the text of a new opera, *Parsifal*, a work about a religious quest and spiritual transformation. Wagner's feelings toward organized religion had been growing of late. His own personal religious experiences and his felt pleasures in the ceremonies of the Protestant church had gradually turned Wagner into a religious man. When F.N. read the text of *Parsifal*, his terse reaction to what he observed as a sell-out to the vulgar churchy tastes of the masses was predictable:

> More Liszt [Franz Liszt (1811-1886), a Hungarian composer and pianist, Wagner's father-in-law, and a notorious religious pietist.] than Wagner— spirit of the Counter-Reformation... it is all too Christian, time-bound, limited; purely fantastic psychology; no flesh and far too much blood (especially at the Holy Communion).... The dialogue sounds like a translation from a foreign language. [Ronald Hayman, *Op. Cit.*, p. 192.]

During this period of the break with the Wagners, F.N.'s health began to seriously deteriorate. Headaches, which he had had since childhood, suddenly began to increase, accompanied by unstoppable bloody vomiting, acute barrages of anxiety, fevers, hemorrhoids, constipation, chills, cramps, night sweats, and swollen eyes. The migraine attacks, for so they were diagnosed, and hypersensitivity to light, and a blindness that began to rob him of three-fourths of his eyesight, now confined him to bed for days and then for weeks at a time as the pain and vomiting would continue unabated. In May 1879 at the age of thirty-four he resigned from the University of Basel. Nearly blind, he was about to begin a life-long search for a cure for his illnesses, a search that would end only with the onset of insanity in 1889 and a tragic but merciful death in 1900.

With Wagner removed from the list of heroes who might have brought honesty and value back into the world, F.N. turned to a hero of his own creation. From 1883 until 1885 Nietzsche worked on and published the work for which he is probably most famous, *Thus Spoke Zarathustra*. It is the chief source that we have for F.N.'s way of philosophy and his answer to the question, What is the best and most worthwhile life that a human being can live?

Zarathustra As the Best and Most Worthwhile Life

Zarathustra is F.N.'s alter ego. The hero is named after the ancient Persian prophet Zoroaster, but the voice and heart are those of Nietzsche. Zarathustra is a savior who preaches self-overcoming, an anti-Jesus figure who speaks of a future in which mankind will have reached salvation but without supernatural or divine aid. *Zarathustra*, the book, is a humanist manifesto for a race that has discovered that while God is dead, all is not lost.

The prophet Zarathustra at forty years of age comes down out of the mountains and from the cave where he has been living in solitude for ten years. Like Moses before him, he brings with him a message for mankind, new rules of behavior backed by a new code of values; but unlike the Mosaic rules and code, this one has no divine origin and it is in many respects the very reversal of the Judeo-Christian ethic. Zarathustra is trying to establish a new religion.

He comes announcing that God is dead and he comes preaching the gospel of the "Overman." He gives his first sermon to a mob of people gathered in a crowded market place:

> I teach you the Overman ("*übermensch*"). Man is something that shall be overcome. What have you done to overcome him? [*Thus Spoke Zarathustra* I. 3, in *The Portable Nietzsche, Op. Cit.*, p. 124.]

Zarathustra cautions his incredulous listeners to remain faithful to the earth and to ignore those "despisers of life" who speak of trans-earthly hopes. Man, Zarathustra maintains, is only a bridge to this future being, the Overman, who will succeed man and man's estate in this world. Compare these new Zarathustrian commandments with the older and more familiar ones:

> But if you have an enemy, do not repay evil with good: for that is shaming. Rather show that he did something good to you.
>
> And rather feel anger than shame. And if you are cursed, it is displeasing to me if you want to bless. It is better to join in the cursing a little.
>
> And if you are greatly wronged, commit five small wrongs quickly. It is not pleasant to see all the wrong on one side....

> A little revenge is more human than no revenge. And unless a penalty is
> also a privilege for the transgressor, I do not like your punishment.
> It is nobler to declare oneself wrong than right, especially when one is right,
> only one must be rich enough for that. I do not like your cold justice.
> The eye of the judge glints with the cold steel of the executioner. ["On
> the Adder's Bite," *Ibid.*, p. 180.]

The rules and the code of values behind it reflect the sound psychological foundations of the new religion. The advice is simple, practical
and natural. And compared to Jesus' Sermon on the Mount in *The Gospel
of St. Matthew* [See below pp. 260-261.], Zarathustra's rules appear to be
not only reasonable but eminently practicable. The new religion seems
off to a good morally common sensical start.

Starting a New Religion: Confucius and Lao-Tzu

A similar beginning of another "new" religion is related in the
Chinese tradition concerning a debate between Confucius and Lao-tzu
(about 6th to 5th Century B.C.). Confucius is here seen as the protector of
the old values and ideals of the society. Lao-tzu, a founder of the new
Taoist religion, is the upstart and common-sense realist, out to challenge
the plainly impracticable ethic sanctioned for decades by the older
Confucian absolutists:

> "Tell me," said Lao-tzu, "in what consist charity and duty to one's neigh-
> bor?"
>
> "They consist," answered Confucius, "in a capacity for rejoicing in all
> things; in universal love, without the element of self. These are the charac-
> teristics of charity and duty to one's neighbor."
>
> "What a lot of nonsense!" cried Lao-tzu. "Does not universal love contradict
> itself? Is not your elimination of self a positive manifestation of self?" [H.A.
> Giles, *Chuang-tzu* (Shanghai: Kelly & Walsh, 1926). Quoted in Alan Watts,
> *The Way of Zen* (Pantheon Books, Inc., 1957), p. 26.]

Lao-tzu goes on to make the same existential point that F.N. is making in
Zarathustra, viz., leave off these abstractions, get back to existing particulars, existing realities. The founder of Taoism concludes:

> Why these vain struggles after charity and duty to one's neighbor, as though
> beating a drum in search of a fugitive. Alas! Sir, you have brought much
> confusion into the mind of man. [*Ibid.*]

F.N. has found a similar confusion being peddled by the modern purvey-
ors of Christian morality in his own devastating critique of conventional

virtue. The old values are no longer sufficient for the tremendous task at hand. In their own ways both Lao-tzu and Frederich Nietzsche are calling for a new religion, a transvaluation of all previous values. That is Zarathustra's message for the 20th century.

Christianity and Resentment

F.N., like Lao-tzu before him, had hit upon a telling psychological point about any universalistic ethics that demands of all humans an attitude that goes contrary to "the earth," i.e., to common sense. To demand, as the Christian ethic does, that everyone be loved, that enemies be forgiven, that immoral conduct be forgiven and the immoralist be loved, and that revenge and retaliation and even self-defense be renounced, all of this may be, in itself, curiously noble but it produces consequences of a most unhealthy sort. What F. N. had discovered, and here he goes beyond the mere "confusion" pointed to by Lao-tzu, is that suppressed violent energies give birth to repressed psychological feelings more violent than the actions that would have initially issued from those energies. Suppressed violent energies in the case of relations to one's enemies and wrongs done to oneself can lead to repressed resentment towards others and guilt and shame towards onesself.

Suppose that in anger you strike me across the face. I want to strike back; it's a natural response. But my Christian code tells me to turn the other cheek. So I suppress my anger, and magnanimously forgive you. Now what happens? My anger is still there. I resent you for what you have not allowed me to do, i.e., to strike back. And I feel guilt and shame that I still what to strike back: I feel resentment and not love for you. Zarathustra cries out:

> The spirit of revenge, my friends, has so far been the subject of man's best reflection; and where there was suffering, one always wanted punishment, too.
>
> For 'punishment' is what revenge calls itself; with a hypocritical lie it creates a good conscience for itself.
>
> [*Thus Spoke Zarathustra*, "On Redemption," *The Portable Nietzsche, Op. Cit.*,p. 252.]

The violent energies are left to fester and grow and to await a more appropriate time to emerge, a time where the code won't get in the way to bar revenge and release the guilt. F.N. was neither a Jesus, nor a Gandhi, nor a Martin Luther King, Jr. But he left a warning about the psychology of non-violence and forgiveness and universal love that bears attention even today.

There is yet another side to this attack on Christian morality and virtue. To practice humility, charity and love when one has no other alternative, when one is too weak to retaliate, is not only hypocritical and base but dangerous, for those practices, too, lead to resentment, hatred and guilt. Outlets for all of this repressed resentment lay, F.N. discovered, through the legal and metaphysical punishments of one's enemies. What one cannot do privately, because the code of Christ prohibits it, one can do publicly and respectably by creating wonderfully acceptable Hells and prisons. Christianity was the visible sign of the unconscious workings of massive resentment. Thus it was, F.N. argued, that Christianity emerged as the major punishment-dominated religion of the modern world, a religion of the weak, of the impotent, of the hypocritical, of the slave. God was indeed dead and this religion of resentment had taken its place.

F.N.'s task now is to establish a new religion that will answer the question, What is the best and most worthwhile life that a human being can live? The old ethic, the old religion, is dead; philosophic, religious and moral nihilism has triumphed. Nothing in the Appolonian dominated Judeo-Christian tradition can answer the questions about reality, value and beauty since all of the answers it had offered have proven to lead to either violence to oneself or to others.

The new religion, the religion of the Overman, will be approached from two paths: F.N. will continue his critique of the older Apollonian resentment-dominated Christian tradition while at the same time continuing to develop his own positive way of philosophy. These two paths, the critical and the creative, the negative and the positive, are inseparable, really, and nowhere is this inseparability more evident than in one of F.N.'s last writings, *Geneology of Morals*, published in 1887.

The Triumph of Slave Morality
Over Master Morality

Geneology of Morals, as the title suggests, is an attempt to discover the origin of morality. In the Preface to the *Geneology*, F.N. raises the question as to whether it might be the case that morality and moral values, themselves, are responsible for the fact that full human potential is never in fact realized, i.e., that our moral values are what prevent us from overcoming ourselves and realizing ourselves, i.e., the values that we hold are responsible for the mess that we're in:

> So that precisely morality would be to blame if the *highest power and splendor* actually possible to the type man was never in fact attained? So that

precisely morality was the danger of dangers? [*On the Geneology of Morals*, in *Basic Writings of Nietzsche, Op. Cit.*,p. 456.]

Nietzsche's thesis is that a master morality of the highest possible ideals, presided over by the best and noblest souls in society, was present in the early history of the West, but that that superior morality was subsequently subverted by a slave morality of ignoble ideals. This slave morality and its origins, not surprisingly, are now most clearly seen in the values of the Judeo-Christian tradition and in the history of that tradition in the West. The mob and the slaves have won, their values have triumphed and therein lies the cause of the problem that F.N. is seeking to solve. That triumph has its origin in what F.N. refers to by its French name, "*ressentiment*," i.e., resentment, and in the common man's reaction to a hostile world composed chiefly of those better than himself. The *ressentiment* welled up in those who were impotent and incapable of retaliation; *ressentiment* is their imaginary revenge against that hostile world of superior beings:

> While the noble man lives in trust and openness with himself, the man of *ressentiment* is neither upright nor naive nor honest and straightforward with himself. His soul squints; his spirit loves hiding places, secret paths and back doors... he understands how to keep silent, how not to forget, how to wait, how to be provisionally self-deprecating and humble. [*Geneology of Morals* 10 *Ibid.*, p. 474.]

And it is these men of *ressentiment* who have sought to impose their sick values on others.

In an earlier work of 1886, *Beyond Good and Evil*, F.N. had first spoken of the moral nature of these men of *ressentiment*. In doing so he had given the world a new vocabulary to distinguish their values, *herdenmoral*, "herd morality," or "slave morality," from the values of their moral superiors, *herrenmoral*, "master morality." Slave morality, of course, is the Christian morality of the masses into whose bones and fiber the obsequious spirit of *ressentiment* has seeped. In a famous passage in *Beyond Good and Evil*, F.N. distinguishes these two basic moralities and describes the two quite distinct owners of these moral qualities (though both qualities may be present, he states, in a single soul):

> The noble human being honors himself as one who is powerful, also as one who has power over himself, who knows how to speak and be silent, who delights in being severe and hard with himself and respects all severity and hardness. [*Beyond Good and Evil* ¶ 260. Translated by Walter Kaufmann (New York: Vintage Books, 1966), p. 205.]

The two outstanding characteristics of the noble man, the upholder of the master morality, that must be noted particularly are, first, that he believes in being severe with himself; and, second, that he is one who has power over himself. Whatever else F.N. may say later, or whatever F.N.'s detractors (and there are many) may say about him, it is important to keep these two characteristics in mind:

> Noble and courageous human beings who think that way are furthest removed from that morality which finds the distinction of morality precisely in pity, or in acting for others, or in disinterestedness.... [Ibid.]

While it is obvious that F.N. has contempt for slave morality, it by no means follows that he admires all of the qualities of master morality. What he does endorse, however, along with self-severity and self-over-coming, is clear:

> ...faith in oneself, pride in oneself, a fundamental hostility and irony against "selflessness," belong just as definitely to noble morality as does a slight disdain and caution regarding compassionate feelings and a "warm heart." [Ibid.]

All of this now stands in grand opposition to the ignoble man, the herd man, the practitioner of slave morality. F.N. begins with a question about this common man:

> Suppose the violated, the oppressed, suffering, unfree, who are uncertain of themselves and weary, moralize: what will their moral valuations have in common? [Ibid., p. 207.]

That is, what would the moral values be for all those who are filled with *ressentiment*?

> Probably, a pessimistic suspicion about the whole condition of man will find expression, perhaps a condemnation of man along with his condition. The slave's eye is not favorable to the virtues of the powerful: he is skeptical and suspicious, *subtly* suspicious, of all the "good" that is honored there —he would like to persuade himself that even their happiness is not genuine. [Ibid.]

There is a truth, no doubt, in what Nietzsche is saying. How often have we heard, "Money can't buy happiness?" Or that "a good education" or "being intelligent" can't make you happy. Doesn't the speaker reveal a resentment of his own in all this?, a resentment against the wealthy, the educated, and the intelligent? F.N. concludes citing some typical warm-fuzzy slave feelings:

> Conversely, those qualities are brought out and flooded with light which
> serve to ease existence for those who suffer: here pity, the complaisant and
> obliging hand, the warm heart, patience, industry, humility and friendliness
> are honored.... [*Ibid.*]

And they are honored by the masses and the herd, but not because they
are genuine and real, but because they come from a hypocritical heart
dominated by utility, self-ignorance, fear, and resentment:

> ...for here these [warm-fuzzies] are the most useful qualities and almost the
> only means for enduring the pressure of existence. Slave morality is essen-
> tially a morality of utility. [*Ibid.*]

Summary

Where do we stand now with Nietzsche? He announces, like
Zarathustra, that God is dead. The old religion, the old tradition, is gone
and all of the old aristocratic values have gone with it. The world is in
chaos as the slaves and the slave morality have come to dominate. Filled
with fear, hatred, and resentment from their previous treatment as infe-
riors, they are now in power and threaten civilization, itself. The age of
nihilism is upon us; darkness covers the land; wars, violence, and mass
destruction dominate the world. A new religion, a new philosophy, is
called for.

And here F.N. turns from his attack on the way of the mob to a positive statement of what is most needful in this time of nothingism, this age
of utter contempt for heroic values and courageous lives. Frederich
Nietzsche calls for nothing less than man's surpassing of himself.
Mankind is but a bridge to this new being, this Overman, who expects
much from himself, who is hard on himself, and who welcomes his own
suffering: Suffering and self-overcoming are the ways of this new man
who will hold off the coming of the holocaust that F.N., himself,
prophesied.

We turn now to F.N.'s way of philosophy as we attempt to pull together the several diverse threads that traverse the extremely diffuse
views of this most important thinker. F.N.'s aphoristic style makes sys-
tematization of these views especially difficult. But if we begin, as we
have with the other ways of philosophy in this book, by asking, What is
the problem that F.N. was trying to solve?, things ought to go well.

THE NEW WAY OF SELF-OVERCOMING:
FREDERICH NIETZSCHE

The Problem

Karl Jaspers (1883-1969), the great German existentialist and a man deeply influenced by the writings of both F.N. and Søren Kierkegaard, developed F.N.'s view that it was Christianity that was primarily responsible for the death of God. In 1938, just before the terror and violence of World War II broke over Germany, Europe and the world, Jaspers explored this view stating that because the "values offered by Christianity are mere fictions, the moment of their exposure must plunge man into a nothingness whose equal has never before been felt in all human history." [Karl Jaspers, *Nietzsche and Christianity* (New York: Henry Regnery Co., 1961), p. 15.] The "tremendous event" that was still on its way, the event prophesied by Nietzsche's madman in *The Gay Science* and by Zarathustra earlier, was to break with a terrible certainty throughout the length and breadth of the 20th century. This nothingness, the death of God, constitutes the problem for Nietzsche. It is the realization that all one's past values and the various beliefs about those values are entirely without foundation: And when the foundation goes, baby, it's a long way down.

The Cause

The cause of the nothingness is really a set of causes for F.N.: Christianity is certainly at the heart of the cause, but "Christianity" is a name for a lot of abuses for F.N. It is what Søren Kierkegaard has called "Christendom" and, in a more secular vein, it is what Karl Marx has called "alienation". The cause lies in the triumph of the slave morality together with the overwhelming of the Dionysian force in the world by the Apollonian force. The life-giving strength of Dionysus has been rendered impotent by reason, technology, science and logic. The corrupt, materialistic, vulgar, self-hating, envious practitioners of *ressentiment* had finally dominated: Mediocrity had triumphed. Herd politics, i.e., democracy; herd economics, i.e., communism and socialism; and herd morality, i.e., utilitarianism; and herd religion, i.e., Christianity, were all causes of the death of God, of the nothingness.

The Solution

The solution to the problem for F.N. would seem to involve reversing the forces of the Apollonian triumph, reducing the influence of the slave morality, and transcending the beliefs, practices and institutions of herd man. The solution for F.N. can probably be described as that of transcending the self, becoming the Overman and reestablishing in oneself the aristocratic ideals of courage, integrity, honor and self-discipline, that had been destroyed. But F.N. has no plan to reorganize society; he was no Karl Marx. His views were, in fact, closer to those of Søren Kierkegaard's. Both had focused on the existing individual and not on man in the mass, herd man. Each held that any change must come with that existing individual and not with abstract man. And each held that the way to that change lay in transcending the self: "I teach you the Overman. Man is something that must be surpassed," Zarathustra says. The Overman can be reached by a leap, a Kierkegaardian leap, over what we presently are. "Man (each of us now) is a rope stretched between the animal and the Overman — a rope over an abyss." That abyss is the nothingness that threatens to engulf us should we fail to pass over. "What is great about man," Zarathustra says, "is that he is a bridge and not a goal." The goal, the solution, is the Overman, one who has created himself, disciplined himself, to completeness and total freedom, the man of tolerance, not from weakness but from his own strength.

The Ways

The ways to self-transcendence, or to man-transcendence, is not through some process of biological evolution; Nietzsche was no Darwinian. His message was not to nor about man as a species; but it is a call, once again, to those who have ears to hear and eyes to see, i.e., it is a cry to and about the particular, existing individual. The history of the world has given us examples of superior men who have risen above themselves and become creators, first of themselves, and then of new values for the world. These superior men, men F.N. greatly admired, were Johann Wolfgang von Goethe, Heinrich Heine, Richard Wagner, Ludwig van Beethoven, Frederick the Great, and Napoleon Bonaparte. He even includes, at times, Caesar and Jesus (but not St. Paul whom he harshly criticizes). As far as the ways to this noble self-overcoming are concerned, F.N. seems to focus on two, viz., the way of eternal recurrence and the way of the will to power.

The Way of Eternal Recurrence

The way to the Overman lay in adopting the life of hardness and struggle and the love of suffering, two adoptions that have become F.N.'s trademark. The way to the Overman is exemplified for F.N. through following the rule of *amor fati*, the love of fate, the acceptance, the joyful, loving acceptance, of whatever happens to oneself. F.N. had become the Stoic philosopher *par excellence:* The Overman is the Stoic sage.

But it is not enough merely to accept life's hardships, sufferings and destiny, however joyfully adopted. Following the Stoics, once again, F.N. held that one must go further and actively will that whatever happens would happen again...and again. And this, ultimately, is what *amor fati* really comes to.

This joyful willing of the repetition of suffering rests upon a fine point in a theory of the cosmos that F.N. believed in and that is worth exploring. Nietzsche reasoned, just like the Stoics before him, that nature in an infinite time must eventually repeat itself. Consider this: If there are, as modern physics tells us, a finite number of atoms in the universe, then there can only be a finite number of non-duplicating arrangements of those atoms. Given the probable number of atoms at 10^{80}, the resultant number of such possible arrangements is obviously astronomically large. But before duplication of those arrangements occurs, the number of possible arrangements is finite. You're looking at one such arrangement right now: The universe's atoms at this instant are in one single configuration composed of you sitting reading this book, the table in front of you, together with trillions of other configurations of atoms in Madison, Mars and the Horse Nebula, all of which form part of this same moment's atomic arrangement of the universe. Further, if time is infinite, i.e., if time is without beginning and without end, then those finite arrangements must begin to repeat themselves eventually. In other words, this moment's identical arrangement of those 10^{80} atoms must, in infinite time, eventually occur again. And it must eventually occur again an infinite number of times, if time is, indeed, beginningless and endless. That is the theory of eternal recurrence.

F.N. was fascinated with the theory. And he argued that to be able to *will*, i.e., to fully and passionately want, this life, your life, to repeat itself over and over again, unchanged, an infinite number of times, is the true meaning of *amor fati*:

> My formula for the greatness of a human being is *amor fati*: that one wants nothing to be different — not forward, not backward, not in all eternity. Not

merely bear what is necessary, still less conceal it...but love it. [*Ecce Homo* (*Behold the* Man) 11.10 in Walter Kaufman, *Nietzsche, Philosopher, Psychologist, Anti- Christ*, Fourth Edition (Princeton University Press, 1974), p. 283.]

"The most scientific of all possible hypotheses," as F.N. called it, [Ronald Hayman, *Nietzsche, Op. Cit.*, p. 234.] had been transformed into the way of the Overman.

The Way of the Will to Power

Coupled with the way of eternal recurrence is a second way to the Overman, i.e., to the best and most worthwhile life. This is the will to overcome oneself through self-mastery, self-overcoming, or *sōphrosynē* as Plato called it. For F.N. self-mastery was merely power over the self, and the will to power was, consequently, the will to self-control. The Overman is the man who has willed power over himself.

Self-overcoming is accomplished through *sublimation*, the process of actively and consciously controlling and rechanneling vital energy into creative activities. One simply dislocates energy, the sexual drive, for example, and puts it to work in creative spiritual activities instead of in the sexual act. F.N. thereby anticipated the Austrian founder of psychoanalysis, Sigmund Freud (1856-1939) who was later to recognize the value of sublimation in the investigation of psychological processes. F.N. knew of its value in his own pursuit of the will to power over himself. "Ultimate power," Walter Kaufman writes, "consists in controlling, sublimating, and employing one's impulses — not in considering them evil and fighting them [as the Christian Church had advised for centuries]." [Walter Kaufmann, *Nietzsche, Philosopher, Psychologist, AntiChrist, Op. Cit.*, p. 253.]

The life of the Overman is the good life that unites and balances Dionysus and Apollo, a creative striving that gives form to itself. [*Ibid.*, p. 282.]. The good man, the man who has found the best and most worthwhile life, is the man who has, through disciplined effort and sacrifice, mastered his passions as Socrates and Goethe had done, and created himself. The Overman, as F.N. stated in his final and posthumous work, *The Will to Power*, is "the Roman Caesar with Christ's soul."

NIETZSCHE'S ACCOMPLISHMENTS

The Christian myth and the God that lay at its center were both dead. They had been slain, on the one hand, by an onslaught of modern, historical, Biblical criticism, all the theological and intellectual fashion in

the 19th and now in the 20th century; and they had been buried, on the other hand, by modern science, religion and democracy, by all the rational elements of an age of reason. But despite the mythicide, the deocide, and all the buryings, the need for redemption, for salvation, for finding the best and most worthwhile life, continued. The question that F.N. asked, and the one that 20th century men and women have been asking more and more insistently ever since, is, How can I be saved, if God is dead?

F.N. will probably be remembered for his psychological insights into the moral and religious hypocracies of the age of nihilism: His penetrating discovery that *ressentiment*, hatred, and envy are the offspring of weakness and impotency; that when power finally comes to those who are weak and impotent, they create a world of values, i.e., goals and ideals, that reflect weakness and impotency; that those values may, considering their origin, destroy not only their originators but the rest of us, as well.

F.N. will be remembered for his devastating critique of the vulgar age of materialism, selfishness and crass conformity. Like Kierkegaard, Marx, and the other great critics of the industrial age, he attacked the popular views of his time and offered an explanation of the causes of the problems that he witnessed. His blistering comments on journalism, women, Christianity, socialism, democracy, art, the bourgeoisie, philosophers, Germans, and popular culture in general have earned him the enmity of the representatives of all those mentioned. But what he said, more than the manner of his saying it, is what has proved to be enduring and valuable. Thus when he stated, "Man was made for war and woman for the entertainment of the warrior," a first reaction may be anger and disgust. But in holding up the mirror to our civilization, however much one may dislike what is reflected, one must admit that Nietzsche was right on this. That's what our vulgar civilzation has produced though perhaps not in the way that F.N. saw it. We still live in a violently competitive society of professional sports, life-consuming business, budget-busting militarism, and me-first science where women, despite attempts to the contrary, remain as much a part of the rewards for success as fast cars, opulent homes, money and honors. Nietzsche told us what we are and we have, unfortunately, paid more attention to the diagnostician than to the diagnosis.

F.N. will be remembered as one of the two 19th century founders of 20th century existentialism. The 20th century atheistic existentialists, such as Martin Heidegger, Albert Camus, and Jean Paul Sartre, and the theistic existentialists, such as Karl Jaspers and Gabriel Marcel, were all strongly influenced, as they all freely admit, by F.N. They all lived during the very age of mediocrity, destruction, and madness that he had prophesied. Men like Martin Heidegger and Jean Paul Sartre have continued F.N.'s search for a meaning to life in a world without God. For them, as with F.N., God is dead, God remains dead, and it is up to the existing, solitary individual to find an authentic and meaningful life by oneself, through one's own anguish and efforts.

PROBLEMS WITH NIETZSCHE

There are three problems with F.N.'s way of philosophy. The first is trivial but needs mentioning; the second is a general critique of existentialism and is probably answerable; the third is devastating and perhaps unanswerable.

First, the critic might say, everyone knows that F.N. was insane. So if he was insane, then so was his philosophy. So why should we even consider the insane way of philosophy of an insane philosopher?

To begin with, we're not really considering the philosopher but only his way of philosophy. That way must be criticized in terms of our three criteria for an adequate way of philosophy, viz., common sense, consistency and completeness. The human origin of the way, while interesting and perhaps even helpful in understanding the meaning and significance of the way, is relatively unimportant. We judge the way of philosophy on the basis of its merits alone.

But suppose it could be proved, the critic might persist, that if you followed this insane philosophy then you'd end up like its author, hopelessly insane. What then?

To begin with, F.N. himself wasn't driven mad by adopting his or anybody else's way of philosophy. The criticism implies that if you follow an "insane philosophy," whatever that means, that you'll become insane yourself. Insanity in F.N.'s case was probably the consequence of a life time of sickness and it came only during the last years of his life. Its origin is not known. Speculation ranges from his having contracted congenital syphilis from his father to a venereal disease that he, himself, may have gotten while a student. All of his later symptoms, including the delusions and the eventual insanity, are due to a disease and not philosophy. F.N.'s life deserves our understanding and sympathy; his way of philosophy deserves our analysis and criticism.

Second, the critic might say, F.N. expects too much on an individual level from human beings. He expects much more than we are able to give. His way of philosophy entails attitudes of go-it-alone, follow the hard and suffering life and to-hell-with-the-group, a way which merely reflects his own tormented and lonely life. But that way overlooks one very important point: The group and society are important and valuable. We can't, and F.N. himself found that he couldn't, live for long without the companionship and fellowship of others: "Only mad men and dogs eat alone," Epicurus said; and F.N. was no dog. To believe as F.N. did that there are anchorites like Zarathustra who can live in solitary splendor in caves, be apart from society, and in their splendid solitude rise above the mob, i.e., the group, and go-it-alone to the icy metaphysical heights of the Overman, points to someone who doesn't understand human nature. F.N.'s way of philosophy and the philosophic way of humanistic existentialism, in general, that exalt the isolated individual over the collective community, are simply impractical and they violate our first criterion of acceptability, viz., common sense.

This second criticism points to our third problem with F.N.'s way of philosophy and that is that in it there really is no way. That is to say, for all of his Zarathustrian posturing of transcending the self by the self in an age of deocide, F.N. nowhere tells us in any particular manner how this transcending is to be done. While it is true that he does, after the manner of the Stoics, tell us to accept life, to will hardness and suffering to the point of eternal recurrence, he never spells out how that is to be undertaken. Should we use yoga?, meditation?, prayer?, long walks? (F.N. loved walking), conjured suffering, i.e., making pain and hardness of life artificially in order to strengthen our characters? What? Or do we just do it, somehow? But how? In lieu of a clear expression from him of what conjuring and overcoming techniques are to be employed, the charge of incompleteness must be leveled at Nietzsche's way of philosophy. And it may be a charge that could be similarly leveled at any philosophic way that exalts solitude and isolation without offering a definite prescription of the precise way of arriving at goals.

One other major representative of the way of existential nothingness is the 20th century French philosopher Jean Paul Sartre. Very briefly, let's look at his way of philosophy and his answer to the question, What is the best and most worthwhile life?

JEAN PAUL SARTRE (1905-1980): THE MAKING OF AN EXISTENTIALIST

The most popular exponent of humanistic existentialism in the 20th century was the French philosopher Jean Paul Sartre. He was born in

Paris on June 21, 1905, and, following the death of his father, grew up in the home of his wealthy and respected maternal grandfather, Charles Schweitzer, an uncle of the physician-missionary, Albert Schweitzer. Though deeply attached to his grandfather, he soon rebelled against what he perceived as the middle class hypocrisy of his grandfather's bourgeois values. By the age of nine, Sartre resolved to become a writer. Having turned away from the Roman Catholicism and the Lutheranism of his parents and family, Sartre sought his youthful identity through writing. It was the beginning of a life-long concern with personal identity, the nature of the person, and an attempt to answer the perennial philosophic question, Who am I? In his autobiography of these early years, *The Words*, published in 1963, when he was almost sixty, he states,

> By writing, I was existing, I was escaping from the grown-ups, but I existed only in order to write, and if I said 'I,' that meant 'I who write.' In any case, I knew joy.... I was prepared at an early age to regard teaching as a priesthood and literature as a passion. [Jean Paul Sartre, *The Words*, translated by Bernard Frechtman (New York: Braziller, 1964), p. 153.]

In 1929 he received a degree in philosophy from the Ecole Normale Superieure and for the next ten years taught philosophy at high schools in Le Havre and Paris. Like Nietzsche before him, he was constantly reminded of the great gulf that existed between the grand idealized generalizations of both philosophy and religion and the concrete way things really were; he was all too painfully conscious of the gross inappropriateness of what was being studied in the schools to the problems of everyday existence and in the daily lives of those whom he taught. Anyone who has ever struggled through a course in philosophy must have felt as Sartre felt; hacking one's way through a jungle of interminable generalizations, trying to find a concrete particular on which to climb and rise above the tangle of ideals and values that always seem to obstruct the view of real understanding. Life as it is lived gives us a far different picture of reality than the abstract and ideal representations of life that the home, church, synagogue, and school would have us believe in and guide our lives by.

Sartre spent the year 1933-34 in Germany studying with Edmund Husserl, one of the leaders in a new philosophic movement called "phenomenology." Its concern with pure experience and with the concrete problems of life and their solutions, i.e., with existence, proved to be strongly compelling for Sartre. It is from phenomenology, and from the influence of philosophers like Friederich Nietzsche, Franz Brentano (1838-1917), a Roman Catholic priest, and Brentano's distinguished pupil, Edmund Husserl (1859-1938), and also from Sartre's experiences during the German occupation of France during World War II, that modern French existentialism will be born. And its birth will be the responsibility of one person alone, Jean Paul Sartre.

Sartre served in the French army following Germany's invasion of France in 1940. He was captured and spent nine months as a military prisoner in Germany. Escaping, he returned to Paris where, along with Albert Camus and Francois Mauriac, he joined the underground resistance movement and served in it from 1941 to 1944. It was these experiences in the day to day struggle for survival that taught Sartre the value of life, of freedom and of "existence," itself. In an atmosphere where freedom was "total responsibility in total solitude," where apprehension meant torture and execution, where one could count on no other power for guidance, safety and survival, other than one's own inner resources and personal prowess, Sartre's way of philosophy was born. And out of all this came the simple motto of humanistic existentialism:

> "Existence precedes essence"... [which means that] Man is nothing else than his plan; he exists only to the extent that he fulfills himself; he is therefore nothing else than the ensemble of his acts; nothing else than his life. [Jean Paul Sartre, *Existentialism and Humanism*, in *Problems in Philosophy: West and East*, Edited by R.T. Blackwood and A.L. Herman (Prentice-Hall, Inc., 1975), pp. 82, 88.]

Following the war, Sartre's reputation as *the* leading French man of letters continued to grow. His philosophic writings, his plays, essays, and novels, but particularly his autobiography of 1963, *The Words*, earned him the Nobel Prize for literature in 1964, an award which he refused to accept contending that it was a literary bribe. Throughout his later years he turned to Marxism and communism and attempted to synthesize his earlier existential insights with his newly formed Marxist beliefs. We will have more to say about this synthesis in what follows. He died, honored and acclaimed, in Paris in 1980 at the age of 74.

Three Sartrean Ways of Philosophy

Sartre's philosophic life may be divided into three ways of philosophy which neatly divide into three chronological periods of his life: First, an existential period, beginning before the Second World War and running up to the end of the war; second, a Marxist and Communist period starting after the war in 1946; and, finally, an existential-Marxist period beginning around 1960 when Sartre attempted to bring the two earlier views together. In our attempt to understand Sartre's answer to the question, What is the best and most worthwhile life that a human being can live?, we shall focus primarily on the first and third of these three philosophic periods and the ways of philosophy that they exhibit.

The Existential Way (1938-1946)

Like Nietzsche before him, Sartre pursued the implications of a world of contingencies, where nothing *must* be and everything is an *accident*, i.e., a world without God. In such a world, a world without necessity, without certainty, without absolute guides and guarantees, life becomes "absurd." For consider this: You might not have been born! So why were you born? Why were your parents and grandparents born? Why is there mankind and the human species? Eventually we arrive at the ultimate question: Why is there anything at all? Without an answer, it's all crazy, meaningless, empty: It's absurd!

Absurdity

Nowhere is this view more penetratingly pursued than in Sartre's early novel of 1938, *Nausea*. Here the author's hero, Roquentin, confronts the basic absurdity and the essential meaninglessness of life whenever he tries to get that meaning from others. Any meaning that life has, he suddenly realizes, must come ultimately from himself, it cannot be bestowed on him by anyone else.

Why is there anything at all?, Why am I here?, Why was I born? Answer those questions but without the usual transcendental responses, such as, God wants me to fulfill His plan, or He loves me so much he wants me to exist, or Providence needs me, and the like. Try an answer from inside yourself. But first must come the question, and before that the great confrontation. Without all three, the confrontation, the question, and the answer, existentialism would have remained just one more philosophic *ism*, one more abstraction, the very thing that Sartre hated.

In the following passage from *Nausea*, the confrontation with the absurdity and the question about the meaning of life are both nicely encapsulated:

> Absurdity was not an idea in my head nor the sound of my voice, it was this long, lean, wooden snake curled up at my feet — snake or claw or talon or root, it was all the same.

Sitting in a park, Roquentin is suddenly struck by the appearance of the sinuous dark roots of an ancient chestnut tree. They are an immediate and direct experience, not mere ideas nor illusions of sound or sight:

> Without formulating anything I knew that I had found the clue to my exis-
> tence, to my nausea, to my life. And indeed everything I have ever grasped
> since that moment comes back to this fundamental absurdity. [Jean Paul
> Sartre, *Nausea*, Translated by Lloyd Alexander (New York: New Directions,
> 1964), p. 69.]

The roots of this ancient tree were struggling beneath the earth, probing
through the darkness, just as he had been probing. There was no meaning, no ultimate sense for their groping, nor could there be for his.
Existence for trees or man has no meaning beyond themselves. It can't.
God is dead!

What is left for man to do is not to speculate nor to theorize about
God, heaven, ultimate goals and purposes, but to act. And in action to
find right now whatever meaning and sense human life has. Sartre's real
genius lies in the conclusions that he now draws from the life of man as
an actor, i.e., a moral agent.

Existence Precedes Essence

Sartre captures the essential meaning of "existentialism" in the key
phrase, "Existence precedes essence." Understanding the several implications of this phrase will enable us to understand man as a moral agent
and to get at the heart of Sartrean existentialism and the consequences of
the realization of the absurdness of life.

Sartre published *Existentialism and Humanism* in 1946 at the end of the
first period of his philosophic life. It was a work designed to answer the
question, What is existentialism?, a philosophy then becoming all the
rage in post-war Europe, and a soon-to-become pop-philosophy around
the world. Three years earlier Sartre had published a massive 772 page-
long, obscure and highly technical book called *Being and Nothingness*. It is
the work on which his reputation as a professional philosopher had been
erected. Published in 1943 in German occupied France, *Being and
Nothingness* attracted little attention. But what now brought readers back
to it was this inexpensive and brief book of 1946, *Existentialism and
Humanism*, a vulgarized abridgement of both Sartre's popular lectures
and his *Being and Nothingness*. To Sartre's surprise and horror
Existentialism and Humanism became "the bible of existentialism."

It contained all the familiar concepts of the rising new philosophy:
freedom, responsibility, individualism, anguish, solitude, commitment,
forlornness and despair. All of these, in turn, were couched in the popular phrases of what was now known as "existentialism," phrases as
significant now as they were splendidly meaningful then: "Existentialism

defines man by his actions;" "It tells him that hope lies only in action and that the only thing that allows man to live is action;" "Man commits himself to his life, and thereby draws his image, beyond which there is nothing;" "We are alone and without excuses. This is what I mean when I say that man is condemned to be free." And he invented the famous definition of existential humanism that neatly encapsulates all of these concepts and phrases: "Existence precedes essence."

Following the violence and horrors of the Second World War, together with the obvious collapse of the values and explanations of the Judeo-Christian tradition, European men and women began looking for new ways of philosophy, new religions. The looking became a frenzied search as new philosophic fads and strange religious sects vied with one another for attention and loyalties; and of all this while the cold war between East and West heated up and dominated the world. Nietzsche had been right: When man discovered that God was dead, he went mad.

In the midst of all of this frantic deocide and chaos, there was *Existentialism and Humanism*:

> Atheistic existentialism which I represent states that if God does not exist, there is at least one being in whom existence precedes essence, a being who exists before he can be defined by any concept, and that this being is man.... [Jean Paul Sartre, *Existentialism and Humanism*, Translated by Bernard Frechtman in *Problems in Philosophy: West and East, Op. Cit.*, p. 82.]

Sartre continues with that key phrase:

> What is meant here by saying that existence precedes essence? It means that, first of all, man exists, turns up, appears on the scene, and, only afterwards, defines himself. [*Ibid.*]

Whatever I am, or whatever I will to be, is precisely what I make of myself. I cannot be defined as a Christian or Jew or an American or a Russian merely by being born into a particular family or country. Man has no *apriori* human nature or religious or political nature. He or she is what he or she *wills* to be:

> If man, as the existentialist conceives him, is indefinable, it is because at first he is nothing. Only afterwards will he be something, and he himself will have made what he will be. [*Ibid.*]

That making lies through action. Which leads to the first principle of existentialism:

> *Man is nothing else but what he makes of himself.*

From this first principle, and from the key phrase, itself, a second principle also follows:

Man is totally responsible for what he is.

Thus I cannot blame God, or the stars, or Fate, or my parents, or my environment, or the state for what I am. I am what I have chosen to be. In *Being and Nothingness* Sartre had earlier expounded this notion of total freedom and total responsibility when he proclaimed:

Thus there are no *accidents* in a life; a community event which suddenly bursts forth and involves me in it does not come from the outside. If I am mobilized in a war, this war is *my* war; it is in my image and I deserve it.

It is my responsibility because I could always choose something else, i.e., "...I could always get out of it by suicide or by desertion." The consequence for everyone is, Sartre concludes, "There are no innocent victims," "we have the war [i.e., the life] we deserve." [Jean Paul Sartre, *Being and Nothingness*, quoted in Jeffrey Olen, *Persons and Their World* (New York: Random House, 1983), pp. 200, 201.]

From this second principle Sartre now adds a corollary:

Each man is responsible for all other men through the choices that he makes.

This corollary really follows from the second principle for when we choose we have affirmed the value or worth of what we choose. Thus, "We always choose the good, and nothing can be good for us without being good for all." [*Existentialism and Humanism, Op. Cit.*, p. 82.]

From this and the other two principles there follows the third principle of existentialism:

The feeling of deep and total responsibility for all mankind leads to the feelings of forlornness and anguish.

We recognize that all of our moral decisions are made without benefit of God; hence there follows the abandoned and lost feeling of aloneness that Sartre denominates "forlornness;" and we recognize that every such decision is made with total freedom by the agent but also with total responsibility for what he chooses, for he chooses as a lawmaker for all mankind; hence the feeling of anguish. The existentialist lives in a state of constant tension and anguish as he discovers that he is condemned to be free. My moral choices entangle all of humanity in my decisions. The tension is real, the tension leads to self-realization and ultimate self-overcoming and maturity. It is no easy thing to become an authentic person, a real human being. This is the way of existential man in the first period of Sartre's way of philosophy.

The Marxist Way (1946-1960)

Like Marx before him, Sartre gradually became convinced that without social justice, philosophical pursuits, no matter how noble, must come to nothing: You cannot persuade a starving man that his existence precedes his essence. With his close friend Maurice Merleau-Ponty, he began a close study of both Marx and Hegel. In 1946 he wrote,

> I know that man has no salvation other than the liberation of the working class; I know this *before* being a materialist and from a plain reflection on the fact. I know that our intellectual interest lies with the proletariat. [Jean Paul Sartre, "Materialism and Revolution," in *Literary and Philosophical Essays*, Translated by Annette Michelson (New York: Collier Books, 1962), p. 220.]

Sartre had come to realize, as he goes on to say, that an individual cannot gain his own freedom until his entire class, until all men, are freed. Marx, he now felt, was right! Since the ruling powers will never relinquish their power or their rule voluntarily, only a revolutionary overthrow of the existing economic and political system can free the proletariat: Sartre was turning from a solitary existentialist into a Marxian collectivist seeking violent revolution.

A trivial incident finally threw him completely into the communist camp. In May 1952 an anti-American rally was called in Paris. French security police halted one of the cars carrying one of the rally's chief supporters, Jacques Duclos, the acting secretary of the French Community Party. The police found two pigeons in his car. They arrested Duclos and accused him of plotting against the state and taking orders from Moscow using carrier pigeons. In fact, Duclos was on his way home to dinner and the dinner was those two pigeons. The upshot of this ridiculous incident was that Duclos spent over a month in jail. Sartre was in Italy when this seemingly trivial event occurred but it was the last straw of frustration for him:

> People may find me very naive, and for that matter, I had seen other examples of this kind of thing which hadn't affected me. But after ten years of ruminating, I had come to the breaking point, and only needed one straw. In the language of the church, this was my conversion. [Jean Paul Sartre, *Situations*, Translated by Benita Eisler (New York: George Braziller, Inc., 1965), p. 269.]

And then in an emotional torrent he concludes:

> In the name of the principles my class [the bourgeois middle class, of course] had inculcated in me, in the name of humanism and humanity, in the name of liberty, equality and fraternity, I swore a hatred of the bourgeoisie which will only die with me. [*Ibid.*]

While he never joined the communist party, Sartre became for several years a dedicated, if not fanatical, follower of the party. In 1954 he visited the Soviet Union, later naively proclaiming:

> The Soviet citizen has full freedom of criticism.... It would be a mistake to believe that the Soviet citizen does not speak and keeps his criticism bottled up inside himself.... In Russia a man is aware of the constant progress of his own life as well as social life. Intellectual and collective interests coincide. [Annie Cohen-Solal, *Sartre, A Life*, Translated by Anna Cancogni (New York: Pantheon Books, 1987), pp. 348, 349. Twenty years later Sartre was to declare about this proclamation that he had lied (p. 351).]

He returned home from Joseph Stalin's police state curiously convinced of its openness and freedom. In 1964 he visited Fidel Castro's Cuba and came away similarly impressed.

There is a poignant truth, of course, in his claim that the individual can be free only when all the workers in the society are free. But it is a complete turnabout from his earlier existential claim that the existing solitary individual, not the collective group or class, is the only unit of freedom and responsibility in the world. And it is a far cry from his previous existential claim, viz., "We were never more free than during the German occupation."

Sartre's philosophical pilgrimage had brought him to recognize the philosophers' social responsibility. Armed now with this new recognition but with his previous dedicated commitment to communism slowly changing, Sartre approached the third and final period of his philosophic life.

Sartre Changes His Mind

He gradually came to realize that orthodox Marxism had reached a dead end. But despite this realization about Marxism he still agreed with several of Marx's central doctrines. To the end of his life Sartre continued to uphold the essential wisdom of the doctrine of economic determinism, the view that class structure, class conflicts, and class exploitation are major causes of social disruption and violence; and he continued to uphold the doctrine that an individual's own philosophy is an expression of his socio-economic class; and, finally, he remained a firm believer in the doctrine that the dominant values and ideologies of a society remain those of the most powerful class. [For a more complete discussion of economic determinism, see below Chapter 13, *The Ways of Individualism and Community*, pp. 282-284.]

What now began to incense Sartre during the time of his transition to the third period of his philosophic life was the powerful exercise of state repression in Communist bloc countries, in particular, countries such as Poland and Hungary. It was the brutal crushing of popular uprisings in Poznan in June 1956 and the Soviet attack on Budapest in the fall of 1956 that soured Sartre on the Soviets and on communism. It was obvious that the internal terrorist purges carried out with official sanction in the communist states were significant signs that the communists had lost their concern for the individual citizen, a concern that remained central to Sartre's philosophy even though seemingly laid aside for 15 years. The Communist party's concern for dogmas and material gain had made them forget, Sartre felt, Marx's dire warning that they themselves could easily become the sad imitators of their capitalist masters.

The Existential-Marxist Way (1960-1980)

In 1960 Sartre published *The Critique of Dialectical Reason* and while he continued recognizing Marxism as *the* central philosophy of our age, he nevertheless launched his criticism of it. In addition, his disillusionment with the Soviet Union as the chief representative of what was good in Marxism also waned. Sartre came to believe that the U.S.S.R. was destroying communism.

The *Critique* had as its central theme the notion of freedom through an analysis of the relationship between Marxism and Sartrean existentialism. The sacredness of the individual, a basic existential tenet, now gives way to the sacredness of the group, the class. The new way involved believing that the individual disappears as soon as he sees his connection with the group, the synthetic bond that joins everyone. Now, only the group can be free, only the group can have the responsibility that was so highly touted for the individual, alone, in the old existentialist days. The *Critique* in attempting to synthesize the best in existentialism and Marxism had with fanfare and with all seriousness brought back onto the stage an abstraction, the group. [See Ronald Hayman, *Sartre, A Life* (Simon and Schuster, 1987), for a good discussion of the *Critique of Dialectical Reason*.] The *Critique*, then, was an attempt at a synthesis of his two earlier philosophic periods, wherein he now described existentialism as an "enclave within Marxism." But, to repeat, Sartre's Marxism is not an orthodox Marxism, for he is not a materialist nor a strict determinist.

He turned now to China, living there for one month in 1955. He saw China as the hope of the future and as the leading exemplar of all that was best in Marxism and Communism. He felt that the Chinese Cultural Revolution of the 1950s was one of the noblest and most valuable undertakings of a people, and a true expression of Marxism. It is one of the ironies of our times that today almost everyone, including the Chinese, themselves, see that cultural upheaval as totally disastrous and destructive of all real Chinese values: It was one of the great errors of Chinese Marxism. Again, Sartre was woefully mistaken in his evaluation of events.

Despite the criticisms that he offered of his earlier bourgeois existentialism, Sartre continued to champion the possibility of the good and worthwhile life. He felt that that life could only be possible in a society where freedom was possible for everyone. He felt that that freedom would not come without a struggle. And he felt that violent revolution, given the existing capitalist conditions of society, was the only way to reify that freedom, and that, shades of the old existentialism!, it was a choice that he would willingly make for all mankind. Finally, he felt that the best and most worthwhile life for anyone was possible only when that life was available for everyone.

THE WAY OF EXISTENTIAL NOTHINGNESS: JEAN PAUL SARTRE

There are really two historically significant philosophic ways that can be generated from Sartre's long and extremely complex philosophic life: An existential way and a Marxist-existential way. For our purposes, while summarizing both, we shall concentrate on the former, since Sartre's influence on contemporary thought has been primarily an existential influence rather than a Marxist influence.

The Problem

The problem for Sartre the existentialist, of course, was to end suffering, that is to find meaning or purpose in life for the existing individual. In our Aristotelian language, his problem was to discover the best and most worthwhile life for the individual.

For Sartre the Marxist-existentialist, on the other hand, the problem of suffering was more complex. It was to discover the best and most worthwhile life for all men and women. The wartime Sartre of *Being and Nothingness* (1943) "had been so impressed with individual human heroism that he had taken it to represent the human condition" [Kenneth and Margaret Thompson, *Sartre: Life and Works* (New York: Facts On File Publications, 1984), p. 126.]; but the Marxist Sartre of *The Critique of Dialectical Reason* (1960) sought to show how an entire people might overcome "their plight of alienation and domination by others" [*Ibid.*, p. 128.] and by collective action seek a Marxist solution to these problems. The shift in Sartre's thinking from the individual to the class or group was necessitated by Sartre's new belief that the problem of the best life could not be solved for one until it was solved for all.

But a new problem arises now for Sartre, viz., What is the relation of the individual to the group. The communists and most Marxists maintained that the value of the individual was nothing in comparison to the importance of the group. Sartre, in rejecting both Communism and the more orthodox Marxist view, must now attempt to find a place for his existing individual within the Marxist collective group.

The Cause

The cause of the problem for Sartre the existentialist is really four-fold. The suffering that the existing individual experiences is reflected in *nausea*, i.e., in the relation of the individual to the chaotic world through which he comes to see what is, i.e., the solid, brute facts of the world; in *anguish*, i.e., in the relation of the individual to himself as he discovers the necessity of making choices for which, out of his complete freedom to choose, he is totally responsible since he chooses not only for himself but for all human beings; in the *absurd*, i.e., in the relation of the individual to life when he realizes that there is no meaning to his existence other than what he, himself, gives it; and the final cause of suffering is expressed in *forlornness*, i.e., in the relation of the individual to the realization that he is alone, that God is dead, and that in his aloneness he is all that there is.

For Sartre the Marxist-existentialist the cause of the problem is alienation, i.e., dehumanization on a massive scale, brought on by the problems in the material conditions of life. Those conditions, as Marx discovered, involve the mode of economic production. In other words the problems in the modern world are all traceable to the exploitation of one socio-economic class by another. But Marxism had reached a dead end, Sartre argued in the preface to *The Critique of Dialectical Reason*. In over-emphasizing class conflict and economic determinism, it had lost interest in and neglected both the existing individual and his freedom. These two existential concerns will remain high on Sartre's list of concerns to the very end of his life. This Marxist neglect, as Sartre saw it, will be corrected through the existential approach to Marxism which Sartre was to take in the third period of his philosophic life.

The Solution

The aim of Sartre's way of philosophy, whether existential or Marxist-existential, is, to use his later manner of expression, to live authentically; and to live authentically is to be truly free, to recreate oneself from nothing.

The Way

The way to becoming an authentic person lies through choosing and acting: Man is what he or she does; to be is to act. But to act means that man must be free. But to be free his class must be free, i.e., all men and women must be free. The concentration on freedom as well as its attainment, consequently, have both remained at the center of Sartre's way of philosophy, whether existential or Marxist, from the very beginning. The way lies in overcoming exploitation, dehumanization and alienation, where man is a thing, an object, and not an individual. It entails making this freedom available to the millions in the world for whom freedom remains an illusion. The way to freedom for one then lies in making that freedom available to everyone: And for Sartre that meant using violent revolution if necessary.

SARTRE'S ACCOMPLISHMENTS

The major questions that we should be asking in recounting Sartre's accomplishments are, What is the best and most worthwhile life for Sartre the existentialist?, and for Sartre the Marxist-existentialist? Four of his major accomplishments would seem to point to Sartre's answers to both of these questions:

First, in stating that existence precedes essence Sartre reminds us all that what we are depends on what we make of ourselves. No one else is responsible for our self-creation; if it gets done, that's us and if it doesn't, that's us, too. In order to live authentically my life must be in my hands, it must be of my making, not of my parents', of my church or synagogue, of my temple or mosque, of my community or state. I am the one who must be in charge.

Second, the terrible freedom that we possess, and that so many are anxious to exchange for security and conformity, Sartre argues, is the prime requisite for this self-creation. Sartre reminds us of the important truth that having freedom, having options, having choices, is the *sine qua non* of the best life, and that without the possibility of that freedom and those choices, what we create cannot lead to the best and most worthwhile life.

Third, Sartre reminds us that to want freedom only for oneself is selfish and immoral. Hence the importance of wanting to extend the possibility of choices to everyone and for everyone.

Fourth, Sartre reminds us all that the moral life, wherein right acts are those done with complete awareness and total responsibility, is not an easy life to lead. When I choose, there is a fundamental sense in which I in fact choose as if it were for the entire human race. The rightness of my action, of any action, depends on my being able to freely will that what I am doing might be willed and done at the same time by any other authentic person.

The best and most worthwhile life is found by my creating myself, in an atmosphere of open choices, wherein I am able to wish or to want or to will that all persons be able to follow my lead in the choices that I make and especially in the actions that I then take. But all of this is not without some difficulties.

PROBLEMS WITH SARTRE

Not surprisingly, problems arise with the accomplishments mentioned above.

First, what does it mean to say that existence precedes essence? Is Sartre making a factual claim and is the utterance then descriptive? Or is Sartre stating what he believes ought to be the case and is the utterance then prescriptive? If the first is the correct interpretation, then, of course, what he is saying is patently false. There are instances, of course, where it may be true that existence comes before essence. For example, it is no doubt true that the actions that I perform and that essentially define me as a person can only be performed after I am born, after I have come into existence. But there are instances where it is false to say that my existence precedes my essence. For example, if it is true that my height, hair color, and body structure are all inherited, and that even my character and temperament, as well as my I.Q. and my general personality, are also genetically inherited, or at least 80% inherited, then part of my essence, my defining characteristics, is rather narrowly circumscribed before birth and set into my D.N.A. foundation. Hence, my essence, 80% or more of it, precedes my existence, and Sartre is wrong.

If, on the other hand, Sartre is prescribing when he says that existence precedes essence then he is saying that existence ought to precede essence. What does that mean, anyway? And he must tell us what the justification is for this prescriptive claim. Will it really make better persons of us if we follow this advice? Will it enable us to lead more authentic lives? Sartre never attempts an answer to either question.

Under the first interpretation, Sartre's existential utterance would appear to be empirically inconsistent; and under the second interpretation the utterance would seem to be incomplete. In either case, the first problem points to failures in satisfying two of our standards for an adequate way of philosophy.

Second, is it not a himalayan exaggeration of the existential moral life, whether humanist or Marxist, to say that every time I make a moral choice, I am choosing for the whole of humanity? If Sartre is contending that this is what happens when one makes a responsible moral choice, then it is simply not true, and it violates ordinary common sense to argue otherwise. I can behave responsibly without getting all of humanity hung around my neck; and if they are so hung in the way Sartre imagines, then they would become either a barrier to action prior to every moral action, or they would be part of the guilt experienced by every moral agent after every moral action: And who needs either? If all that Sartre is saying is, Think about the long term effects of your action on everyone concerned, i.e., if he is making a simple utilitarian claim, all well and good. But, in fact, Sartre seems to be saying something far more jumbled than that. And what he says violates our standard of common sense: I simply don't choose for all of mankind every time I make a moral choice, I can't!, nor should I!

Third, to want to extend the possibility of freedom to other persons is a noble, and not a merely Marxist, wish. But what are the methods or means to be used to implement such an extension? For example, didn't Hitler and Stalin share this same dream of extending human freedom? Does the end, freedom, justify the use of any means whatever, e.g., Soviet tanks in Budapest and Prague?, of Kidnapping? Terrorism? and Genocide? Sartre appears to violate our criterion of common sense for in using the language of freedom he obfuscates a very real problem, viz., the bringing of freedom to many while denying that same freedom to many more. Any way of philosophy in which the end sought justifies the use of any means available runs afoul of the same difficulty.

Fourth, how can a universal willing of the act to be performed and the bearing of total responsibility for the choice made ever be psychologically bearable. In other words, how is it ever possible for sensitive moral consciences to accept the responsibility for these actions where horror and violence become necessary in order to extend the boundaries of freedom? Sartre's humanistic existentialism, as well as his Marxist existentialism, both tend to run afoul of our criterion of completeness if they cannot provide a solution to this psychological problem.

Fifth and finally, Sartre has raised a question which he never managed to answer, viz., What is the relation of the individual to the group? That relation entails further questions and problems concerned with rights, values, duties, loyalties, and responsibilities, of the group or class to its members and *vice versa*. The nothingness that loomed so large for existentialists such as Nietzsche and Sartre was the open grave that was left following the death of God. That grave was quickly filled, as the existentialists were quick to point out, by the abstractions and abstractionists eager to take God's place. The new conforming mass man of both the industrial age and the information age is all-too-eager to live, die and kill for the current popular abstractions, his country, his religion, his economic theory, his way of life, however described. For Sartre the existential humanist, *freedom* had been one such abstraction; and now, at the end of his life, for Sartre the Marxist, the new abstraction is the *group*. Sartre must step a very narrow line, indeed, to avoid the paradox of the group: if the group is too strong then we have totalitarianism; if the group is too weak then we have anarchy. Common sense bids us seek a mean between these extremes.

But one question remains, How is the existing individual to find his or her authentic life in a world where first loyalties may lie with the group to which one belongs? In other words, should I seek my own salvation, i.e., the best and most worthwhile life, first?, or should I put it off and help others and myself to find the best life collectively, together? This is what Sartre's question comes to, and that question remains unanswered.

One answer to that question is found in the way of philosophy of the Hindu social and political reformer, Mohandas K. Gandhi. His answer constitutes his response to Aristotle's question regarding the best and most worthwhile life that a human being can live.

ELEVEN
THE WAY OF SATYAGRAHA
❯•❮

MOHANDAS KARAMCHAND GANDHI (1869-1948):
THE PROPHET OF NON-VIOLENCE

Gandhi's Life

Mohandas Karamchand Gandhi was born in 1869 in Gujarat, a province on India's Western coast. He came from the vaishya class, the merchant class, of the Indian social system, though both his father and grandfather had been prime ministers in the governments of local princely states. In his famous *Autobiography*, which he subtitled *The Story of My Experiments With Truth*, Gandhi tells of his early life and marriage in India. He tells of his adventures as a student in London where he went in 1888 for study at the age of 18 and where he obtained his degree in law three years later. He also tells of his early life in South Africa where he practiced law, and of his life later in India where he had his most popular success as both a political and a spiritual leader of millions of his countrymen.

But it was Gandhi's experiences in South Africa that shaped him for his later work of social reform and active political resistance against the British occupation of India. And it was these early experiences in South Africa, applied subsequently in India, that were to lead in no small measure to the eventual freedom of his country from the British in 1947.

Gandhi returned to India from London in 1891 but he was unable to earn a living as an attorney. It was, actually, his uncontrollable shyness that cost him his professional career in the law courts of India. As he tells it, his first case was typical and a disaster:

This was my *debut* in the Small Causes Court. I appeared for the defendant and had thus to cross-examine the plaintiff's witnesses. I stood up, but my heart sank into my boots. My head was reeling and I felt as though the whole court was doing likewise. I could think of no question to ask.... The judge must have laughed.... I sat down and told the agent that I could not conduct the case.... [Mohandas K. Gandhi, *Autobiography, The Story of My Experiments With Truth* (Boston: Beacon Press, 1966/1927), p. 94.]

The adversarial method of arguing cases in courts, a method first introduced by the Sophists in 5th century B.C. Athens, [See above Chapter 2, *The Way of Relativism,* p. 17.] was a technique that Gandhi was psychologically incapable of using. So, in place of the adversarial approach to legal defense, Gandhi introduced in its place a new technique in which he was eventually to become a master: The method of compromise. In the adversarial method there are winners and there are losers, and the stage is thereby set for future adjudication, future appeals, more hatred and even violence. In the method of compromise there are no losers for, ideally, everybody wins as both parties sit down and talk out their differences achieving justice through mutual concession.

But, after two years, unable to earn a living for himself and his family in India, Gandhi accepted an invitation from some overseas Indians in South Africa to represent their company in certain legal disputes. Totally unprepared for the prejudice and hatred present in South Africa, Gandhi arrived in that country in 1893 with his new degree, his new English clothes, and looking very much the British gentleman that he thought he had become. In attempting to ride in a first-class railway compartment, for which he held a first-class ticket, he was, because of his skin color and his refusal to vacate his seat, thrown off the train by the conductor. Gandhi tells the story of his first encounter with racism:

The train reached Maritzburg, the capital of Natal, at about 9 p.m. Beddings used to be provided at this station. A railway servant came in and asked me if I wanted one. 'No,' said I, 'I have one with me.' He went away. But a passenger came next, and looked me up and down. He saw that I was a 'colored' man. This disturbed him. Out he went and came in again with one or two officials. They all kept quiet, when another official came to me and said, 'Come along, you must go to the van compartment.'

'But I have a first class ticket,' said I.

'That doesn't matter,' rejoined the other. 'I tell you, you must go to the van compartment.'

'I tell you, I was permitted to travel in this compartment at Durban, and I insist on going on in it.'

'No you won't,' said the official. 'You must leave this compartment, or else I shall have to call a police constable to push you out.'

'Yes, you may. I refuse to get out voluntarily.'

The constable came. He took me by the hand and pushed me out. My luggage was also taken out. I refused to go to the other compartment and the train steamed away. [*Ibid.*, p. 111.]

Gandhi was to learn the hard way about racial prejudice in South Africa.

He spent nearly 20 years in that country with his wife and growing family, during which time both he and the unjust laws that he fought against slowly changed. He gave up his English clothes and aristocratic ways in exchange for simple Indian peasant dress; he disciplined himself after the manner of the traditional Indian holy man with prayer, fasting, celibacy, and an increasingly ascetic life. During this time he developed his way of philosophy and his philosophy of political and social action which may be summed up in one word: Satyagraha.

Satyagraha in South Africa

The practice of satyagraha was first used successfully by Gandhi in South Africa. On September 11, 1906 a mass meeting of over 3,000 British Indians was called in Johannesburg, South Africa. The Indians had been brought together in order to protest a proposed bill being offered by the Colonial Government, called the "Asiatic Law Amendment Ordinance." Gandhi, one of the leaders of the meeting, had referred to the bill as a "crime against humanity," and had urged the people to refuse to comply with it if it were adopted. In effect the Ordinance if enacted would require all Indians eight years of age and over to register and be finger-printed by the Government; further, all Indians could be forced to produce the required registration certificate on demand, on any occasion, for any reason; finally, their houses and their persons could be searched without warrant and without cause. Failure to comply with any of the above orders, and failure to carry the certificate at all times could mean a fine, or imprisonment, or deportation from the Transvaal, or all three. The Indians at the mass meeting made a solemn vow amongst them-selves, Hindus, Moslems and Christians, to stand together as one people and to resist the Ordinance should it become law.

The events that followed may be briefly recounted. On December 6, 1906 the Transvaal was granted self-government, and despite the protests and warnings of over 13,000 of her Indian citizens, the new Government passed the Transvaal Asiatic Registration Act (the old "Asiatic Law Amendment Ordinance") on March 22, 1907. On March 29 the Transvaal Indians met again in a mass protest, but under Gandhi's tutelage they offered a compromise to the Government which was to agree to register voluntarily if the Act were repealed. Gandhi called on the Colonial Secretary, General Jan Christian Smuts, the great hero of the Boer War, and submitted to him this compromise plan — voluntary registration for repeal of the Act. Nothing came of the offer for on July 1, 1907 the Act was enforced in Pretoria and the Indians were told to register within a month. The campaign to resist began on the same day with Gandhi offering to defend anyone arrested under the law. General strikes (hartals) were organized throughout the Transvaal, public meetings were called to arouse the citizens to back the resisters, letters and telegrams were sent to London, and a newspaper letter writing campaign was begun to the papers in South Africa, England and India. The whole mass effort turned out to be a great success for the Indians. On the last official day of registration, November 30, 1907 only 511 out of 13,000 eligible British Indians had registered under the new law.

The government made arrests throughout the summer and Gandhi defended the arrested until December 27, 1907 when he himself was finally taken into custody. He defended himself in court and while he was told on December 28 to leave the Transvaal within 48 hours, nothing ever came of his indictment and trial. Again it was a victory of sorts against the Government.

The protest continued into January of 1908, with Gandhi again offering to compromise, voluntary registration in exchange for repeal of the law. The alternative again, he told the Transvaal Government, was that Indians would go to prison, or be deported, 10,000 strong, but they would never comply with the unjust law and accept forcible registration. On January 10 Gandhi was arrested, tried and sentenced to two months in jail. On January 28 a representative of the Government came to Gandhi in jail to discuss the compromise offer, and tentative agreement regarding it was reached at that time. Two days later, Gandhi was escorted to Pretoria to meet with General Smuts. In their interview Smuts promised to rescind the law if all Asiatics would register voluntarily. Both Gandhi and Smuts agreed on the compromise and the former called off the disobedience to the law and the resistance to the Government. All protesters were released from jail in a general amnesty and on February 10, 1908 voluntary registration began. By May 9, the last day of registration, well over 8,700 Indians had voluntarily registered with the Transvaal Government.

But the law was not repealed. General Smuts went back on his word, and the "Black Law," as the Indians called it, remained in force. Gandhi accused Smuts of "foul play" and on May 30 the campaign of non-violent civil disobedience, now called *satyagraha*, was resumed. What followed, the public burning of registration cards by the Indians, their working in violation of the law which said only card holders could hawk or vend or sell in the cities, a new refusal to register, mailing back old cards, etc., became part of the new satyagraha campaign. This then was the history of the struggle for Indian rights in South Africa from September 1906 until sometime in July of 1908, a struggle in which a new philosophy of non-violent civil resistance was used for the first time.

The practice of satyagraha was to become the most potent weapon to be used by the Gandhians against the British in India from its first use in Bihar in 1917 until 1947 when Indian independence was finally granted.

Satyagraha, as developed by Gandhi, is composed of four essential elements: First, civil disobedience must be offered to unjust laws. The Gandhians believe that if the law injures human dignity or causes unwarranted human suffering, then one must choose to disobey the law by intentionally courting ridicule, jail, physical injury, imprisonment or death. The *satyagrahi*, as the Gandhian follower of satyagraha came to be called, must be prepared for the physical, the legal, and the moral consequences of the act of civil disobedience. Civil disobedience to unjust laws is important because it attracts and marshals public attention, i.e., the attention of those who support the unjust law and of those who are against it, as well as the attention of those who are indifferent to it because they never thought about it before.

Second, the disobedience must be carried out with an attitude of non-violence and love. The satyagrahis, after fasting and prayer, must conduct themselves in a morally exemplary fashion so as not to hurt or harm those who would attempt to prevent their disobedience.

Third, Gandhi exhorted his satragrahis to look upon the act of disobedience as an offering of their bodies, souls and lives to God. Thus an element of what Hindus call *bhakti yoga*, the way of loving devotion to God, enters into satyagraha. The business of disobedience becomes a sacrifice, a spiritual act, a religious rite within a social or political environment where the consequences of the act, through what Hindus call *karma yoga*, the way of selfless action, are renounced by the satyagrahi.

The fourth and final element of satyagraha followed hard upon the second and third. Gandhi felt that it was more important to change people than to change laws, hence, the aim of satyagraha ought to be to change the hearts and minds of the oppressor rather than the laws through which they oppressed: Only when those who had previously supported and defended the unjust law had been converted, only then could one say that satyagraha had been successful.

Satyagraha, therefore, is simple but intentional disobedience to unjust laws, carried out with an attitude of love, courage, selflessness and non-violence as a religious sacrifice to God Who, Gandhi felt, would then bless and aid such an undertaking. All of this is done for the sole purpose, not of defeating and triumphantly subduing one's opponent, but of converting and changing him or her. As Gandhi wisely saw, when one *defeats* an opponent in a struggle, one merely sows the seeds of hatred and dissension for future struggles. But when one *converts* the "enemy" that enemy then joins you in future struggles for justice, peace and brotherhood. These four elements of satyagraha were to become the essential ingredients of Gandhi's later way of philosophy, a philosophy that he used in solving the day to day problems of human existence.

Salt and Satyagraha: The Great Salt March

One of the most spectacular uses of satyagraha took place in India in 1930. Let me explain this particular action by putting it into perspective. The British government in India, in order to operate the machinery of the state, collected taxes in the usual ways. In particular, the Crown had put a tax on salt which it then proceeded to manufacture. To protect its monopoly the legislation which put the Salt Act into existence provided stiff penalties for anyone who bootlegged salt or made it illegally. Gandhi knew that the law was unjust. In a letter to the Viceroy, Lord Irwin, the British Crown's representative in New Delhi, dated March 2, 1930, and sent only nine days before his satyagraha against the Salt Act was to begin, Gandhi explained his position and his intention. The letter was addressed to his "Dear Friend" and it was an attempt to get the Viceroy to change not only the legislation that put an unfair burden on the poverty-driven masses of the country, since salt was a necessity for existence, but it was also an attempt to convert the Viceroy and to get him to see the error of the very presence of himself and of the British in India. In this extraordinary letter that makes as much an appeal to the heart as to the mind Gandhi went on to inform the Viceroy what he intended to do should the Viceroy fail to respond to his letter: He intended satyagraha. The Viceroy dictated a rude and indifferent reply to Gandhi. The way was then open for the most dramatic act of civil disobedience against the British since the Boston Tea Party of 1773.

On March 12 Gandhi, together with seventy-eight dedicated follow-ers, set out from his *ashram*, or communal retreat, near Ahmedabad, a city north of Bombay, to walk 241 miles in twenty-four days to the sea at Dandi in order to make salt in defiance of the law. Gandhi explained to the crowds of people that they met along the way, "We are marching in the name of God." Wherever he stopped thousands gathered and Gandhi adjured them to give up alcohol and drugs, abandon child marriage, an ancient custom that Gandhi fought with particular vehemence, and to live virtuously and cleanly. Finally, he exhorted them to join with him in breaking the Salt Law.

He was sixty-one at the time and he endured the long march with no visible discomfort while those younger and seemingly more robust were forced to ride part of the way by cart or even to drop out. The people threw flowers and spread leaves before the satyagrahis as they walked. When finally they arrived at Dandi on April 5, 1930 the band had grown from the original few to tens of thousands.

On April 6th, at 8:00 in the morning, Gandhi walked into the sea, picked up some salt from a frothy, foaming wave and returned to the shore. He had broken the law. The pinch of salt, the simplest gesture imaginable, following a long and dramatic march, caught the imagina-tion of the world. The act was a signal to the people of India. Those who accompanied Gandhi waded into the sea to make salt while up and down the coast of the Arabian Sea entire villages sought to catch the water in palms and pans and to make salt. And thousands were arrested.

Suddenly across the country contraband salt was sold openly while thousands of Indians intentionally and non-violently broke the law. In Bombay, salt was made on the roof of the Congress Party headquarters. A crowd of over 50,000 gathered, and hundreds were tied and hand-cuffed and led off to jail. In Ahmedabad, near the city where the salt march had originated, over 10,000 people received illegal salt in the first week following the Dandi satyagraha. Jawaharlal Nehru, the leader of the Congress, and later the first prime minister of the Republic of India, and the father and grandfather of two future prime ministers, was ar-rested in Allahabad for violating the Salt Law.

The Salt satyagraha was also a signal for other non-violent disobedi-ence to the British presence in India. The people were urged to boycott the British where it would hurt them the most: the pocketbook. The re-sult was a nation-wide campaign against all British imports, but espe-cially textiles. Indians began wearing homespun clothing. The spinning wheel, which today appears at the center of the Indian flag, was reintroduced into the cities from the villages. Thousands and then millions of people began to spin their own Indian cloth from Indian wool and cotton, or they bought their clothing from other Indians who did. The spinning wheel, like the defiance of the Salt Law, became a symbol of national honor, a badge of dignity and solidarity.

Within thirty days following Gandhi's disobedience of the Salt Law at Dandi, the entire country seemed to be acting as a single person in its defiance of the government. Except for freakish and isolated acts of violence on the part of a few Indians, the entire campaign was carried out non-violently and in the true spirit of satyagraha.

Finally on the night of May 4th armed Indian policemen led by a British magistrate came to Gandhi's camp near Dandi and arrested him. Gandhi was given permission to brush his teeth while the arrest order was read. He said his prayers, the satyagrahis around the encampment sang a hymn, and Mohandas Karamchand Gandhi was taken off to a waiting truck and from there to prison.

The Accomplishments of the Salt March

For all practical purposes, and though the Salt Law was not repealed until one year later, the satyagraha salt campaign of 1930 accomplished three things:

First, it demonstrated that satyagraha could be used on a massive scale to draw world-wide attention to Indian social injustices and political persecution. The conscience of the world community could be aroused by such a simple, elemental act as making salt when the laws prohibiting it were embedded in a wider and more massive net of social and political injustice.

Second, it demonstrated that satyagraha as a non-violent instrument of action could unite a people more securely, more unselfishly, than could a massive violent campaign. In meeting force, violence and hatred with love, non-violence and passive resistance the Indians blunted the edges of the violent weapons used by their oppressors. Public and individual responses to the new instrument of liberation defeated the British more truly and certainly than bombs and canons ever could.

Third, and finally, it demonstrated that Indians, held together by a common love rather than a common hatred, could, if they could defeat the British, defeat any power on earth. They were demonstrating that love, trust, selflessness and non-violence could move the hearts of men and, as a consequence, move whole nations and entire worlds. They suddenly found that this bond of love united them more surely as a nation than any religion, creed or philosophy had heretofore been able to do. The Hindu, Christian, Jew, Buddhist, Jain and Moslem of India discovered a brotherhood beyond their sects and beyond their dogmas, and they realized, perhaps for the first time, what it meant to be an Indian. Satyagraha helped to define them as a people by giving them a common cause and a common means with which to develop that cause. It was the beginning of the modern Republic of India.

Gandhi's Death

Gandhi believed deeply in his instrument for liberation and used satyagraha numerous times in his struggle for the independence of India. On January 30, 1948, a year after that independence was granted, and while Gandhi was on his way to public prayers, he was shot and killed by an assassin.

With his simple habits of food and dress, with his unadorned doctrines of love and forgiveness, Gandhi was to become an inspiration to millions of people all over the world (including the late Dr. Martin Luther King, Jr.) who watched admiringly as one man's philosophy moved the mighty British empire. It is out of this tumultuous and strife-ridden worldly activity that Gandhi's way of philosophy was born. [The literature on Gandhi and satyagraha is immense. *Publishers Weekly* in 1985 estimates that there are over 400 biographies alone of his life. In addition, some 80 volumes of his collected works are now in print and the collection is not yet complete. Some of the more useful books by and about Gandhi will be found listed at the end of this volume.]

Self-realization

Mohandas Gandhi was once asked, Can a man or woman attain self-realization, i.e., ultimate happiness or liberation, by mere recitation of Ramanama (repeating, or meditating on, the name of God, Rama) and without taking part in worldly actions, such as national service? The questioner (a woman) adds that her sisters have told her that one need not do anything "beyond attending to family requirements and occasionally showing kindness to the poor." The *Mahatma*, an honorific name meaning "great souled," somewhat like the word "saint," answers:

> This question has puzzled not only women but many men and has taxed me to the utmost. I know that there is a school of philosophy which teaches complete inaction and futility of all effort. I have not been able to appreciate that teaching, unless in order to secure verbal agreement I were to put my own interpretation on it. In my humble opinion *effort* is necessary for one's

own growth. It has to be irrespective of results. Ramanama or some equiva-
lent is necessary not for the sake of repetition but for the sake of *purification*,
as an aid to effort, for direct *guidance from above*. It is therefore never a substi-
tute for effort. It is meant for intensifying and guiding it in a proper channel.
If all effort is vain, why [engage in] family cares or an occasional help to the
poor? In this very effort is contained the germ of national service. A national
service, to me, means service of humanity, even as *disinterested service* of the
family means the same thing. Disinterested service of the family necessarily
leads one to national service. Ramanama gives one detachment and ballast
and never throws one off one's balance at critical moments. *Self-realization* I
hold to be impossible without service of and identification with the poorest.
[M. K. Gandhi, *Hindu Dharma* (Ahmedabad: Navajivan Publishing House,
1950), p. 404. Italics added.]

Mohandas Gandhi's doctrine of satyagraha is beautifully encapsulated in this brief answer quoted from a 1926 editorial column in *Young
India*, his own weekly newspaper. That doctrine and that answer are both
expressions of a philosophy of action that begins with self-*purification*
which, in turn, leads to *disinterested* or unselfish moral *effort* which is,
itself, *guided by God*. It is a commitment to a way of engaging in actions
without which self-realization would be impossible. The foundation of
this philosophy of action is derived primarily from Gandhi's interpretation of the *Bhagavad Gita*, the most popular sacred text to come out of the
entire Hindu tradition.

The *Bhagavad Gita*: The *New Testament* of Hinduism

The *Bhagavad Gita* has been justifiably called "the *New Testament* of
Hinduism," an indication of its enormous influence and popularity, and
Mohandas Gandhi knew almost all of its 700 verses by heart. To under-
stand Gandhi's own enormous influence and popularity, as well as to
understand his philosophy of action, it is necessary to understand the
Gita and its way of philosophy.

The *Bhagavad Gita* ("the message of God") probably dates from
around the 4th to the 2nd centuries B.C. It purports to be the record of a
conversation that took place in India's mythical past between Krishna, a
human incarnation of the Hindu God Vishnu, and a human warrior hero,
Arjuna. As the *Gita* opens, a great and decisive battle is about to begin in
a war between two sides of the same family; the war and the battle are
concerned with who shall be king of India. One side of the family,
Arjuna's and Krishna's side, has been repeatedly cheated by the other
side, and after all attempts at compromise have failed, the war begins: A
final battle will decide the right.

Krishna has been chosen to be Arjuna's charioteer and as the 700 verses of the *Gita* unfold, Krishna's identity as God, Himself, descended to earth in human form, is gradually revealed to Arjuna. As the *Gita* begins, Arjuna has asked Krishna to drive their chariot to a place between and overlooking the two armies. From this prospect Arjuna now sees the "enemy" across no-man's-land. That enemy, as it turns out, consists of members of his own family, the side that has cheated and wronged his four brothers and himself. We are in the midst of a civil war, of course, and Arjuna recognizes uncles, grandfathers, cousins, teachers and friends that he has known, loved and respected all of his life. And he knows that it is wrong to kill members of his own family. But being a warrior, a member of the class dedicated to protecting his family and clan, he is caught in an overwhelming moral dilemma; for the clan that he is called upon to defend is now the very same clan that he is called upon to destroy.

Arjuna's moral dilemma can be stated in the following way:

1. If Arjuna fights then he will be committing murder.

2. If he doesn't fight then he will have failed to do his duty.

3. But he must either fight or not fight.

4. Therefore, he either commits murder or he fails to do his duty; in either event he does what is wrong.

The first of the brief eighteen chapters of the *Gita* ends as Arjuna, heartsick and despondent, casts his weapons aside and sits down on the floor of his chariot, refusing to fight.

Arjuna's dilemma stands upon another dilemma, more fundamental to both Hinduism and to Gandhi's philosophy of life, and in many ways a dilemma far more troublesome than Arjuna's dilemma. This other dilemma, call it "the dilemma of action," carries with it a number of assumptions which both Hinduism and Gandhi accept, assumptions which ought to be mentioned. We shall see that if this dilemma, the dilemma of action, can be solved, then Arjuna's dilemma can be solved, as well.

All Hindus believe that human beings are held in bondage to successive and unending rebirths into this world. Further, they believe that the chief cause of this bondage is human desire, whether that desire be good desire or evil desire. Thus, curiously enough, whether one desires to bring about good or whether one desires to bring about evil, the results are still going to lead to rebirth and bondage. The reason for this lies in the law of karma which says that eventually all good desires must be rewarded and all evil desires must be punished. Either way bondage and rebirth, either for reward or punishment, are the inevitable results. Further, all Hindus believe that bondage and rebirth, no matter how well reborn one might come to be, are conditions or states to be avoided. The ultimate goal for all humans is, consequently, liberation from bondage and rebirth. Finally, liberation from rebirth is achieved through the yogas which we shall touch on shortly.

The dilemma of action can now be stated in the following way:

1. If one does evil acts (such as fighting one's own family), then this produces evil results that lead to bondage and rebirth.

2. If one does good acts (such as doing one's duty and defending the family), then this produces good results that also lead to bondage and rebirth.

3. But one must do either evil acts or good acts.

4. Therefore, whatever one does, bondage and rebirth will be the inevitable consequence.

Arjuna's problem is stated in both the dilemma of action and in Arjuna's dilemma. The ways to solve these dilemmas and to achieve liberation from suffering is now carefully explained to Arjuna by Lord Krishna. It is God speaking to Man, offering a way of life that can escape the evils and suffering that all action in the world inevitably brings. Krishna will show Arjuna three ways or yogas, and all three of them speak directly to the two dilemmas mentioned above. All three yogas, as we shall see, slip between the horns of our dilemmas by showing that there is an alternative to either fighting or not fighting, as with Arjuna's dilemma, or an alternative to either doing evil acts or doing good acts, as with the dilemma of action.

The *religious* way is referred to by Hindus as *bhakti yoga*, the way of devotion to God. It says, in effect, keep all attention on God, Lord Krishna in this case, and then all of one's actions become sacrifices to God. Show love and devotion to Lord Krishna and the dilemmas cease to be problems. Krishna tells Arjuna:

> He who with devotion offers to Me a leaf, a flower, a fruit or water, that offering of love, from the pure in heart, I accept.

> Whatever you do, whatever you eat, whatever you offer, whatever you give away, whatever austerities you perform, do that as an offering to Me.

> In this way you will be freed from the good and evil consequences of karma which are your bonds. [B.G. IX. 26-28]

> Abandoning all duties, come to Me alone for refuge. Be not sorrowed for I shall give you liberation from all sins. [B.G. XVIII. 66]

The *mystical* way is referred to by Hindus as *jnana* (pronounced "gyahna") *yoga*, the way of knowledge. *Jnana yoga* relieves one of the responsibility of the karmic consequences of one's action through the intuitive discovery that one's true inner-nature (*Atman* or Self) is identical with the Holy Power of the universe (*Brahman*). This mystical knowledge of the divine nature of one's true Self is also taught by Krishna to Arjuna:

> Only by the knowledge of the *Atman* (Self) through the destruction of ignorance, only by that will true knowledge (*jnana*) shine forth like the sun, revealing the Highest.

> Thinking on That (*Brahman*), merging the *Atman* with That, making That the sole aim and object of their devotion, they reach a state from which there is no rebirth, their sins destroyed by truth and knowledge. [B.G. V. 16-17]

The dilemma of action is destroyed and with it Arjuna's dilemma as well, for Lord Krishna has shown Arjuna an alternative to right action and wrong action that will end suffering and bondage forever. That way lies beyond all action and inaction and leads to the discovery of the divine Self.

The *ethical* way is referred to by Hindus as *karma yoga*, the way of action. It is probably with this third and final yoga that the *Gita* speaks most directly to modern men and women. Lord Krishna counsels Arjuna to give up the desire for the ends or consequences of his actions. And it is this letting go of the anticipated results of action that lies at the heart of *karma yoga*:

> Let your concern be with action alone and never with the fruits of action. Do not let the results of action be your motive, and do not be attached to inaction.

> ...perform your actions renouncing attachments, indifferent to success and failure....

Those endowed with unattachment leave behind in this world both good and evil. Therefore, unite yourself to (*karma*) *yoga*. (*Karma*) *yoga* is, indeed, skill in action.

The wise, united to unattachment, renounce the fruits which action produces, and freed thereby from the bondage of rebirth, they go to that place free from pain. [*B.G.* II. 47-48, 50-51]

What Krishna is really asking Arjuna to do through *karma yoga*, however, is to abandon all desire:

When he abandons all desires that are in his heart and finds satisfaction in the real Self alone then, oh Arjuna, that one has truly reached steadfast wisdom.

When in sorrow his mind is not disturbed, when he is indifferent to pleasures, when his passions, fears and hatreds have departed, then he is called a holy man of steadfast mind.

He who has no attachments toward anything, and who, having gotten this or that good or evil, neither delights in it nor hates it, then his mind is steadfast. [*B.G.* II. 55-57]

The best exponent of *karma yoga* in the modern world was without a doubt Mohandas Gandhi who, through his life and writings, attempted to introject this way of action of the *Gita* into the 20th century.

Gandhi and the *Bhagavad Gita*

Gandhi was deeply influenced by the *Gita*. He called it his "spiritual reference book" adding, "When doubt haunts me... and when I see not one ray of light on the horizon, I turn to the *Bhagavad Gita* and find a verse to comfort me." And Gandhi found in the *Gita* a technique for implementing satyagraha, viz., *karma yoga*. As we have seen, *karma yoga* is the method by which desireless activity can be accomplished, and the successful exercise of satyagraha would be impossible without this element of desirelessness, the renunciation of the results of all action.

Gandhi's interpretation of the *Gita* is novel in that he saw the *Gita* as a spiritual allegory and not as an historical text advocating the dutiful use of war and violence to solve human problems. In the introduction to his own translation of the *Gita* he states:

Even in 1888-89, when I first became acquainted with the *Gita*, I felt that it was not a historical work, but that, under the guise of physical warfare, it described the duel that perpetually went on in the hearts of mankind, and that physical warfare was brought in merely to make the description of the internal duel more alluring. [Mahadev Desai, *The Gita According to Gandhi* (Ahmedabad: Navajivan Publishing House, 1946, p. 127]

The battlefield of the *Gita* lies in the heart of every person. And it is there, within each person, that Lord Krishna, God, gives His counsel. God lives then in the hearts of all human beings and, Gandhi says, man is not at peace until this divine part within him is known, i.e., until real self-realization has been achieved:

> Man is not at peace with himself till he has become like unto God. The endeavor to reach this state is the supreme, the only ambition worth having. And this is self-realization.

Further, self-realization is, Gandhi contends, the central concern of the *Gita*:

> The object of the *Gita* appears to me to be that of showing the most excellent way to attain self-realization.

And the way to that object is, of course, *karma yoga*:

> That matchless remedy is renunciation of fruits of action.... This is the center round which the *Gita* is woven. This renunciation is the central sun, round which devotion [*bhakti*], knowledge [*jnana*] and the rest revolve like planets. [*Ibid.*, 128, 129.]

GANDHI'S ACCOMPLISHMENTS

Like many of the Roman Stoics before him, Gandhi was in the forefront of politics and social change throughout his turbulent life. He was in and out of jail, agitating for reform, calling for strikes and boycotts, speaking and writing to capture the attention of the world over the plight of his fellow Indians in a country ruled by a colonial power. In many ways this outstanding champion of non-violent direct action against injustices was, more than any other single figure, responsible for India's eventual independence, an independence, let it be noted, that was without violence and bloodshed against that colonial power.

Gandhi shared with those same Stoics several common beliefs about the human self, the world and God. These beliefs helped to justify and ground both of their activities in the world, but these shared beliefs also led to divergent practices, as well. The Stoics argued that there was a natural law, which they variously called Zeus, God, Destiny, Providence, Reason and Nature, a law which was rational, divine and knowable, which stood above all man-made law but was present in man as the

Logos, man's true and divine Self. It was this commonly shared natural law which made all men and women equal in the eyes of God, and it was this commonly present indwelling Self that made all humans brothers and sisters in the eyes of their fellow man. In the same fashion, Gandhi and the *Gita* both claim an equality among human beings in virtue of man's common and shared destiny in the eyes of God, on the one hand, and in virtue of the presence of God, the real Self (*Atman*), in the hearts of all persons, on the other, guiding and counseling those who will listen. Finally, the Stoics held that desires must be controlled, reduced and checked, if happiness was to be achieved. This, as we have seen, is what in the end karma yoga is all about, as well. Renouncing the fruits of action is tantamount to controlling and eliminating desire. It is this conclusion that stands behind Gandhi's and the *Gita's* concept of liberation from rebirth, and it may be in the background to much that is said by the Stoics, as well; that is to say, the best and most worthwhile life is ultimately lived by the person who has no desires (self) at all.

But beyond all this, Gandhi's greatest accomplishment probably lay in proclaiming to the world that the individual can alone, by himself or herself, move mountains. It is possible to start a one man revolution, as Henry David Thoreau proclaimed, and in virtue of that revolution overturn injustice everywhere. Gandhi by his example showed the world what one just man could do in the face of the mighty British empire and, as such, he left a reminder, a hope, and a legacy for all just men and women who would follow after him.

THE WAY OF SATYAGRAHA: MOHANDAS K. GANDHI

The Problem

For Gandhi the problem that he sought to solve was the problem of suffering, his own suffering as well as that of others. This suffering at the personal level had already been identified for him in virtue of his religion, Hinduism. As a Hindu, and as a loyal devotee of the *Bhagavad Gita* Gandhi recognized *samsara,* the suffering of rebirth, as the major problem to be solved. But as a man sensitive to the poverty, ignorance and chaos present in the plight of his fellow human beings Gandhi was all too aware of the wider social dimension to suffering, as well. The problem of suffering, then, lay on two levels, personal and social, and Gandhi sought to address both levels in his way of philosophy.

The Causes

For Gandhi the causes of the two kinds of suffering were distinct but related. The personal suffering that he experienced was, as the *Gita* had explained, caused by both the ignorance of the Self and Its divine nature, as well as by the selfishness and desire that led to pain and bondage in actions. The societal suffering that he experienced was caused by practices ranging from child marriage, untouchability, caste discrimination and the presence of a foreign power on Indian soil to the poverty, disease, and appalling conditions of bare survival rife throughout the entire subcontinent of India. Removing one set of causes of suffering, Gandhi felt, would affect the existence of the other set of causes. Thus achieving self-realization by removing selfishness and desire in one's own life could have dramatic repercussions in the social sphere in which one attempted to act and think like a satyagrahi. And altering the appalling social conditions would provide the arena in which self-realization could be developed and encouraged.

The Solutions

For Gandhi the two problems and the two causes needed two solutions. The problem of personal suffering was solved by liberation from self-ignorance and uncontrolled desire. The problem of societal suffering was solved by the creation of a better society. The solutions could be simply labeled "liberation for oneself" and "liberation for society."

The Ways

For Gandhi, the ways to the two solutions of the two problems were found by attacking the two causes of the problems. These two ways were to be found in the *Bhagavad Gita*, and Gandhi used the concept of satyagraha to cover both of them. First, the problem of personal suffering was met by adopting *bhakti yoga* and *karma yoga*, the way of devotion to God and the way of non-attached, desireless action. By dedicating all of one's actions to God, the satyagrahi lets go of the consequences of his or her actions and learns to act in a desireless, unselfish manner. Second, the problem of societal suffering was met by adopting non-violent, compassionate and direct means to change the hearts and minds of those who follow the unjust laws and customs as well as of those who make them. Both ways lead ultimately to self-realization and release from *samsara*, as well as social liberation and release from societal suffering.

PROBLEMS WITH GANDHI

One of the chief difficulties with Gandhi's philosophy lies with the way of *karma yoga*. How does one go about reducing one's desires? or letting go of the anticipated results of one's actions? What's the plan or formula that I ought to follow? I know I can give up wanting two cars but can I give up wanting one car? or one of anything? How do I do it? Isn't it true that the only people who don't want two cars are the ones who have two cars already? Isn't the key to getting rid of desire really that of satisfying desire and not trying to control it or stamp it out? But then aren't the hedonists right after all?

Further, how can I desire to give up desire? Surely there's a paradox in that, a paradox of desire not unlike the paradox of hedonism familiar from our discussion of John Stuart Mill and utilitarianism. [See above Chapter 9, *The Way of Utilitarianism*, pp. 192-193.] If reduced desires or even desirelessness are the desired ends or goals to be pursued, then how can I pursue, i.e., desire, those ends without ending up in a terrible tangle?; that is to say, How can I ever desire to give up desire?

Further, if satyagraha, as recommended by Gandhi, depends on finding some ultimate source of Power in the universe, whether it be Self or *Brahman*, or self or God, and obeying the laws or rules prescribed by that Power, then how do I find that Power?, and how do I go about obeying those laws? The conflicting traditions all seem to have inconsistent views, not only about the nature of that Power, e.g., is it personal God?, is it self?, is it reason?, is it impersonal?, but they also seem to have inconsistent views regarding what man is commanded to do, e.g., should one use violence to correct injustice?, or should one never use violence and always turn the other cheek? But doesn't all of this then make the way of satyagraha not only inconsistent, if it entails the paradox of desire, but now incomplete, as well, should it fail to answer the questions of *how* to get rid of desire?, or let go of consequences?, or turn the other cheek?, or how to find that power within oneself or outside of oneself that makes that ridding, that letting-go, that turning and that finding possible?

Finally, can satyagraha say that it is always right to turn the other cheek? Should I turn the other cheek to a Hitler?, a fanatic racist?, an intolerant ideologue? Isn't changing the heart of the oppressor too much to hope for?, too idealistic? Shouldn't we only be satisfied with changing man's laws and not man's minds?, hoping the conversion of minds will follow. And doesn't satyagraha through all of this simply fly in the face of good old-fashioned common sense?

These are all questions and problems that the follower of the Gandhian way of philosophy must attempt to answer and solve, and they are puzzles to which we shall return for answers when we investigate the application of satyagraha to racial intolerance in the United States in the philosophy of Martin Luther King, Jr.

TWELVE
THE WAY OF CHRISTIAN SATYAGRAHA
❧•❧

MARTIN LUTHER KING, JR.: A CHRISTIAN *SATYAGRAHI**

The question, What is it to be a Christian? was the central question asked
and answered by Martin Luther King, Jr., a Black clergyman from
Atlanta, Georgia. Moved to action by the violence and injustices that he
witnessed while growing up in the South, King answered the question
with a theory of Christian action that blended the pacifist ethic of Jesus of
Nazareth with the civil disobedience methodology of Mohandas Gandhi.
It proved to be a unique synthesis of Western and Eastern elements, of
Christianity and Hinduism. At the same time King's way of Christian
action offered a practical alternative to the ways of hatred, violence and
war that even now confront millions of men and women in the 1990s.
King's answer to the question, What is it to be a Christian?, is to be
found, as we shall see, in King's attempt to answer another question, the
question with which our long study began, What is the best and most
worthwhile life that a human being can live?

KING'S LIFE

Martin Luther King, Jr. was born on January 15, 1929, in Atlanta,
Georgia. His father, Martin Luther King, Senior, was pastor at the
Ebenezer Baptist Church in Atlanta and expected his namesake to follow
in his ministerial footsteps. Martin was a bright, quick, perceptive child
and early learned the hard fact, which he will have to pass on to his children, that he is a Black man in a world dominated by White racism. Like

---

* A *satyagrahi*, again, is one who practices satyagraha.

Gandhi before him, he learned the dirty implications of being "colored" through two experiences both involving public transportation:

> When I was fourteen, I had traveled from Atlanta to Dublin, Georgia, with a dear teacher of mine, Mrs. Bradley; she's dead now. I had participated there in an oratorical contest sponsored by the Negro Elks. It turned out to be a memorable day, for I had succeeded in winning the contest. My subject, I recall, ironically enough, was "The Negro and the Constitution." Anyway, that night, Mrs. Bradley and I were on a bus returning to Atlanta, and at a small town along the way, some white passengers boarded the bus, and the white driver ordered us to get up and give the whites our seats. We didn't move quickly enough to suit him, so he began cursing us, calling us "black sons of bitches." I intended to stay right in that seat, but Mrs. Bradley finally urged me up, saying we had to obey the law. And so we stood up in the aisle for the ninety miles to Atlanta. That night will never leave my memory. It was the angriest I have ever been in my life. [Martin Luther King, Jr., "Playboy Interview" in *A Testament of Hope, The Essential Writings of Martin Luther King, Jr.*, Edited by James Melvin Washington (San Francisco: Harper & Row, Publishers, 1986), pp. 342-343.)]

A second incident involving bigotry and public transportation comes even closer to Gandhi's first racist experience in South Africa. King had passed the entrance examination to Atlanta's prestigious Morehouse College enrolling at the age of 15 without graduating from high school. To earn money for his college tuition he worked summers on a tobacco farm in Connecticut. He expressly enjoyed the personal and social freedom that the New England atmosphere provided, entering the front doors and sitting wherever he wished in restaurants and theaters just like White folks. But the train trip back to Atlanta at the end of summer drove home to him once more the terrible reality of his situation as a Negro. On one such occasion as the train entered Virginia,

> ...King made his way to the dining car and started to sit down anywhere, as he had done on the way through New York and New Jersey. But the train was in Dixie now, and the waiter led him to a rear table and pulled a curtain down to shield the white passengers from his presence. He sat there, staring at that curtain, unable to believe that others could find him so offensive. "I felt," he said, "as though the curtain had dropped on my selfhood." [Stephen B. Oates, *Let the Trumpet Sound, The Life of Martin Luther King, Jr.* (New York: New American Library, 1982), p. 17. The story is recounted by Lerone Bennet, a close friend of King's and a fellow student at Morehouse.]

On February 25, 1948, King was ordained to the Baptist ministry and in June he graduated from Morehouse with a B.A. in sociology. In September he entered Crozer Theological Seminary in Philadelphia intending to become a well-educated Christian minister. One Sunday he heard Dr. Mordecai W. Johnson, the president of Howard University, give a lecture on the life and teachings of Mohandas Gandhi. Johnson talked of Gandhi's philosophy of soul force, satyagraha, the power of love and non-violence as a way of social change. King was overwhelmed by Johnson's suggestion that the moral power of Gandhian non-violence could revolutionize race relations in the United States: "I had heard of Gandhi... [but Johnson's] message was so profound and electrifying that I left the meeting and bought a half-dozen books on Gandhi's life and works." [*Ibid.*, p. 31-32.] King was to become convinced that Gandhi's way was the only just and practical way for oppressed people everywhere to overcome social and political injustice. King was to write some eight years later, and following the early success of the practice of his own Christian satyagraha, a paragraph that was to become the inspiration for the Black non-violent struggle for justice in the United States:

> American Negroes must come to the point where they can say to their white brothers, paraphrasing the words of Gandhi: "We will match your capacity to inflict suffering with our capacity to endure suffering. We will meet your physical force with soul force ["satya-graha"]. We will not hate you, but we cannot in all good conscience obey your unjust laws. Do to us what you will and we will still love you. Bomb our homes and threaten our children; send your hooded perpetrators of violence into our communities and drag us out on some wayside road, beating us and leaving us half dead, and we will still love you. But we will soon wear you down by our capacity to suffer. And in winning our freedom we will so appeal to your heart and conscience that we will win you in the process." [Martin Luther King, Jr., *Stride Toward Freedom: The Montgomery Story* (New York: Harper & Row, 1958), quoted in *A Testament of Hope, Op. Cit.*, p. 485.]

This chapter is about the influence of Gandhi's way of philosophy on the Christian way of philosophy of Martin Luther King; it is a chapter about Christian satyagraha.

King's March to Higher Education

In 1951 King graduated with honors from Crozer with a B.D. degree and in the fall he went to Boston University on a scholarship to pursue a Ph.D. in systematic theology. King intended to become a research scholar, find a quiet ivory tower somewhere, write inspiring books and articles, and let the rest of the troubled world roll by. He married Coretta Scott in June 1953 and, exams behind him, started work on his Ph.D. thesis that summer.

256 THE WAYS OF PHILOSOPHY

He chose as his topic for the dissertation the divergent 20th century theologies of Paul Tillich and Henry Nelson Wieman; and divergent they were, indeed. Tillich, a theological descendent of Søren Kierkegaard, had devoted his intellectual life to demonstrating and arguing that God was a transcendent pure Being, impersonal, and utterly beyond the world of particulars and sufferings. Wieman, on the other hand, a theological ancestor of current liberation theology, had held an equally supportable Christian position, maintaining that God was immanent in the world, ever present, and ever involved in that world. It was super-monist versus super-pluralist in Christian theology. King attempted a radical synthesis of the two views, and it was Mohandas Gandhi and satyagraha that gave him the insight into how the synthesis could be worked.

Years later King was to reflect on the role that Gandhi played in his own attempts to understand the role of an ethic of love and non-violence in the church's concern with strict Pauline, or Kierkegaardian, faith and the salvation of souls. The problem that he saw then in his seminary days was to haunt him even later:

> Any religion that professes to be concerned about the souls of men and is not concerned about the slums that damn them, the economic conditions that strangle them and the social conditions that cripple them is a spiritually moribund religion waiting burial. [Martin Luther King, Jr., *Christian Century* 77 (April 13, 1960), a restatement really of part of Chapter 6 of his *Stride Toward Freedom, Op. Cit.*, p. 38.]

The problem of synthesizing the social gospel of Jesus of Nazareth as it is found in the Sermon on the Mount with the soul-saving faith of St. Paul and Paul's Danish apologist, Søren Kierkegaard, was neatly expressed when King again reflected back on this earlier period of his life at Boston University:

> During this period I had almost despaired of the power of love in solving social problems. The "turn the other cheek" philosophy and the "love your enemies" philosophy are only valid, I felt, when individuals are in conflict with other individuals; when racial groups and nations are in conflict a more realistic approach is necessary.

But it was Gandhi who provided the way out:

> Then I came upon the life and teaching of Mahatma Gandhi. As I read his works I became deeply fascinated by his campaigns of nonviolent resistance. The whole Gandhian concept of *satyagraha* (*satya* is truth which equals love, and *graha* is force; *satyagraha* thus means truth-force or love-force) was profoundly significant to me.

...I came to see for the first time that the Christian doctrine of love operating through the Gandhian method of nonviolence was one of the most potent weapons available to oppressed people in their struggle for freedom. [*Ibid.*]

The dissertation gave him the opportunity to join together the two indispensable elements of Christianity, faith and works, and the conclusion that he arrived at was this:

Wieman's ultimate pluralism fails to satisfy the rational demand for unity. Tillich's ultimate monism swallows up finite individuality in the unity of being. A more adequate view is to hold a quantitative pluralism and a qualitative monism. In this way oneness and manyness are preserved. [Stephen B. Oates, *Let the Trumpet Sound, Op. Cit.*, p. 47.]

But before beginning a scholarly life King felt he owed the world and his father his talents as a working minister. He hoped that after finishing his dissertation there would be time to find a teaching post and take up a life in academe. It was not to be.

Civil Rights in the United States

In April 1954 King accepted an offer to become pastor of the Dexter Avenue Baptist Church in Montgomery, Alabama. Reluctant at first to return to the deep South with all the racial problems that he had known as a child, the church made him an offer that he couldn't refuse. Together with an annual salary of $4,200, the highest salary of any Negro minister in the city, they gave him a parsonage and guaranteed him released time and expenses to complete his dissertation.

He preached his first sermon as pastor in May 1954. It was the same month that the United States Supreme Court handed down a landmark decision that was to change the life of Martin Luther King, Jr. as well as the life of the entire country. The decision was in the case of *Brown versus Board of Education of Topeka* in which the Supreme Court ruled that racial segregation in the public schools of the country was unconstitutional. It immediately set aside the Court's previous decision of 1896 in the case of *Plessy versus Ferguson* that had ruled that segregation of the races was constitutional, hence legal, as long as equal facilities were provided for both races. In setting aside the "separate but equal" decision of fifty-eight years earlier, the Court under Chief Justice Earl Warren found that "in the field of public education the doctrine of 'separate but equal' has no place" because "separate educational facilities are inherently unequal." The reason then given by the Court for overturning *Plessy* was that segregation in schools on the basis of race "has a detrimental effect upon the colored children" by developing "a feeling of inferiority as to their status in the community" which may "affect their hearts and minds in a way unlikely ever to be undone." [*Brown v. Board of Education of Topeka*, 347 U.S. 483 (1954).] With that decision and with that reasoning to substantiate the ruling, the legal path was now open to a plethora of legitimate challenges to *all* separate but equal public facilities, from lunch counters, restaurants, motels and hotels, to theaters and housing, and, of course, to trains and buses.

In Boston on June 5, 1955, his dissertation completed, accepted, and successfully defended, Martin Luther King received his Ph.D. in Systematic Theology from Boston University.

The Montgomery Bus Boycott

In Montgomery on December 1, 1955, her work at the city's leading department store finished for the week, Mrs. Rosa Parks, a forty-two year old Negro seamstress, boarded a bus for home. She was tired, her feet hurt, and she sat down in the first seat in the Negro back section of Montgomery's segregated Cleveland Avenue bus. The law throughout the South's segregated bus systems was that of sitting segregation, and it was very simple: If you were Black, you sat in the back half of the bus; if the White half of the front section filled, you could then be forced to surrender your seat in order that Whites might sit in your seat even if it was in the Black section.

Rosa Park's bus had filled and the bus operator ordered her to stand up and to move back in order that boarding White passengers might be seated. There were no other vacant seats that Friday, it was the Christmas shopping season. But Mrs. Parks was not about to surrender her seat so that a White male could sit while she stood all the way home. Unlike Gandhi decades before her in South Africa, and unlike King years earlier in Georgia, Rosa Parks quietly refused to give up her seat. She was promptly arrested and jailed. Four days later on December 5, after lengthy discussion with other Negro leaders, the Montgomery bus boycott began. [It was not the first such boycott. In 1953 the Reverend Theodore J. Jemison of Baton Rouge, Louisiana, a close friend of King's, had led a successful bus boycott in that city. Nor were they the first to recommend non-violent direct action in opposing segregation. The Congress of Racial Equality (CORE) had advocated its use as early as 1942. See Aldon D. Morris, *The Origins of the Civil Rights Movement: Black Communities Organizing for Change* (New York: The Free Press, 1984), pp. 17-22, 128-130.]

The Negroes of Montgomery were asked to stop riding city buses and to find alternate means of transportation. King was elected president of the Montgomery Improvement Association (MIA) which was to direct the strike against the buses and to find alternative transportation for 17,500 former bus riders. The strike was to have far broader implications, however, as other grievances were presented by the MIA to the city of Montgomery, grievances relating to the employment of Negroes in city jobs.

On February 2 the MIA went to Federal District Court to ask that segregated transportation be declared unconstitutional. The boycott in Montgomery became nearly 100 percent effective as the Negroes of Montgomery managed to stand together and find alternative transportation. The city fought back with injunctions and arrests, accusing those waiting for rides of loitering and of those riding in car pools of hitchhiking. Standing together for the first time, and doing it without retaliation and without violence, refusing to be intimidated by beatings, arrests and harassment from the racists, the city, and the police, the Negroes began to find what Gandhi and his South African *satyagrahis* had found fifty years earlier, viz., a new sense of pride, worth, and dignity.

On January 30, 1956, after days of obscene phone calls, hate mail, and an arrest for driving 30 mph. in a 25 mph. zone, King's house was bombed. On February 21 King and one hundred other MIA members were indicted and later found guilty of not obeying an outdated antiboycott law. But on June 4, 1956, the Federal District Court ruled that segregation on Montgomery's bus lines was unconstitutional. The city appealed but on November 13, 1956, almost a year after Rosa Parks refused to obey an unjust law, the United States Supreme Court affirmed that Alabama's state and local laws requiring segregation on buses violated the Constitution. A month later segregation on buses officially ended and on December 21, 1956, the MIA ended the boycott.

Christian Satyagraha

Now it was King's turn, like Gandhi before him, to reflect on the success of his own non-violent protest; and reflect he did, drawing up the necessary and sufficient elements of what we shall call "Christian satyagraha."

On January 10, 1957, one hundred Negro clergy came to Ebenezer Baptist Church in Atlanta and agreed to form what came to be called "the Southern Christian Leadership Conference," (SCLC). They elected Martin Luther King their president. In speaking to them King outlined his philosophy and the philosophy that was to guide SCLC in the violent days ahead. It was a philosophy that would enable committed Christians everywhere to defeat the evils of segregation as well as, as it turned out, to non-violently confront the evils of poverty, hatred, and war. Christian satyagraha became Martin Luther King's answer to Aristotle's question, What is the best and most worthwhile life that a human being can live?

King began with a bow to Gandhi:

> The alternative to violence is nonviolent resistance. This method was made famous in our generation by Mohandas K. Gandhi....

And then he stated four of the five points for his program, points that included all of the familiar elements of Gandhian satyagraha:

> Five points can be made concerning non-violence as a method in bringing about better racial conditions.
>
> First, this is not a method for cowards; it *does* resist.... [The nonviolent resister] is not physically aggressive towards his opponent. But his mind and emotions are always active, constantly seeking to persuade the opponent that he is mistaken....
>
> A second point is that nonviolent resistance does not seek to defeat or humiliate the opponent, but to win his friendship and understanding.... The end is redemption and reconciliation.
>
> A third characteristic of this method is that the attack is directed against forces of evil rather than against persons who are caught in those forces.... As I like to say to the people in Montgomery, Alabama: "The tension in this city is not between white people and Negro people. The tension is at bottom between justice and injustice, between the forces of light and the forces of darkness...."
>
> A fourth point that must be brought out concerning nonviolent resistance is that it avoids not only external physical violence but also internal violence of spirit. At the center of nonviolence stands the principle of love. [*A Testament of Hope, Op. Cit.*, pp. 7-8.]

The Sermon on the Mount

This principle was grounded in the *New Testament* and in particular in Jesus of Nazareth's *Sermon on the Mount.* This sermon lay at the heart of the non-violent pacifist message preached by both Gandhi and King. Here is a portion of that sermon most often quoted by each of them:

> You have heard that it was said to the men of old, "You shall not kill; and whoever kills shall be liable to judgment." But I say to you that every one

who is angry with his brother shall be liable to judgment; whoever insults his brother shall be liable to the council, and whoever says, "You fool!" shall be liable to the hell of fire.

. . . You have heard that it was said, "An eye for an eye and a tooth for a tooth." But I say to you, Do not resist one who is evil. But if anyone strikes you on the right cheek, turn to him the other also; and if any one would sue you and take your coat, let him have your cloak as well; and if any one forces you to go one mile, go with him two miles. Give to him who begs from you, and do not refuse him who would borrow from you.

. . . You have heard that it was said, 'You shall love your neighbor and hate your enemy.' But I say to you, love your enemies and pray for those who persecute you. [*The Gospel of St. Matthew*, Chapter 5, *passim*. Revised Standard Version.]

The non-violent core of Jesus' entire ministry was elegantly summarized for both Gandhi and King, when Jesus said, "The second commandment is this: 'You shall love your neighbor as yourself.' There is no other commandment greater than this." The *New Testament* Greek word for love was *agapē* which King defined as "a willingness to go to any length to restore community." [*A Testament of Hope, Op. Cit.*, p. 20.] And that restoration became the ultimate goal of all of his Christian satyagraha efforts.*

King concluded his reflections on his program with a fifth and final Gandhian characteristic of the new method:

Finally, the method of nonviolence is based on the conviction that the universe is on the side of justice....the nonviolent resistor has...cosmic companionship. This belief that God is on the side of truth and justice comes down to us from the long tradition of our Christian faith. [*Ibid.*, pp. 7, 8, 9. The piece is from *Christian Century 74* (February 6, 1957) but the five points were repeated many times in the years ahead in various church and secular journals. Jesus' love and Gandhi's strategy pervade the entire method outlined here by King. See above Chapter 11, *The Way of Satyagraha*, especially pp. 237-238.]

Christian satyagraha is, consequently, the way wherein, as King put it, "Christ furnished the spirit and motivation while Gandhi furnished the method." [*Ibid.*, p. 447.] Later, in reflecting back on the boycott victory in Montgomery, King was to state:

---

* Compare below Chapter 13, *The Ways of Individualism and Community*, pp. 294-295, Aldo Leopold's definition of rightness: "A thing is [ethically and aesthetically] right when it tends to preserve the integrity, stability, and beauty of the biotic community."

From the beginning a basic philosophy guided the movement.... It was the Sermon on the Mount.... As the days unfolded, however, the inspiration of Mahatma Gandhi began to exert its influence. I had come to see early that the Christian doctrine of love operating through the Gandhian method of nonviolence was one of the most potent weapons available to the Negro in his struggle for freedom. [*Ibid.*, p. 16, from *Stride Toward Freedom, Op. Cit.*]

Letter from Birmingham City Jail

Following a visit to India in early 1959 to study directly Gandhi's techniques of non-violence, King and his family moved to Atlanta, Georgia, in 1960 where King became co-pastor with his father of the Ebenezer Baptist Church. It is from here that he put his Christian satyagraha to the test over the next several years, traveling to speak, to preach, to confront, to challenge, to march, to go to jail, to commit himself again and again to the struggle to integrate lunch counters, interstate buses, and living facilities, to start the drive to register Negro voters, to nullify the poll tax and literacy tests as requirements for voter registration, and to protest the laws of racism that had made Negroes second class citizens for over 100 years. While publicly demonstrating against the segregation of eating facilities in downtown Birmingham, King was arrested. On April 16, 1963, he wrote one of the most moving and famous moral and social documents in American history, the "Letter from Birmingham City Jail."

The letter, a rare defense to his critics of the philosophy and tactics of Christian satyagraha, was written in response to an open letter published in January by eight White clergy who called upon King to let the fight for integration be waged in the courts and not in the streets. King's reply is not only a reply to the eight clergy, but a reply to Christians anywhere who had ever asked the question, What is the best kind of life for a Christian to lead in a world filled with violence and injustice? It is King's credo of Christian satyagraha set into the context of that kind of world.

He begins, "My dear Fellow Clergymen," acknowledges their claim that his present protests are "unwise and untimely," and goes to the heart of the charge against him that he is an "outsider," here in Birmingham, where he clearly does not belong. He responds, "I am in Birmingham because injustice is here," and like Christ's apostles before he has come in response to the Christian community's call for help:

Birmingham is probably the most thoroughly segregated city in the United States. It's ugly record of police brutality is known in every section of this country. [It had come to be called "Bombingham" by its Black citizens and

one section of the city in particular was known as "Dynamite Hill."] Its
unjust treatment of Negroes in the courts is a notorious reality. There have
been more unsolved bombings of Negro homes and churches in
Birmingham than any city in this nation. These are the hard, brutal and
unbelievable facts. On the bases of these conditions Negro leaders sought to
negotiate with the city fathers. But the political leaders consistently refused
to engage in good faith negotiation. [*Ibid.*, p. 290. The entire letter was
reprinted in *Why We Can't Wait* (New York: Harper & Row, 1963) and by the
American Friends Service Committee as a pamphlet. It is probably the most
well-known and often reprinted of all of King's works.]

Likening himself to a Socratic gadfly, King explains his mission:

Just as Socrates felt that it was necessary to create a tension in the mind so
that individuals could rise from the bondage of myths and half-truths to the
unfettered realm of creative analysis and objective appraisal, we must see
the need of having nonviolent gadflies to create the kind of tension in society that will help men to rise from the dark depths of prejudice and racism
to the majestic heights of understanding and brotherhood. [*Ibid.* p. 291.]

To the central question that he set out to answer, viz., Why can't you
wait until the law changes by the means provided by the Constitution?,
King answers that "justice delayed is justice denied" and then eloquently
proclaims:

We have waited for more than 340 years [from the time when the first Black
African slaves arrived in the New World] for our constitutional and God-
given rights. The nations of Asia and Africa are moving with jet-like speed
toward the goal of political independence, and we still creep at horse and
buggy pace toward the gaining of a cup of coffee at a lunch counter.

The latter was the very reason that King, followed by a worldwide press
of reporters and journalists, and an army of photographers, radio and
television crews, was now in Birmingham. He then recounts centuries of
degradation, fear, and slavery:

I guess it is easy for those who have never felt the stinging darts of segregation to say, "Wait." But when you have seen vicious mobs lynch your
mothers and fathers at will and drown your sisters and brothers at whim;
when you have seen hate-filled policemen curse, kick, brutalize, and even
kill your black brothers and sisters with impunity; when you see the vast
majority of your twenty million Negro brothers smothering in an airtight
cage of poverty in the midst of an affluent society; when you suddenly find
your tongue twisted and your speech stammering as you seek to explain to
your six-year-old daughter why she can't go to the public amusement park
that has been advertised on television, and see tears welling up in her little
eyes when she is told that Funtown is closed to colored children [When his

daughter, now 8 years old, cried for him, wanting him to come home, her mother explained to Yolanda that Daddy was in jail so that all people might go wherever they liked, the child stopped crying and said, "Good, tell him to stay in jail until I can go to Funtown," Stephen B. Oates, *Op. Cit.*, p. 198.], and see her begin to distort her little personality by unconsciously developing a bitterness toward white people; ...when your first name becomes "nigger" and your middle name becomes "boy" (however old you are) and your last name becomes "John," and when you wife and mother are never given the respected title "Mrs."; ...when you are forever fighting a degenerating sense of "nobodyness"; then you will understand why we find it difficult to wait. [*Ibid.*, pp. 292-293. All this is reminiscent, of course, of the 19th century philosopher, naturalist and pacifist, Henry David Thoreau, who, in his "Civil Disobedience" of 1849, stated: "As for adopting the ways which the State has provided for remedying the evil, I know not of such ways. They take too much time, and a man's life will be gone." Thoreau disobeyed unjust laws, went to jail, and his life and works were well known to both Gandhi and King. The Thoreauian influence throughout this entire letter is inescapable.]

To the question, How can you advocate breaking some laws and obeying others?, King responds,

> The answer is found in the fact that there are two types of laws: there are *just* and there are *unjust* laws. I would agree with Saint Augustine that "an unjust law is no law at all."

He goes on to explain the difference in a fashion that would have pleased Gandhi:

> A just law is a man-made code that squares with the moral law or the law of God. An unjust law is a code that is out of harmony with the moral law... Any law that uplifts human personality is just. Any law that degrades human personality is unjust. All segregation statutes are unjust because segregation distorts the soul and damages the personality. [*Ibid.*, p. 293.]

To the questions, Doesn't your disobeying of the law end up in the same way that the segregationist's disobeying ends up — in anarchy? So what's the difference between your illegal disobedience and theirs?, King answers that the difference is great. First, unjust laws ought to be disobeyed in order that the searchlight of public attention might be drawn to them. Second, like Gandhi before him, but unlike the segregationist, the Christian *satyagrahi* must be willing to go to jail or to give up life, itself, if necessary:

> In no sense do I advocate evading or defying the law as the rabid segregationist would do. This would lead to anarchy. One who breaks an unjust law

must do it *openly*, *lovingly* (not hatefully as the white mothers did in New Orleans when they were seen on television screaming, "nigger, nigger, nigger"), and with a willingness to accept the penalty. I submit that an individual who breaks a law that conscience tells him is unjust, and willingly accepts the penalty by staying in jail to arouse the conscience of the community over its injustice, is in reality expressing the very highest respect for law. [*Ibid.*, p. 294. King obviously knew Plato's dialogue, *Crito.*]

One of the last questions that King answers is the oft-repeated question, If your non-violent action is going to precipitate violence then ought it not be condemned? King's response is masterful. It is reminiscent of a remark he will make some months later when he is about to lead a demonstration in Danville, Virginia, the last capital of the old Confederacy. Someone told him that there was a local injunction against civil disobedience: "I have so many injunctions that I don't even look at them anymore. I was enjoined January 15, 1929, when I was born in the United States a Negro." [Stephen B. Oates, *Op. Cit.*, p. 254.] And so he was:

In your statement you asserted that our actions, even though peaceful, must be condemned because they precipitate violence. But can this assertion be logically made? Isn't this like condemning the robbed man because his possession of money precipitated the evil act of robbery? Isn't this like condemning Socrates because his answering commitment to truth and his philosophical delvings precipitated the misguided popular mind to make him drink hemlock? Isn't this like condemning Jesus because His unique God-consciousness and never-ceasing devotion to His will precipitated the evil act of crucifixion? We must come to see, as federal courts have consistently affirmed, that it is immoral to urge an individual to withdraw his efforts to gain his basic constitutional rights because the quest precipitates violence. Society must protect the robbed and punish the robber. [*A Testament of Hope, Op. Cit.*, pp. 295-296.]

King continues with a reference to the forces of law and order in Birmingham:

But before closing I am impelled to mention one other point in your statement that troubled me profoundly. You warmly commend the Birmingham police force for keeping "order" and "preventing violence." I don't believe you would have so warmly commended the police force if you had seen its angry violent dogs literally biting six unarmed, nonviolent Negroes. [And throughout the world, anyone with a television set and access to news reports had seen that—and more.] I don't believe you would so quickly commend the policemen if you would observe their ugly and inhuman treatment of Negroes here in the city jail; if you would watch them push and curse old Negro women and young Negro girls; if you see them slap and kick old Negro men and young boys; if you will observe them, as they did on two occasions, refuse to give us food because we wanted to sing our grace together. I'm sorry that I can't join you in your praise for the police department. [*Ibid.*, p. 301.]

The letter ends as King praises the non-violent army that has demonstrated for justice in Birmingham:

One day the South will know that when these disinherited children of God[*] sat down at lunch counters they were in reality standing up for the best in the American dream and the most sacred values in our Judeo-Christian heritage, and thusly, carrying our whole nation back to those great wells of democracy which were dug deep by the Founding Fathers in the formulation of the Constitution and the Declaration of Independence. [*Ibid.*, p. 302.]

It was probably the South's and the Nation's finest hour.

Two weeks later, on May 3-5, Eugene "Bull" Connor, Director of Public Safety of Birmingham, ordered the use of police dogs and fire hoses on the protesters. The world sat in witness to the brutal effects on the young, unarmed, and peaceful demonstrators. But by May 20, 1963, it was legally all over as the Supreme Court of the United States ruled Birmingham's segregation ordinances unconstitutional. The lunchrooms were desegregated, and restrooms, sitting rooms and drinking fountains were similarly desegregated during the days that followed.

The Final Years

Martin Luther King helped to launch what was to become the hardest campaign of his entire life: The drive to register Negro voters throughout the South. The effort began in earnest in 1964. Busloads of young men and women, Black and White, from North and South, attempted to register Negroes as King and others realized the importance of political reform if there was ever to be economic and social reform. The fight for political rights was most bitter but again it was carried out non-violently by the protesters and registrars.

On March 9, 1965, a White Unitarian minister, James Reeb, was beaten by four White segregationists in Selma, Alabama. Reeb had left his wife and four children and a job as director of a low income housing project in Boston to come to Selma "to make a direct witness" for human freedom. He had come with some four hundred other ministers, rabbis,

---

[*] This was Gandhi's name for the untouchables of India: *harijan* or "children of God."

priests, nuns, students, lay leaders, Black as well as White, in response to the violence in Selma when King called for a dramatic "ministers' march" from Selma to Montgomery, the capital of Alabama. The marchers had been viciously attacked by state and local police and by mobs of Whites. James Reeb died from his beating on March 11.

On March 21, as the nation watched, Martin Luther King led the march on which Reeb had started, guarded this time by federal troops, and arrived in Montgomery four days later. Gandhi's 1930 satyagraha Salt March to Dandi that had captured world-wide attention had been duplicated with the same dramatic and spectacular results. The marchers sang "We shall overcome" and "Ain't no-one gonna turn us around" and everyone knew that they meant every word of it.

As dozens and then hundreds of protesters had been killed, maimed and injured by the violence in Selma and elsewhere throughout the South, the Federal Government finally stepped in, first, with armed troops at Selma and then with federal marshals. Gradually the situation began to change. The political results of Selma were, first, the Civil Rights Act of 1964 which barred discrimination on grounds of race, color, religion, or national origin in restaurants, hotels, lunch counters, gasoline stations, movie theaters, stadiums, arenas, and lodging houses with more than five rooms, and which also authorized cutting off government funds from any federally assisted program in any state practicing discrimination; and, second, the Voting Rights Act of 1965 which sent federal registrars protected by federal marshals into the South to register at government expense all eligible voters in federal, state and local elections. These two acts guaranteed voting rights to all Americans with heavy penalties for anyone convicted of interfering with those rights. The climax was the passage of the 24th Amendment to the Constitution in 1964 which effectively outlawed the poll tax as a criterion for the right to vote in federal elections. [See James Q. Wilson, *American Government, Institutions and Policies* (D. C. Heath and Company, 1986), pp. 411, 536, 547-549.]

"I Have a Dream"

The famous march on Washington, D. C. for civil rights on August 28, 1963, organized by King, the SCLC, and others, undoubtedly precipitated the passage of those civil rights bills in 1964 and 1965. King, himself, gave the keynote address in front of the Lincoln Memorial while hundreds of thousands stood and listened and cheered. It was another never-to-be-forgotten recounting of a vision of a country freed from prejudice, discrimination, hatred and violence. Coretta King has said of the speech, "At that moment it seemed as if the Kingdom of God appeared. But it only lasted a moment." To the hundreds of thousands who heard King that day, or the millions that have heard this speech since, his vision seemed lasting enough:

> So I say to you, my friends, that even though we must face the difficulties of today and tomorrow, I still have a dream. It is a dream deeply rooted in the American dream that one day this nation will rise up and live out the true meaning of its creed—we hold these truths to be self-evident, that all men are created equal.
>
> I have a dream that one day, on the red hills of Georgia, sons of former slaves and sons of former slave-owners will be able to sit down together at the table of brotherhood.
>
> I have a dream that one day even the state of Mississippi, a state sweltering with the heat of injustice, sweltering with the heat of oppression, will be transformed into an oasis of freedom and justice....
>
> I have a dream that one day in Alabama, with its vicious racists...little black boys and black girls will be able to join hands with little white boys and white girls as sisters and brothers. I have a dream today!

And King concluded:

> And when we allow freedom to ring, when we let it ring from every village and hamlet, from every state and city, we will be able to speed up that day when all God's children—black men and white men, Jews and Gentiles, Catholics and Protestants—will be able to join hands and to sing in the words of the old Negro spiritual, "Free at last, free at last; thank God almighty, we are free at last." [*A Testament of Hope, Op. Cit.*, pp. 219, 220.]

With the legislation of 1964 and 1965 about to be passed, King's dream seemed close to reality, indeed.

On December 10, 1964, Martin Luther King received the Nobel Peace Prize in Oslo, Norway.

The struggle continued as King carried the fight against discrimination to the North. He rented an apartment in a Chicago ghetto in early 1966 and led marches and protests against discrimination in housing and the work place. When asked why he marched, he said, "I'm marching for something that should have been mine at birth," i.e., the right to live and work anywhere I wish. He exhorted his fellow Chicago marchers,

> We're going to march with the force of our souls, we're going to move out.
>
> We're going to mobilize bodies in concern for justice.

We're going to take the ammunition of determination, we're going to move
out with the weapons of courage.

We're going to put on the breastplate of righteousness and the whole armor
of God and we're going to march.

He concluded, "I march because I must, because I'm a man, because I'm
a child of God." [From the film, *Martin Luther King, Jr.: From Montgomery
to Memphis.*] And march they did while vicious mobs jeered, threw
stones, burned their cars, and beat them and spit at them. But the effort
to integrate housing and to do something about the poverty and the
ghettos of Chicago ultimately failed. King later described Chicago as the
most hate-filled city he had ever encountered.

On May 16, 1966, King read an anti-war statement at another large
rally in Washington, D.C. Now he was protesting the war in Vietnam. He
was to remain until his death one of the most outspoken opponents of
the United States military involvement in Vietnam and South Asia.
Speaking again on February 25, 1967, he prophetically described the war
as "one of history's most cruel and senseless wars," referring to "our"
tragedy and "our" guilt in Vietnam along with "our paranoid anti-com-
munism, our failure to feel the ache and anguish of the have-nots," he
concluded,

> I speak out against it not in anger but with anxiety and sorrow in my heart,
> and above all with a passionate desire to see our beloved country stand as
> the moral example of the world.... We must combine the *fervor* of the civil
> rights movement with the peace movement. We must demonstrate, teach
> and preach, until *the very foundations of our nation are shaken*. [Stephen B.
> Oates, *Op. Cit.*, p. 431.]

And preach he did. The war hawks in the United States were furious,
President Lyndon Johnson, in particular. The White House and the F.B.I.
began a campaign of harassment against a man they considered trea-
sonously unpatriotic. The country as a whole in 1967 opposed King and
it volubly supported the war in Vietnam. He was branded an extremist, a
communist, and a traitor. His non-violent international position on the
Vietnam war, on all wars, for that matter, was consistent with his
Christian satyagraha, but the mood of the nation was like that of the
mood of the nation before Montgomery in December 1955.

The End

In February, 1968, one thousand three hundred Black sanitation
workers in Memphis, Tennessee had gone on strike protesting working

conditions and viciously low wages. They called King for help and he responded bearing witness against the economic injustice in Memphis, just as he had witnessed against the military injustice in Vietnam and the racial injustice in the South. On March 28 he led six thousand strikers and their supporters on a march through Memphis. Violence broke out; one person was killed and fifty people were injured. On April 4, 1968, Martin Luther King was murdered at his motel in Memphis by a White racist.

He was laid to rest in South View Cemetery in Atlanta on April 9 and on his tombstone are carved the words which his vision for America enshrined: "Free at last, free at last; thank God almighty, we are free at last."

KING'S ACCOMPLISHMENTS

The non-violent, pacifist, social gospel of Jesus as found in the *Sermon on the Mount* and as mirrored in the satyagraha of Mohandas Gandhi combined to form the Christian satyagraha that became King's answer to the hate-filled racism of the South and then to the violence-filled militarism of what became Vietnam. His major accomplishment was, consequently, that he showed Christians, and non-Christians alike, the way of Christian satyagraha, i.e., how to *behave* non-violently and with love in a nation and in a world gone mad with injustice, hatred and violence.

In addition to this central accomplishment of his life, King will be remembered for several other major accomplishments:

He helped to give back to Negroes their pride and dignity in being Black by reminding them who they were and what they could become; and he showed them that what one Black man, Martin Luther King, could do they could do as well.

He, more than any other single individual in the 20th century, brought segregation legally to an end in the South. By his efforts, not alone but in concert with MIA, SCLC, CORE and others, discrimination *de jure* and *de facto* ended in restaurants, lunch counters, buses, theaters, trains, barber shops, voting booths, and public schools. The nation would probably never have moved non-violently to where it is today on civil rights if Martin Luther King had become a research scholar and university lecturer instead of a working preacher.

He showed that economic, political, social and moral values are all part of one whole; that, in the words of Socrates, the virtues are one, and that it is impossible to have justice in one part without justice prevailing in all of the others. He drew attention to the role that economics plays in the development of human values and he showed that it is woven into the very fabric of the mores of a people. To get more jobs for Blacks in department stores and in city government were both as important in Montgomery in 1956 as was integrating the buses. For to integrate the buses made no sense unless one had a decent job to pay for the ride. Like John Stuart Mill before him, he showed that the right to vote is essential to gaining economic power, social welfare and human dignity. But unlike Mill he knew that the reforms needed could only come about through an obedience to Christian principles, that power, whether economic, political or social, rested on a religious foundation that was neither violent nor sentimental. Of that foundation King once said:

> Now we've got to get this thing right. What is needed is a realization that power without love is reckless and abusive, and love without power is sentimental and anemic. [*A Testament of Hope, Op. Cit.*, p. 247. This is from King's last SCLC presidential address.]

In other words, King reminded the world, as Plato had before him, that for there to be justice in the whole of society, there must first be justice, i.e., balance and harmony, in each of the parts, i.e., in the political, social, economic, and psychological parts, of that society.

Finally, Martin Luther King put the armor of beauty and the sword of elegance onto the American English language and sent it into battle against racism and injustice. The political forcefulness of spoken English had never been more powerfully and dramatically exhibited than in the moving sermons and speeches of Martin Luther King. They combined the familiar repetitions of the Negro gospel songs, and patriotic American clichés, with the images, symbols, phrases and stories from the *Bible*; all of which was then blended with King's rational Greco-Roman philosophical, theological, and logical heritage. Everyone who heard him speak, the literate and the illiterate, the educated and the uneducated, the sophisticated and the simple, invariably came away moved by his eloquence. Who can forget lecture-sermons like "I have a dream" in 1963?, "Our God is marching on," his Selma, Alabama speech of 1965?, "I was a drum major for justice," preached at Ebenezer Baptist church in 1968?, "I've been to the mountain top," his last speech in Memphis in 1968, the night before his murder, when he movingly prophesied his own death? King loved language, he was a master communicator, and what John F. Kennedy said about Winston Churchill's speeches in World War II applies even more aptly to the battles that King fought in the United States and the world from 1955 to 1968: "He marshaled the English language and sent it off to war."

THE WAY OF CHRISTIAN SATYAGRAHA:
MARTIN LUTHER KING, JR.

The Problem

As King came to see the problem facing Blacks in the South and Christians in the world, the issues were far more complex than were at first apparent. Let's treat that complexity under *Causes* below, and simply state here that the problem was a combination of untold misery, fear, bitterness and hatred, and that these were felt as much by Blacks as by Whites, by Americans as much as by Europeans, Africans and Asians.

The Causes

In the beginning the cause was seen simply as racial discrimination; but as time passed, King saw that racial discrimination was imbedded in a larger network of injustices that enclasped Whites as much as Blacks. The unjust laws were born in fear, hatred, greed and selfishness, and these same laws bred, in turn, further psychological vices. Later in his career King added economic injustice and poverty to his list of causes of suffering, degradation and human indignity. Finally, with his firm pacifist stand he realized that the net of injustices was not confined to one region, one country, but was thrown around the world itself. His congregation became all the earth's suffering human beings, his church the world, his pulpit the national and international news media.

The Solution

The solution remained in the end what it had been in the beginning, viz., the conversion of one's opponent. To turn around the racist, the murderer, the thug, the international terrorist, as well as to energize and convert those who sit silently on the side lines, uncommitted and aloof, all that became part of the solution. Gandhi had taught him an important lesson about winning and losing, viz., that where there are winners, there are losers, and that where there are losers, everyone loses in the end. The aim was not merely then to change laws, for changed laws can't alter attitudes and hearts as the 1990s are demonstrating all too clearly. That King got it right and got the segregation laws changed was not an empty victory by any means; but it never was the primary goal of all of his satyagraha efforts.

The Way

The way to change the hearts and minds of one's oppressors and opponents is through Christian satyagraha. This involved the five stages of non-violent direct action against the impersonal forces of injustice and evil, action to be carried out with non-violence and love for one's opponent, with the aim of persuading the opponent that he or she is wrong, and bringing about redemption, reconciliation and community.

PROBLEMS WITH THE WAY OF MARTIN LUTHER KING, JR.

There are two problems that anyone must face who intends to adopt King's Christian satyagraha as a way to the best and most worthwhile life. These problems are part of the same problems that a Gandhian *satyagrahi* faces who attempts to follow Mohandas Gandhi's way.

The first problem is the problem of injustice and it is this: How does one know when one is faced with injustice? King says that injustice is present whenever the community is torn apart and whenever human dignity is threatened. But how does one know when community and dignity are in jeopardy? King asserts that conscience tells us, if the matter is not already obvious. Racial segregation was an obvious case where both community and human dignity were sundered. But how about those less obvious cases where injustice is claimed to be present? Good men and women conscientiously and honestly disagree over abortion, divorce, capital punishment, gun control, flag burning, contraception, war, terrorism, and the myriad other ethical issues on which the public law and individual morality clash repeatedly. King early in his career closed the door to the more obvious solutions to such problems, solutions of the sort that a utilitarian like John Stuart Mill might have found. Mill held that one simply practiced or enacted those laws that led to the greatest happiness for the greatest number of people. King will have none of this, proclaiming instead,

> The end of life is not to be happy. The end of life is not to achieve pleasure and avoid pain. The end of life is to do the will of God, come what may [i.e., whatever the consequences.] [*A Testament of Hope, Op. Cit.,* p. 10. This is from a sermon preached in Montgomery, Alabama on November 6, 1956, seven days before the United States Supreme Court found Alabama's bus segregation laws unconstitutional.]

All well and good, if one knows the will of God, an area, once again, as with conscience, where men and women of good will notoriously differ.

Martin Luther King's way of Christian satyagraha would seem to be, *prima facie*, incomplete since it cannot furnish us with an incontrovertible method for solving any but the more notorious instances of injustice. But King would probably respond that the way of Christian satyagraha has never been a way of easy solutions to problems of injustice.

The second problem is the problem of commitment and it is this: Suppose that I know when I am faced with a case of injustice; but how can I possibly take a stand and become committed to doing something about the injustice? King is asking the impossible of people, if he expects us to picket, to march, or even to lay down our lives in protest to injustice. Protesting publicly takes bravery, heart and endurance, qualities that the average person is simply incapable of generating. The problem of commitment points to the impracticality of King's Christian satyagraha which is a way for saints, Overmen, Stoic sages, and martyrs like Socrates, Jesus, Gandhi and Martin Luther King, Jr. It is not a way for the average man and woman who haven't the time, the energy or the temperament to follow an ideal, an impractical way of life. And any philosophy of life that is impractical usurps commonsense and stands in violation of yet another of our criteria of adequacy for a way of life.

King may have had the problem of commitment in mind when he preached on February 4, 1968 at Ebenezer Baptist Church in Atlanta two months before his murder. He concluded with these memorable lines on commitment:

> I won't have any money to leave behind. I won't have the fine and luxurious things of life to leave behind. But I just want to leave a committed life behind. [*Ibid.*, p. 267. Excerpts from this sermon, "The Drum Major Instinct," were played at King's nationally televised funeral at the same church on April 9, 1968.]

Christian satyagraha was never meant for the average man or woman, King might say, because the Christian is not an average person. The Christian was never meant to be ordinary for Christ called on men and women to be extraordinary and to do extraordinary things. Søren Kierkegaard was right when he said that it is a difficult thing to become a Christian. But things difficult of attainment, even impractical in practice, are not necessarily impossible to grasp. King's example of a committed life, of an examined life in the Socratic sense, is an example to all who would come after him that the best and most worthwhile life is possible but that such a life demands the best and the most that human beings can give. Martin Luther King Jr.'s birthday, January 15, is now a national holiday. It is belated and deserved recognition from a grateful Nation of a life that was fully committed to non-violence, dignity, and justice.[*]

The questions and issues that King has raised regarding the place of the committed individual within the larger context of the uncommitted community of individuals are matters that will be with us as we take up the next chapter of this book. The relationships between the individual and the community are reflected in the kinds of questions that arise in religion, philosophy, the social sciences and, in the natural, non-human and even inorganic, sciences. They may all, ultimately, come down to one central question, however, which is, What or who is to take precedence, in any conflict between the individual and the community?, i.e, Who is to be master, the individual or the community? Two final ways of philosophy are going to attempt an answer to that question together with several other related questions. We now turn to Charles Darwin, the exponent of individualism, and Aldo Leopold, the proponent of community, as each takes up his answer to the questions, What is the best and most worthwhile life that a human being can live?

[*] Recent revelations regarding King's private life have no place in an evaluation of his way of philosophy. Those revelations can neither add to nor subtract from his stature as a Christian *satyagrahi*.

THIRTEEN
THE WAYS OF INDIVIDUALISM AND COMMUNITY

CHARLES DARWIN (1809-1882) AND ALDO LEOPOLD (1887-1948)
AND THE WAYS OF INDIVIDUALISM AND COMMUNITY

EAST AND WEST

In an essay written in 1957, the famous Zen Buddhist scholar, D. T. Suzuki, juxtaposed two poems, one Eastern, the other Western, for consideration and analysis. Here is the first:

> When I look carefully
> I see the nazuna blooming
> By the hedge!

And here is the second:

> Flower in the crannied wall,
> I pluck you out of the crannies;-
> Hold you here, root and all, in my hand
> Little flower - but if I could understand
> What you are, root and all, and all in all,
> I should know what God and man is.

The two poems epitomize several significant differences between East and West, and the ideas about man, God and the world that flow from those differences. More specifically, they illustrate two divergent approaches to the natural world and to the land on which and in which we all live.

The first poem comes from the Japanese tradition of Zen Buddhism. It was composed by Basho (1644-94) as a *haiku,* a three line, seventeen syllable poem. While on a walk, Basho notices by the roadside a rather insignificant wild flower, the white flowering herb, nazuna or shepherd's purse. The poem ends with the Japanese word *kana* which signifies a strong feeling of admiration, praise, joy or even sorrow. The word is untranslatable and Suzuki uses the exclamation point to render Basho's untranslatable feeling. Basho's haiku, like much Eastern poetry, is monistic and devoid of object-subject dichotomy; and it is impersonal as it avoids all obvious appeal to the reader's emotions by movingly understating the poet's own feelings: By indirections it yet brings directions out.

The second poem is by the Victorian poet laureate, Alfred Lord Tennyson (1809-1892). Instead of merely contemplating the flower *in situ,* the poet pulls it out of the wall, "root and all," and then, holding the withering dying flower in his hand, he begins his lucubrations. Tennyson's poem, like much Western poetry, is dualistic, personal, probing, inquisitive and full of emotion as it appeals to the reader's feelings by letting the poet's spill out over the page.

The two poems call forth reflections of one's own, of course, and Suzuki's comments are most insightful on the essential differences between the poems, the poets and the traditions from which they came:

> Basho does not pluck the flower. He just looks at it. He is absorbed in thought. He feels something in his mind, but he does not express it. He lets an exclamation mark [*"kana"*] say everything he wishes to say. For he has no words to utter; his feeling is too full, too deep, and he has no desire to conceptualize it. [D.T. Suzuki, Erich Fromm, and Richard DeMartino, *Zen Buddhism and Psychoanalysis* (Harper Colophon Books, 1970), p. 3]

Tennyson, on the other hand, tears the flower from the cranny where it naturally belongs, so that it must surely wither and die. He then analyzes and dissects his feelings just as surely as he analyzes and dissects the flower.

Basho never touches the flower, preferring merely to look and to look with complete attention at the flower and not beyond it. The flower, for Basho, becomes neither a springboard into his own agonized feelings nor an excuse for a flight of philosophic fancy. Basho is not inquisitive and inquiring but silent and restrained. His experience is ineffable and that ineffability is eloquently communicated by his silence.

Suzuki continues, saying of Tennyson:

His appeal to the understanding is characteristically Western. Basho accepts, Tennyson resists. Tennyson's individuality stands away from the flower, from "God and man." He does not identify himself with either God or nature. He is always apart from them. His understanding is what people nowadays call "scientifically objective." Basho is thoroughly "subjective"....Basho sees the *nazuna* and the *nazuna* sees Basho. [*Ibid.*, p. 4]

Basho and the nazuna at this moment become unified, i.e., inseparable. Basho has become at-one with the object, leaving behind the dualism of subject-object; and with that he leaves behind the intellect which probes and preys on subject-object distinctions:

In Tennyson, as far as I can see, there is in the first place no depth of feeling; he is all intellect, typical of Western mentality.... He must say something, he must abstract or intellectualize on his concrete experience. He must come out of the domain of feeling into that of intellect and must subject living and feeling to a series of analyses to give satisfaction to the Western spirit of inquisitiveness. [*Ibid.*, p. 5]

Suzuki then concludes by generalizing on these two diferent approaches to the natural world:

Basho is of the East and Tennyson of the West. As we compare them we find that each bespeaks his traditional background. According to this, the Western mind is: analytical, discriminative, differential, inductive, individualistic, intellectual, objective, scientific, generalizing, conceptual, schematic, impersonal, legalistic, organizing, power-wielding, self-assertive, disposed to impose its will upon others.... [*Ibid.*]

From this list of Western traits, Suzuki goes on to characterize the East with the following interesting list, asserting that the East is:

...synthetic, totalizing, integrative, non-discriminative, deductive, unsystematic, dogmatic, intuitive (rather, affective), nondiscursive, subjective, spiritually individualistic and socially group minded.... [*Ibid.*]

We have been at some pains to follow this discussion about Eastern and Western attitudes to nature and the world for in it there lies several interesting insights about the ways that Western man and Eastern man look at the land. To make the point more clearly, let's look at a typical Western approach to the environment and then juxtapose it to an Eastern approach. Let it be noted that one doesn't have to be born East of Suez in order to be called "Eastern man" any more than one has to be born west of Suez in order to be called "Western man." For if Professor Suzuki is right, East and West are states of mind that satisfy in some fashion the predicates in the above two lists; "East" and "West," in other words, are no longer mere geographical locations. To demonstrate this point and to make the previous point as well, let's juxtapose the great naturalist and evolutionist, Charles Darwin, our Western man, with the famous ecologist and conservationist, Aldo Leopold, our Eastern man. Following a discussion of their two approaches to the environment, we'll turn to an evaluation of the two approaches and to the question of which way of philosophy adequately answers our question, What is the best and most worthwhile life that a human being can live?

CHARLES DARWIN AND EVOLUTION BY NATURAL SELECTION: THE WAY OF INDIVIDUALISM

Charles Darwin (1809-1882) was born in Shrewsburg, England, and attended the Universities of Edinburgh and Cambridge. Intending to specialize in medicine and later theology to please his father, he gave up both for botany, driven by an enthusiasm for collecting beetles. From 1831 to 1836 he served without pay as the naturalist on board the *H.M.S. Beagle* in its historic voyage to the coast and islands of South America and around the world. Observing and collecting an enormous variety of new species of plants and animals, the voyage laid the foundation for his later life and interests. On his return he remained in London for six years where he came to know as intimates such scientific luminaries as T. H. Huxley, Sir Joseph Hooker, Sir Charles Lyell, and other leading scientists and educators of a now rapidly industrializing Victorian England. In 1842 Darwin, now married and with a growing family, moved permanently to Down, a quiet village in Kent. There, with a personal income that guaranteed his privacy, he settled down to do his research and write his articles and books. It was from Down that *The Origin of Species* came in 1859 and *The Descent of Man* in 1871. Darwin died in 1882, famous and honored, and his body now rests in Westminster Abbey close to the grave of Sir Isaac Newton, another originator of revolutions.

The Survival of the Fittest

The Origin of Species, the most renowned of all Darwin's works, bore the revealing subtitle, *By Means of Natural Selection or The Preservation of Favored Races in the Struggle for Life*. In the book Darwin attempted to establish several common biological theories about the natural world: First, that complex higher organisms, including man, had evolved from simpler organisms by a gradual process of change; second, that natural selection was the mechanism whereby certain individuals and, by inheritance, certain species, are selected by nature for survival because they have successfully adapted to deleterious environmental changes that eliminated individuals and species less favored for survival. Thus the neck of the giraffe, it might be argued, has gotten progressively longer over the centuries as more individuals responded to a sparseness of grass on the African plains; the longer neck ultimately favored the survival of these individuals since the longer necked giraffe could feed on leaves of high trees at a time when short-necked feeders would die out. Just as breeders of horses practice artificial selection in ensuring that only the fastest horses survive to pass on their swiftness to their progeny, so also nature practices natural selection in ensuring that only those individuals, and ultimately those species of plants and animals, survive that are capable of meeting nature's strenuous selection. The fit survive the struggle for life and pass on their fitness to their progeny. That is to say, natural selection ensures the survival of the fittest.

Thomas Malthus and the Population Explosion

But it wasn't until 1838 when Darwin read the Reverend Thomas Malthus' *Essay on Population* that all these matters suddenly began to come together for him. What Malthus showed was that human population grows at a faster rate than the food suply. One consequence of the unbridled growth of population was, Malthus felt, that human population would eventually outstrip the earth's supply of food leading to the ultimate "elimination of the `poor and inept' by the ruthless selecting agencies of hunger and poverty, vice and crime, pestilence and famine, revolution and war!"

Here was precisely the kind of evidence that Darwin was looking for to fuel the rather well-known theory about natural selection. Even to Malthus nature assured that the strong and the industrious, the brightest and the best, i.e., the most fit, would not only survive but they would prevail over the weak, the lazy and the dullest; hence the worst, i.e., the least fit, would not survive. It was obvious that life is a struggle, an unending war, wherein nature is blood red in tooth and claw, as Tennyson had said in one of the most popular poems of the Victorian Age, *In Memorium*; and the fact that human nature driven by human appetite would eventually outstrip the available food supply seemed to define precisely the essence of the struggle for existence that Darwin felt drove all living things into a frenzy of competition from which only the fit could and would emerge. In other words, the theory of natural selection became Thomas Malthus' theory about human population as applied by Darwin to the whole of the animal and vegetable kingdoms.

To begin with, the theory of evolution by natural selection produced a storm of criticism. Biologists, originally reluctant to accept the theory, had generally been won over by 1889. This acceptance was made all the more possible with Darwin's publication in 1871 of *The Descent of Man* with its massive new evidence and bolstering arguments that focused on the human species, alone. But the popular reaction against Darwin and Darwin's theory remained in force long afterward fueled in part by Darwin's friend and supporter, T. H. Huxley, who took pains to tease and challenge the orthodox theologians and religious fundamentalists. Appointing himself as "Darwin's bulldog," Huxley gave expression in public to what Darwin, himself, had begun to say and believe only in private about the impact of the theory of evolution on religion, society, the *Bible*, the church and Christianity.

Karl Marx and Economic Determinism

Darwin was much admired by another Victorian writer of the period, the economist Karl Marx (1818-1883), who called *The Origin of Species* "a basis in natural science for the class struggle in history." [Quoted in Geoffrey West, *Charles Darwin: A Portrait* (New Haven: Yale University Press, 1938), p. 334.]

In order to understand Darwin's impact on the 20th century with respect to the comparison we are undertaking between Eastern and Western attitudes towards the environment and in order to understand the influence of Darwin's own time on his theories of natural selection and species evolution, let's look a bit more closely at Karl Marx. In particular, let's see what Marx and Marx's theories have to say about the unmentioned and *apriori* "Western" assumptions that may have lain beneath Darwin's theories. Prior to the publication of his *Das Kapital* in 1867, Marx wrote to Darwin kindly asking his permission to dedicate to him his great book on economics. Darwin, just as kindly, declined the compliment apparently fearing guilt by association with the notorious economist with the resultant jeopardizing of his own work in biology by that association. Frederick Engels, Marx's close associate and collaborator, wrote in a letter of 1875 explaining Marx's and his own feelings about Darwin:

> The whole Darwinist teaching of the struggle for existence is simply a transference from society to nature of Hobbes' doctrine of *bellus omnium contra*

*omnes** and of the bourgeois economic doctrine of competition, together with Malthus' theory of population. [Marx and Engels, *Selected Correspondence,* translated by I. Lasker (Moscow: Progress, 1965), p. 302.]

To Marx and Engels Darwin's teaching was corroboration of their own assumption that there were in the universe fixed laws, part of the dialectic of change and development in history, that neither God nor man could change.

But Karl Marx and Friedrich Engels had put forward a new theory outstandingly "Western" in Suzuki's sense, about man and the laws of history. This new theory was called "economic determinism" and it said, in effect, that the material conditions of life determine or cause or have a profound effect on the beliefs, philosophies and theories about the universe that classes of people hold. For example, your beliefs, as well as your parents' beliefs and your children's beliefs, about God, the self and the world are all engendered and shaped by the economic class to which they belong. Marx is simply making the point that what we are depends on our environment, and the most important thing in that environment is the economic and social class from which we come:

> The production of ideas, of conceptions, of consciousness is directly interwoven with the material activity and the material relationships of men; it is the language of actual life. Conceiving, thinking, and the intellectual relationships of men appear here as the direct result of their material behavior.

No longer are our likes and dislikes or our "morality, religion, metaphysics, and all the rest of ideology and their corresponding forms of consciousness" independent of material life processes. And natural science, itself, together with its theories and laws, is also no longer independent of the same material and economic conditioning factors:

> But where would natural science [Marx has physics and chemistry chiefly in mind] be without industry and commerce? Even this "pure" natural science receives its aim, like its material, only through commerce and industry, through the sensuous activity of men. [*The German Ideology* in *Writings of the Young Marx on Philosophy and Society,* translated and edited by Loyd D. Easton and Kurt H. Guddat (Anchor Books, 1967), pp. 414, 415, 418.]

That Marx is talking about the influence of economic classes on the way one thinks and believes is made abundantly clear as he proceeds:

> In every epoch the ideas of the ruling class are the ruling ideas, that is, the class that is the ruling *material* power of society is at the same time its ruling

---

*   "the war of all against all"

intellectual power. The class having the means of material production has also control over the means of intellectual production, so that it also controls, generally speaking, the ideas of those who lack the means of intellectual production.... Their ideas are the ruling ideas of the epoch. [*Ibid.*, p. 438.]

According to Marx's theory of economic determinism, then, Darwin's own ideas about natural selection and species evolution would have been the ideas of the ruling economic class of his own time. And that class was, of course, the new and rising industrial class of 19th century England.

Natural Selection As a Product of Its Time

If Marx was right, and if, for example, Darwin's ideas and theories about the natural world were the product of the images, models and language of the Victorian industrial world, and if the *Origin* itself is, as Oswald Spengler put it, "in some way merely the application of economics to biology," reeking of the "atmosphere of the English factory" [Quoted in Gertrude Himmelfarb; *Darwin and the Darwinian Revolution* (New York: W. W. Norton, 1959), p. 345] then a good many matters relating to Darwin's theories must be looked at carefully and critically. For with the decline of the industrial age it now would seem to be an appropriate time to re-examine the concepts and language that we have used to describe and explain the natural world and to re-evaluate the images, models and metaphors that have influenced our attitudes toward that world.

That Darwin's theory of evolution and the various views that went with it are the products of his time and class and that they are not merely descriptive of the environment are the opinions of a number of contemporary thinkers. The opinions that these thinkers hold is important for our purposes. For if our attitudes about the environment and the land are the consequence of an outdated and now wrong set of assumptions relevant only to the Victorian age, then what we have to say about and what we do with the environment and the land is similarly going to be outdated and wrong. In other words, if our present Western ways of philosophy are the product of outmoded models and dangerous metaphors, then it is best to recognize this fact and change our ways of philosophy now while change is still possible.

Social Darwinism

Making this same point from the political side, the historian, Gertrude Himmelfarb, comments on the general effects of social Darwinism, i.e., the application of Darwin's models and metaphors to society:

> From the "preservation of favoured races in the struggle for life," it was a short step to the preservation of favoured individuals, classes or nations - and from their preservation to their glorification. Social Darwinism has often been understood in this sense. [Gertrude Himmelfarb, *Op. Cit.*, p. 343.]

Social Darwinism has continued, Himmelfarb adds, to exalt "competition, power and violence," over "convention, ethics and religion." As a result, social Darwinism became the chief argument for "nationalism, imperialism, militarism, and dictatorship, of the cults of the hero, the supermen, and the master race." [*Ibid.*] Further, social Darwinism has had similar disasterous results, in many ways even more devastating, on the land and the environment. Jeremy Rifkin in his popular book, *Algeny*, observes:

> Darwin's cosmology sanctioned an entire age of history. Convinced that their own behavior was in concert with the workings of nature, industrial man and woman were armed with the ultimate justification they needed to continue their relentless exploitation of the environment and their fellow human beings without ever having to stop for even a moment to reflect on the consequences of their actions. [Jeremy Rifkin, *Algeny, A New Word—A New World* (Penguin Books, 1984), p. 108]

The origin of this attitude held by many of the social Darwinists and their apologists is not difficult to find. It lies in the 19th century theory of natural selection bolstered by the language of economics and industrialization.

One of the dominant ideas underlying the new industrial world, an idea that seemed open to empirical confirmation on all sides, political, economic, as well as biological, was the notion that only the fit survive; more particularly, only "the best-adapted biological forms were seen as surviving the struggle for life in the wild, in exactly the same way that the fittest individuals were thought to survive the rigours of industrialisation in *laissez-faire* Britain." [Michael Mulkay, *Science and the Sociology of Knowledge* (London: Allen & Unwin, 1979), pp. 105-106.] Darwin, himself, had voiced the same sentiment in the *Origin*, reflecting, perhaps, what every Englishman of the industrial age already knew, viz., that there was "one general law leading to the advancement of all organic beings, namely, multiply, vary, let the strongest live and the weakest die." [Charles Darwin, *The Origin of Species* (New York: Watts, 1929), p. 209. Quoted in Rifkin, *Algeny*, *Op. Cit.*, p. 83] Hence, in at least one instance it would seem that Darwin's biological views had come out clothed in the non-biological language of the 19th century. If Darwin's other views are similarly clothed, and if the clothing expresses or conceals subjective and non-scientific prejudices which we in the 1990's have inherited from the 1880's, then we'd best know it now and be prepared.

DARWIN'S ACCOMPLISHMENTS

Charles Darwin, as an exponent of what we shall call *the way of individualism*, rather than as a biologist, now accomplished two things in *The Origin of Species*: First, he found in nature a parallel to the struggles occurring in the English industrial society in which he was nurtured. Nature and society were both red in tooth and law, the fit did survive in the jungle and they survived in London, Manchester and Leeds, as well. But, second, he also discovered a justification for the English industrial society, "a scientific guarantee of the rightness of the property and work relations of industrial society" [Robert Young in *Charles Darwin's Natural Selection*, ed. R. C. Stauffer (Cambridge, England: Cambridge University Press, 1975), p. 375]. For if the same relationships were found in nature as were found in industrial society, and if those relationships were "natural," i.e., normal and just, in nature, then they must be natural in industrial society, as well.

Charles Darwin's theory of natural evolution also tended to support another dogma in addition to the survival of the fittest, viz., the dogma of individualism, i.e., the biological and social sacredness of the individual. One is reminded yet again of D. T. Suzuki's list of the properties that characterize Western man. It would appear that that list could easily have grown out of the British, Victorian, colonial, and industrial ideals of the 19th century.

Rifkin, again, states the matter:

> The political and economic dogma of the day extolled the virtues of individualism, and everywhere one turned there was great support for the notion of unfettering the individual from the chains that bound him to a larger whole, so that he might be free to pursue his own interests and inclinations. [*Op. Cit.*, pp. 92-93]

It was a further dogma of the time, given credence by Adam Smith's view, that the individual must be given complete freedom "to maximize his own material interests," and that this selfish and self-serving activity would ultimately benefit society as a whole. Hence, private vice is ultimately society's gain, i.e., public virtue. Darwin's discoveries were used to assuage any guilt that any Victorian might feel over the selfish pursuit of his own interests by christening those pursuits not only "beneficial" to society but wholly and entirely "natural."

THE WAY OF INDIVIDUALISM: CHARLES DARWIN

It is not entirely accurate to hold Charles Darwin, alone, responsible for the uses that were subsequently made of his views in *The Origin of Species* (1859). For Darwin came to hold another view, widely publicized in *The Descent of Man* (1871), that is not representative of the way of individualism. In the *Descent* Darwin appears to argue that human sympathy can be developed and spread out like a moral net:

> Sympathy beyond the confines of man, that is, humanity, to the lower animals, seems to be one of the latest moral acquisitions...unfelt by savages, except toward their pets.

And Darwin concludes,

> This virtue, one of the noblest with which man is endowed, seems to arise incidentally from our sympathies becoming more tender and more widely diffused, until they are extended to all sentient beings. [Charles Darwin, *The Descent of Man* (New York: J.A. Hill and Company, 1904), p. 124.]

Should such sympathy become necessary for survival then the Darwin of 1871 is not a follower of social Darwinism. With this *caveat* in mind, let's look at the way of individualism of the Darwin of 1859:

The Problem

The problem for Victorian and industrial man was how to survive in a world with too many people and too few necessities to support them. In particular, the problem for social Darwinism was, How can I survive in such a world when my neighbor is also trying to survive.

The Cause

The cause of my anxiety over my survival is the realization that only the fit in the struggle for existence will survive and that I may not be one of the fit. How can I ensure that I will be a survivor and not some poor, unprepared nerd destined for extinction?

The Solution

Let's face it—the solution is survival!

The Way

If it is a jungle out there, then I had better become the best predator in that jungle. I can survive in that wolf-eat-wolf world only by eating the other wolves first. Rugged individualism is the name of the game and I must either play it better than the other wolves or else convince those others not to play the game at all. Thus the way of individualism.

PROBLEMS WITH THE WAY OF INDIVIDUALISM

The legacy of Darwin in the *Origin* and the 19th century neo-Darwinian defenders of social Darwinism then comes to this: The 19th century produced a cosmology or view of the universe that justified a kind of rugged individualism modeled after what they thought were the incessant struggles in the natural world, a world in which they believed only the best do and, consequently, ought to survive. It was convenient for 19th century Victorians to have such a view because it served their purposes in justifying a vicious industrial and commercial guilt-producing economic system: Darwin in the *Origin* seemed to have taught them that their social view was right because it was natural; and whatever is natural, as every Victorian knew, is right.

In addition to the problems already mentioned, problems relating to natural selection as a product of its time and the Victorian moral myopia of social Darwinism, in general, there are two other outstanding problems with the way of individualism: The first problem relates to our criterion of common sense insofar as the way of individualism assumes that the natural world is simply a world in competition, "a jungle red in tooth and claw," where only the brutally voracious survive. Common sense must surely be affronted by this one-sided and violent ascription to the community of nature. Enlightened common sense, reinforced by careful observations of the natural world, bids us focus now on the global ecosystem as a balance of energies in which the organisms of that system continue to survive through, *inter alia*, a process of interconnected and mutual cooperation. The original assumption was an ecological howler.

The second problem relates to our criterion of consistency insofar as the way of individualism argues from observations about human society, where only the strong and powerful *do* or *seem* to survive, to a conclusion that states that this is the way that human society *ought* to be. The logical error lies in trying to derive a *prescription* for human behavior, "only the rich and powerful *ought* to survive," from a *description* of the competitive world where "only the rich and powerful *do*, or *seem*, to survive." But as every student of logic and ethics knows, you cannot derive an *ought* statement from an *is* statement without creating philosophic pandemonium. The original argument was a logical howler.

We turn now from our "Western man," Charles Darwin, to our "Eastern man," Aldo Leopold. Following our discussion of Leopold's view of the natural world, we shall attempt an answer to our central question, What is the best and most worthwhle life that a human being can live?

ALDO LEOPOLD AND ATTITUDE UTILITARIANISM: THE WAY OF COMMUNITY

Aldo Leopold was born in Burlington, Iowa in 1887 and spent most of his life in the Midwest. He was graduated from Yale University in 1909 with a masters degree in forestry and in that same year joined the United States Forest Service. By 1912 he had become supervisor of the one million acre Carson Forest in New Mexico. A founder of the Wilderness Society, he initiated the first Forest Wilderness Area in the United States in 1924, an area which eventually became the Gila National Forest. He subsequently moved to Madison, Wisconsin as Associate Director of the Forest Products Laboratory. In Madison he founded the profession of game management, authoring the first significant book on the subject in the United States, and in 1933 the chair of game management was created for him at the University of Wisconsin. He died in 1948 while fighting a grass fire on a neighbor's farm.

Aldo Leopold's most memorable contributions to the field of environmental ethics are contained in several papers in professional journals of the 1920s and 1930s and in a small volume of his collected essays, *A Sand County Almanac*, published in 1949, one year after his tragic death. The latter work contains the chief philosophic endeavor of his career, "The Land Ethic."

In his brief Forward to *A Sand County Almanac*, Leopold drew attention to what we might refer to as "the industrial ethic," an ethic familiar from our earlier discussions of Suzuki's identification of the properties of Western man and of the way of individualism:

Conservation is getting nowhere because it is incompatible with our
Abrahamic concept of land. We abuse land because we regard it as a com-
modity belonging to us. When we see land as a *community* to which we
belong, we may begin to use it with love and respect. [Aldo Leopold, *A Sand
County Almanac* (A Sierra Club/Ballantine Book, 1970), pp. xviii-xix. The
"Abrahamic concept of land" probably refers to the promise that God makes
to Abraham at *Exodus* 17.8: "And I will give to you, and to your descendents
after you, the land of your sojournings, all the land of Canaan, for an ever-
lasting possession." Presumably, Abraham may then, thus owning the land,
do with it as he pleases.]

Leopold's love and respect for the land is evident throughout the volume, whether he is sawing up an ancient oak for firewood, or merely observing geese and ducks returning to the spring pond. This love and respect for the land are necessary constituents of the land ethic, as we shall
see.

The Industrial Ethic

The industrial ethic espouses an adversarial rather than a communal
relationship between man and the land, a relationship that has its roots
in the book of *Genesis* in the *Old Testament*. In a very important sense,
Genesis provides the very foundation on which modern misuse of the
land rests. For if the sacred texts of a culture influence the values of that
culture, and if *Genesis* is such a text, then *Genesis* is going to influence the
values of, in this case, Western culture, with passages that advocate or
hold as valuable the following:

1. the domination of the land by man to do with as he sees fit;

2. the use, by Divine example, of both personal violence and
    catastrophic physical destruction as legitimate ways of
    solving problems;

3. the separation between, and alienation of, that which is ul-
    timately valuable, God, from that which is only derivatively,
    hence less, valuable, the land or creation.

Appropriate passages might be called to mind, passages such as:
"...let man have dominion over the fish... the birds... cattle... all the
earth;" "...the fear of you [man] and the dread of you shall be upon every
beast... bird... creeping thing... fish... into your hands they are delivered;"
"...cursed are you [man] above all things;" "And the Lord was sorry that
He had made man.... So the Lord said, 'I will blot out man....' *Genesis*

1.26; 9.1-2; 3.14; 6.6-7. [Revised Standard Version.] In these passages lies the genesis of the industrial ethic.

Where the land ethic presupposes that man is part of the community of those entities that compose the 'land', which for Leopold includes man, animals, birds, insects, fish, plants, water and soil, the industrial ethic presupposes that man is a potential survivor in a jungle red in tooth and claw where, through intense competition, only the best survive because only they deserve to survive.

The industrial ethic is narrowly utilitarian in thrust holding, with John Stuart Mill, that moral rightness is to be decided by calculating the amount of happiness or pleasure in the consequences of actions. Value, in other words, resides in the action's results and not in the agent's intentions or the nature of the act.

The industrial ethic is empirical rather than intuitive in holding that the sole determinants of value, the consequences, are publicly available for all to quantify, calculate, and compare. Utilitarianism maintains that what benefits the greatest number of *human beings* by giving them the greatest amount of pleasure or happiness is what ultimately determines what is morally right or morally wrong: Thus industrial utilitarianism.

The industrial ethic is anthropocentric since the determinor of value is man, and it is an aristocratic ethic since the men and women who determine value are survivors, i.e., the "best" that nature and society can produce; hence, it is an ethic of and for those most fit human survivors. The rugged individualism of a 19th century free enterprise economy might be the best example yet of this *Genesis*, utilitarian, empirical, anthropocentric, aristocratic ethic in operation. The defender of the industrial ethic finds ultimate value in personal survival, specifically in the obligation to perfect oneself both in this life and, as is often believed, in the life to come. To achieve this end the industrial ethic covertly encourages the domination of, and the use of, other humans; and it overtly encourages the exploitation of animals, birds, fish, insects, plants, water and soil, in order that humans might realize their potential and perfect themselves, at least in this world. The implications of this industrial ethic for the world's human citizens and their environment are all too obvious as air becomes unbreatheable, water becomes undrinkable, soil becomes unuseable, vegetation inedible, and animal and human life intolerable; man's insatiable drive to self-realization seems, paradoxically, self-defeating. The best and most worthwhile life that a human being can live is not going to be found by following the way of individualism with its industrial ethic.

The Land Ethic

In *A Sand County Almanac* Aldo Leopold puts forward a plan to develop what he refers to as "a land ethic." For Leopold, "the land" is not merely soil, dirt, and rocks; but it also includes water, plants and living creatures, all existing in a communal relation with one another. Something to watch for in Leopold's development of his land ethic is this: If value lies in all of the members of the land community, then what kind of moral obligation do I have to the individual members of that community? For example, am I under some sort of moral obligation to squirrels? But squirrels are easy. I am obliged even now, someone might say, not to injure or cause suffering to sentient beings like squirrels, dogs, and horses. 'Be kind to animals' expresses this obligation, and we honor it because we recognize that these animals have use, hence value, and with that certain derivitive rights in virtue of that value.

The Judeo-Christian tradition and the industrial ethic that flows into and out of it don't recognize such value as being *inherent* in animals, however. *Genesis* bids Adam do with the creation what he pleases; and there is no commandment against killing or abusing squirrels. Still, squirrels, dogs and horses have use, hence value; not inherent value such as beings with immortal souls have, but derived value.

Part of Leopold's task will be to convince us that all members of the land community have inherent value, and that includes not only squirrels but also trees and ponds and mountains. His attempt at establishing a land ethic is fascinating, and it leads to challenges to those of us who still live by the industrial ethic and all that it implies.

Leopold begins,

> There is as yet no ethic dealing with man's relation to land and to the animals and plants which grow upon it. Land, like Odysseus' slave-girls, is still property. The land-relation is still strictly economic, entailing privileges but not obligations. [*Ibid.*, p. 238]

Private property has derived value but no inherent value. Economic value is the chief reason for granting derived value to things. Deer, ducks, salmon, and swamps have a value then, like the slaves, because, like the squirrels above, they represent economic opportunity to those who would use them or own them. And things that are owned can be used as the user or owner sees fit.

But when your use of your possessions affects my use of my possessions, the law steps in to prevent your rights from infringing on my rights. For example, you can't or ought not to use a herbicide to kill weeds on your land if the wind is going to blow the lethal particles onto my lettuce. Private land, like public land, we are slowly beginning to realize, carries certain obligations for its proper use along with the privileges of ownership.

This view of the inter-relatedness of objects, the holistic interconnectedness of things, is what lies behind the land ethic:

> An ethic, ecologically, is a limitation on freedom of action [i.e., a recognition of an obligation] in the struggle for existence. An ethic, philosophically, is a differentiation of social from anti-social conduct. [*Ibid.*]

As Leopold goes on to explain, an ethic entails not only the recognition of obligations but also "the tendency of interdependent individuals or groups to evolve modes of cooperation." In such a cooperative atmosphere "the original free-for-all competition has been replaced." [*Ibid.*] In other words, the industrial ethic has been replaced by another wider and more inclusive ethic, an ethic that will ultimately prove to be neither anthropocentric nor aristocratic but that will be instead communocentric and democratic:

> All ethics so far evolved rest upon a single premise: that the individual is a member of a community of interdependent parts. His instincts prompt him to compete for his place in the community, but his ethics prompt him also to cooperate.... (*Ibid.*, p. 239)

Leopold's aim will be to alter the entire notion of what constitutes a community, and to move from an industrial ethic with its talk of competing individual human units to the land ethic with its talk of cooperating members of an interconnected community.

Leopold's land ethic, the ethic that grants inherent value to all of its cooperating members, brings those members into community:

> The land ethic simply enlarges the boundaries of the community to include soils, waters, plants, and animals, or collectively: the land. [*Ibid.*]

In other words, the industrial ethic with its hierarchical structures is now superceded by a new ethic with a horizontal networking structure:

> In short, a land ethic changes the role of *Homo sapiens* from conqueror of the land community to plain member and citizen of it. It implies respect for his fellow-members, and also respect for the community as such. [*Ibid.*, p. 240]

The conqueror role was fitting for the older age and it formed yet another of those dualisms that the land ethic perforce rejects.

The Land Ethic As Community Ethic

The land ethic appeals to feelings or intuitions of rightness and obligation that seem to transcend anything in utilitarian and self-interest ethics. Those feelings exist wherever there is a sense of community. Such feelings exist in places where people do rise above self interest "in such rural community enterprises as the betterment of roads, schools, churches and baseball teams." [*Ibid.*, p. 245] We are speaking about doing an action, not because it benefits me or because we calculate that in the long run more happiness will be produced by it for me (egoistic ethics) or even for all concerned (universalistic ethics) but because it is right. And here is where those special feelings in human nature spring up. Leopold calls those feelings "conscience":

> Obligations have no meaning without conscience, and the problem we face is the extension of the social conscience from people to land. [*Ibid.*, p. 246]

But to do this calls for a moral conversion, an ethical turning around, without which the land ethic is useless. What is called for is an ethical relation to land and not just to other human beings and their interests, pleasures, or happiness. This relation is one of "love, respect and admiration for land, and a high regard for its value" [*Ibid.*, p. 261]:

> No important change in ethics was ever accomplished without an internal change in our intellectual emphasis, loyalities, affections, and convictions. [*Ibid.*, p. 246]

We must arrive at the point where we cease to see economic advantage as the sole arbiter of right and wrong. Leopold points to a major weakness in the self-interest economic theory of ethics, viz., that most members of the land community have no economic value:

> Of the 22,000 higher plants and animals native to Wisconsin, it is doubtful whether more than 5 percent can be sold, fed, eaten or otherwise put to economic use. Yet these creatures are members of the biotic community, and if (as I believe) its stability depends on its integrity, they are entitled to continuance. [*Ibid.*, pp. 246-247]

And that continuance is right, not for economic advantage and not for self-interest, but solely because "these creatures are members of the biotic community." The appeal, once again, transcends economics and pleasure, and leads to a new definition of rightness:

> The 'key-log' which must be moved to release the evolutionary process for an ethic is simply this: quit thinking about land-use as solely an economic

problem. Examine each question in terms of what is ethically and aesthetically right.... A thing is right when it tends to preserve the integrity, stability, and beauty of the biotic community. It is wrong when it tends otherwise.
[*Ibid.*, p. 262.]

Aldo Leopold's land ethic calls then for the abandonment of traditional land use ethics, industrial or hierarchical ethics; and it calls for a
vision, an intellectual intuition of the interconnectedness of all things, it
calls for a realization and acceptance of a moral duty to those things in
virtue of membership in a community.

The land ethic exists whenever there is a unique relation between the
land, i.e., soil, water, air, plants and animals, and the moral conscience.
This relation is the realization of a responsibility that the individual has
to the land, a responsibility that is felt in the discovery that one is a
member of a community. Concerning the land, Leopold says:

Land, then, is not merely soil; it is a fountain of energy flowing through a
circuit of soils, plants, and animals. Food chains are the living channels
which conduct energy upward; death and decay return it to the soil. (*Op.
Cit.*, p. 253)

The sense of moral responsibility for the land or ecosystem, exists whenever the ordinary moral conscience is transformed into the ecological
conscience:

A land ethic, then, reflects the existence of an ecological conscience, and this
in turn reflects a conviction of individual responsibility for the health of the
land. (p. 258)

In other words, the feeling of ecological responsibility and the sense that
I have a duty to the biotic community, the land, is the result of discovering my place in that community. This in turn transforms my ordinary
conscience, which recognizes duties only to members of my own family
or my own species, into an ecological conscience, which recognizes duties to the entire ecosystem. Finally, this sense of duty is expressed in a
new ethic, viz., the land ethic.

THE WAY OF COMMUNITY: ALDO LEOPOLD

The Problem

The problem is and remains survival in the 20th and 21st century in a
world dominated by environmental pollution and ecological degradation.

The Cause

The cause of our environmental problems lies primarily with the outdated and dangerous attitudes and beliefs found in the industrial ethic. That ethic with its indifference to the environment, its inherent selfishness with respect to other members of the biotic community, and its adamantine ignorance of where the indifference and selfishness are carrying us are what have brought about our environmental crisis and the suffering that accompanies it.

The Solution

The solution, quite simply, to the problem of environmental pollution and ecological degradation lies in the development of the concept of community and all that that concept entails. The best and most worthwhile life, Leopold seems to be saying, can only be found when we realize what community is and then see to its implementation.

The Way

The way to the solution of the ecological problems that we face and the suffering that those problems entail lies in removing the selfishness, indifference and ignorance that caused them. In short, the solution lies in shaking off the industrial ethic and the Abrahamic concept of the land. Leopold is calling for nothing less than a moral conversion, a self-transformation, through the development of love, respect and admiration for all the members of the biotic community. This occurs when I begin to feel or intuit that I belong to a community of interrelated living and non-living entities. What this community is like and where I am within it is found in Leopold's model of the land pyramid.

LEOPOLD'S ACCOMPLISHMENTS: THE LAND PYRAMID

The way of community can be further understood through the model of the land pyramid. Leopold's pyramid is not the power pyramid of the industrial ethic as his discussion makes abundantly clear:

> The image commonly employed in conservation education is 'the balance of nature'.... this figure of speech fails to describe accurately what little we know about the land mechanism. A much truer image is the one employed in ecology: the biotic pyramid. [*Ibid.*, p. 251]

He continues, describing the biotic pyramid:

Plants absorb energy from the sun. This energy flows through a circuit called the biota, which may be represented by a pyramid consisting of layers. The bottom layer is the soil. A plant layer rests on the soil, an insect layer on the plants, a bird and rodent layer on the insects, and so on up through various animal groups to the apex layer, which consists of the larger carnivores. (p. 252)

And he concludes:

Each successive layer depends on those below it for food and often for other services, and each in turn furnished food and services to those above. Proceeding upward, each successive layer decreases in numerical abundance.... Man shares an intermediate layer with the bears, raccoons, and squirrels which eat both meat and vegetables. (p. 252)

The vision of life which Leopold's pyramid enshrines is remarkable and for several reasons: First, as we have indicated before, it is astonishingly non-Western in scope and content. As with Basho and his *nazuna* plant, there is no real distinction, morally and perhaps aesthetically, among the members of the ecological pyramid; they are all morally and aesthetically non-different, as it were. The land ethic, after all, gives moral status and moral value to things like dirt, ponds, and trees; and each such thing has as much value as any of the other things in the biotic pyramid. And this is remarkable.

Second, not only is man not at the apex of the pyramid but he counts just as little, or just as much, as dirt, ponds, and trees in the community. In other words, everything is interconnected and interrelated in such a way that nothing counts for more, or less, *prima facie*, than anything else. And this is remarkable, indeed.

Third, the language Leopold uses in discussing the land pyramid and its ethic is Eastern in Suzuki's sense, and the vision that that language describes goes far beyond the ordinary Western ways of talking about man and man's place in nature. And that, again, is remarkable.

But the ways of community and the land ethic are not without their problems. We turn to those problems next.

PROBLEMS WITH THE WAY OF COMMUNITY

The land ethic as developed by Aldo Leopold raises a number of puzzles and questions that need attention. They all seem to relate to our standard of common sense as a criterion of adequacy for the way of community.

First, and most importantly perhaps, is the very pressing question, Do I have moral obligations to every member of the land community? More particularly, Can I have a moral obligation to a squirrel? to a white oak? to a pond or a mountain? And if I can have a moral obligation to them, then do I? More generally there is the question, Can nonhuman animal species have rights?, and Can these rights ever supercede the rights of other living species like man?, and finally, Can these rights then impose obligations on me? For example, given my place in the land pyramid, a place occupied by bears, raccoons and squirrels, am I duty-bound not to injure or kill those on the same pyramid level as myself? or not to injury or kill living species from other levels, such as deer, mosquitos, and roses? and not to mess up or pollute grassy hills and silvery ponds?

Second, if I am a member of the land community, then, of course, I can and do have some such obligation or other. But does this make any sense? Does equal moral consideration for all members of the land community mean equal treatment as well? Does the land ethic impose on me an obligation to open the pens at livestock markets, at farms and ranches?, to burn down slaughter houses, green houses, and any other enclosure where living species are held in chains, pens, and captivity? To answer this question about moral obligations, moral duties, and moral responsibilities to nonhuman living species, it might be well to move on to one other more basic question that seems to lie behind all of these: What sort of ethical theorist is Aldo Leopold? Answering this question should put us in a better position to consider obligations, responsibilities, and duties to squirrels, oaks, ponds, and mountains.

Aldo Leopold as an Attitude-Utilitarian

Aldo Leopold's definition of rightness was that "a thing is right when it tends to preserve the integrity, stability and beauty of the biotic community." [See above, p. 295.] The definition, despite Leopold's apparent feelings about utilitarianism, seems plainly utilitarian: for wherever rightness is measured by some future state of affairs, and where that state can be called "happiness," and where that happiness is for the sake of all concerned, then we have all the rudiments of classical utilitarianism. [See above, Chapter 9. *The Way of Utilitarianism*, pp. 180-182.] Leopold's talk about "tendency," "integrity, stability and beauty," and "biotic community" is talk about future states of happiness for all concerned; and that's utilitarianism.

But Leopold's utilitarianism is complicated by his talk about "the ecological conscience," and "inherent value" residing in each element of the community, and the necessity of their being self-transformation together with "special feelings" and "intuitions" that lead to the development of the ecological conscience, and having "obligations" to the community that seem to transcend the ordinary utilitarian calculations of benefits and usefulness. In other words, obligations to the land and to the community are, for Leopold, very special obligations, indeed, since they are not calculated on the basis of utility alone; and a transformed ecological conscience is a conscience that recognizes this special obligation. So what kind of theory of ethics is this anyway?

I think that if we can see Leopold's ecological conscience as a particular kind of special attitude, and if we can see the development of this attitude as the transformation of the ecological conscience, then, some interesting things happen; for not only might Leopold's land ethic make some kind of utilitarian sense, but also the problem of adequacy relative to our standard of common sense might be solved, as well.

Aldo Leopold's ethics, if it must have a label, is probably a variety of what has been called "attitude-utilitarianism." Attitude-utilitarianism takes as the starting point of moral action, not the consequences nor the acts which we perform, but the attitudes, the motives and feelings, with which the acts are done. John Hospers has put the position most clearly:

> According to *attitude-utilitarianism*, we should do our best to cultivate those attitudes which would be the most likely to produce the most good if generally adopted. [John Hospers, *Human Conduct, Problems of Ethics* (New York: Harcourt Brace Jovanovich, Inc., 1972), p. 334].

Hospers continues, drawing out the implications of attitude-utilitarian-sim, sounding at the same time as if he had the land ethic in mind:

> The goal is not simply that people should help others - grudgingly [which would have been enough for classical utilitarianism], or even from a sense of duty — but that they should *enjoy* doing so.

The "others" that Hospers mentions might, by simple extension, be the members of the biotic community of which Leopold speaks. Hospers continues, focusing next on the development of "an outgoing attitude," which sounds like what Leopold had called "the ecological conscience," the sense of oneness and community with the land:

> If people have developed within themselves an outgoing attitude which permits them to help others quite willingly and spontaneously, without

begrudging it as a sacrifice, then there will be more happiness in the world
than if they helped grudgingly or not at all.

The community as a whole will benefit from the adopting of these attitudes, and when all persons have such attitudes, the benefits will be that
much greater still:

A universal attitude of mutual concern for one another — "no man is an
island" — will yield a society in which the most possible good exists. [*Ibid.*,
p. 335]

This is as close as Hospers comes to expressing the sense of Leopold's
holistic community within the biotic pyramid. No one is an island, the
parts are interlocked by the development of communal feelings of sympathy, love and interdependency, where each is equal to each in the
community:

The best society would be brought about through the cultivation of universal human sympathy. Not pity, which is the feeling of the one on top for the
miserable creatures down below; but sympathy, a concern by equals for
equals. [*Ibid.*, p. 336].

Hospers continues, linking the attitude of sympathy to the survival of life
itself:

Indeed, the cultivation of such an attitude increases the chances not only of
mutual well-being but, in extreme circumstances, of life itself, on which all
well-being depends. When one person must give his life to enable others to
live (as Arctic explorers did) there is more chance for survival in a group
possessing these attitudes. [*Ibid.*]

Even granting that man is the only species likely to develop this
moral attitude, the big question that remains for the attitude-utilitarian
is, How is this attitude to be developed or cultivated? Leopold called for
a moral transformation, an internal change that would recognize the
interconnectedness and interdependence of all things toward which the
ecological conscience can then recognize its duty and responsibility.
While Leopold is silent on the specific way that the change is to be
brought about, Hospers is of some help, first stating the problem and,
then, showing the direction from which a solution, even Leopold's solution, must start:

"But how can we develop these attitudes?" you continue. "Since you say
they *are* semipermanent things [all feelings and attitudes are semiperma-
nent], how can we achieve them? [*Ibid.*, p. 337]

Again, a good question. How do I transform my ordinary feelings into an ecological conscience? How do I come to intuit that the land is a living and valuable being to which I have a moral obligation? How, in other words, do I develop the attitudes of sympathy, affection and respect? Hospers continues, sounding like the Charles Darwin of *The Descent of Man*:

> We can, over a period of time, develop the habit of identifying ourselves with other people so that we can share their experiences and take joy in their successes.... But the process is gradual and admittedly difficult to develop to a high degree. As Aristotle said, it is only by engaging in virtuous activity that one can become virtuous.

The way to the goal is slow and laborious:

> At first we do it outwardly without inner willingness; but then, as we cultivate the habit, gradually "second nature becomes first nature" and we find ourselves enjoying what we once performed mechanically. [*Ibid.*]

It's like learning to swim, Hospers suggests. Difficult at first, then, as ability develops, we come to enjoy it.

A critic might wonder, again, how genuine sympathy and concern can be developed in a society where others are selfish or indifferent to your concerns, which is precisely the case for Leopold's land community where other humans are indifferent by choice and other nonhumans are indifferent by nature:

> Admittedly things would be more difficult if nobody else has the human sympathy which you possess. You will have to "play it cautious" with them while yet retaining your concern for their welfare. But it is still to your own interest, and to that of society in general, for you to develop and retain your attitude even under these hard conditions. [*Ibid.*]

Even instilling sympathy in a few will eventually increase the world's happiness by that tiny amount until the attitude is spread to more and more members:

> Ideally, you will have a state of society in which there is no conflict of interests, because what is to the interest of others will, because of the nature of your own attitudes, also be to your own. [*Ibid.*]

In such a society, where genuine universal sympathy has led to a community of common, interdependent mutually reinforcing interests, a right action would indeed be one that tended to preserve the integrity, the stability and beauty of the entire biotic community. Thus the argument of attitude-utilitarianism.

CONCLUSION

If Aldo Leopold is an attitude-utilitarian, I think that we can now answer the questions with which we began the present section, viz., Can I have a moral obligation to a squirrel? a white oak? a pond? or a mountain? and if I can, then do I?, and solve the problem of common sense, as well? Under attitude-utilitarianism I can and I do have such an obligation. And I am obliged to cultivate those attitudes which will lead to the most good for the land, the biotic community, if they are adopted. And this means adopting attitudes of love and respect which will lead to the best and most worthwhile life for all the members of the ecosystem. Leopold's way of community, supplemented now by attitude utilitarianism, lead to enlarging our vision of the community by widening the circle of sympathy, proceeding imaginatively down and then up the land pyramid, as it were, to include animals, insects, plants, and the very soil itself. Sympathy, love, and respect supplemented by imagination allow me to envision the entire land community and to see or perceive my moral obligation to all of its members.

It is a mighty vision, indeed, that Aldo Leopold had, a vision that invites us to broaden our very *common* common sense and transform it into an *uncommon* common sense. And Leopold's vision is not unlike the one that D.T. Suzuki bids Western men and women adopt, if they would save themselves in what remains of the 20th century.

FOURTEEN
SOME CONCLUSIONS:
MASCULINE AND FEMININE WAYS OF PHILOSOPHY

There is a single prominent theme that has been rumbling through the pages of this book. That theme will be the subject of this final chapter and it will serve as a summary of the entire text. This theme does not have a name as yet but it has appeared in every chapter in the form of a dichotomy between two or more contrasting actions or factions, parties or persons, concepts or properties, and as a dichotomy dividing the ways of philosophy, themselves.

In the previous chapter this theme appeared as West versus East and as individualism versus community. In the opening chapter of the text it appeared as *nomos* (convention) versus *physis* (nature). This dichotomy or opposition, whatever it is called, generated controversy, problems and conflict and, in a very real sense, the tension between these and similar opposites has been the driving energy behind practically all of the ways of philosophy that we have been discussing. If the best and most worthwhile life is ever to be found and properly analyzed, this opposition, this confrontation between opposites, ought to be recognized and discussed.

In what follows, I want to recall the instances of this dualism that we have been encountering, and offer a tentative name to the dualism using the language of Chinese Taoism to do it; second, I want to illustrate, by way of summary of the text, the role that this dualism has played in answering our central question, What is the best and most worthwhile life that a human being can live?; third and finally, I want to conclude with an attempted balancing of the opposing elements of our dualism, a balancing or integrating that might promise a fruitful place in which to continue the search for the best and most worthwhile life.

YIN AND *YANG* AS FEMININE AND MASCULINE ORGANIZING PRINCIPLES

It was probably the Chinese Taoists in the 4th century B.C. who first made the discovery of two central forces that moved the universe and which made things behave the way that they do. [See Arthur Waley, *Three Ways of Thought in Ancient China* (Doubleday Anchor Books, 1939), pp. 16, 31, 69, and *The Way and Its Power* (New York: Grove Press, Inc., 1958), pp. 110-112.] The Taoists referred to these opposing forces as the *yin* and the *yang*. The two forces are exemplified in the absolute and the relative, the weak and the strong, the dark and the light. *Yin* and *yang* represent the forces of vital energy, the breath of life of the earth, as well as the breath of life of the heavenly world, the infinite and the finite, the contemplative and the active. They are frequently depicted at work, for there is nothing static about them nor their opposition, in the well-known diagram of the *Tai-chi T'u* ("the model of the Supreme One"). In the diagram a circle enclasps two inner S shaped parts with each part representing one of the two forces of the universe:

The darkened part of the circle is the *yin*, the feminine principle, and the lightened part is the *yang*, the masculine principle. Within each *yin* and *yang* component there appears another smaller circle, its own opposite and the source of the change that drives the darkened *yin* to become lightened, and the lightened *yang* to become darkened. The Taoists say that the diagram is to be likened to the shadow cast by a mountain as the sun rises, passing over the mountain, and then setting. The shadow is long and dark at the rising, shrinks as the sun climbs into the sky, reappears on the opposite side of the mountain where it gradually lengthens as the sun begins its setting, and then reappears once again as the sun rises the next day. The sun, mountain and shadow analogy is full of the same play of opposites as the *Tai-chi T'u*, a play of rising-setting, light-dark, and long-short.

What we are observing in the model is a two-dimensional symbol of the multi-dimensioned, dynamic universe. The *Tai-chi T'u* describes that universe macrocosmically as well as microcosmically: For it says, on the one hand, that masculine and feminine forces are at work on a grand and cosmic scale, creating, preserving and then destroying the totality, only to start the entire process over again, endlessly and ceaselessly; on the other hand, it says that within each particular thing in the universe the masculine and feminine forces of the *yang* and *yin* are at work there as well, opposing now, harmonizing later, but tirelessly and effortlessly moving and altering.

The Taoists list a number of properties associated further with each of these dynamic forces, many of which might have merely antiquarian interest for 20th century seekers of dichotomies and their meanings. The *yin* is associated with the feminine, winter, cold, damp, the receptive, intuitive and mystical, synthesizing (bringing together), absolute, beyond categorizing and classifying, being holistic in thought, communal, non-logical, dealing in values, and having a regard for what is natural. The *yang* is associated with the masculine, summer, hot, dry, the active, rational and scientific, analyzing (taking apart), the conditional or probable, classifying and categorizing, being sequential in thought, individualistic, logical, dealing in facts, and having a regard for the artificial.

What the ancient Taoist list of *yin-yang* properties gives us, I would suggest, is a set of categories for discussing not only the ways of philosophy but the forces within those ways that led to both the problems and the solutions that we have encountered throughout this book. In what follows, let's refer to these forces as masculine and feminine forces. And, following the lead of the Taoists, let's now attempt to see our ways of philosophy as masculine or feminine ways as we catalogue the various predominant elements within them as either *yang* (masculine) or *yin* (feminine). When we finish, we should have two things before us: First, a new way of talking about ways of philosophy; and second, an insight into how to construct a more adequate way of philosophy as an answer to the question, What is the best and most worthwhile life that a human being can live?

FEMININE AND MASCULINE WAYS OF PHILOSOPHY

With the previous list of characteristics of the *yin* and *yang* before us, it should be an easy matter to attempt to characterize our various ways of philosophy as feminine or masculine. While the very act of seeking such classifications may be notoriously *yang*-ish, some interesting conclusions can be wrung, nonetheless, from such an attempt. As a start, we might begin at the end of our text and, working our way backwards; that is to say, we shall go from what must seem more obvious to the apparently less obvious.

The way of community of Aldo Leopold seems obviously *yin* and feminine in its definition of the best and most worthwhile life. The way of community is earth oriented, its depiction of the problem, its causes and solution are developed around the concept of the ecosystem, a holistic concept, and the solution to the problem depends on a realization, a kind of intuitive apprehension, of the oneness and unity of that community. In contrast the way of individualism is the way of competition not of cooperation wherein the physically strong survive the contest with the environment. It seems obviously *yang* and masculine. The way of individualism is calculating and future looking; its way lies through clashes and confrontations, through action and combat.

Recall D. T. Suzuki's juxtaposition of the Eastern Zen poet, Basho, and the Western English poet, Tennyson. Basho anticipates Leopold's feminine way of community, a way that entails quietly observing the environment, accepting it, joining with it, and intuiting its hidden power. Tennyson anticipates the neo-Darwinian masculine way of individualism that entails separating oneself from what is to be observed, ripping and disturbing the environment, tortuously speculating on its observable properties and classifying and analyzing its obvious powers. The tone of, as well as the properties of, the feminine and masculine ways of philosophy are neatly encapsulated here in Suzuki's explication of the Eastern and Western approaches to nature as they are exemplified in the way of community and the way of individualism, respectively. Let's use these properties now in our summary of and search for the feminine and masculine elements in the ways of philosophy. It might be helpful in what follows to keep the *Appendix: A Summary of the Ways of Philosophy and Their Problems* on pp. 313-315 ready at hand. It might also be helpful to remember that we are talking about the feminine ways and the masculine ways as *tendencies* in these philosophies rather than hard and absolute categories.

With the way of relativism, Protagoras gave to us a whole host of *yang* elements. In saying that man was the measure of all things, Protagoras introduced us to empiricism, relativism, subjectivism, scepticism and the masculine rationalistic philosophies of metaphysical materialism and, as the founder of secular humanism, religious atheism. The Sophists, in general, laid the standard for all judgments at the feet of the individual who makes the judgments. The result was that the way of individualism was really born with Protagoras.

With the way of *psychē*, Socrates led us into a feminine way of philosophy that contained, nonetheless, several interesting masculine elements. The eternal and indestructible soul that Socrates sought to know stood beyond the purview of the senses and the empirical world. The way to that soul was through the rational process of the dialectic. Insofar as the dialectic process was confrontational, it was masculine; but insofar as it led to the transcendent reality of the soul, it was feminine. The result was that Socrates' way of philosophy was feminine in its solution but masculine in its way. The best and most worthwhile life becomes an interesting balancing of the feminine and the masculine. The balancing of *yin* and *yang* properties will be the subject of the last part of this chapter.

With the way of justice, Plato continued this balancing of the feminine and the masculine. The community that Plato envisioned was the arena in which the best and most worthwhile life was to be lived. The way of community that Plato introduced supported the view that the search for justice or happiness must be carried on within a feminine way of philosophy. Further, the mystical vision of the Forms on which much of that happiness depended was always an intuition that transcended both the senses and the mind, lending further credence to the conclusion that the way of justice was, indeed, a feminine way. But Plato's drive for order and security, his concern for absolute and authoritarian civil control together with the centralized manipulation of the citizens in the state where happiness was to be generated must needs give us pause in judging the way of justice as wholly the product of a feminine way of philosophy. As with Socrates before him, the end which he sought for his guardians and philosopher kings was intuitive, mystical, trans-rational, and feminine; but the arena in which these searchings were to be achieved was controlled from top to bottom by a masculine way of classifying, controlling, and manipulating. Again, Plato seems to have attempted a balance between the *yin* and the *yang*.

With the way of self-realization, Aristotle continued the tradition begun with Protagoras that will put the masculine way of philosophy on a sound, as well as a popular, footing. The ways of empiricism, the sciences, and reason are more or less born with Aristotle. After all, it was with Aristotle that the classification of the sciences and the organized interest in the empirical world probably began. The way of self-realization was largely an empirical undertaking wherein the elements for ordinary happiness do not depend, as with Plato, on transcendental, intuitive leapings. What is hidden in the soul, for Aristotle, became actualized, manifested and obvious under the right kinds of empirical conditions. Aristotle's community is reasoned, ordered and as common-sensical as any community can be. His neglect of love and compassion as elements significant in moral behavior, and his rejection of women as equal partners with men in the realization of the soul's potentialities say more than anything else could about his masculine way of philosophy. The way of self-realization is, it must appear, a philosophy out of balance.

With the way of *nirvana*, the Buddha offered us, once again, an interesting compounding of the feminine and the masculine ways of philosophy. The Buddha adopted an empirical and pragmatic attitude toward the problems of men and women arguing that since the problem of suffering was entirely naturalistic and psychological, so also was the solution wholly naturalistic and psychological. On this interpretation the atheism, relativism, non-self doctrine and empiricism of the Buddha followed from the Buddha's essential belief in *anitya*, ceaseless change. And yet coupled with this generally masculine attitude there went an attitude of compassion and community that is distinctively feminine in tone. The Buddha had actually laid the foundations for both communalism, as found in later Mahayana Buddhism (ca. 100 A.D.) and individualism, as found in later Theravada or Hinayana Buddhism (ca. 250 B.C.). For in stressing the possibility for the individual attaining *nirvana* for himself or herself, alone, but only in a monastic or community setting, the Buddha was really integrating both feminine and masculine elements. Finally, the way of the eight-fold noble path was a compounding of both *yin* and *yang* elements, itself, as both good works and meditation were synthesized into a profound and original insight.

With the way of pleasure, both Aristippus and Epicurus offered a distinctly feminine way of philosophy. There was not the urge to separate and divide, to strive and conquer, to reason and classify, that we saw with the Sophists and Aristotle. The hedonists constructed their way of pleasure on an insight about human nature, viz., that humans are by nature pain avoiding and pleasure seeking creatures. Psychological hedonism is the essential insight that leads to ethical hedonism which says, in effect, life is short so we ought to enjoy it (Aristippus) or life is short so we ought to seek out the stable and lasting pleasures of the mind (Epicurus).

With the ways of letting-go of the Cynics, the Stoics and the Skeptics, a hearty and vigorous compounding of the *yin* and *yang* elements took place. Where the hedonists bade us easily and naturally let go of all pains, the Cynics told us to simplify our lives by letting go of all the desires and junk that clutter those lives. Diogenes of Sinope's vision of a world brotherhood living in peace and security in a true community without the encumbrances of the luxurious and the unnecessary was a vision we might all wish on ourselves today. The Stoics urged us to go even farther and to reduce our desires altogether by making our wills conform with the will of God. Sharing the vision of Diogenes, Zeno of Citium counseled us to see all men as brothers and in a great human cosmopolis to find the best and most worthwhile life together. The Skeptics, finally, having discovered all the problems and pains that vain masculine reasoning and judging can cause, urged us to give up making judgments altogether about those things that in the end can only cause us concern and suffering. Pyrrho and Sextus, like their Cynic and Stoic brethren, let go of all that was not truly needful, seeking tranquility and quietude, *yin* characteristics, rather than action and continued striving, *yang* characteristics, in the simple and natural life. But there is a balance, of sorts, in these reasonings of the Cynics, Stoics and Skeptics, for they were ways of philosophy that depended after all on reasoning and argumentation, on rational defense. We might see them consequently, as ways of philosophy not wholly one-sided but proportioned and balanced.

With the way of utilitarianism, John Stuart Mill offered a synthesis, a balance, between the feminine and the masculine ways of philosophy. Act utilitarianism which asked one to measure the rightness of each individual action was an expression of the go-it-alone-ism of the rugged individualist, and it expressed its *yang* characteristics all-too-clearly. But rule utilitarianism which asked one to measure the rightness of an action against the already proven rules of the community was an expression of the community-oriented commitment of the feminine way of philosophy. This balance was nicely maintained as we saw throughout Mill's personal and public life. One expression of this balance lay in his concern for the tyrannies of the minority over the majority and of the majority over the minority. That concern expressed itself in Mill's attempt to balance the rights of the individual against the rights of the community without doing harm to either.

With the way of existential nothingness, both Frederich Nietzsche and Jean Paul Sartre spoke primarily of a masculine way of philosophy then ended with a feminine way of philosophy of total acceptance. Nietzsche's focus on the self-overcoming of the individual and his depiction of the disorder, madness and meaninglessness of life as lived by the great mass of mankind in community, led him to reject the community of men and to speak to the lone individual. Sartre as the existentialist spoke to this aloneness, with its attendant anguish and despair. His existential way of philosophy, like Nietzsche's, was the way for the solitary man wherein living authentically involved accepting oneself together with the terrible burden of private freedom that went with that acceptance. Nietzsche attempted a balance between the Apollonian (reason) and the Dionysian (will), the *yang* and the *yin* forces in his philosophy, a balance which ultimately didn't work as the Dionysian force overwhelmed him. Sartre also attempted a balance as he turned from existentialism to a community-centered, people-centered, form of Marxism, and then to a synthesis of the two in the end. Thus, finally, each philosopher realized that the *yang* nothingness from which they had started, the realization that all Absolutes were dead, must needs be balanced with a *yin* some-thingness, viz., a gentle acceptance of their own life and fate.

With the way of satyagraha, Mohandas Gandhi prominently displayed the feminine way of philosophy but with a nice balance with the masculine way. Satyagraha, the way of non-violent overcoming of injustices, was obviously an attempt to bring the disperate community together. Satyagraha was a simple blending of both *yin* characteristics, non-violent, community oriented commitment, and *yang* characteristics, vigorous, ideally selfless action directed at threatening injustices wherein the agent remained unattached to the results of the action. Satyagraha for Gandhi was a unique blending of *yin* and *yang* elements.

With the way of Christian satyagraha, Martin Luther King, Jr. attempted a similar blending of masculine and feminine elements. As with Gandhi, there was an attempt to focus on the community as the center of human energy and activity. Recall that for King, Christian *love* was defined as "a willingness to go to any length to restore community," and it was this love, of course, that dominated King's way of philosophy. But mixed and balanced with it was the *yang* striving that refused to merely accept things the way they were: That masculine "going to any length" was effectively balanced with the feminine end of "restoring community."

With the ways of individualism and community of Charles Darwin or neo-Darwinism and Aldo Leopold we have come now full circle. The *yang* elements in the masculine way of philosophy of neo-Darwinism lay in the competitive and combative confrontations that led to the production of strong survivors both inside as well as outside the community. The *yin* elements, on the other hand, within the feminine way of philosophy of the proponents of the land ethic argued for what seemed to be an extended utilitarianism that attempted to enlarge the community of those to whom moral duties were due. This attitude utilitarianism attempted to promote the virtues of cooperation in an ecosystem wherein, as Aldo Leopold put it, "A thing is right when it tends to preserve the integrity, stability, and beauty of the biotic community." Aldo Leopold's moral vision laid stress on the *yin* elements within his way of philosophy. But Leopold's call to ecological arms, a call to fight to save the biotic community from pollution and destruction, was sufficiently *yang* in tone to allow us to say that, once again, we have a feminine way of philosophy balanced by and integrated with a masculine way of philosophy.

Let me now turn to a final comment following this excursion into feminine and masculine ways of philosophy. What does all this talk about balancing *yin* and *yang* forces have to do with answering our question, What is the best and most worthwhile life that a human being can live?

BALANCED AND UNBALANCED WAYS OF PHILOSOPHY

At the beginning of this long study of the ways of philosophy we stated that an adequate, as opposed to an inadequate, way of philosophy would have to satisfy three criteria: common sense, consistency and completeness. We have been at some pains to draw attention to the putative inadequacies of all of the ways of philosophy herein examined. But now we may have another dimension for adequacy-inadequacy that may have to be taken into account in measuring adequacy. From our previous discussion we have seen the necessity of a balance between theory and practice, feeling and action, God and the world, intuition and reason, the mystical and the scientific, values and facts, between what we have called the *yin* and the *yang*, the masculine and the feminine. All of this may add a new standard for measuring philosophic adequacy. Let me explain.

The Taoists who gave us the *Tai-chi T'u* argued that an imbalance of the *yin* and the *yang* would always lead to suffering and that to avoid that suffering a balance between the two forces must always be maintained. They put the matter in this fashion: A fully realized being is one who knows the masculine and yet keeps to the feminine. Their advice is not unlike the advice of the Oracle of Apollo at ancient Delphi, *medēn agan*, "nothing in excess," or Plato's definition of *dikē*, justice, as a balance in the soul or in the state. This avoidance of extremes finds perfect expression in the life and wisdom of Gautama the Buddha who preached *madhyamika*, "a middle path," between sensuous luxury and mindless asceticism, and in the golden mean between extremes of both Confucius and Aristotle. It would appear then, if what we have said makes some sense, that an adequate philosophy of life must needs be a blending and balancing of opposing forces. The gentle advice of these more adequate ways of philosophy would appear to bid us avoid extremes and thereby find a balance between the *yin* and *yang*. The best and most worthwhile life, in other words, would appear then to be a kind of harmonious blending and balancing of those very elements in our own lives.

APPENDIX: A Summary of the Ways of Philosophy and Their Problems

PHILOSOPHERS: Ways of Philosophy	The Way of Relativism: Protagoras	The Way of Psyche: Socrates	The Way of Justice: Plato	The Way of Self-realization: Aristotle	The Way of Nirvana: The Buddha	The Way of Popular Pleasure: Aristippus	The Way of Enlightened Pleasure: Epicurus
Rx for Liberation from Suffering: Problem	Suffering in this life. Anxiety over future success.	Suffering-fear that life may not be worth living-fear of life after death.	Suffering-personal and social in the soul and in the state.	Suffering-personal and social in the corrupt soul and the corrupt state.	Suffering. i.e. duhkha or anxiety	Suffering-physical pain, absence of pleasure.	Suffering-anxiety over death, Gods, pain, the WORLD: "Pain in the body, trouble in the soul"
Causes	Ignorance on how to get along in this world in private and public affairs.	Neglect of the Soul; caring more for money and reputation; not examining one's self and one's life.	Ignorance of the Forms, of the self and of one's true vocation.	Ignorance of the self; bad habits; improper government; failure to reach goals.	Fear of old age, sickness and death: Desire and ignorance.	Lack of wealth, energy, power.	Ignorance of causes as matter, atoms, power of mind. Fear of Gods, death and the alien world, in general.
Solution	Happiness as living well; becoming a success.	Happiness as the improvement of the Soul.	Happiness as justice in the soul and justice in the state.	Happiness-living in accord with reason (man's *virtus* or *areté*).	Nirvana: Desirelessness and tranquility.	Pleasure-intense physical pleasure.	Ataraxia-peace of mind.
Ways	Learn virtue, learn how to get along, accept the mores of your community as your guide to morality. Learn the art of gaining wealth, reputation, fame and honor in the 50 drachma course of study.	Self knowledge through the dialectic. Self analysis leading to self discovery	Self-realization; vision of ultimate reality, the Idea of the Good; following the right vocation led by reason.	Action guided by reason; follow the golden mean; contemplative life: luck, leasure, wealth and good habits are all necessary, do what is fitting for that leads to the best results; self-realization.	Following the Eightfold Noble Path: Good works and meditation.	Seek pleasure of the senses, the body and the moment, for all pleasures are the same.	Stay in the Garden. Seek katastematic or stable pleasure, e.g., knowledge, friendship; control desire. Shrink WORLD. Remove fear of Gods, death, hell and the world.
Problems and Questions	But can the virtues be taught? Can anyone be taught to be good?	How does one discover the Self anyway? Can Self-knowledge ever make anyone happy?	Who would ever care to live in Plato's authoritarian state just to be happy?	The problems of women, slavery and self-realization.	The problem of anitya (ceaseless change) and nirvana.	The problems of bad pleasures and of the choices between pleasures.	The problems of whose pleasures? and how much pleasure?

PHILOSOPHERS: Ways of Philosophy	The Ways of Letting-Go			The Way of Utilitarianism: **J.S. Mill**	The Way of Existential Nothingness: **Frederich Nietzsche**	The Way of Existential Nothingness: **J. P. Sartre**	The Way of Satyagraha: **Mohandas Gandhi**
	of Pleasures: **Antisthenes the Cynic**	of Desires: **Epictetus the Stoic**	of Judgments: **Sextus the Skeptic**				
Rx for Liberation from Suffering: *Problem*	Suffering-the problem of self-WORLD.	Suffering-anxiety over death, Gods, and the WORLD	Suffering-anxiety over making wrong decisions or judgments.	Suffering-social and personal.	Disorder; madness in the world; meaninglessness of life.	Suffering: nausea at world, anguish at self; absurdity; forlornness.	Suffering-social and personal.
Causes	Wanting too much; desire in general.	Ignorance of the Self; desire.	Making decisions or judgments.	Selfishness and indifference which cause poverty and injustice. Tyrannies of the majority and the minority.	Herd morality; the realization that God is dead - Christianity, democracy, mediocrity; triumph of Apollonian forces.	Essentialism - to be out of control; alienation; economic degradation.	Selfishness; greed; uncontrolled desire.
Solution	Indifference.	Apatheia - peace of mind	Ataraxia - tranquility, quietude.	Happiness.	Become the übermensch.	To live authentically.	Self-realization.
Ways	"To have no wants at all." "I would rather go mad than feel pleasure." -Antisthenes- Shrink both self and WORLD.	Learn that God is a Divine Force in you (Logos); death is a mingling of fires, yours with God; a wise and good Force governs all: *Amor fati.*	Epochē - suspend all judgments; dogma → trope → equipollence → epochē → ataraxia	Seek G.H.G.N. Become a utilitarian and seek social reform and personal happiness, thereby.	Rebirth of Dionysius; overcome yourself; *amor fati;* accept eternal recurrence as a final test.	Accept oneself and one's actions in freedom; accept one's forlornness and anguish.	Satyagraha and service to others through karma yoga.
Problems and Questions	The problem of self-WORLD.	The problems of free will and evil.	The problem of universal doubt.	The paradox of hedonism.	The problems of what to do and the isolated individual.	The problems of existential anguish and universal choosing. How does the individual relate to the community?	How do I give up all desire? What use is non-violence in a world committed to violence?

PHILOSOPHERS: Ways of Philosophy	The Way of Christian Satyagraha: **M. L. King**	The Way of Individualism: **Charles Darwin**	The Way of Community: **Aldo Leopold**
Rx for Liberation from Suffering *Problem*	Suffering: misery, fear, bitterness and hatred.	Anxiety over just surviving.	Environmental pollution and ecological degradation.
Causes	Economic, social and political injustice.	Competition for limited goods caused by over-population.	Human indifference and ignorance and following the industrial ethic.
Solution	Conversion of one's opponent.	Survival of the fittest.	Realization that we are a community.
Ways	Christian satyagraha.	Develop a sense of individualism by following nature's ways and practicing competition in order to weed out the weak and the unfit in order that the fit and the strong may survive.	Develop a sense of community by adopting the land ethic and abandoning self-interest ethics through attitude utilitarianism.
Problems and Questions	How does one know when one is faced with injustice? The problem of commitment.	The problems of what is natural? and deriving an *ought* from an *is*.	How can I have moral obligations to squirrels and trees and rivers?

READING QUESTIONS FOR THE WAYS OF PHILOSOPHY

Chapter 1. The Ways of Philosophy

1. This chapter claims that we live in a time of crisis. What reasons or evidence are given to support this claim? Do you agree with the claim? Explain.

2. Explain the meaning of "crisis," and "philosophy."

3. What is "the prescription for happiness"? How does it relate to "the way of philosophy"?

4. What is an "adequate way of philosophy"? Define or explain the criteria of common sense, consistency, and completeness that define "adequacy."

5. Answer the following ten questions. Write about three sentences on each one: 3 sentences minimum

YOUR PHILOSOPHICAL AUTOBIOGRAPHY (preferably typed)

1. Name two persons, living or dead, but not relatives or friends, that you consider to be the two greatest persons that ever lived. Why do you think that they are the greatest?

2. Is there any ideology, doctrine or belief that you'd be willing to give up your life to protect?, or kill someone else to protect? Explain briefly. (If you would die or kill, doesn't this make you a fanatic? If you wouldn't die or kill, doesn't this mean that you're

wishy-washy? So you're either a fanatic or you're wishy-washy. What do you think about that?)

3. If, as a result of examining the ways of philosophy, you suddenly discovered that God didn't exist (or if you're an atheist, suppose you suddenly discovered that God did exist), would this bother or upset you? Please explain.

4. If, as a result of examining the ways of philosophy, you suddenly discovered that you were becoming a Hindu or a Buddhist, (or a Platonist, Hedonist, or a Stoic), i.e., beginning to give up your present beliefs and adopting these new ones, would this bother or upset you? Please explain.

5. Suppose that you suddenly discovered that you had 30 days left to live, and who knows, perhaps you do. How would you want to spend those last 30 days? Why?

6. Suppose that an all-powerful and Divine Creator made the world, and suppose that He wanted to make some changes in its present organization and structure? Suppose that He came to you for advice. What improvement or change would or could you suggest? Please explain.

7. Do you think that there are certain kinds of ideas or philosophies that should not be taught, advocated or discussed in our society? Give an example or two, if you can, and explain your reason.

8. Name the one thing, event, or idea that really frightens you the most, i.e., what are you most afraid of? Why do you fear it, and what protects you from it? Or if you aren't really frightened of anything, why do you suppose you aren't? Explain either one briefly.

9. Right now, what do you think is the most *real* thing that exists? What makes that thing *real* for you? Explain. ("Real" means "eternal, unchanging, independent.")

10. What's the one thing, do you think, that is so *certain*, or so *true*, that no one, but no one, could ever convince you that it was false or wrong? Just name, if you can, that certainty. Explain. ("Certain" means "incapable of ever being false.")

Chapter 2. The Way of Relativism

1. Be able to recount the major battles and dates of the Persian Wars. What were some of the consequences of the Persian Wars?

2. Identify: the Persians, Themistocles, Xerxes the Great, Pericles, and Pythagoras of Samos.

3. Who were the Sophists? What were their major accomplishments? What was so objectionable about them?

4. Distinguish *physis* from *nomos*. Why was the distinction important? What is *aretē*? and *technē*?

5. Identify in three sentences Gorgias of Leontini and Protagoras of Abdera.

6. "Man is the measure of all things." Explain the significance of this statement. Do you believe it? Is it true? How do you know that it is or is not true? Does it really lead to relativism, scepticism, pragmatism, empiricism, anthropocentrism and humanism? Explain.

7. Distinguish ethical relativism from epistemological relativism.

8. Read Plato's *Republic* 489 b, c, where Plato argues that since there are experts in various fields (people who *know* how to practice medicine, pilot ships, etc.) then all opinions are not equal (you wouldn't want your roommate to remove your inflamed appendix or steer an oil tanker through a fog). But then relativism is false! What do you think about that?

9. Consider this seemingly relativist assertion: "To you it's true that God exists; to me it's false that God exists. So we're both right." But Aristotle says that a statement must be either true or false and that it cannot be both. So who's right? The relativist or Aristotle? Why?

10. What were Protagoras' (or Sophism's) major accomplishments?, and what were the central problems with his (or their) way of philosophy? Do you agree? Explain.

Chapter 3. The Way of *Psychē*

1. Be able to recount the birth and death dates and the major events in Socrates' life.

2. Explain *psychē*, Socratic irony, and Socratic dialectic, *daimōn*. What is the debate between Socrates and Laches all about?

3. If you had been on the jury that tried Socrates, how would you have voted? For acquittal? For death? Why?

4. "The unexamined life is not worth living." What does that mean? How do you examine your life? What makes such an examination

worthwhile? Was Oedipus, for example, better off after he examined his life than before? Explain.

5. "Socrates was the Jesus Christ of the ancient Greek world." In what sense might this be true? What parallels can you find between their lives? What differences?

6. At Delphi the temple of the God Apollo had three maxims, or guides for life, carved in the stone: "Know thyself; nothing in excess; promise nothing to anyone." Write an essay on the significance of these mottoes as the essence of the way of philosophy of the ancient Greeks.

7. "It is not a rational justification for a belief b to claim for it that you were taught b as a child, or that you have always believed b, or that b is the only belief that you understand." Do you believe this? Explain. Would Socrates agree with the statement? Explain.

8. What were Socrates' major accomplishments?, and what were the central problems with his way of philosophy? Do you agree? Explain.

Chapter 4. The Way of Justice

1. Be able to recount the birth and death dates and the major events in Plato's life.

2. Identify the Academy, Parmenides, Heraclitus, the tri-partite soul, and the three vocational classes.

3. In what way did Plato synthesize the philosophies of Parmenides and Heraclitus?

4. What is the dilemma of knowledge? How does Plato solve it?

5. What is justice (*dikē*)? List the first six definitions that are offered in *Republic* and be able to indicate one problem with each. What do you think justice is? Why is the meaning of "justice" so important anyway?

6. What is Glaucon's point in recounting the story of the ring of Gyges? If you had that ring, how would you act? So maybe Glaucon is right after all.

7. Distinguish Plato's justice in the large from his justice in the small.

8. Pretend that you are Socrates and that you have just visited Plato's new state utopia. Write a letter home describing what you have seen, mentioning the good as well as the not-so-good. Begin your letter, "Dear Xanthippe." Suppose it was *you* and not Socrates writing the letter. Would it be a different letter? Explain.

9. "The state is like an organism, a living body." Is it? Explain. "The ecosphere with the land, the trees, waters, grass and animals, is like one great, organic, living body." Is it? Explain.

10. Sketch the allegory of Plato's cave and then, after reading *Republic* 509-511, just beneath it draw the divided line, matching the four parts of the latter to the parts of the former, thereby demonstrating the relation between epistemology and metaphysics in Plato.

11. Explain one of Plato's Forms, like love, redness, or truth and explain how each Form relates to particular instances of that Form in the world. For instance, is the ideal of love more real for you than the experiences of love that you have encountered thus far in your life? Doesn't that then make you a Platonist? Explain.

12. What were Plato's major accomplishments?, and what were the central problems with his way of philosophy? Do you agree? Explain.

Chapter 5. The Way of Self-realization

1. Explain what it means to say that every person is born either a Platonist or an Aristotelian. Is it true? Which are you? Explain.

2. Explain rationalism, empiricism, tender-minded, tough-minded, substance, Prime Mover, prime matter, *eudaimonia, sōphrosynē,* leisure (*scholē*) and the Lyceum.

3. Be able to recount the birth and death dates and the major events in Aristotle's life.

4. Explain the major differences between Aristotle and Plato in regard to the Forms, knowledge, reality in general, women, and the ideal state.

5. It is said that Aristotle has a God but no religion. Explain.

6. How does Aristotle bring value into a world of facts?

7. What are the golden mean and the practical syllogism? Give an example of each.

8. What things do I need in order to lead the happy life?

9. Why is the rule of law superior to the rule of men? In what ways is it just as imperfect as the rule of men? Which rule do you now live under? Is there anything wrong with that system now? Explain.

10. What were Aristotle's major accomplishments and what were the central problems with his way of philosophy? Do you agree? Explain.

Chapter 6. The Way of *Nirvana*

1. Be able to recount the birth and death dates and the major events in Gautama the Buddha's life.

2. Define or explain the Four Signs, the five ascetics, "*nirvana*," the Four Noble Truths, and "*anitya*." If *anitya* is true universally, then what five implications does it have? Explain.

3. Can one be religious without being moral (ethical)? or vice versa? Explain.

4. Consider the Buddha's final words. Could they lend support to the view that Buddhism is an atheistic religion? Explain.

5. What was the attraction in early Buddhism that led to so many conversions?

6. What were the Buddha's major accomplishments?, and what were the central problems with his way of philosophy? Do you agree? Explain.

Chapter 7. The Way of Pleasure

1. Be able to recount the birth and death dates and the major events in the lives of Aristippus of Cyrene and Epicurus of Samos.

2. Define "hedonism," "popular ethical hedonism," "enlightened ethical hedonism," "*phronēsis*," "empiricism," and "metaphysical materialism."

3. What were popular hedonism's major accomplishments?, and what were the central problems with this way of philosophy? Do you agree with any of the items in either list? Explain.

4. How does Epicurus solve the problem of choices between pleasures?

5. What led to the downfall of the city-state in ancient Greece? What implications did this have for the citizens of those political-social units? How did the rise of the new philosophies relate to this collapse of the city-state and to the problem of self-WORLD?

6. How did Epicurus solve the problem of self-WORLD?

7. What were enlightened hedonism's, or Epicureanism's, major accomplishments?, and what were the central problems with this way of life? Do you agree? Explain.

Chapter 8. The Ways of Letting Go

1. Be able to recount the birth and death dates and the major events in the lives of Antisthenes of Athens, Diogenes of Sinope, Zeno of Citium, Epictetus, Pyrrho of Elis, and Sextus Empiricus.

2. Define "corporeal-pyro-pantheism," "*Logos*," "*epochē*," and "*ataraxia.*"

3. Distinguish Cynics from Stoics from Skeptics. Despite their differences they had certain things in common. What were those common things?

4. What is the problem of fatalism? How might it be solved?

5. What is the problem of evil? What is the Stoic solution? What is yours?

6. What is the problem of self-WORLD? How is it solved by the Cynics, the Epicureans, the Stoics, and the Skeptics. How would you solve it?

7. Pyrrho claims that to be happy you need to answer his Three Questions that Lead to Happiness. Ask yourself those questions. Now, are you happy? What purpose then do the questions serve? What's the point? Try to defend Pyrrho in your own words.

8. What are the problems of God, immortality, and the world? How are they solved by the Cynics?, by the Stoics?, by the Epicureans?, by the Skeptics?, and by yourself?

9. What were Stoicism's major accomplishments?, and what were the central problems with this way of philosophy? Do you agree with the items in either list? Explain.

10. What were Skepticism's major accomplishments?, and what were the central problems with this way of philosophy? Do you agree? Explain.

Chapter 9. The Way of Utilitarianism

1. Be able to recount the birth and death dates and the major events in the lives of James Mill, John Stuart Mill, Jeremy Bentham, and Harriet Taylor. What influence did the other three have on the life of John Stuart Mill?

2. Define "psychological hedonism," "ethical hedonism," "egoistic-, altruistic- and universalistic ethical hedonism," and "utilitarianism."

3. How does John Stuart Mill's utilitarianism differ from that of Jeremy Bentham's utilitarianism?

4. What were the central problems of act utilitarianism? How does rule utilitarianism solve these problems?

5. "Utilitarianism can justify the most heinous crimes. All one has to show is that the "crime" brings the greatest happiness to the greatest number of people and, Lo!, the "crime" ceases to be a crime and becomes a virtuous and right act." Comment by first agreeing and then by disagreeing with the critic.

6. Mill's *On Liberty* has been called "the most liberal document ever penned," on the one hand, and "the most conservative document ever penned," on the other. Citing your own examples and passages from *On Liberty*, defend one of these views against the other.

7. Suppose I want to commit suicide, take heroin, burn the flag, or become a prostitute. What might Mill respond as the writer of *On Liberty* on the one hand, and as the author of *Utilitarianism*, on the other? What were the major accomplishments and what were the central problems with his way of philosophy? Do you agree? Explain.

Chapter 10. The Ways of Existential Nothingness

1. Explain what it means to say that God is dead? Given that meaning is it then true?

2. In what sense is this age the age of nihilism?

3. Be able to recount the birth and death dates and the major events in the life of Frederich Nietzsche.

4. What effects did Arthur Schopenhauer and Richard Wagner have on Nietzsche's life and way of philosophy?

5. Identify or explain Zarathustra, the Overman (*übermensch*), resentment, Apollonian and Dionysian forces, master morality and slave morality, eternal recurrence.

6. Suppose you wanted to start a new religion. What would you need to do it?

7. What is an existentialist?

8. Be able to recount the birth and death dates and the three major periods in the life of Jean Paul Sartre.

9. Explain "existence precedes essence," absurdity, forlornness, anguish and nausea.

10. What were the major accomplishments and the central problems with the ways of philosophy of Frederich Nietzsche and Jean Paul Sartre?

Chapter 11. The Way of Satyagraha

1. Be able to recount the birth and death dates and the major events in the life of Mohandas Gandhi.

2. Define or explain the adversarial method of legal representation, "satyagraha," self-realization, *yoga*, and the paradox of happiness.

3. Describe in detail the Salt March of 1930 and what it accomplished.

4. What is the *Bhagavad Gita*? Describe Arjuna's dilemma, the dilemma of action, *bhakti yoga*, *jnana yoga* and *karma yoga*.

5. What were Gandhi's major accomplishments and what were the central problems with his way of philosophy? Do you agree? Explain.

Chapter 12. The Way of Christian Satyagraha

1. Be able to recount the birth and death dates and the major events in the life of Martin Luther King, Jr.

2. Define or explain "satyagrahi" and "Christian satyagraha."

3. In what ways were the lives of Gandhi and King similar?

4. Describe the Montgomery Bus Boycott of 1955 and 1956. What other alternatives did King and his friends have to segregation? Were they similar to the alternatives that Gandhi had in South Africa 50 years before? Are those *realistic* alternatives to what both men ended up doing?

5. Would the Buddha, Socrates, or J.S. Mill have approved of Gandhi's and King's satyagraha techniques? Try writing the letter that either one of the first three might have written to Gandhi and King about their ways of philosophy.

6. Read King's "Letter from the Birmingham Jail." How do you think that the ministers that he was writing to would have reacted to it. Write, if you can, a letter in reply from their point of view.

7. Suppose Gandhi had been in Montgomery in 1956 and King in South Africa in 1906. How would each have behaved in the face of these new climates of bigotry? The same? Differently? Explain.

8. Both King and Gandhi were assassinated. Socrates and Jesus of Nazareth were executed by the state. What conclusions can you draw from these violent deaths, these men, their ways of philosophy, and the world's reaction to those ways?

9. What were King's major accomplishments and what were the central problems with his way of philosophy? Do you agree? Explain.

Chapter 13. The Ways of Holism

1. Be able to recount the birth and death dates and the major events in the life of Aldo Leopold.

2. Define or explain ecology, biosphere, the biotic pyramid, utilitarianism, and attitude-utilitarianism.

3. What basic differences do you see between Basho's poem and Tennyson's poem about a flower?

4. Do you think the lists of properties differentiating Eastern man from Western man are accurate?, too simple?, mistaken? Explain.

5. What influence on our contemporary attitudes toward ethics and the environment is found in the work of Charles Darwin, Karl Marx, and Thomas Malthus.

6. Distinguish the industrial ethic from the land ethic.

7. "If Leopold's land ethic became a reality, we'd all starve to death— you can't eat clouds, rocks and rain, and still survive." Respond to the critic.

8. What major problems can you see in the development of a land ethic as envisaged by Aldo Leopold? Would it be worth trying to develop and implement such an ethic? How would you judge its ultimate worth? By utilitarian standards? Does that present a problem?

Chapter 14. Some Conclusions

1. Define or explain the *Tai-chi T'u, yin* and *yang*, feminine and masculine ways of philosophy, balanced and unbalanced ways of philosophy.

2. Are there really feminine and masculine ways of philosophy? Try to imagine two extreme ways of philosophy; make the first wholly feminine and the second completely masculine. What observations can you now make about these two extreme ways of philosophy? For example, would either be a way that would lead to the best and most worthwhile life? Could anyone ever successfully live by either one? Could these two extreme ways survive side by side in the same household, state or country? What might the result be? Please Explain.

3. What makes a way of philosophy become unbalanced? Are the Taoists correct in suggesting that an imbalance, an excess, always produces suffering? Could suffering produce the imbalance? Explain.

4. Recalling Socrates' notion of moderation (sōphrosynē), and Plato's definition of justice (dikē) as a balance in the soul, and Aristotle's concept of the Golden Mean, and the Oracle of Delphi's declaration of Nothing in Excess, and the Buddha's espousal of a Middle Way between pleasure and asceticism, and now the Taoists' claim that the best and most worthwhile life lies in balancing the yin and the yang, what conclusions might one draw about the best and most worthwhile life?

5. Could a balanced way of philosophy contain excesses of yin and yang and still be considered balanced? Notice that "balanced" need not mean "equal parts of." So what does "balanced" mean anyway?

6. Return to the ten questions for Chapter 1, above, called "Your Philosophical Autobiography." Have you changed your mind about any of the answers that you gave? Please explain.

SOME SUGGESTIONS FOR FURTHER READING

In addition to the works already mentioned in the text the reader is urged to consult the following popular and highly recommended writings:

CHAPTER 1. THE WAYS OF PHILOSOPHY

Robert F. Davidson, *Philosophies Men Live By* Second Edition, (Holt, Rinehart and Winston, Inc., 1974). A grand introduction to philosophies that have guided the life of man by a fine scholar and a real pioneer in the field of practical philosophy.

Will Durant, *The Story of Philosophy* (Washington Square Publishers, 1969). Since its first appearance in 1926 this work remains one of the best popular introductions to the history of Western philosophy.

Erich Fromm, *The Sane Society* (New York: Fawcett Publications, 1967/1955. A hard criticism of Western society, as biting and applicable today as it was forty years ago.

Marvin Harris, *America Now* (New York: Simon and Schuster, 1982). A more conservative look at American society that many will find speaks with authority and insight about today's social problems.

CHAPTER 2. THE WAY OF RELATIVISM

N.L. Gifford, *When in Rome, An Introduction to Relativism and Knowledge* (State University of New York Press, 1983). A good and readable little book about the nature of and the problem of relativism.

W.K.C. Guthrie, *History of Greek Philosophy* (Cambridge University Press, 1962-1981) is available now in six volumes. A massive and excellent study, part of which is now available in two short paperbacks, *The Sophists* and *Socrates*. Get them!

Edith Hamilton, *The Greek Way* (W.W. Norton & Company, 1983/1930). This is still one of the best introductions to ancient Greece ever written.

G.B. Kerferd, *The Sophistic Movement* (Cambridge University Press, 1984). An exciting and authoritative account about the Sophists and their impact on Western civilization.

CHAPTER 3. THE WAY OF PSYCHĒ

Plato, *Euthyphro, Apology, Crito, Phaedo, The Death Scene*, Translated by F.J. Church (The Macmillan Publishing Company, 1986). Four dialogues about Socrates in a handy, inexpensive edition.

Sophocles, *Three Theban Plays, Antigone, Oedipus the King, Oedipus at Colonus*, Translated by Howard Banks (Oxford University Press, 1980). The best way to know Socrates is to immerse yourself in the Athenian culture of which he was a part—here's a start.

A.E. Taylor, *Socrates, The Man and His Thought* (Doubleday Anchor Books, 1953/1932). Probably the best of the older and briefer works on Socrates by a great scholar.

Xenophon, *Recollections of Socrates* and *Socrates' Defense Before the Jury*, Translated by Anna S. Benjamin (The Library of Liberal Arts, 1965). For another view of Socrates from another one of his devoted friends and as an alternative to Plato's account, try Xenophon, the practical philosopher *par excellence*.

CHAPTER 4. THE WAY OF JUSTICE

The Collected Dialogues of Plato Including the Letters, Edited by Edith Hamilton and Huntington Cairns (Pantheon Books, 1961). The best complete edition of Plato's writings available in English.

Karl R. Popper, *The Open Society and Its Enemies,* two volumes (New York: Harper Torchbooks, 1963). Still the classic diatribe against, as Popper sees it, the founder of modern totalitarianism, viz., Plato.

Paul Shorey, *What Plato Said* (The University of Chicago Press, 1965/1933). A resumé and analysis of Plato's writings with synopses and critical comments.

A.E. Taylor, Plato, *The Man and His Work* (London: Methuen & Co., Ltd., 1978/1926). Still the best analysis of Plato's writings, dialogue by dialogue.

CHAPTER 5. THE WAY OF SELF-REALIZATION

J.L. Ackrill, *Aristotle on Eudaimonia* (Longwood Publishing Group, 1974). Aristotle's writings are analyzed around the topic of the best and most worthwhile life.

Mortimer J. Adler, *Aristotle for Everybody* (Bantam Books, 1980). A very successful attempt to apply Aristotle's way of philosophy to today's problems and issues.

G.E.R. Lloyd, *Aristotle: The Growth and Structure of His Thought* (Cambridge at the University Press, 1968). Written for the modern reader, a delightful overview of the great philosopher's intellectual development.

The Oxford History of the Classical World, Edited by John Boardman, *et al* (Oxford University Press, 1988). Probably the best and most recent collection of articles on ancient Greece and Rome by many of the world's leading scholars.

CHAPTER 6. THE WAY OF *NIRVANA*

Edward Conze, *Buddhist Thought in India* (London: George Allen & Unwin, 1962). A great study of Buddhism in India by a first rate scholar of Buddhism.

David J. Kalupahana, *Buddhist Philosophy: A Historical Analysis* (Honolulu: The University Press of Hawaii, 1976). A grand introduction to the historical background and philosophical implications of the major schools of Buddhist Thought.

Nancy Wilson Ross, *Buddhism, A Way of Life and Thought* (Vintage Books, 1981). A delightful introduction to Buddhism as a way of philosophy.

Edward J. Thomas, *The Life of Buddha as Legend and History* (London: Routledge & Kegan Paul, Ltd., 1949/1927). Despite its date it is still the best introduction to Buddha, his life and times.

CHAPTER 7. THE WAY OF PLEASURE

Diogenes Laertius, *Lives of Eminent Philosophers*, Two Volumes, Translated by R.D. Hicks (Harvard University Press, 1950). This work of around 220 A.D. contains the best ancient account yet of the great Greek philosophers, such as Socrates, Plato, Aristotle, the Cynics, Stoics, and Skeptics. And for enlightened pursuers of pleasure there is Epicurus, Volume II, pp. 529-677. Full of gossip, anecdotes, wild tales, and sober wisdom, Diogenes is required reading for all seekers of the best and most worthwhile life.

Lucretius, *The Way Things Are: The De Rerum Natura of Titus Lucretius Carus* (Indiana University Press, 1968). The greatest hedonist of the Roman world was Lucretius, an ardent follower of Epicurus. Still today a great work of philosophic art.

Luther E. Martin, *Hellenistic Religions, An Introduction* (Oxford University Press, 1987). A fine introduction to the age that spawned so many of the ways of philosophy including hedonism.

Rubaiyat of Omar Khayyam, Translated into English by Edward Fitzgerald (New York: Random House, 1947). There are many editions of this fine old work, required reading for all serious pursuers of pleasure.

CHAPTER 8. THE WAYS OF LETTING-GO

The Encyclopedia of Philosophy, 8 Volumes, Paul Edwards, Editor in Chief (Macmillan, 1967). This is probably the most important reference work in the field of Eastern and Western philosophy. The articles on Cynicism, Stoicism and Skepticism are exceptionally well done.

Marcus Aurelius, *Meditations* and Epictetus, *Enchiridion*, George Long, Translator (South Bend: Regnery-Gateway, 1956). The most popular and brief of all Stoic writings, both works made grand subway and bedside reading.

The Skeptical Tradition, Edited by Myles Burnyeat (University of California Press, 1983). A fine collection of scholarly papers ranging from the ancient Stoics to the ancient and modern Skeptics.

The Stoics, Edited by John M. Rist (University of California Press, 1978). Another grand collection of scholarly papers on the history, purpose and basic doctrines of the Stoics.

CHAPTER 9. THE WAY OF UTILITARIANISM

Robert L. Heilbroner, *The Worldly Philosophers* (Time, Inc., Book Division, 1962). A superb introduction to the jungle of economic theory that dominated the 19th century.

Michael St. John Packe, *The Life of John Stuart Mill* (New York: Capricorn Books, 1970). An eminently readable and well-researched biography of Mill.

Utilitarianism and Beyond, Edited by Amartya Sen and Bernard Williams (Cambridge University Press, 1982). A grand collection of papers on utilitarianism, its various meanings, its impact on contemporary society, and its use as a theory of personal morality.

Works of John Stuart Mill, Edited by Max Lerner (Bantam Books, 1965). A good collection of Mill's most influential writings including his *Autobiography*.

CHAPTER 10. THE WAYS OF EXISTENTIAL NOTHINGNESS

William Barrett, *Irrational Man, A Study in Existential Philosophy* (Doubleday Anchor Books, 1962). A fine analysis of the leading existential thinkers of the 19th and 20th centuries for whom existentialism was a way of life.

Ronald Hayman, *A Critical Life of Nietzsche* (Penguin Books, 1982). A highly acclaimed and extremely well-presented examination of Nietzsche's life and thought.

Ronald Hayman, *Sartre, A Life* (Simon and Schuster, 1987). An extremely well-written and exciting account of Sartre's life that keeps good literary company with Hayman's previous book on Nietzsche.

Walter Kaufman, *Nietzsche: Philosopher, Psychologist, Antichrist* (Princeton University Press, 1974). Undoubtedly, Kaufmann has no equal in his understanding and presentation of Nietzsche's complex thoughts.

CHAPTER 11. THE WAY OF SATYAGRAHA

Margaret Chatterjee, *Gandhi's Religious Thought* (University of Notre Dame Press, 1986). A delightful recounting of Gandhi's way of satyagraha by a fine scholar.

Louis Fischer, *The Life of Mahatma Gandhi*, Translated by Mahadev Desai (Harper & Row, 1983). This is still the biography that beats all of the others focusing as it does on Gandhi's way of philosophy, its successes and failures; by a man who knew the Mahatma personally.

M.K. Gandhi, *Satyagraha in South Africa*, Translated by Mahadev Desai (Greenleaf Books, 1979). A first-hand and very exciting account of the first successful use of satyagraha in the world by the man who started it all.

Dhananjay Keer, *Mahatma Gandhi, Political Saint and Unarmed Prophet* (Bombay: Popular Prakashan, 1973). A massive, almost day by day, biography of Gandhi but extremely well written and well documented.

CHAPTER 12. THE WAY OF CHRISTIAN SATYAGRAHA

David J. Garrow, *Bearing the Cross, Martin Luther King, Jr., and the Southern Christian Leadership Conference* (William Morrow and Company, Inc., 1986). A well-researched and readable scholarly account of King and the history of the S.C.L.C.

Stephen B. Gates, *Let the Trumpet Sound, The Life of Martin Luther King, Jr.* (New American Library, 1982). Probably one of the most

moving biographies ever written; a grand introduction to the
life and writings of King.

A Testament of Hope, The Essential Writings of Martin Luther King, Jr.,
Edited by James Melvin Washington (Harper & Row,
Publishers, 1986). Everything that the beginning student would
ever want that King wrote and spoke is contained herein. An
extremely well-done collection.

CHAPTER 13. THE WAYS OF INDIVIDUALISM AND COMMUNITY

J. Baird Callicott, *In Defense of the Land Ethic: Essays in Environmental
Philosophy* (State University of New York Press, 1989). Extremely
well written and moving writings about Leopold by the man
who pratically invented environmental ethics.

Darwin, A Norton Critical Edition, Edited by Philip Appleman (W.W.
Norton & Company, Inc., 1970). A really fine introduction to the
life and times of Charles Darwin. The volume includes selections from Darwin's contemporaries, his letters, the *Origin*
(1859), the *Descent* (1871), and modern commentaries on his
works and influence.

Aldo Leopold, *A Sand County Almanac, With Essays on Conservation from
Round River* (Oxford University Press, 1966). Get it!, read it!, it
could save your life!

Curt Meine, *Aldo Leopold: His Life and Work* (University of Wisconsin
Press, 1988). A highly readable, well-researched account of
Leopold and the reason why his life and work can change our
own way of philosophy.

Roderick Nash, *The Rights of Nature* (University of Wisconsin Press,
1989). A history of environmental ethics written clearly and
well.

CHAPTER 14. SOME CONCLUSIONS: MASCULINE AND FEMININE WAYS OF PHILOSOPHY

D.T. Suzuki, Erich Fromm and Richard De Martino, *Zen Buddhism &
Psychoanalysis* (Harper Colophon Books, 1970). The essay by
Suzuki is still the best work on *yin-yang* and the balancing of
opposites in order to bring balance and order into one's own
way of philosophy.

Lawrence G. Thompson, *Chinese Religion*, Fourth Edition (Wadsworth Publishing Company, 1989). A particularly fine introduction to Chinese thought, to the workings of the essential forces of *yin* and *yang*, and to the transformative powers of Chinese Taoism.

INDEX